DECEPTION

DECEPTION

From Ancient Empires to Internet Dating

Edited by Brooke Harrington

With a Foreword by Murray Gell-Mann

Stanford University Press
Stanford, California

Stanford University Press
Stanford, California

Printed in the United States of America on acid-free, archival-quality paper

Library of Congress Cataloging-in-Publication Data

Deception : from ancient empires to Internet dating / edited by Brooke Harrington ; with a foreword by Murray Gell-Mann.
    p. cm.
Includes bibliographical references and index.
ISBN 978-0-8047-5649-5 (cloth : alk. paper)
1. Deception. 2. Deception--Social aspects. 3. Truthfulness and falsehood.
I. Harrington, Brooke, 1968-
    BF637.D42D46 2009
    177'.3--dc22   2009006216

Typeset by Bruce Lundquist in 10/14 Minion

Contents

Foreword

Murray Gell-Mann

DECEPTION and especially lying are typically ascribed to human beings and often distinguished from other forms of conveying incorrect or misleading information by intentionality. If a person is merely ignorant of the truth, then telling something other than the truth would not usually be considered lying, except that pretending to know the truth is itself a kind of deception. (Different ideas about intentionality are presented elsewhere in this volume, along with proposals to distinguish lying from deception.)

As we consider more and more primitive forms of life, we are presumably dealing with less and less intentionality or conscious awareness. So when we discuss other animals as well as people we may find it useful to employ a different way of talking. Perhaps we can say that conveying incorrect or misleading information is deception when some perceived benefit accrues to the deceiver. If you cheat me out of money by exaggerating the value of an object you are selling, then you obviously are getting something out of lying. Even if you are a compulsive liar and tell tall tales all the time, you are presumably gaining a subtler benefit, say feeling like a big shot by exaggerating your accomplishments or impressing an audience with your fibs. At the very least, you get the benefit of scratching the itch that you have: the need to lie.

MURRAY GELL-MANN is a Distinguished Fellow of the Santa Fe Institute. He received the Nobel Prize in physics in 1969 for his achievements in elementary particle theory. He is noted particularly for his work on quarks, antiquarks, and gluons as the constituents of strongly interacting particles such as the neutron and proton. He is the author of *The Quark and the Jaguar* (1994), a popular book reflecting his interest in simplicity and complexity and in complex adaptive systems.

A government department that keeps lying (as in the Soviet Union, for example) gets, at least, the benefit of not having to change the habit, even if nobody believes the lies anymore. Our Atomic Energy Commission, later called ERDA and finally a part of the present-day Department of Energy, is an interesting case in point. Many years ago someone discovered a little tritium in the water supply near Hanford, Washington, and immediately ERDA issued a statement saying in effect: "We didn't do it." The assistant administrator of ERDA for Health Safety and Environment was a splendid Texan who went storming into the office of the administrator, Dixie Lee Ray, and told her, "Dixie, we gotta stop lying!"

I was told that in some species of fireflies the female stays in one place and flashes at a constant rate, which is identified by the male, who then mates with her. But I was told in addition that in some species the female can also blink at the rate characteristic of another species, thus attracting that alien male, whom she then devours.

Now in biology there is an important distinction between habits that are learned in a lifetime and others that are acquired over many lifetimes through the genome. In one way of talking, we can say that the first is a kind of learning or adaptation while the second is part of biological evolution. The distinction gets blurred a bit by processes such as the Baldwin effect, in which learned behavior can gradually become geneticized by favoring genetic changes that reinforce it. In any case, we want to include both sorts of behavior and anything in between.

Batesian mimicry is a very well-known example of evolved deception in biology. The monarch butterfly, raised on milkweed, is said not to taste very good to birds. The viceroy butterfly, which closely resembles the monarch although it is usually a bit smaller, is also passed over by many birds because of the resemblance. Supposedly the viceroy tastes all right, and so deception is being carried out.

When in flight, the *Buteo albonotatus*, or Zone-tailed Hawk, resembles a Turkey Vulture, holding its wings in a similar dihedral and doing a lot of gliding. Its prey, rodents and small birds, can mistake it for a vulture, which eats carrion, and thus not be afraid of it.

A very direct benefit accrues to an animal in a group that gives a warning signal when there is no danger and then grabs some food while the other members of the group are scrambling for safety. Chimps, for example, are known to do that.

My friend Charlie Munn studied birds in the lowland rain forest of the Manu National Park in Peru. There are mixed feeding flocks of several species in the lower canopy and other such flocks in the middle and upper canopy. In each case, one of the species supplies the sentinel that gives a warning cry when a predator, say a bird of prey, approaches. Charlie noticed that every so often the cry would be uttered in the absence of any danger and, sure enough, the sentinel grabbed a choice morsel to eat while the other birds were seeking cover. It occurred to Charlie to ask how often this occurred, that is, what fraction of warning calls were fake. For the lower canopy, it was around 15 percent. He then checked the middle and upper canopy flocks and found the same answer, around 15 percent.

I included this result in my book, *The Quark and the Jaguar*, and before publication I showed a version of the text to Charlie Bennett, the brilliant theoretical researcher at IBM. He commented that his late father had served in the Royal Canadian Air Force (RCAF) in Britain during the Second World War. Together with the Royal Air Force (RAF), the RCAF sent bombers over Germany and occupied Europe, typically with a fighter flying above to protect the bomber. Once in a while, they would send the fighter below the bomber to try to fool the enemy into attacking the fighter instead of the bomber. To determine when to carry out the act of deception, they used a disk divided into equal sectors and a spinning pointer that landed in one of the sectors when it stopped. A single sector was marked with color, and when the pointer ended up in that sector, the ruse was attempted. How many sectors were there? Seven. One-seventh is, of course, close to 15 percent. Could there be some principle involved?

Evidently, there is a trade-off here. If the act of deception is attempted too often, it will not be believed, as in the case of the boy who cried wolf. If it is attempted too rarely, then an opportunity for perceived benefit is being missed. But why is the proper ratio about one over seven? Is six or seven a natural order of magnitude, not based, like ten, on the number of human fingers? Is it connected with two pi?

Is it perhaps related to George Miller's collection of a large number of cases in which the numerals six or seven enter into human psychology? For example, one can immediately count a number of small objects in one's palm with very little chance for error as long as the number is less than seven or so. For somewhat higher numbers, a mistake by one is fairly likely, and so forth.

It would seem that the ratio in question would depend on the amount of benefit conferred by the deception and the amount of risk that the victim would fail to be deceived. Why, then, should the resulting quantity be a particular number? Perhaps it is the ideal ratio in some limit and thus not dependent on the particular amounts involved.

It would be interesting to investigate, if that has not already been done, what these ratios look like in a variety of new cases. For example, how often does a particular bird pass up a viceroy meal compared with the frequency with which it turns up its beak at a monarch meal? How often does a chimp give a false alarm signal compared with giving genuine signals? And so on.

Behavior that is learned (rather than passed on through the genome and thus "instinctive") need not simply be acquired over a single generation. It can be acquired through culture, that is, taught by other, often older members of the species. Although culture is less rich for other animals than it is for people, it certainly exists. In *The Quark and the Jaguar*, I cite the example of a species of tit in England that learned to open milk bottles on doorsteps. The trick was passed on from one member of the species to another and on and on. That is not deception, but we may ask whether some of the deceptions practiced by nonhuman animals are learned in this way rather than by inheritance or by direct experience of the individual.

What about penalties for deception in nonhuman animals (other than failure to be believed)? Sometimes a chimp will try to hoard some food instead of sharing it in the approved way. It has been remarked that, in such cases, the animal will give the food call, even though doing so undermines the animal's intent. This example has been cited in comparing human communication with that of other animals. A human could withhold such a cry in a parallel situation, but the chimp seems unable to do so. Others have pointed out that chimps have been seen to be punished for not giving the food call and that perhaps such punishment, rather than an innate inability to withhold the call, is responsible for the phenomenon.

Before making a few remarks about human beings, let me proceed in the opposite direction. What about computers, or robots run by computers? We are only too familiar with enormous numbers of cases in which computers give false or misleading information. But what about benefit? What is the reward for deception here? Let us consider science fiction, as suggested by Brooke Harrington. In the film *2001*, the notorious computer HAL deceives two astronauts and even brings about the death of one of them, and the expected reward is to avoid being turned off by the surviving astronaut. Thus survival is the key here. In the film *Matrix*, machines engage in wholesale deception of humans, including the construction of a whole false world, so as to be able to suck out of them the so-called "bio-energy." Again, we deal with survival. In *Blade Runner*, the "replicant" machines lie in order to have their expiration dates canceled.

Looking back at the animal examples, we see that the rewards—getting food and not becoming food—are both connected with survival as well. Turning to human beings, I should like to ask first to what extent we have habits of deception that are inherited rather than learned in a single generation by the individual or over many generations through culture. It would be very interesting to hear what experts have to say about this matter.

Next, to what extent do we have habits of deception that are spread by culture? Certainly these exist. For example, when ethnic groups or nationalities demonize one another, they tend to distort history rather badly, and distorted histories are taught to schoolchildren and passed on to later generations. The perceived reward here is the allegiance of children, grandchildren, and so on to the struggle against the hated group.

In a much gentler vein, we teach our children to follow us in telling so-called white lies that prevent people from feeling bad. We sometimes conceal the gravity of an interlocutor's medical problems or the severity of his or her children's misbehavior, or even the degree to which a child's musical performance failed to come up to snuff. Clearly, the habit of telling these lies is spread by culture over many generations.

The habit of avoiding lies can also be transmitted culturally. Karen Blixen, writing under the name of Isak Dinesen, uses as the epigraph for one of her books an ancient Persian saying about how children are taught "to ride, to shoot with the bow, and to tell the truth." In our culture, too, telling the truth is supposed to be a great virtue, but we adults often fail to provide good models for children in that respect.

One case of truth telling is especially interesting. In Rwanda, during the last days of Belgian rule around 1959–60, one of the occasional massacres occurred involving baTutsi and baHutu. In this case, some Tutsi leaders, hoping to perpetuate their domination over the Hutu, tried to wipe out most of the Hutu with a modicum of education. For some of the murders, they made use of a third group, the baTwa, who are short people somewhat resembling pygmies. Unfortunately for the guilty Tutsi, the Twa were trained to tell the truth. When they came before the Belgian authorities, according to news reports the Twa confessed their crimes and named the Tutsi individuals who had ordered them to commit those crimes.

In the chapters covering human deception, its many forms, and the complex ethical considerations involved, we are carried far from the kinds of things I discuss here. Outlining it all would make this Foreword far too lengthy and would soon outrun my capabilities, but perhaps the remarks I have made will nevertheless serve as a useful preface by addressing a scattering of intriguing questions about the endlessly fascinating subject of deception.

DECEPTION

Introduction

Beyond True and False

Brooke Harrington

I T SEEMS FITTING to follow Murray Gell-Mann's Foreword with a story involving two other illustrious physicists. During the 1940s, Leó Szilárd—who discovered the nuclear chain reaction—decided to keep a diary of his work on the Manhattan Project. He told Hans Bethe, one of his colleagues on the Project, that he did not intend to publish the diary, but only "to record the facts for the information of God." "Don't you think God knows the facts?" Bethe asked. "Yes," Szilárd responded, "He knows the facts, but He does not know *this version of the facts*."[1]

This quip actually raises a serious point about the aims of the present volume: If, as Szilárd suggested, humans merely produce a "version of the facts" while absolute truth is known only to God, how can we even begin to define deception? That is, if we cannot agree on what is true, we cannot hope to agree on what is false. As a result of this basic epistemological problem, we are still grappling—after thousands of years of inquiry—with basic questions about what constitutes deception and how it should be evaluated, morally and ethically. Where the greatest thinkers in history have failed to converge, this volume can hardly hope to succeed. So let us acknowledge at the outset that while we, too, confront the difficult questions of defining deception and its positive and negative effects, this volume does not resolve those issues. Rather

BROOKE HARRINGTON is the Alexander von Humboldt research fellow at the Max Planck Institute for the Study of Societies in Cologne, Germany.

than making conclusive or programmatic statements, we have sought to integrate and synthesize research on deception from across the humanities and the sciences.

It may be surprising to learn that this is a significant advance in its own right: while deception and its manifestations have long held a central place in many realms of inquiry, knowledge remains fragmented. At the same time, the need for synthesis is urgent, as new forms of deception arise in a wide variety of arenas, from online communication to modern warfare. So, while this volume will not by any means be the last word on deception, it is the first to invite the long-overdue cross-disciplinary discourse about it. The chapters that follow thus provide a kind of status report on deception, bringing readers up to date on what biologists and sociologists, poets and computer scientists, among others, have learned and can learn from each other.

Reluctance to force a definitional consensus should not be interpreted as a sign of intellectual laziness or hopelessness about the task. Instead, we are trying to avoid the kind of premature, misleading conclusions that have vexed our understanding of deception and encouraged the fragmentation of knowledge. As many of the following chapters attest, the sciences and humanities are littered with incomplete and unsatisfactory definitions of deception; rather than adding to their number, we attempt to make a more enduring contribution by gathering together a wide range of research streams and putting them into dialogue about deception, in many cases for the first time. Where fruitful connections among the disparate research traditions are possible, we make them, but we also acknowledge the irreducible differences and points of contention that remain. By pointing up areas of both convergence and controversy, this approach can contribute to more rapid advances in deception research and a more robust platform for future inquiry than has hitherto been available.

A second reason we avoid developing a conclusive consensus definition of deception is the problem of selection bias, which affects virtually every domain of research on the topic. That is, as psychologist Maureen O'Sullivan puts it in this volume, "We think lies look like the poor-quality, easily detectable ones we have uncovered." Her observation can readily be generalized to all forms of deception: indeed, the evidence from across the sciences and humanities is consistent in suggesting that many more deceptions are perpetrated than are detected. For all we know, the deceptions that philosophers and scientists and artists have been pondering for thousands of years—that is, deceptions that have been detected—may be qualitatively very different from deceptions that succeed in eluding our awareness. This suggests the need for caution in making conclusive statements about the phenomenon, as well as the advantages of the kind of disciplinary multivocality and methodological pluralism adopted in this volume.

What Deception Is Not

While definitions of deception have varied across disciplines, time periods, and cultures, there has been a strikingly broad and enduring consensus about what deception is *not*. For instance, there is long-standing agreement that deception is *not* synonymous with lying. As St. Augustine pointed out in his essay *De Mendacio*,[2] deception may occur in the absence of any intentional falsehood; one can thus deceive others by making false statements that one believes to be true. So, unlike lying, which requires intent to promulgate a falsehood, deception can take place without either intent or awareness on the part of the deceiver. Among humans, this raises problems of self-delusion that complicate definitions of deception in interpersonal settings. Similar issues arise in biology: as natural scientists remind us, animals and plants employ deception to facilitate reproduction and survival; to the best of our knowledge, these phenomena—such as changing color or shape to attract prey or mates—occur without conscious intent. These insights led us to strive in this volume toward accounts of deception that could encompass both its intentional and unintentional forms.

Similarly, we sought to formulate our understanding of deception without overconstraining it in ethical terms. On the one hand, the Western religious and philosophical canon would seem to condemn deception unambiguously, in all forms and circumstances. Dante famously reserved the largest circle of Hell in his *Inferno* for deceivers, treating them to some of his most imaginative punishments, including being thrown into a lake of boiling pitch, and being buried upside-down with their feet on fire.

However, there are opposing strains within Western thought that often go unacknowledged—arguments in favor of what might be called "ethical deceptions." In the realm of statecraft, for example, Plato argued in *The Republic* that political leaders not only could but often *should* "lie for the public good";[3] similarly, Winston Churchill said that "in wartime, truth is so precious that she should always be attended by a bodyguard of lies."[4] Deception can also follow from Hippocrates' dictum to physicians: "First, do no harm." Thus, deception arises in many forms within medicine, from the administration of placebos in research studies to the deliberate concealment of truths likely to cause pain or damage to vulnerable persons, such as the gravely ill.[5] An article published in the *New England Journal of Medicine* summed up the position held by many physicians that "it is meaningless to speak of telling the truth, the whole truth and nothing but the truth to a patient. . . . So far as possible do not harm. You can do harm by the process that is quaintly called telling the truth."[6]

The uses of deception to save lives may constitute more than exceptions that prove the rule: several chapters in this volume suggest that deception is actually *necessary* to social and physical survival. For example, psychologists Mark Frank and Maureen O'Sullivan show how socialization leads us to commit certain routine forms of deception so that social interaction may proceed from day to day. In addition, natural scientists have long argued for the value of deception in ensuring evolutionary fitness through increasing attractiveness for mating purposes and decreasing visibility to predators.[7] This theme is illustrated with particular timeliness in the chapter by communications scholar Jeff Hancock, who reviews some results of his study of deception in online dating forums.

The ways in which deception is connected, seemingly inextricably, to mating and survival among humans and other animals may help explain why, despite the many social and ethical proscriptions against it, deception remains so common in everyday life. Among humans, recent psychological research indicates that lying is actually the norm rather than an anomaly in social interactions.[8] Indeed, one study found that, in the course of a ten-minute conversation, over 60 percent of subjects lie at least once; the average person tells two or three lies during that period.[9] Although deception generally decreases in frequency with the increasing closeness of a relationship, participants in these recent studies report lying in one-third to one-half of the interactions they have with their lovers and their mothers. Some linguists have even argued that deception was at the root of the development of human language.[10] Thus, as Maureen O'Sullivan (this volume) points out, connection to others inevitably entangles us in webs of deception: "In ordinary social life, all but saints, sinners, and madmen collude with liars."

The prevalence of deception in interpersonal settings also suggests the need to consider why there are so many instances of "authorized" deception within societies that otherwise condemn the practice. For example, in sporting events and the performing arts, deception is regarded with appreciation and admiration. What would baseball be without deceptive pitches such as the changeup, the slider, the sinker, or that recent Japanese innovation, the "gyroball"? From the batter's point of view, they all leave the mound looking like fastballs, but arrive at the plate moving with a totally different speed or trajectory than expected. These pitches win games, and the pitchers who throw them are lionized for their deceptive skill, much as Odysseus was for the tricks recounted in the *Odyssey* (see Kenneth Fields's concluding chapter in this volume for more on trickster heroes). By the same token, excellence in the performing arts—from theater pieces and magic tricks to the special effects in films—is defined in part by successful artifice: their ability to make audiences suspend disbelief or forget altogether that they are watching a performance.

So, why do societies that condemn deception accept it in these cases where necessity—to save lives, for example—cannot be argued? One possibility is suggested by the treatment of deception in the visual arts. While *trompe l'oeil* and photorealism in painting historically have been prized and rewarded as marks of artistic skill, altered photographs (as described in Hany Farid's chapter, this volume) have been condemned as frauds. The distinction between art and fraud depends on context: it is not only a matter of where one finds such works (on a museum wall versus the front page of a tabloid newspaper), but also of the expectations elicited by those settings. The context "newspaper" customarily implies information (and thus accuracy and truth), while the context "art" implies the aesthetic enjoyment of artifice.

With entertainment, as in love and war, "consensual reality" is premised on the expectation that individuals know in advance that when they enter settings such as a theater or a playing field, deception may (or will) occur. By participating in such events, even as an onlooker, one is presumed to be giving his or her consent to be deceived. As Mark Frank (this volume) puts it, "in some scenarios, like acting, we permit deception and actively participate in it. . . . Other scenarios, in which we are not notified by the person or the context that deception is happening—such as when a lie is told—are deadly to trust, if uncovered." Obviously, the boundaries around these areas of "authorized deception" vary considerably by location and time period; even within the same society at the same time, individuals and groups can disagree violently about what kinds of deception are acceptable (see my chapter on caveat emptor and deception in financial markets, this volume). However, it is noteworthy that in many research domains, a defining characteristic of deception is its nonconsensual character: that is, a regular feature of the phenomenon is that one or more parties to the interaction has not agreed—implicitly or explicitly—to be deceived.

To draw out other regularities among the domains of inquiry represented in this volume, and to point up key points of contention, the chapters have been organized around four broad thematic areas: defining and detecting deception, the role of technology in deception, the relationship between deception and trust, and the key social institutions through which deception is perpetrated and regulated. Mindful that many edited volumes can read like disconnected essays linked only by a common topic, this one attempts something more ambitious: to capture in print the cross-disciplinary dialogue we began in person at the Santa Fe Institute. To this end, each chapter explicitly defines its links to others in the volume, pointing up similarities and differences in terms of basic premises, levels of analysis, methodologies, and conclusions. Our intent is to create a richer and wider perspective on the topic than is available through a single-disciplinary lens.

Part I: Defining and Detecting Deception

The first section of the book is comprised of four chapters that directly address the problem of definitions. We begin in the animal kingdom, as evolutionary biologist Carl Bergstrom introduces us to a realm in which "organisms deceive one another in every imaginable way in order to attain every conceivable advantage." Behind the matter-of-fact title of his chapter, "Dealing with Deception in Biology," we find a flamboyant rogues' gallery of deceivers—like the carnivorous fireflies that send out false mating signals to lure their prey—along with marvels such as "the bluffing threats of a molting stomatopod." The volume leads with this chapter for two reasons. First, it offers an elegant model of deception—one that sets the context for the rest of the chapters in the book by showing why and how deception, despite its costs, can serve the survival interests of many living things. Second, Bergstrom's text elegantly blends the sciences and humanities, modeling the kind of transdisciplinary approach that this volume seeks to advance.

From the animal kingdom we move to the realm of philosophy. "Paltering," by Frederick Schauer and Richard Zeckhauser, not only reviews the philosophical and legal definitions of deception but does so by highlighting the distinction between two of deception's most common manifestations: lying and paltering. Readers may find it noteworthy that *paltering* is a not a neologism coined by the authors but a word that came into English centuries ago by way of the Vikings. Modern Danish and Swedish preserve the word to this day as *pielter* and *paltor*, respectively, meaning "rags" or "worthless shreds," leading to speculation that the connection between paltering and deception involves telling worthless shreds of truth to create a false impression. Thus if lying is commonly understood to involve fabrications, paltering involves manipulations of truth, including fudging, twisting, slanting, exaggerating, and selective reporting. So, while nothing in a palter may be factually untrue, it nonetheless belongs under the rubric of deception.

Impression management and interpretation are the subjects of the next two chapters, both authored by psychologists whose research careers have been devoted to detecting deception. Mark Frank's chapter, "Thoughts, Feelings, and Deception," deconstructs the micromechanisms by which facial muscles—particularly those around the eyes and mouth—give away would-be deceivers. Frank, who trains law enforcement and counterterrorism officials based on his research, shows how accurate detection depends on attention to context and patterns of behavior, rather than on spotting a single indicator. Biases—such as the tendency to be too trusting or too suspicious—can undermine observers' ability to interpret what they see and hear. This points up the interactive, contextual nature of deception: another theme that recurs throughout the volume.

Maureen O'Sullivan's chapter delves further into the impact of interaction on deception by examining "truth wizards"—an elite group of research participants who were found by chance to have unusually (and consistently) high accuracy in detecting deception in others. While the truth wizards come from all walks of life, one feature they share is the willingness to bear the significant cognitive and emotional costs of deception detection. Not only does spotting deception require close attention within interaction settings, but it carries the social burden of "accusatory reluctance": the hesitancy many people feel to risk destroying a relationship by voicing their suspicions that someone is acting deceptively. Thus, O'Sullivan argues that truth wizards are rare in part because the high socioemotional costs of accuracy in this regard often outweigh the benefits of being right or preserving the integrity of truthful communication. As La Rochefoucauld—a keen observer of the court of Louis XIV—put it in one of his best-known maxims, "Social life would not last long if men were not taken in by each other."[11]

This raises a question that recurs throughout the book: what harm is there in deception, if any? In the case of paltering, what could be the harm in a confection of partial truths? Schauer and Zeckhauser take the position that while paltering may be "less than lying" in content, the effects are, if anything, *more* dangerous than that of outright fabrication; this is because mechanisms for detecting and punishing palters are so few, and the "truthiness" of palters (to borrow a neologism by way of *The Colbert Report*) makes them harder to detect. The social cost of degrading trust and truth arises in other chapters throughout this book (notably that of Tom Lutz), as does the problem of institutional safeguards against the subtler forms of deception, such as paltering (see in particular the chapter by Ford Rowan). In examining deception in this detailed manner, we inevitably must grapple with the meaning of trust and truth, which are the subjects of the third section of the book.

Part II: Deception and Technology

No 21st-century discussion of deception could be complete without addressing the role of technology. While public discourse often focuses on the role of technology in aiding the detection of deception, the three chapters in this section review the ways in which the digital age has made deception easier than ever, and in some cases more difficult to detect. Hany Farid's chapter, "Digital Doctoring: Can We Trust Photographs?" takes on an issue that many of us confront every time we stand in the supermarket checkout line: the ways in which the evidence of our senses, which many of us are used to treating as reliable, can be used to mislead us. While we may have grown sophisticated enough to know that tabloid journalists routinely doctor photos for "dramatic" effect—mixing and matching heads and bodies, or creating "couples" by the cut-and-paste method—it may be more disconcerting to learn that iconic photographs (such as the full-length portrait of Abraham Lincoln that appears in many American history books) are just as fraudulent as the celebrity collages featured in the *National Enquirer*. Such revelations can inspire something alarmingly close to the paranoia of those who believe that other historically significant photographs (such as the images of the Apollo 11 moon landing in 1969) have also been faked. The implications of this erosion of trust are explored at greater length in Gary Alan Fine's chapter on the social psychology of urban legends, "Does Rumor Lie? Narrators, Trust, and the Framing of Unsecured Information."

Jeffrey Hancock's chapter, "Digital Deception: The Practice of Lying in the Digital Age," delves further into the deceptive uses of technology by exploring how different modes of interpersonal communication—e-mail, telephone, and face-to-face encounters—influence the frequency and content of deception. Hancock's research explores the question of "which properties of technology affect how honest and self-disclosive we are, and why." His findings indicate, somewhat surprisingly, that electronic communication is *not* the most hospitable environment for would-be deceivers. Rather, that distinction belongs to the telephone, which—by stripping away the visual cues that people use to detect deception in face-to-face settings, and failing to create the kind of documentation provided by e-mail—remains the most common medium for deception. Within the realm of electronic communication, it will likely surprise no one to learn of Hancock's finding on the abundance of deception on dating websites: not only do people doctor photographs of themselves, but they lie in the text of their online personals (men usually claim to be taller, and women slimmer, than they actually are).

Paul Thompson's chapter, "Cognitive Hacking: Detecting Deception on the Web," delves into the conceptual structure and implementation of these deceptions, uncovering the mechanisms that have brought us some of the banes of 21st-century life, such as "phishing" and identity theft. Addressing both the technical and social sides of the phenomenon, Thompson investigates how hackers create programs that send millions of plausible-looking e-mails to trick recipients into divulging personal information such as their bank account and Social Security numbers. Executing such deceptions successfully requires the ability to develop what psychologists call "theories of mind" about others; thus a successful hacker is not only technically skillful but psychologically astute as well, able to imagine what signals would be interpreted as trustworthy within the relatively impoverished medium of e-mail communication.

Part III: Trust and Deception

This leads directly into a discussion of trust: the hackers described in Thompson's chapter, along with the digital deceivers who figure in Farid's and Hancock's research, succeed in large part because they are free riding on the trustworthiness and integrity of the vast majority of interactions we have with each other and with institutions. As O'Sullivan points out, our disposition to believe that most people are honest until proven otherwise is borne out by research evidence; that is, *not* expecting deception is in fact the most rational course of action. Unfortunately, as Guido Möllering points out in his chapter, "Leaps and Lapses of Faith: Exploring the Relationship Between Trust and Deception," this generalized trust provides useful cover for would-be deceivers. If most individuals expected deception in their interactions, it would be more difficult for any given deception to pass undetected.

Möllering's thoughtful theoretical discussion of trust makes explicit several themes that are implicit in the earlier essays in this volume, including the interactive and performative nature of both deception and trust. We behave toward each other in an "as if" mode, he writes, investing individuals and institutions with our trust and thereby imposing an obligation on them (which they may or may not accept, but that is nonetheless felt as consequential) to act in accordance with our expectations. As Möllering writes, "trust exerts an almost compulsory power." Thus trust—and, by implication, deception—does not exist a priori, but arises as a consequence of interactions and expectations.

As a result, two parties interacting could just as well find reasons to assume deception from one another as they could reasons for trustworthiness: it all depends on how they draw meaning from what Möllering astutely terms "the semiotic chaos and ambiguity in most real-life situations." This indeterminacy is vividly illustrated in Gary Urton's chapter, "Tying the Truth in Knots: Trustworthiness and Accountability in the Inka Khipu," in which mutual trust suddenly turns to mutual suspicion and accusations of deception. The story begins with the encounter between the Inka empire and the Spanish conquistadors; the latter initially accept at face value the "inviolable," quasi-sacred truthfulness of the Inka accountants—the guardians of the knotted *khipu* strings by which the empire's wealth was measured. The cause of the abrupt demise of this equilibrium is unknown, but one can imagine how this interaction might have turned disastrously antagonistic. As Möllering writes (this volume), it takes very little to catalyze a vicious cycle of negative attributions and interpretations: "one act of unnoticed deception often triggers further such acts and possibly an escalation of deception, because the deceiver wants to conceal the initial deception or has self-reinforcing incentives to exploit the situation further and further." Perhaps one of the Inka or one of the Spanish made a mistake, or intentionally exploited the trust that initially flourished between the two groups; that single act might have started a chain reaction in which the relationship, already vulnerable due to cultural and language differences, fell apart rapidly. A similar interpretation is suggested by considering Urton's chapter in light of Mark Frank's work, which mentions the "Othello error"; that is, expressing the expectation that another person will deceive you in some sense creates an invitation to deceive by lowering the reputational costs of the behavior. Thus, if one has heretofore been honest and then becomes an object of suspicion, it is sometimes easier to "live down" to others' expectations (for example, that one is deceptive) than to prove one's honesty.

The problem of expectations also figures prominently in Gary Fine's chapter, "Does Rumor Lie?" As Fine explains, rumor "works" in part because it confirms prior expectations; as a result, certain stories can become "too good" *not* to be true, making them virtually indestructible, even in the face of compelling evidence of their falsehood. Part of rumor's robustness stems from the kind of cognitive laziness described in O'Sullivan's chapter. Another element, however, is the entertainment value of deception: the "will to believe" or to suspend disbelief that sustains our enjoyment of magic tricks, films, and *trompe l'oeil* paintings, just to cite a few examples. This issue is revisited in greater detail in my own chapter, "Responding to Deception: The Case of Fraud in Financial Markets," and in "The Pleasures of Lying" by Kenneth Fields.

But to return to Möllering's insight about the "semiotic chaos" of interaction, the concluding chapter of Part III—"Crocodile Tears, or, Method Acting in Everyday Life" by Tom Lutz—problematizes the very notion of trust and deception as clear-cut categories. As Lutz illustrates in his autobiographical account of the early days of his relationship with his future wife, deception can occur without the conscious intent of the deceiver. This challenges the definition of deception proposed by Frederick Schauer and Richard Zeckhauser in their chapter, "Paltering," which lists intent as one of three necessary conditions for an act to be deemed deceptive. The intent requirement creates a bright line between deception and other types of interaction, and accounts for some of the elegance and clarity of Schauer and Zeckhauser's contribution. However, if one removes the intent requirement, the domain of inquiry instantly expands to include animal behavior as well as important realms of human behavior that are otherwise captured only in the arts. As Joan Didion observed in one of her best-known essays, "Self-deception remains the most difficult deception. The tricks that work on others count for nothing in that very well-lit back alley where one keeps assignations with oneself."[12]

Such deceptions are difficult to trace within oneself, let alone in others. And acknowledging the existence of self-deception complicates our understanding of deceit, implying—like the tears Lutz describes as *simultaneously* sincere and contrived—that imposing discrete true / false categories distorts and does violence to the empirical reality. As this section of the book moves from the macro to the micro levels of analysis, from that of whole civilizations to that of dyads, the risks of reductionism become increasingly apparent. Lutz sums up the problem by noting the way "the binary thinking we are pushed toward in all of our considerations of trust and deception . . . necessarily fails to account for the endlessly recursive variety of motives and understandings informing any intimate encounter." This is reminiscent of Conrad's observation in *Lord Jim* about "the essential sincerity of falsehood"—the way in which the most skillful and effective deceptions begin with self-deceit. This suggests why we need insight from the humanities to engage with deception and perhaps other complex phenomena in the social realm: literature seeks to describe behavior accurately before (or instead of) imposing reifying categories. The power of Conrad and Didion derives from the accuracy of their observations, and the clues they have left us in their writing can help scholars embark on the study of phenomena that may not fit readily into existing conceptual frameworks, but that are nonetheless eminently deserving of attention.

Part IV: Deception and Institutions

The fourth and final section of the book looks at the role of institutions as agents and regulators of deception. While previous chapters examine deceit among individuals and groups, this section takes institutions—in the government, financial, military, and cultural realms—as the unit of analysis. These institutions are (dis)credited with innovating techniques of deception on a mass scale: the best-known examples being propaganda and disinformation campaigns, which employ lies in the conventional sense of the term. But newer methods are more akin to paltering, in that institutions are becoming more skillful at deception without falsehood. This may be driven by mass communication technologies, particularly the World Wide Web, which make it easier to check the evidence for factual claims (and thus to expose lies), but that can also provide new opportunities for deception, such as overdisclosure.

In the present era, when "transparency" is among the most highly prized descriptors applied to political and corporate institutions, providing an excess of information can be an extremely effective tool of deception. The technique consists simply of disclosing far more information than is required or requested, making it difficult to find the essential data points among the extraneous ones. It might be compared to piling hay around a needle, or manure around a pony; at any rate, it exploits well-known limitations of human cognition when it comes to information search—a phenomenon termed "bounded rationality."[13] For example, as this introduction was being written, staffers for John McCain—the Republican candidate for the 2008 presidential race—executed this move brilliantly: responding to public demands for disclosure of the 70-something senator's health records, they literally buried the story in an avalanche of information. Instead of the 400 pages the press expected, reporters received 1,173 pages on the Friday afternoon of Memorial Day weekend and were given four hours to examine the documents. Not surprisingly, McCain's health ended up being a nonstory because it was too difficult to sort through that much information in such a short time. What is significant for this volume is the change of tactics: unlike the traditional and much more common response of withholding sensitive information, institutions such as political parties have swung to the opposite extreme, which might be termed the information-saturation approach to deception. This provides deceptive cover while retaining the moral high ground through the appearance of disclosure.

While such *trompe l'oeil* transparency can frustrate further demands for institutional disclosure, it has not necessarily promoted trust in those institutions. For example, as Ford Rowan documents in his chapter, "Deception and Trust in Health Crises," expectations of deception by the U.S. government are so widespread now that a majority of Americans polled said that in case of a bioterror incident they would be more likely to trust information from their local fire chief than from the Centers for Disease Control. On the one hand, this can be explained as the logical outcome of Watergate, AbScam, Iran-Contra, MonicaGate, and the myriad of other instances in which representatives of the federal government have been caught lying (or paltering) to the people they are purported to represent in good faith. On the other hand, the quantity of information may have as much to do with the problem as the quality of the information: the vast amount of conflicting data available on bioterrorism—both supporting and contradicting the positions of the CDC—might mean that local figures such as fire chiefs attain greater importance simply because they can serve as filters, reducing the overwhelming flow of information to a more manageable size.

To add a Lutzian twist to this section of the book, the last three chapters deal with institutional arenas in which deception is often rewarded, celebrated, and expected. My own work is informed by the evidence that much of what is accepted as sensible, rational business practice in financial markets involves deception. Language such as "caveat emptor" and "information asymmetry" put a polite face on these behaviors—there is no "fraud" until someone gets caught—but they suggest the degree to which paltering and outright lies are understood and accepted as part of standard operating procedure. As a result, the claims by some people accused of financial fraud—such as Martha Stewart—that they were not aware of committing any wrongdoing seem at least partially plausible, which once again raises the tricky issues of intent and awareness in defining deception.

The ambiguous status of deception as an "authorized" behavior in financial transactions is paralleled by deception's changing role in military strategy. As William Glenney IV reviews in his chapter, "Military Deception in the Information Age: Scale Matters," deceptive tactics embraced in Asian contexts (and recorded in texts such as the *Art of War* by Sun Tzu) were until recently rejected by Western military strategists as both uncivilized and unmanly—a last resort of the weak and dishonorable. But the rise of guerrilla and extranational warfare, including terrorist networks that transcend political boundaries, has brought about a reconsideration of deception's role in Western military strategy. The change has been extremely slow, however, lagging far behind the empirical evidence: despite long-standing acceptance of disinformation and propaganda as weapons of war, the bias against other forms of deception is so strong in the West that lessons from conflicts that occurred decades earlier (such as the Vietnam War) are only now having an impact on the organization and deployment of American and European military forces.

Finally, the volume closes with Fields's chapter, "The Pleasures of Lying," which sums up several thousand years' worth of celebration of tricksters, liars, and cheats. This essay brings the book back to its starting point by featuring animals as agents of deception—as Bergstrom's chapter does—and by challenging the long Western tradition of moral condemnation of deception (as reviewed by Zeckhauser and Schauer). Fields, in contrast, shows us how many cultures have taken exactly the opposite view, including ancient Greece (which lionized Odysseus for his skillful deceptions) as well as early-modern Africa (cradle of the folktales featuring Ur-deceiver Brer Rabbit that came to America via the slave trade) and Native America, where the antihero of many stories is the lying, sneaky coyote. In all three cases, deception is an integral part of cultural institutions and serves multiple purposes: as a teaching tool (especially when it comes to lessons about survival), as a socialization mechanism, and as a rhetorical vessel for safeguarding traditions threatened by warfare or colonialism.

Beyond True and False

While the deceptions by government institutions recounted in Rowan's chapter come across as wholly negative events, those described in the chapter by Fields make it difficult to come away from this volume with a clear-cut moral stance, or even a pragmatic cost-benefit analysis of deception. That is very much by intent. Ultimately, this book aims to represent deception as the complex, multifaceted, and elusive phenomenon it is: to deny those qualities would be to rob deception of much of its significance to world history and its power to fascinate and puzzle some of the greatest thinkers in history.

While this volume resists reductionism, it is nevertheless possible to observe and highlight a number of regularities across its chapters. For example, the following themes recur throughout the text, tying together disparate fields of inquiry in the sciences and humanities:

- Defining deception has always been a matter of controversy, but there is broad agreement that deception can occur without any intent or deliberate falsehood; examples include adaptive deception in the animal kingdom as well as self-deception by humans.
- Lying is among the least problematic modes of deception, since definitions of the phenomenon and sanctions against it are generally clearcut; but we have far fewer institutional and conceptual mechanisms for dealing with partial truths and self-deception, making deception without falsehood a more insidious and potentially damaging issue.
- Despite historically and culturally variable definitions of deception, the concept is inevitably linked to notions of truth and trust; we cannot discuss deception without considering the other two, implicitly or explicitly.
- Deception ordinarily involves *interaction* between two or more parties; the amount and type of deception in any given case are shaped by the

institutional and technological contexts: wartime versus peacetime, for example, or online versus face-to-face communication.

- Judeo-Christian cultures are conflicted on the moral status of deception; while numerous religious and philosophical sources condemn it in all circumstances, there is tacit acceptance of deception in love and war, as well as for "palliative" purposes (that is, to shield people who are deemed physically or psychologically fragile from upsetting truths that might cause their condition to deteriorate) and for entertainment (as when the deceived collaborate with the deceivers by suspending disbelief).

- Many non-Western cultures treat deception in an explicitly positive light and use it to serve important functions, including adaptation, teaching, socialization, and survival.

Research on truth wizards indicates that the highest forms of awareness of deception involve remaining open to the data and avoiding premature conclusions. As the bulleted items above imply, this book asks something similar of readers. In this sense, the book is as much about the *process* of inquiry into the workings of a complex system as it is about providing insight.

I DEFINING AND DETECTING DECEPTION

1 Dealing with Deception in Biology

Carl T. Bergstrom

L IFE GETS INTERESTING when it gets complicated—and nothing complicates life so much as society. Flowing through the network of social conventions, institutions, obligations, and expectations that make civilization possible are a complex suite of individual motivations, sometimes common and sometimes conflicting, upon which tenuous alliances are formed and broken. We humans are fascinated by this complexity and drawn naturally to it. Here, gossip seeps through the bedrock of friendship; here, the politics draw us in against our better judgment; here, theater becomes gripping as intrigues multiply; here, Walter Scott's tangled web demands every iota of our cognitive ability to carry out our deceptions while unveiling those of others.[1] Society becomes possible through a matrix of trust, coordination, and communication, which provides countless alcoves where deception lurks and threatens to undermine the very social order that brings it into being.

Biology is no different. Biology gets interesting when simple structures aggregate and diversify to form larger and more complex units of organization.

CARL T. BERGSTROM is associate professor of biology at the University of Washington and an external faculty member at the Santa Fe Institute. His research explores the role of information in social and biological systems. His recent projects include contributions to the game theory of communication and deception, applications of information theory to understanding complex networks, bibliometric work on ranking and mapping scientific journals, and a number of more applied studies in disease evolution.

Cells bring together once-independent organelles, bodies aggregate billions of cells, colonies collect together thousands of bodies, and ecosystems comprise a "webwork" of competing, cooperating, and coexisting species. The diversity and complexity of the biological world emerges from the hierarchies of social organization—and from the intricate mechanisms required to keep these hierarchies from splintering along lines of individual incentive.

Such is the central thesis of the influential 1995 monograph, *The Major Transitions in Evolution*, which laid out a research program for a generation of evolutionary biologists.[2] Its authors, John Maynard Smith and Eors Szathmáry, envision the history of life as the story of a series of major evolutionary innovations and transitions allowing organisms and societies to increase in complexity and efficiency.[3] Some of these transitions, such as the shift from unicellularity to multicellularity, or the shift from asociality to eusociality, facilitated cooperation by aggregating previously independent agents into ensembles with linked reproductive fates. These transitions allowed the agents to exploit economies of scale, and in particular, gains to specialization. Other transitions engendered cooperation and trust by changing the rules of the games without physically aggregating the individuals involved. In these latter transitions, the agents impose upon one another strategic incentives that once again facilitate the economies of scale and gains to specialization, but in this case the agents continue to operate independently while also facilitating the economies of scale.

What does this have to do with deception? A great deal. First, in order to benefit from aggregation or cooperation of the sort discussed above, participants need ways of coordinating their actions. For coordination, they need communication. This opens the door for deception; where one can communicate, one can manipulate.[4] Somehow, the deception problem must be overcome in order to move through the major transitions that Maynard Smith and Szathmáry contemplate.

Second, when it comes to cooperation, one of the easiest things to share is information. A key insight from Maynard Smith and Szathmáry is the idea that most if not all of these transitions increase the scale upon which organisms and societies can acquire, store, process, and transmit *information*. Innovations, such as the shift from RNA-based to DNA-based genetic information, or the shift from simple signals to combinatorial representational language, offer leaps in information technology that allow organisms to better extract information from their environments and transmit this information to other individuals. Why is information and information sharing so important in generating major evolutionary transitions? Cooperation and sharing are particularly likely to emerge for information resources rather than physical goods, because of the unique stoichiometry of information. As Lachmann and colleagues showed in an elegant model of information acquisition and exchange, information sharing works differently than the sharing of physical resources.[5] A quotation commonly attributed to George Bernard Shaw summarizes the underlying concept that drives their model:

> If you have an apple and I have an apple and we exchange apples then you and I will still each have one apple. But if you have an idea and I have an idea and we exchange these ideas, each of us will have two ideas.

Those readers whose political inclinations leave them skeptical of sermons on sharing delivered by celebrated socialists may consider Thomas Jefferson to be a more reputable source:

> He who receives an idea from me, receives instruction himself without lessening mine; as he who lights his taper at mine, receives light without darkening me. That ideas should freely spread from one to another over the globe, for the moral and mutual instruction of man, and improvement of his condition, seems to have been peculiarly and benevolently designed by nature, when she made them, like fire, expansible over all space, without lessening their density in any point.[6]

Whatever one's leanings, there is clearly a highly favorable stoichiometry for sharing information. But where receiving shared information can be beneficial, it can be dangerous as well. Signalers have the means to effect changes in the behavior of those to whom they signal. Where the interests of signaler and signal receiver diverge, there exist both incentives and opportunity for manipulation by sending misleading information. Deception is the major obstacle to information sharing—and the living world is rife with deception. From the lure that an anglerfish uses to attract prey to the false alarm that a flycatcher raises to dissuade competitors, from bluegill sunfish males that sneak matings by masquerading as females to the mimic octopus that can imitate a wide range of poisonous creatures and other underwater objects, from the false mating signals of carnivorous fireflies to the sham regenerated claw of a fiddler crab, and from the chemical mimicry that caterpillars use to invade the nest chambers of ants to the bluffing threats of a molting stomatopod, organisms deceive one another in every imaginable way in order to attain every conceivable advantage.[7]

So this creates a puzzle. On the one hand, communication provides organisms with the means to deceive, and indeed deception is common in animal signals. On the other hand, for animal communication systems to evolve, they have to be beneficial—and thus presumably somewhat honest—on average. After all, if they were not beneficial, the intended signal receivers would evolve to ignore them. If signal receivers ignored these messages, they would be useless, and signalers would eventually evolve not to send them. Maynard Smith and Harper put this in game-theoretic terms: "It is not evolutionarily stable for the receiver to alter its behaviour [in response to a signal] unless, on average, the signal carries information of value to it."[8] This insight can be formalized within game theory using the concept of information value.[9]

To resolve this puzzle, let us explore the ways in which living organisms deal with all of this deception. In order to do so clearly, we will distinguish between two different forms of deception that organisms must deter or detect.

1. *Deception by society members.* The "legitimate participants" in a social interaction or signaling situation have different interests from one another, and thus have incentives to manipulate one another by deception.[10]

2. *Subversion by rogue outsiders.* The legitimate participants in a social interaction or signaling system have coincident interests, but "rogue outsiders" may attempt to parasitize the system by subterfuge.

We might see the first type of deception in animal (or human!) courtship. For example, when a suitor displays to a potential mate, both are legitimate participants in the interaction, but the suitor has an incentive to overrepresent his or her virtues in an effort to impress. We might see the latter type of deception when a caterpillar mimics the hydrocarbon signals that ants use for nestmate recognition, in order to gain access to the brood chambers and a ready meal of ant larvae. I will explore further examples of both types in the subsequent sections.

Before doing so, we can draw out the comparison by taking a slight detour to consider a relatively recent human institution. The Internet auction site eBay has been remarkably successful at extending the scope of small-scale interpersonal commerce from local to global. As eBay draws upon explicitly in its business model, this requires the creation of trust within the community, and requires that there be effective mechanisms in place to deal with the threat of deception.[11] Think about the various perils that one might confront when shopping for a rare book on eBay. An otherwise honest dealer might palter, accurately listing a book as "first edition" but omitting the additional detail that this particular volume was printed in such great quantities as to render the first edition nearly worthless. In a more serious deception, an unscrupulous antique dealer might exaggerate the condition or quality of a rare book in order to generate a higher selling price.

These are examples of deception by society members. Both the dealer and the potential buyer are the intended participants in the auction system; the only problem is that the dealer has an incentive to deceive so as to increase his or her profits. The eBay system deals with this threat in a number of ways: with an extensive reputation system, with a suite of dispute-resolution tools and procedures, and with limited third-party guarantees over some transactions.

Compare this to deception by rogue outsiders, such as the "phishing" schemes that Paul Thompson describes in detail later in this volume. For example, a perpetrator might set up a fake website designed to look like eBay and send e-mails to eBay users in an attempt to lure them to the site, where these users may be tricked into entering credit card information or other valuable data. In this scenario, the perpetrator is not an intended participant in the interaction, and the con artist uses deception to insert him- or herself into the communication flow between the intended parties. The company goes to extensive lengths to help users protect themselves against this form of deception, such as providing a tutorial on how to avoid falling prey to phishing scams and other deceptive tactics.[12] Moreover, eBay communicates with users only through a highly protected channel, its own site-internal message system, and never by general e-mail that can more easily be "spoofed."

So that is eBay's situation; numerous other Internet communities and, more generally, human social institutions face similar problems. But what about biology? Where in nonhuman biological systems do these opportunities for deceit arise, and what sorts of mechanisms have evolved to deter deception?

Deception by Society Members

The basic problem of honest communication is as follows:

> *Information asymmetry*: A signaler has private information not available to a signal receiver.
>
> *Gains to exchange*: Both parties could gain by honestly sharing this information.
>
> *Strategic conflict*: The signaler and receiver have different preferences with regard to the receiver's actions—and thus the signaler may have an incentive to manipulate the receiver by means of deception.
>
> *How can honest communication be ensured?*

From the profusion of signals that saturate the living world, we can infer that this problem is somehow resolved. Whether we are walking along a rocky ocean shore, bicycling along a forest path, or simply soaking up the sunshine in a mountain meadow, a huge fraction of our sensory experience comes from stimuli that evolved precisely for the purpose of operating as signals. Calls, patterns, colors, fragrances—these are just a few of the modalities by which signals are sent and received.

In the early 1970s, economist Michael Spence and biologist Amotz Zahavi independently proposed what was essentially the same solution to this problem.[13] Spence proposed his solution to explain how higher education serves as a signal from employee to employer and developed a formal game-theoretic model in its support; for this work, he shared a Nobel Prize with George Akerloff and Joseph Stiglitz. Zahavi proposed his solution in an effort to understand why animals often produce extravagant ornaments and displays, and his strictly verbal formulation was met with skepticism until it was formalized mathematically many years later by other researchers.[14] Before proceeding to a concrete example, let us summarize the general solution.

> *Spence-Zahavi solution*: If signals are costly and lying costs more than honesty, everyone may do best by simply telling the truth.

But why would this be? Why would lies be more costly than honest signals? To answer this question, we turn to Zahavi's paradigm case, the tail of the peacock (*Pavo cristatus*).[15]

In this example, the peacock is the signaler, and his perspective mate, the peahen, is the signal receiver. The cock has private information about his own condition: he alone knows whether he is strong or weak, well fed or undernourished, healthy or parasite ridden. The hen would benefit from knowing this information, because she could then make a good choice as to whether to accept the peacock as a mate. (We assume that she benefits from choosing a high-quality male to father her offspring.) But the cock may have an incentive to deceive her. If he is in poor condition, he would do well to feign otherwise so as to avoid being rejected.

How can honest communication occur in this circumstance? The peacock's extravagant tail is the key. A weak or sickly male can scarcely afford to divert energetic resources from basic upkeep to the production of ornaments, and moreover he would have a hard time escaping from a predator if his flight were hindered by a long tail. A strong and healthy male, by contrast, can readily afford the additional costs of producing bright colors and a long tail, and he can usually escape a predator despite the length of his tail.

Because only the high-quality males can afford bright colors and long tails, peahens prefer mates with these characteristics. High-quality males, for their part, produce these bright colors and extravagant plumes to ensure that they are chosen as mates by females. Low-quality males cannot afford to do so, thus they will produce duller colors and shorter tails. Perhaps next year they will be stronger and able to be more ambitious with their plumage.

This was a wonderful idea on Zahavi's part, because it resolved two huge puzzles in evolutionary biology by showing that each puzzle was actually the solution to the other. The puzzles are these: (1) Why are signals honest despite incentives to deceive? (2) Why are so many biological signals extravagant if natural selection favors efficient use of resources?

But does Zahavi's solution work? Game-theoretic models indicate that it does. To show why with full rigor, we need to deal simultaneously with the signaling strategy of the signaler and the response strategy of the signal receiver, and to show that each is a best response to the other; Bergstrom et al. provide a general methodology for doing so.[16] Without going into the mathematical complexities of that approach, we can still capture much of the intuition for why this mechanism works with a simple graphical model.[17] Here, we treat the receiver's response to different signals as fixed, and we look at the properties of the optimal signaling strategy for signalers, given these responses.

Figure 1.1 shows a hypothetical set of fitness costs and benefits for peacocks playing the "mating game" described above. The dark, concave-down curve labeled *fitness benefit* indicates the advantage—in terms of mating success—that accrues to a male as a function of the size of his tail. The lighter, concave-up curves illustrate the fitness costs—in terms of energy expenditure, increased predation risk, and the like—of producing a tail for peacocks of low, medium, and high quality, respectively. High-quality peacocks can produce larger tails more readily than can medium-quality peacocks, which in turn can do so more readily than low-quality ones.

Each peacock is selected to maximize his fitness and to choose a tail size that maximizes the difference between the fitness benefit received and the fitness cost of producing it. The dashed lines in Figure 1.1 indicate optimal

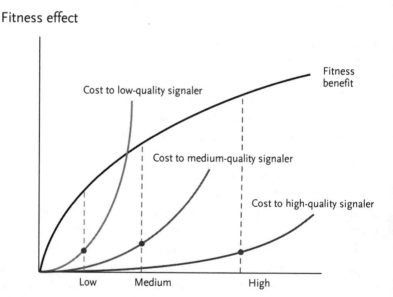

Fitness effect

Cost to low-quality signaler

Fitness benefit

Cost to medium-quality signaler

Cost to high-quality signaler

Low   Medium   High

Tail size

FIGURE 1.1 Costly signaling

SOURCE: Adapted from M. Lachman, S. Számadó, and C. Bergstrom, "Cost and Conflict in Animal Signals and Human Language," *Proceedings of the National Academy of Sciences, USA,* 98 (2001): 13189–94.

tail sizes for low-, medium-, and high-quality peacocks; the dots indicate the fitness costs incurred by these qualities of birds.

From this figure, we can see costly signaling in action. Even though peacocks are free to "choose" the optimal tail length given their condition, we see that here:

1. *Signals are costly.* Each cock incurs a nonzero fitness cost from producing its showy tail.

2. *Signals are honest.* Higher-quality birds produce larger tails, and the hen can thus infer quality from the size of the peacock's tail.

We can view the diagram in Figure 1.1 as an illustration of the mathematical vindication of Zahavi's idea. Costly signals can provide a way of dealing with deception in biological systems. Yet this seems to be an extremely wasteful way of transmitting information. Indeed, in some cases, costly signaling systems such as the one described can leave signaler and signal receiver worse off than if no signal were sent at all.[18] Can there not be some way of sending honest signals at reduced cost?

To answer this question, we can take a cue from the house sparrow (*Passer domesticus*). This species (and many related ones, including the often-studied Harris's Sparrow, *Zonotrichia querula*) signal dominance or fighting ability using relatively minor and inconspicuous variations in plumage, such as variable throat bibs or forehead patches.[19] In the case of the house sparrow, the signal is the size of the black throat patch. The size of the throat patch honestly signals fighting ability: birds with larger badges are less likely to be challenged and more likely to win if challenged than are birds with smaller badges.

In the sparrow's case, in contrast to that of the peacock, the cost of actually *producing* the signal is very low: it involves only the negligible expense of altering the shade of a few feathers. So what keeps this signaling system honest? Why do the lower-status birds not produce a deceptively large throat patch so as to feign dominance? The answer comes from the behavior of the other individuals in the social environment. Sparrows that "cheat" by exaggerating their own condition in their choice of badge are attacked and punished by conspecifics.[20]

Here we see a different kind of honest signaling. Producing the signal is not costly in and of itself, but rather the costs only accrue through the actions of other birds that enforce the signaling conventions, attacking any bird that produces a throat patch that is too large for its status. When signal costs arise from the punishing behavior of the signal receiver, signals can be entirely free when honest, and expensive only when deceptive.[21] Figure 1.2 provides a geometric representation of this type of honest signaling. Here signals are honest, just as in the peacock example of Figure 1.1, but now the optimal choices of signal for each signaler, indicated by the points labeled low, medium, and high, are not costly. This figure illustrates that what enforces signal honesty is not the total cost of signaling a particular quality, but rather the marginal cost. In other words, it is not the expense of honest signals that enforces honesty, but rather the increase in expense that comes from sending dishonest signals.

Why does the peacock get stuck having to construct and maintain an elaborate and expensive tail in order to signal his quality, whereas the sparrow can signal quality with a simple and inexpensive adjustment to throat coloration? The difference is that, in the peacock's case, the female signal receiver has no ready way to verify the accuracy of the message. To ascertain whether the cock really had the good genes that he was advertising, a peahen would have

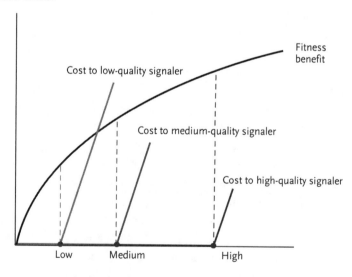

FIGURE 1.2 Cost-free signaling

SOURCE: Adapted from M. Lachman, S. Számadó, and C. Bergstrom, "Cost and Conflict in Animal Signals and Human Language," *Proceedings of the National Academy of Sciences, USA,* 98 (2001): 13189–94.

to mate with him, raise her offspring, count the survivors among them, and do the necessary statistics to determine whether her mate has deceived her as to the quality of his genome. By then, of course, he is long gone. In this system, there is no ready way for receivers to detect and punish misleading signalers, thus honesty must be enforced by the cost of signal production. The sparrow, on the other hand, can easily assess the honesty of a throat-badge signal. It need only provoke a fight with the signaler to determine whether the signaler is indeed as tough as it has indicated by its coloration. Here, since assessment is quick and easy, signal costs can be imposed by the receiver and need not be associated with signal production.[22]

As we move beyond the types of animal signals described above to more complicated forms of communication, such as the combinatorial syntax and referential meaning that we see in human language, two things happen: (1) it becomes impossible to stabilize honest signals by assigning appropriate production costs to specific signals,[23] and (2) a whole new suite of extended possibilities for deceptive communication arises.[24] Costs associated with deception will almost always derive from the responses of receivers. Nonetheless, much of the basic logic illustrated in Figures 1.1 and 1.2 may continue to apply. For *Homo economicus* as well as *Pavo cristatus*, the choice of whether to deceive or not comes down to a cost-benefit analysis between the expected benefits from sending a particular signal and the costs associated with doing so. A signaler will advance his cause until the marginal cost of pushing further exceeds the marginal benefit of doing so.

For human communication, much of this may be mediated through systems of reputation. If I lie to you, you may retaliate directly; but you will more likely simply adjust your assessment of my character, trustworthiness, and desirability as a partner—be it in commerce, scholarship, or love. While human communication may lean on reputation in order to enforce honesty, human language also has the property of facilitating social enforcement by reputation. Through complex referential communication, I am able to share information about those who have wronged me and gain information about others' reputations, even in the absence of firsthand experience.

In this section, we have seen how biological systems facilitate honest communication despite incentives to deceive. In short, the game-theoretic answer to how one deals with deception is this: *The structure of the communication "game" must include appropriate strategic incentives against dishonesty.* These incentives may take the form of signal costs, reputation effects, or any of the other mechanisms—such as reciprocity, partner choice, and sanctions—that bolster cooperation.[25] The game-theoretic study of signaling draws its continued research interest from exploring the myriad forms that these incentives can take, and from studying the dynamical processes that give rise to these forms. How can the appropriate incentives and disincentives evolve by natural selection (in the case of animal signaling) or be constructed by those designing institutions (in the case of many human communication systems) to deal with deception?

And, with talk of constructing the appropriate incentives, we come back around to eBay. What eBay has done, and what allowed eBay to extend the social and geographic range of trusted commerce, was to set up highly efficient ways of distributing reputation information: a centralized, searchable database for each participant listing the experiences of all others who have previously dealt with that individual.[26] Compared to previous approaches of inquiring about another's character through one's own social network, this is a much more powerful way to obtain information about potential trade partners and their likelihood of acting deceptively. Thus eBay was able to capture the long tail of the market without requiring the long tail of the peacock as collateral against deception.[27]

Now let us return to biology and look at how biological systems avoid deception by rogue outsiders. Thus far we have concentrated on an example in which one bird signals to another bird. In order to focus on deception by rogue outsiders, we will shift our attention from communication between animals to communication among the cells within a single animal. We will use the cells of the vertebrate adaptive immune systems as our paradigm "society," and we will consider pathogens such as bacteria and viruses as the rogue outsiders. In particular, we will look at the way in which immune cells, in their communications with one another, avoid being deceived by pathogens that may attempt to interfere.

In this discussion of signaling among intended participants, I have been able to lay out a clean and, I hope, clear picture of the strategic conflicts that arise and how they can be resolved. The theory treated above is grounded in a well-developed foundation of simple game-theoretic models that highlight the important aspects of the problem while abstracting away unnecessary details. The study of subversion by rogue outsiders has not yet reached this point; researchers have yet to identify the clear, simple models that capture the essence of the problem but include nothing more. In part, this is because the problem of deception by rogue outsiders has received less attention in the theoretical behavioral ecology and game-theory literatures to date. In part, it is due to the difficulty in circumscribing the range of possible deceptions that an outsider can employ. As a result, the following section is somewhat more speculative and open ended than has heretofore been the case. This is exciting: the discussion in the next section describes an area that is ripe for future theoretical development.

Subversion by Rogue Outsiders

Think about the staggering challenge that the human immune system faces in doing its job. To function properly, it needs to be able to acquire information about what is self and nonself. It must continually scan the cells of the body for any sign of nonself. It has to process this information to mount appropriate responses. It must coordinate those responses among the millions of cells involved. Ideally, it should store this information as immune memory for subsequent use.

In doing all of these things, our immune system has to be extremely sensitive to detect rapidly reproducing pathogens early on in an infection. It has to identify the proverbial needle of a nonself protein (for example, one produced by a virus) among a haystack of self proteins within any individual cell. It must recognize and respond to any of the countless varieties of pathogens that could arise over evolutionary time. It must very narrowly target the pathogen or pathogen-infected cells, without attacking other parts of the body. Finally, our immune system must have a very low rate of Type I error (false positive), because any such mistake can trigger a potentially disastrous autoimmune reaction.

The inevitable trade-offs between these requirements pose a control-theorist's nightmare, but this is only the beginning. To make matters immeasurably worse, pathogens typically replicate within the body of the host and thus have ample opportunity to subvert immune function by sabotage or subterfuge.[28] For example, pox viruses such as chickenpox and smallpox have evolved not so much to avoid detection by the immune system, but rather to confuse the immune system and render it impotent.[29] Among other stratagems, they target the chemokine-signaling molecules that the immune system uses to regulate and coordinate its responses. Pox viruses interfere with the chemokine-signaling system in almost every imaginable way. They sabotage some chemokine signals by producing enzymes that degrade the signal molecules. They spoof other chemokine signals by producing false-signal proteins that stimulate chemokine receptors. And they tamper with gene expression on the part of the host organism, altering chemokine-signal production in that way. Pox viruses also sabotage the receptors, both by attacking them directly and by producing decoy chemokine receptors that attract the host's chemokine signal molecules and prevent those signals from reaching their true targets.[30]

Due to the threat of this kind of deception, immune systems have to be robust not only to noise, but also to targeted misinformation and other forms of deceptive signals or information attacks: they have to be *strategically robust*. Another computer analogy can help to elaborate on this distinction between robustness and strategic robustness. When constructing a mission-critical computer system, the engineers need to build in sufficient robustness to noise and accidental component failure such that the system will function despite occasional power spikes and electrical interference. They need to make sure that it will keep working across a range of temperatures and even when a few resistors burn out or one of the memory chips fails. That would be a robust system. Designing a strategically robust system is an even greater challenge; here, one has to construct a computer system that will continue to function even if an expert technician with access to the inner workings of the machine tries to sabotage it by jamming it with targeted electrical interference, by introducing malicious software, or by removing key physical components.

How can immune systems meet this challenge? How can they carry out the coordination and communication necessary to respond with specificity, breadth, precision, and accuracy, *while simultaneously remaining strategically robust to deceptive signals from pathogens*? As immunologists come to an increasingly refined understanding of the intricate molecular biology of immune learning, recognition, signaling, regulation, and memory, they are starting to uncover the answers to this question. And by comparing the tricks and tactics that the vertebrate adaptive immune system uses to avoid internal deception with the tactics used by other immune systems, evolutionary biologists can uncover general themes in the way that biological systems evolve to deal with deception from within.[31]

This type of study is still in its early stages in biology; we lack a detailed theory of how systems evolve to avoid internal deception and subversion. But to illustrate the sorts of insights that biology does offer, in the paragraphs that follow I will briefly describe just a few of the common mechanisms of avoiding internal deception and subversion, with examples drawn from the vertebrate adaptive immune system. A more detailed discussion and examples from other immune systems are provided in Bergstrom and Antia's 2006 paper.[32]

Redundancy   One of the most straightforward mechanisms for ensuring that a system continues to function smoothly despite noise, component failure, or sabotage and deception is to use multiple, redundant pathways to carry out the desired functions. For example, if one needs to ensure an uninterrupted source of power, it is very useful to have one or more backup generators in place in case something happens to the primary power source. If a system has redundant pathways and any single pathway fails with probability x, the chance of all pathways failing—and thus the system as a whole failing—is the much smaller value x^k. We see this strategy of redundant pathways in the vertebrate adaptive immune system, which deploys multiple branches—including nonspecific and other forms of innate immunity, cell-mediated immunity (killer T-cells), and humoral immunity (the antibody response)—in its efforts to guard against invading pathogens. If one branch is shut down by sabotage or deception, the other branches remain and may well be sufficient to eliminate the threat. Having multiple redundant defenses also makes it harder for a pathogen to evolve ways around an immune system. Even if the pathogen manages to deceive one branch of the immune system, the others can eliminate it—and thus a pathogen derives little if any fitness benefit from outfoxing a single one of the immune pathways.

Distributed Control   In systems where internal deception is not a concern, one of the most effective ways to achieve coordination among multiple dispersed components is to have a *central controller* that instructs the many components of the system via *broadcast signals.* In living systems, we see precisely this approach in endocrine (hormonal) regulation. For example, the pituitary gland is a central controller that regulates numerous metabolic, developmental, and reproductive processes by emitting a suite of hormone signals that control the behavior of numerous organs and tissues. But systems that are regulated by a central controller can be highly vulnerable to deception. If some antagonistic agent (such as a pathogen) takes over the central controller to alter the nature and timing of signals, or even spoofs the broadcast signals, it can deceive the dispersed components that receive these signals, and alter the behavior of the entire system for its own purposes.

By way of analogy, suppose I want to coordinate the actions of a set of colleagues so that everyone submits a paper on the same day. One way to do this is to give each a small radio, and to broadcast a message "submit now!" at the appropriate time. But this method is vulnerable to subversion: someone could steal my transmitter, or spoof my message, and thereby alter the behavior of all of my colleagues in any way that she desired. If subversion is a concern, a safer alternative would be to give each of my colleagues a wristwatch with a calendar and to let them check their own watches and then act at some prearranged time, say, noon on January 1st. Once a plan of this sort is put into place, there is no central target for an antagonistic agent and no single broadcast signal that the agent can spoof to take control of the individuals' actions. To change the behavior of the group, the saboteur would have to access and alter each and every wristwatch.

The vertebrate immune system, which functions to eliminate pathogen threats and is thus a natural target for disruption and deception by pathogens, makes scant use of central control and broadcast signals. Instead, we see an extensive reliance on *distributed processing*. Decisions and commands are "pushed to the periphery": sensing and control occurs over small local scales via signaling among the individual components—immune cells—circulating throughout the body. While the immune system has multiple mechanisms for turning off immune reactions that are directed toward the self or that are ineffective, these are highly local in operation. There is no command center that a pathogen can take over or spoof in order to cancel an immune reaction with one simple signal. We see a similar logic of control in the intracellular immune system of RNA interference.[33]

Commitment Instead of Feedback Control   One of the foundations of control-system design is the use of feedback or "closed-loop" control. A feedback controller measures the output or progress of a system, compares this output with the desired trajectory, and adjusts its input accordingly.[34] Feedback controllers allow systems to function effectively across a range of conditions, stabilize otherwise unstable dynamic processes, and facilitate closer tracking of the desired trajectory. Relative to open-loop control, in which there is no mechanism for monitoring a system's progress and responding accordingly, closed-loop control is a highly efficient way to regulate and coordinate behavior. Thus it is of little surprise that feedback control is widely used in biological systems, from adjusting the circadian clock to the control of metabolism, from cell signaling to hormonal regulation, and from bacterial navigation to DNA replication to limb development.[35]

But feedback control is risky in the face of potential internal deception. Implicit in the idea of feedback control is that the system responds to certain kinds of stimuli—and where these stimuli can be faked, the system can be co-opted. In other words, when one cannot trust the controller, or one cannot trust one's measurements of a system's progress, feedback control can be dangerous.

Thus perhaps it is unsurprising that the vertebrate adaptive immune system omits feedback control in some of its regulatory machineries. In one of the most striking examples, recent experiments and mathematical models indicate that the growing populations of CD8 T-cells that deal with viral infections do not track the current density of pathogens within the body, contrary to the common belief.[36] Instead, the population of CD8 cells targeting a specific pathogen often continues to grow long after that pathogen is cleared by the immune system or by artificial means. Rather than relying on feedback control, CD8 cell lines appear early on to commit the course of an infection to a "programmed" period of expansion that cannot be halted even if the pathogen disappears entirely. This makes sense; early in the course of an infection, a pathogen is at low density and is less likely to be able to tamper with immune sensing and signaling. Thus the cells of the immune system commit to a plan of action at this point, and despite some inefficiency from operating without feedback control, they do not adjust this plan later, when the pathogen could potentially be at higher density and better able to tamper with immune regulation.

Cross-Validation   Another way to avoid being tricked by subversive signals from rogue outsiders is to make sure that no single signal is sufficient to initiate a potentially dangerous course of action. If I want to make sure that I am not fooled into doing something by a single charlatan, I may require not only a primary message from a primary signaler, but also a set of supporting messages from other individuals. While closely related to the concept of redundancy, in which multiple independent systems back one another up in case one is subverted, cross-validation features a single system that requires multiple inputs from varied sources before taking action.

For example, if an immune response could be cancelled by a single chemokine signal, the system would be highly vulnerable to deception by false chemokines of the sort that the pox viruses commonly produce. But if it takes several different signals of several different chemical classes to down-regulate an immune response, deception is less likely. If these multiple requisite signals are interrelated in complex ways (if one serves as a checksum for the others, for example), deception by spoofing is even harder. For these reasons, it seems likely that cross-validation will be important in the structure of immune signaling systems.

The field of immunology—with its endless roster of cell types and signals, receptors and modulators, with its hopelessly entangled pathways of communication and regulation—is among all of the biological sciences perhaps the most notoriously hard to learn. One might conjecture, not entirely in jest, that this is no accident. Perhaps it has evolved to be so. The same cascades of complexity that have stymied legions of medical students and that have fascinated generations of researchers may have evolved precisely because what students and researchers could learn quickly, pathogens could learn as well through the action of natural selection on trillions of virus particles reproducing many times a day within each of billions of host individuals over the time span of millions of years.

In this section, we have considered how one particular biological system, the vertebrate immune system, carries out the extensive information gathering and signaling that it requires, despite the threat of deception by rapidly evolving pathogens. The structures of other immune systems offer comparable lessons.[37] To prevent deception by rogue outsiders, it is not sufficient to evolve or impose strategic incentives on the intended signaler; the intended signaler is not the one that is potentially causing the trouble. Rather, there can be an unending line of additional individuals trying to find ways in to exploit the system, and they must be deterred as well. Perhaps there are no hard-and-fast rules about how to do this, but in examining the structure and control logic of immune systems, we do see repeated use of a few key design principles, including redundancy, distributed control, commitment, and cross-validation.

Society requires coordination, which in turn requires honest communication among the participants in a social group. Therefore, to facilitate any sort of social structure and interaction, there has to be some way to deal with the threat of deception. Natural selection has been grappling with this problem for several billion years, innovating and testing approach after approach, solution after solution in the crucible of biological competition. Perhaps as we seek ways to deal with deception in our own societies, in our institutions, in our own communication systems, we can learn from what natural selection has devised, much as we have benefited from biologically inspired design in so many other areas of engineering.

2 Paltering

Frederick Schauer and Richard Zeckhauser

T O IMMANUEL KANT (as well as to Aristotle, St. Augustine, St. Thomas Aquinas, and countless others) lying was simply and absolutely wrong.[1] For Kant, the intentional assertion of a knowingly factually false proposition was a morally impermissible act that derived from its incompatibility with the liar's own dignity as a human being. By contrast, others have located the wrong of the lie in its deprivation of the victim's ability to choose and thus of the victim's autonomy.[2] And still others have assessed lying's impermissibility in utilitarian terms.[3] But regardless of whether it be through a focus on the liar, the victim, or the well-being of society at large, we have inherited a venerable tradition that has little hesitance in condemning lying as wrong.

FREDERICK SCHAUER is Frank Stanton Professor of the First Amendment, Emeritus, at the John F. Kennedy School of Government, Harvard University, and David and Mary Harrison Distinguished Professor of Law, University of Virginia. He works on constitutional law, freedom of speech, and the forms of legal reasoning and legal argument. Among his books are: *Free Speech: A Philosophical Enquiry* (1982), *Playing by the Rules: A Philosophical Examination of Rule-Based Decision-Making in Law and in Life* (1991), *Profiles, Probabilities, and Stereotypes* (2003), and *Thinking Like a Lawyer: A New Introduction to Legal Reasoning* (2009).

RICHARD ZECKHAUSER is Frank P. Ramsey Professor of Political Economy at the John F. Kennedy School of Government, Harvard University. A pioneer in the field of policy analysis, he conducts conceptual and policy studies using decision analysis and microeconomics. His most recent (coauthored) books are *Targeting in Social Programs: Avoiding Bad Bets, Removing Bad Apples* (2006) and *The Patron's Payoff: Conspicuous Commissions in Italian Renaissance Art* (2008). His experience with deception comes from playing bridge; he won the 2007 United States Mixed Pair Championship.

Although few nowadays subscribe to the Kantian view in its unalloyed form, lying is still widely considered morally objectionable. Yet despite the virtual unanimity of the view that lying is presumptively even if not absolutely wrong, it is not entirely clear which component of a lie is the principal contributor to the lie's wrongness, or whether one or more of those components is sufficient on its own. To be more precise, we commonly understand a liar to be someone who *intentionally* utters words that he or she knows to be false, where what is uttered is in fact *literally false*, and where utterance of the literally false words produces the *effect* of the listener believing or being likely to believe in the truth of something that is not in fact true.[4] A lie in its full glory, therefore, involves elements of intent, literal meaning, and effect. When one or more of these elements is missing, we would be hesitant to designate the activity as lying, even though it might in other ways be morally questionable or socially detrimental.

Just as a lie involves the confluence of all three of these elements, so does the absence of all of the three constitute truth telling in its purest form—the sincere assertion of a proposition both believed to be true and actually true, under circumstances in which the assertion either creates or reinforces a belief by the listener in a true proposition. Yet although we can thus distinguish truth telling from lying, numerous statements are, intriguingly, neither lies nor truth tellings. Rather, they make up a universe of morally and socially problematic statements and propositional actions in which one or more of the elements of the genuine lie is missing, but in which one or more of the elements of authentic full-bore truth telling is missing as well. Sometimes we talk about "misstatements," and sometimes we (or the law) criticize or punish people for "misleading" others, understanding that in such instances we are concerned with the effect on the listener more than with the moral worth of the speaker or the literal meaning of the words used.

Our goal in this chapter is to explore this area of "less than lying" and to focus in particular on the widespread practice of fudging, twisting, shading, bending, stretching, slanting, exaggerating, distorting, whitewashing, and selective reporting. Such deceptive practices are occasionally designated by the uncommon word *paltering*, which the *American Heritage Dictionary* defines as acting insincerely or misleadingly. Although the intended effect of a palter is the same as that of a lie, both the dictionary definition and everyday usage of related ideas make a palter somewhat troublesome while still less than a full-fledged lie. More specifically, the palter falls short of being a lie in two important dimensions.

First, the palter may not be literally false. One of us is a furniture maker and is known by his friends to be a furniture maker. When a friend comments on the excellent workmanship of a store-bought desk in his office and he responds by saying "thank you," he has paltered, because he has left the false impression that he made the desk himself, even though none of his words said so explicitly.[5] Relatedly, and more commonly, paltering is somewhat more active and creative. The other of us is a tournament bridge player. When asked about his successes, he might remark: "When I played in the World Pairs Championship recently, we got to the finals," intentionally omitting mention of the fact that in pairs tournaments a sizable fraction of the pairs—10 percent in this case—reach the finals, and omitting mention as well of his more frequent worse results. Thus the typical palter achieves its misleading effect without the use of literal falsity.

In addition to not relying on literal falsity to produce its misleading effect, the typical palter, like the ones just noted, often seems at least slightly less harmful than the typical lie. We treat palters as sometimes unfortunate and sometimes not, but to accuse someone of paltering—even assuming he knows what the word means—falls short of calling someone a liar. Indeed, in many cases we make no charge at all against the palterer, in part because we are embarrassed to have been fooled, but in part because the Kantian legacy has left a residue of belief that the lack of literal falsity is indicative both of lesser harm and of a lesser wrong.

Although palterers often escape unscathed and even uncriticized, part of our claim in this paper is that it is nevertheless a mistake to regard palters as generally harmless or near harmless. Often a particular palter seems as wrongful as would a lie in the same or similar circumstances, and often its consequences are as severe. Indeed, the expected harm of a particular palter may occasionally be greater than the harm of a similar lie, *ceteris paribus*, just because palterers are more likely than liars to escape detection. And insofar as a particular palter, even if detected, is less likely to be subject to either legal or nonlegal blame, the expected harm may again on occasion exceed the expected harm of an analogous lie. These factors together suggest that the use of a palter is often as reprehensible as the use of a lie, and perhaps at times more so just because choosing to palter rather than to lie, assuming equivalent intent to deceive and equivalent harm to the victim, is typically a much safer strategy.

Given that the expected punishment of a palter is typically minimal, it is no surprise that paltering is widespread, and although a tally would be difficult to prepare, we would conjecture that the aggregate palters in the world do more harm than the aggregate lies, precisely because they are underpunished and underdeterred as compared to pure lies and hence are widely employed. In addition, palters are likely to be common relative to lies because, although there may be only one way (or just a few ways) to lie about a proposition, there are many ways to palter. Palters can abound therefore, even when effective lies are likely to be relatively rare.

In seeking to explore the dimensions of paltering, this chapter is motivated by our belief that individual palters are not only often more harmful than lies, but also that paltering in the aggregate is almost certainly much more common than lying. Yet the fact that paltering exists largely outside of the reach of the law, and indeed often outside the reach of the harshest of nonlegal social sanctions, may explain why it has not been well studied. If paltering is as harmful and as widespread as we believe, however, and if the typical palter leads the recipient—the palteree, if you will—to have an incorrect perception of reality, then the omnipresence of paltering may in fact be more of a social problem than many people suppose. This chapter thus aims to explore the practice of paltering, alongside of and in contrast to its cousin lying, and to examine the various ways in which the two activities might be controlled.

Definitional Preliminaries

Bearing in mind the three-part definition of the genuine lie as involving (1) an intent to deceive, (2) the use of words that are literally false, and (3) the presence of a recipient who is caused by the lie to have a misimpression of reality,[6] we can hypothesize the relaxation of one or two of these three components. If we relax the requirement of intent, we wind up with the category of statements in which speakers say something they erroneously believe to be true, in which that belief leads them to say things that are literally false, and in which those false statements lead listeners to have a false view of some actual state of affairs. Under many accounts, for example, the statements of President Bush about Iraqi weapons of mass destruction fit this characterization, for it is unlikely that he actually knew there were no weapons of mass destruction at the time he announced that they existed. Although the president might be charged with making a negligent misstatement, and thus with being somewhere between slightly and highly imprudent, we would not, contemporary political hyperbole aside, normally call the unintentional misstatement a lie, no matter the degree of negligence or recklessness. This requirement of actual intent to deceive is consistent with the common law of fraud, at least in its purest traditional form, which requires that there be some actual intent to mislead in order to support legal liability.[7] When the actual intent to deceive is missing, there is no fraud and there is no lie.

The unintentional misstatement does not amount to fraud in law, even when the other requirements of fraud are satisfied, but there are circumstances in which the law does impose other sorts of liability for unintentional misstatements. The common law of libel, for example, made libel (and slander) strict liability torts, such that the mere utterance of a reputation-harming falsehood could support legal liability—even absent the speaker's or writer's knowledge of falsity and, indeed, even absent the intent to harm, and even absent negligence. Similarly, various aspects of the securities, consumer protection, and food and drug laws impose liability upon the makers of false statements even where there exists no intent to deceive.

Although the nature of legal liability or moral responsibility for the unintentional utterance of a falsehood on which someone relies to his detriment is an important topic, it is not our topic here. Paltering, as we understand it, is an intentional act, even though the act is different from (although not necessarily less harmful than) lying, and paltering is typically an act intended to mislead or to defraud.[8] Thus our concern is with a certain form of calculated deception, and not with acts that unintentionally, even if negligently or recklessly, mislead others.

Nor is our concern in this paper presented when the listener is not ultimately led to believe something that is not true. In some circumstances, listeners will understand falsehoods as just that, and then even an intent to deceive coupled with a false statement will still produce no misimpression. This is how, for example, we decode inflated letters of recommendation, or adjust for the nonrepresentativeness of what are described on résumés as "representative" lists of publications. In other circumstances, speakers may exaggerate or distort the truth when they believe a listener's existing beliefs make a clear understanding or evaluation of the unadulterated truth unlikely. For example, parents may overstate the dangers of drinking, driving, smoking, or sex to children who probably would underestimate those dangers.[9] Such misstatements, intended to compensate for biased inferences, is a category of some interest, but not to us here, largely because, by producing accuracy rather than misperception, they are far from obviously morally, socially, or legally problematic.

Finally, we are not interested here in the genuinely beneficial social lie or white lie. Telling sick people that they are looking better, or saying to our spouses that their clothes are becoming when they are not, or declining an invitation by inventing a prior engagement rather than truthfully expressing distaste for the host are lies, pure and simple, but they are lies whose consequences are either beneficial or at least believed, sometimes *ex ante* and sometimes *ex post*, by the liar as likely to be beneficial. Palters may be employed in the same fashion, and they may receive the same assessment. But while white lies and white palters comprise a fascinating topic, it is again one that we are content to leave to others.

By contrast, our interest *is* in the category in which the second criterion for a lie is relaxed while the first and the third are retained. That is, we are interested in the category of statements in which the speaker intends for the listener to have a misimpression, and in which the listener does wind up with a misimpression as a result of the speaker's statement, but in which the connection between the speaker's intent to deceive and the listener's state of having a misimpression is not the literal falsehood, as in the true lie, but something short of literal or exact falsity. This is the category of the successful palter, and this category will be our primary focus in the balance of this chapter.

Varieties of Paltering

Examples of paltering are widespread. Sometimes paltering seems to occur when people take advantage of vague language, as when a used-car dealer describes a car as a "cream puff," when a real estate agent describes a location as "prestigious" or "highly desirable," when a stockbroker describes a new public offering as "hot," or when a restaurant announces on the menu that its own signature pastrami and cheese sandwich is "famous." But since almost all of the consumers of such loose exaggerations are well aware of the practice, and consequently accept the vagueness of the language used, it is not clear that vague language by itself, in most circumstances, even qualifies as mild paltering.[10]

True examples of paltering, therefore, are the ones that occur when something the palterer says (or does not say) or does (or does not do) is intended to leave the impression that a specific state of affairs obtains, and when the recipient as a result of the palterer's actions or inactions believes that this specific state of affairs obtains, but when in fact the reality is quite different and perhaps just the opposite. Often the recipient's misimpression is a consequence of failing to correct a wrong impression. People who physically resemble a famous person may be treated better than they would otherwise expect and, knowing what is happening, may simply let the misimpression stand. So, too, with people who share names with famous persons.[11] Such examples only scratch the surface, with people often taking advantage of the countless misimpressions that are held by people all around us.

Much more common, however, is creating a wrong impression through deliberate action. PhDs will often make restaurant or hotel reservations as "Dr. So-and-so," hoping in the process to lead the establishment to believe that they are (typically wealthy) physicians and not (typically nonwealthy) academics. Advertisers wishing to draw consumers' attention to the contents of an envelope will frequently put a government warning about tampering with the mail on the outside of the envelope, while also omitting a return address, thus intentionally attempting to create the misimpression that the envelope contains an official letter from a government agency. People will often refer to a famous person by his or her first name, attempting to create the impression of close friendship. The Internal Revenue Service is alleged to deliberately select the period immediately preceding the April 15 tax-filing deadline as the time to initiate tax-fraud criminal prosecutions and to send out routine press releases about audit practices, presumably hoping in the process to lead taxpayers to believe in a probability of audits and criminal prosecutions that is considerably higher than the actual objective probability of those occurrences. Politicians will often take advantage of the availability heuristic by presenting extreme and unrepresentative examples of various problems and benefits—discussing Willy Horton, for example—hoping thereby to lead their listeners into a predictably mistaken generalization.[12] These are but a few examples, but even such a short list should be sufficient to establish that paltering—the deliberate attempt to create a misimpression in someone by means other than by uttering a literal falsehood—is as widespread as it is interesting.

The Political Economy of Paltering

Most people would much prefer to palter than to lie. Perhaps this is due to their upbringing, and perhaps the preference has other causes. Some might even attribute these preferences to evolution or adaptation, as identified (although not necessarily fully endorsed) by Mark Frank (this volume). But whatever the cause, it is hardly clear why paltering should be thought preferable to lying, or deemed less reprehensible. The law is of course concerned with problems of proof, and thus much of the law's tolerance for paltering is likely less a function of its social acceptability and more a function of the difficulty of proving that paltering has occurred. The current state of the law aside, however, once we understand paltering as involving the same intent as lying and the same effect as lying, and lacking only the exact mechanism of literal falsehood, it is hard to understand why the law, except for the obvious problems of proof involved, would be less concerned with paltering than lying.

Indeed, if we forget about the law for a moment, and just think more generally about the political economy of paltering and lying, we might suspect that paltering is in some sense worse than lying.[13] Because lies involve literal untruths, they are easy—or at least easier than palters—to identify, whether legally or through loss of reputation. And because lies are easier to identify with some certainty, they are also easier to punish. Conversely, because palters are harder to identify, there is a considerable incentive for those who wish to deceive others to turn to paltering rather than to lying. First, the personal discomfort from paltering is likely to be less than that from lying. After all, no one talks about galvanic skin responses attending the clever misrepresentation. Second, the same problems of proof that may lead the law to be comparatively unconcerned with paltering make paltering easier to get away with than lying, regardless of the law. Those who intend to deceive will thus have multiple incentives to palter rather than lie. But if the harm of the palter is no less than the harm of the lie, then the very fact that it is safer to engage in one rather than another equally harmful act would suggest that it is the safer but equally harmful act—the palter—that is likely to become the greater social problem.

This comparative propensity to palter rather than to lie is likely exacerbated by the way in which many—probably most—people have a somewhat hard time telling a straight (and nonwhite) lie. Whether this reluctance is caused by hardwired moral sensibilities or, more likely, by socially reinforced condemnation of lying as such (George Washington refused to lie about the cherry tree, we were taught,[14] but we were not taught what he might have done had there been paltering options available[15]), it seems plain that most of us have developed an internal "reject" button that makes it hard for us to lie. But this internal reject button exists within a psyche that also resists taking actions that are to our detriment, and so the palter often emerges as the self-interested but internally palatable alternative to lying.

Although incentives thus exist for people to palter, it is also likely that the cost of identifying a palter is higher than that of identifying a pure lie, in part because many palters, like President Clinton's statement that "I did not have sexual relations with that woman," have the element of deniability.[16] That is, the palterer can, if exposed, often claim, unlike the liar, to have been misunderstood. Because careful wordings often tend to be misheard in direct hearing—and even more often in secondhand accounts—the palterer gets the benefit of the likely understanding coupled with a defense based on the exact and careful wording that is actually used.

Deniability, combined with the absence of a plainly demonstrable false-hood, thus makes it more costly to identify a palter than to identify a lie. And so, if it is cheap to palter and expensive to identify a palter, and beneficial to palter if undiscovered, we can expect the practice to be widespread. We thus find ourselves with a practice that is often beneficial to those who engage in it, difficult to identify, and hard to penalize through the law and outside the law, all of which combine to make the practice likely to be common. The palter, therefore, presents almost all of the same harms as the lie,[17] but because the lie is easier to identify, easier to penalize with and without the law, and subject to internal controls on its use, it may turn out—surprisingly perhaps—that lying is less common and less of a problem, in the aggregate, than paltering.

Penalizing Paltering

Although neither the law of perjury nor the traditional law of fraud penalizes paltering, the situation is changing. The securities laws, for example, penal-ize "material" omissions,[18] and in modern times civil penalties for deceit or fraudulent misrepresentation (see Harrington, this volume) cover conduct as well as words and encompass a wide range of nondisclosures, passive acts, half-truths, and evasions.[19] So, too, with crimes of larceny. Obtaining prop-erty by false pretenses nowadays covers a broad range of potential targets, and people with larcenous motives to induce false beliefs in their victims—such as the contractor who wants a homeowner to make a substantial advance pay-ment for repairs that are unlikely to be completed, for example—may find themselves subject to legal liability.[20]

Although the law is broadening, it still remains a narrow and (compara-tively) rarely used weapon against paltering. The law indeed has its place, but it often plays a subordinate role in the control of antisocial behavior, especially when compared to the role played by social norms, informal sanctions, and various other extralegal remedies. (See Fine, this volume.) And because of this, we turn, at least here, primarily to the question of nonlegal remedies for paltering and to the crucial role played by reputation in explaining the dynamics of paltering.

In considering nonlegal remedies, a number of interrelated dynamics come into play. First, the palterer's gains—financial or otherwise—from paltering are likely to be greater where paltering produces more misimpressions. Moreover, the effectiveness of a palter will depend both on how difficult it is to distinguish a palter from the truth and on the percentage of palterers in a given group or society. When distinguishing palters from the truth is difficult, and when the number of palterers is relatively small, paltering is likely to be effective.

Consider the question of frequency. For some activities, like driving in excess of the speed limit, the incentives to break the law vary positively with the prevalence of the activity, because the prevalence reduces the probability of enforcement, and at times even of detection. The driver on the Massachusetts Turnpike who drives at 78 miles per hour (the speed limit is 65) along with scores of others is far less likely to be apprehended than the driver who drives at 78 when everyone else is going no faster than 66. If all motorists were identical, and if prevalence increased attractiveness, there would then be two equilibria: one in which no one exceeded the speed limit, and another in which everyone did. But for other activities, like murder, the incentive to commit the crime is largely independent of the prevalence of the activity. Whether there are more or fewer murders in a given time frame or area is largely irrelevant to the individual murderer.

Unlike speeding, in which frequency increases the incentive to participate, however, and unlike murder, in which the incentive is independent of frequency, paltering is an activity in which the practice becomes less attractive as more people participate. As used-car dealers and rug sellers have come to lament, paltering is far more effective when only a small number of people engage in it. And, indeed, the limiting case is the one in which the behavior is so widely expected (and accepted) that no one is deceived and we do not have paltering at all. But even short of this limiting case, the more common paltering is, the harder it is for the individual palterer, since recipients will set higher standards for accepting some statement as true. A palter will thus be most effective in an environment in which palters are rare, and hence where recipients are especially likely to be trusting. An individual palterer, therefore, has an interest in there not being much paltering.

An additional problem, however, is the way in which this dynamic may limit the effectiveness of sanctions. The reduced ability of sanctions to dissuade the behavior they are directed against—at least in the case of paltering, as we have just seen—will increase an individual palterer's incentive to palter.[21] The less paltering there is, the more a potential palterer will have an incentive to engage in it, thus limiting the effectiveness of any scheme of sanctions and suggesting that an irreducible positive level of paltering is likely.

This dynamic works the other way as well, however, and thus it might initially appear that paltering is to some extent a self-enforcing, self-limiting, and self-correcting activity. The more paltering there is, the higher the cost (greater probability of detection, more elaborate palters necessary to produce the same effect, and so on) of engaging in it, and thus paltering might appear to some people to be a problem that can, at least to a significant degree, take care of itself. It will not go away, but it may be inherently self-limiting and thus not in need of external sanctions in order to keep its incidence to manageable proportions.

Although at the extremes such self-limitation may be expected to occur, short of the extremes there is a familiar coordination problem: a problem exacerbated because paltering often cuts across preexisting social or professional groupings and to a lesser extent within the groupings, and individual palterers will have an interest in there being less paltering so that their own palters will be more effective. When one palters, one is more likely to be trusted when everyone is trusted than when some are not trusted (see Möllering, this volume, and also Glenney, this volume, who makes a similar point with respect to military deception). Thus the best palter of all is the first in any given arena. But this dynamic affects everyone, at least on the assumption that there is a bit of the palterer in each of us. Without external enforcement of some sort, therefore, no one will have an incentive not to palter, but everyone will have an incentive to have others not palter, and it is precisely in this situation when outside help is most needed. If this outside help takes the form of punishment, the palterers who are punished will clearly be worse off and the world will be better off. Even if there is a cost to punishment, it will typically be the case that the loss to the palterer will be greater than the loss to the punisher, which is why the incentives encourage gossip and other forms of reputation-damaging sanctions against palterers.

Before turning to an analysis of the externalities that have been hinted at among players, we should identify the three reasons why a society—comprised of senders and receivers, with many players in both roles—should want fewer palterers in its midst. First, the senders do not like palterers because paltering makes it harder to be believed themselves. Second, receivers do not like palterers because it makes them more likely to be deceived. And third, any instruments designed to ameliorate the effects of paltering—either by enabling senders to demonstrate that their statements are whole truths, or receivers to discern the truthful essence of a statement—will come with costs of employing them. These costs will rise as the number of palterers increases.

In assessing various approaches to outside help, which in this context would consist largely of calibrated social sanctions, we need to focus on two kinds of errors. In doing so, we can first put ourselves in the shoes of an individual confronting someone who makes a statement that may or may not be a palter. In this situation, to borrow the language of statistics and decision theory, the Type II error will be in believing someone who is paltering. And the Type I error will be in not believing someone who in fact is telling the whole truth. Obviously, there are degrees of truth and untruth and degrees of believing and nonbelieving, but we will stick to this simplified form of presentation.

Now imagine we have an environment, call it World A, in which one hundred people each deliver one message every day. And to simplify further, imagine that in World A another, distinct group of one hundred people each receive one message every day. Now assume that a 5 percent chance exists in World A that any given message is a palter, perhaps because all of the message deliverers palter 5 percent of the time, or because 95 percent never palter and 5 percent always palter. Whatever the cause, any individual message is 5 percent likely to be a palter. The task of the message recipient is to make a decision under these conditions about whether to believe a given message.

Assume that if the recipient accepts all messages at face value, he will make 5 percent Type II errors and no Type I errors. If the recipient scrupulously sorts all of the messages in order to exclude those that could conceivably be palters, assume that he would screen out all of the palters but also 10 percent of the truthful messages. Thus he would make no Type II errors and 9.5 percent (95% x 10%) Type I errors.[22]

Now let us move to another society, which we will call World B. In World B, assume that 10 percent of the statements are palters, and only 90 percent are truthful. A recipient who accepts all statements in World B will thus make 10 percent Type II errors. And if the recipient rejects all even slightly suspicious messages, she will make 9.0 percent (90% x 10%) Type I errors. Thus the recipient's possible trade-off rate between Type II and Type I errors is greater in World B than it was in World A. She should be more skeptical and disbelieve more messages. Using this more formal analysis, therefore, we can see why it is that the honest used-car salesman, like the midnight stroller in a neighborhood plagued with burglaries, is at a particular disadvantage. Ultimately, of course, the enhanced doubting by receivers in World B would feed back to affect the behavior of senders.

Recall P. T. Barnum's statement that "there's a sucker born every minute." Assuming that Barnum was right (we are confident that his estimate was actually on the low side), he was smart enough to recognize that a plentiful supply of suckers would make being a huckster more attractive. Barnum's implicit model was based on two types of receivers, suckers and sophisticates, where sophisticates knew how to avoid being taken in by a palter. Barnum, who was particularly smart in these matters, was presumably interested in the ratio of suckers to hucksters, hoping for a higher ratio. Thus if the supply of suckers increased, the returns to hucksters would increase. But this, in turn, would stimulate the supply of hucksters, leading to a falloff in business, and eventually an equilibrium would be reached.

If switching from being an honest sender to being a huckster were costless, the ultimate returns to both suckers and hucksters would be the same as before the suckers were born, and nothing would have changed. Thus Barnum was obviously interested in a world containing many suckers and few hucksters, and his interest in there being fewer hucksters was not just about being able to divide up the pie into fewer sections. Rather, it was primarily in his interest in raising the returns of huckstering, which would result from there being fewer hucksters to increase wariness among suckers and fewer sophisticates who could costlessly detect hucksterism. As long as the ratio of suckers to hucksters remained high, Barnum would do very well. And what is interesting is that this is a world in which society would also benefit. A world in which a small number of hucksters preying on a large, basically trusting population that is rarely fleeced is, under reasonable empirical assumptions, probably a better world than one in which a large number of hucksters seek to fleece an equivalent number of wised-up potential suckers. Thus a world with fewer hucksters, even if it contains fewer older but wiser suckers, would be a world with few actual fleecings. The task, then, is to devise strategies for getting to this better world and avoiding the worse one. And the goal is certainly to avoid the worst world, one in which a large number of hucksters serially fleece the same suckers, suckers who rarely learn from their own bad experiences.[23]

Chief among the strategies for getting to this better world is likely to be one focusing on reputation. Although the law may have a role to play, and although direct condemnation—"You dirty palterer!"—can occasionally be valuable, we believe that reputational mechanisms that spread condemnation, and hence raise the expected costs of paltering, are more likely to be effective. To be caught in a serious palter may not hurt much, but to be caught in half a dozen may truly tarnish a reputation. The businessman of yesteryear, who could establish that "my word is my bond," had a reputation that protected against both lying and paltering. The more a society rewards those who scrupulously avoid harmful palters and are known as straight shooters, the more important it will be for people to avoid being known as even minor palterers.

We do not think it wise for reputational enforcement to rely (even if it could) on brittle barriers, in which reputations would remain good in the absence of harmful palters, and would turn bad if but one were detected. Reputational enforcement needs to be more flexible than this. That is partly a function of the fact that all of us would probably like to palter a bit, and also partly of the fact that, given current standards, all of us probably palter from time to time. But more important, it is frequently difficult to determine whether a statement is a palter. Between Type I errors (rejecting a truthful statement as a palter) and Type II errors (responding to a palter as if it were the truth), optimal detection will lead to some Type I errors. Thus sending someone to the gallows for a single detected palter will be undesirable. But over the longer term, particularly if perceived palters to one individual are passed on to others, it should be easy to distinguish the palterer from the truth teller.

The need for measured drops in reputation is also partly a function of the fact that, as hinted above, the optimal level of paltering may not be zero. Just as there is a line between the palter and the lie, and between the palter and the truth, so too is there a line between the harmful palter and the beneficial white lie or, to keep the parallelism, between the harmful palter and the white palter. If there were no paltering, especially in a world of uncertainty about the line between the palters that are harmful and those that are beneficial, there might be too much blunt and harmful truth, and thus the optimal level of paltering, although likely low, is also unlikely to be zero.

The task then is to imagine a reputational mechanism that recognizes that people will be deterred from paltering not primarily by the inner voice that tells them not to, because there are also inner voices telling us that sometimes it is good for us to palter even if it is not good for society that we do so. Indeed, some of us get a sneaky but good feeling from fooling others, partly because a palter requires more ingenuity than a lie. Moreover, still another voice is telling us that some palters are socially beneficial and that this might just be one of them. Under these circumstances, the fear that we will be regarded poorly by others or that others will not deal with us can prove to be a much more significant regulatory mechanism than self-policing.

How might such a regulatory mechanism work? Leaving to others (Farid, this volume; Hancock, this volume; Thompson, this volume) the very important question of how modern technology may be as important for controlling deception as for facilitating it, we focus here on what a regulatory approach would seek to achieve, and how—whether through technology, incentives, or simply altered awareness of the problem. First, a regulatory approach must separate and sanction most severely the intentional palters, leaving the negligent or innocent palters for different forms of punishment. Let us focus, then, on the palters that we most want to limit, the self-interested intentional palters that are meant to and in fact will hurt others. Even for these, the reputational repercussion cannot simply be one that imposes large penalties in a small number of instances. Although such strategies seem appealing in theory, low enforcement / high penalty regulatory strategies tend to work least well when the high penalties are socially unacceptable.[24] And high penalties are socially unacceptable in this context for a variety of reasons. One is that there is a bit of the palterer in each of us, and the line between self-interested palterers and harmless ones is not easy to draw. Is it wrong, for example, and, if so, how wrong, to enhance our own athletic accomplishments in order to impress a member of the opposite sex? People tend to be comfortable with imposing heavy penalties for crimes that they themselves cannot imagine committing, but when it is a socially harmful activity that they can see themselves doing—driving under the influence is the classic example of a socially harmful activity that is underpenalized because of the "there but for the grace of God" phenomenon—the willingness to punish heavily is severely weakened.

Moreover, it is considered bad form to mistakenly accuse someone of being less than honest. This is well known to students who ask for extensions on final papers for reasons of computer failure, death of a grandparent, and the like. Although the student knows that the story is false (these, by the way, are typically lies and not palters), and knows that the teacher knows that the story is likely false, the student also knows that the penalties to the accuser for making a false accusation of dishonesty are high. Few teachers want to accuse the student of dishonesty only to be presented with a death certificate for the student's deceased grandmother, or the dated repair bill for the computer, or the verified record of a genuine medical emergency. Thus under conditions of uncertainty, even suspicious conditions, we often do not accuse when an accusation is merited, and for similar reasons we often are unwilling to impose severe reputational penalties even when they appear to be justified.

Thus the imposition of reputational penalties is impeded by the way in which imposition of such punishment can cost the punisher as well as the punishee, by the fact that the optimal level of paltering is above zero, and by the fact that our universal desire to palter now and then makes us squeamish about heavy penalties. The task, therefore, is to devise a system of social or reputational sanctions for paltering that takes account of the unavailability of the theoretically efficient high-penalty/low-enforcement devices that might otherwise seem optimal. So if we are restricted to lower-penalty enforcement mechanisms, we are also restricted—unless we are unwilling to be effective— to low-penalty/high-enforcement devices.

Such devices are hardly rare. Indeed, the typical parking ticket is a classic example, even if we assume (counterfactually in some locations) that the law enforcement goal is to minimize the activity rather than to maximize revenue. In the context of paltering, therefore, the task is to imagine a set of reputational sanctions that is the equivalent of the parking ticket. That is, the sanctions should be easy to apply, but not so costly that they would not be applied. Gossip is one such sanction that comes to mind. But gossip, itself appropriately regulated by second-order social norms penalizing loose gossip, can be a useful first-order social norm in the control of antisocial behavior. Gossip can be a powerful social deterrent; while a single item of gossip will rarely have a serious negative effect, multiple tidbits will transform gossip into large-scale reputational penalties. Some jurisdictions raise the marginal cost of parking tickets as they accumulate during a year, just to discourage those who regard parking fines basically as a convenience that save money on average, or as a beneficial trade-off between ease of parking and money. Such an escalation scheme thus separates the true scofflaws from those who accidentally overstay the meter's limit. So, too, one item of gossip about a palterer may do little, two items may do some harm but not too much, and three or more may produce a widespread reputation for dishonesty. Such an approach is quite consistent with rational decision making, given the occurrence of multiple events, each of which would be low probability, given good behavior.[25] Similarly, an extremely harmful palter would incur a large reputational penalty. Thus if reputations spread fluidly, then appropriately directed and regulated gossip about palterers may succeed in imposing large deterrents on serial palterers, but only small deterrents and penalties on those who occasionally palter.[26] If properly calibrated, this might well achieve the optimal result of aligning the societal interest in limiting large-scale paltering with the individual tendency in almost everyone to occasionally fall prey to the temptation to palter.

3 Thoughts, Feelings, and Deception
Mark G. Frank

W HAT PEOPLE DO WHEN THEY LIE, and how those lies affect social life, has been of interest to the layperson and the professional alike since the beginning of recorded history. To tackle these issues, first we must understand what is meant by a lie, then examine how known human physiological and expressive behaviors might manifest themselves when someone tells a lie, and only then apply this analysis to real-life lie detection and its resultant social impact.

The ability to lie is a "skill" that has benefits and costs. By definition, a social group must have some level of cooperation among its members or else it ceases to be a cohesive group. In order to facilitate cooperation and achieve smooth interactions, groups must communicate their behavioral intentions. Human beings can communicate their intentions with language; for example, we can discuss what time the football game takes place, where we will meet for dinner, when we need to be left alone to finish our work, and when we wish the company of others. However, other species (and our own species in its first year or so of life) do not have complex language. This means that at the earliest points of our phylogeny and ontology we had to communicate through nonverbal means—tones of voice, body movements, and facial

MARK G. FRANK is associate professor and director of the Communication Science Center at the University at Buffalo, State University of New York. His research is on facial expressions and deception, and he has received $4 million in external funding in the past five years to study interpersonal deception and facial expressions in real-world contexts.

expressions. Without the ability to communicate honestly in some form, we cease being social and devolve into islands of individuals.

Darwin was the first to rigorously propose that our species has specific nonverbal communication skills, including a repertoire of specific messages to indicate various behavioral intentions or states, particularly states related to survival such as imminent attack (anger), imminent danger (fear), potentially sickening substances (disgust), approachability (happiness), and so forth.[1] These signals are reliable, honest indications of these states; they are primarily expressed in the face and are amplified or deamplified by body actions.[2]

At times, our species has found it advantageous to feign these signals, or to hide them, to gain an advantage. Research has shown that when people keep diaries of their lies, they report telling one to two falsified accounts each day.[3] This option cannot be exercised too often, as once one is identified as an unreliable signaler, all future signals will tend to be discounted (see O'Sullivan, this volume).[4] Yet we as a society tend to trust each other, despite the fact that not all signals we receive from others are trustworthy (see Möllering, this volume). In other words, more often than not when we are lied to, those lies are effective: research shows that when people are asked to recall lies they uncovered, they mention detecting deception through subsequent factual discoveries, rather than from the behavioral clues of the deceiver.[5]

What Is a Lie?

Deception researchers have been concerned with more than just verbal and nonverbal clues to lying and our abilities to catch lies. Research programs have looked at deception as a means to understanding other topics—such as interpersonal communication—by examining the strategic use of deception in interpersonal encounters.[6] They have also examined such topics as cognitive development through the study of children's abilities to develop a theory of mind;[7] comparative cognition, through the observation of other animals' abilities to engage in behaviors that look remarkably similar to human deception;[8] and the evolution of human signaling systems, through the coevolution of signs of deception and "cheater detectors."[9] These programs often overlap their interests, while at other times they apparently contradict each other—depending on how one defines deception and lying.

In the real world, there are a number of ways in which information we receive from others can be deceptive or misleading, and we need to articulate what we mean by various terms to fully understand what it is that we are studying. People can provide inaccurate information through means other than deception—such as an honest difference of understanding, mistaken recall, or false memory.[10] For example, someone who is assaulted at 8:30 PM has mistaken recall if he thinks it was at 9:30 PM; he has false memory if the assault never happened at all but he really believes it happened. In fact, two people who witnessed the same event rarely give identical accounts because they are limited to their particular point of view, they forget things, and so forth. What distinguishes a lie from these other forms of inaccurate information is that only a lie involves the *deliberate* presentation of information that a person hopes will mislead others. Paul Ekman, the preeminent scholar on emotion and nonverbal behavior associated with deception, made this intentional aspect the cornerstone of his definition of a lie as a deliberate attempt to mislead, without the implicit or explicit prior consent or notification of the target.[11] In other words, lying is synonymous with what would be called perjury in a courtroom. Thus a man who truly believes he is the father of a woman's baby is not lying—he may be wrong, but he is not lying. A man who knows he never had sexual contact with the woman, but claims to be the father, is lying. Even a person who truly believes that space aliens impregnated this woman would not be lying. The person who believes that space aliens did not impregnate her, but insists that they did, is lying. Lying is a deliberate, fully conscious act performed by individuals, regardless of the statement's believability. We note that, as pointed out by Rowan and Fine (both in this volume), individuals in group situations can certainly make mistaken assessments of, say health care regimens or rumors, and that these would only become lies by Ekman's definition if these groups *knew* what they were saying was factually incorrect.

However, according to Ekman, a person can lie not only by fabricating information but also by concealing information, telling the truth falsely (for example, saying a truth with such a tone of sarcasm that the target of the lie believes the liar really means the opposite of what he or she just said, thus misleading the target), and even engaging in the "incorrect inference dodge."[12] This latter refers to making statements that are actually truthful but that the target of the lie will misinterpret (make an "incorrect inference"). For example, an artist may ask another artist about her opinion of his work, and the second artist may respond with "Wow—I cannot believe you did this," which may leave the inquiring artist with the impression that this expressed disbelief was about his great skill, rather than his great lack of skill. This type of statement is similar to paltering, as described by Schauer and Zeckhauser in Chapter 2, which involves statements that may be factually correct but that are assembled in such a way as to create a false impression in the listener, this being seen as somehow less harmful than a full-blown fabricated lie. However, palters are still lies, particularly if one applies the courtroom oath to "tell the truth, the whole truth, and nothing but the truth," as that requires one to expand upon one's testimony to ensure that it is not misleading or misunderstood, thus rendering concealment, incorrect inference, and paltering as perjury. However, informal and unsystematic observations of courtroom trials by ourselves and others suggest that a person who answers only the immediate question would not be considered to be lying, despite the failure to mention pertinent details that are not technically part of the immediate question.[13]

This definition of lying separates it from the broader category of deception. Deception would be anything that misleads another for some gain. Thus a tiger misleads its prey by having a fur coat pattern that is orange with black stripes, enabling it to blend into the high, dry grass of its environment. However, the tiger does not awake in the morning, look into its closet, and choose to wear the stripes rather than the solid or spotted coat. Evolution may, in a longer time scheme, be choosing this color pattern, but it is not a deliberate choice on the part of the tiger. Likewise, other similar examples of deception in the animal kingdom are up for debate as to whether they are simply deception or the deliberate lie. Bergstrom (this volume) and other biologists who study deception in animals other than humans wrestle continually with this concept because of the difficulty of accessing the thoughts and intentions of animals, as compared to those of humans. For example, some work with chimpanzees has perceived behavior that looks very much like the chimpanzees lied to their troopmates about the location or presence of food. Given that it is difficult to ascertain what a chimpanzee was trying to do—that is, to have access to its thought patterns—we cannot conclude with any confidence that the chimpanzee was lying, although it looked suspiciously close to lying. However, we can clearly conclude that the chimpanzees deceived their troopmates.[14]

This definition also suggests that some other forms of deception are authorized and involve an explicit or implied prior notification of the targets that what they are about to see or hear is not quite the reality. In some situations the deception is explicit, as in the unspoken notification by actors in a play or movie that they are pretending to be someone else, or when a poker player engages in bluffing. In other situations, the deception is more implicit, as when a polite dinner guest expresses enjoyment over a meal he or she may not have liked, or when home sellers list the price of a home above the price they will accept. The decision a researcher makes about what sort of deception to study—whether passive deception, such as the tiger, or active deception, as in a politeness situation, or a lie, which involves the active, unauthorized misleading of another—may have implications for the observed behaviors and situations that might be generalized in the results.[15] Regardless, researchers must be cautious in what they can generalize based on the type of lie or deception used in their work, be it observational or laboratory experiments.

These definitional distinctions have implications for trust. In some scenarios, like acting, we permit deception and actively participate in it. There is trust that the boundaries of that scenario will be honored (that the actors will stay in character). Other scenarios, in which we are not notified by the person or the context that deception is happening—such as when a lie is told—are deadly to trust, if uncovered.

Although deception is a large topic, we will focus on how a human telling a lie may betray that lie through his or her behavior. For example, some nonverbal behaviors include facial expressions, eye movements, and other facial actions; head, hand, leg, and other body movements, gestures, or postures; and voice tones and other paralinguistic information. Other verbal behaviors may include word choice, content of the statements, and so forth. In this process we will attempt to detail the process underlying deception and the signs that indicate trustworthy and untrustworthy behavioral intentions

What Happens When Someone Lies?

The evidence suggests that in day-to-day life most lies are betrayed by factors or circumstances surrounding the lie, and not by behavior.[16] However, sometimes demeanor is all one has at one's disposal to detect a liar. In security settings—such as a customs inspection in which luggage may be only randomly searched unless contraband is visible on a person—the security screener must base his or her judgment on people's behavior. As a society, we have entrusted and trained some individuals to be able to spot those intent on causing harm to themselves or others, as well as to detect and impede such plots prior to their execution.

The research on detecting lies from behavior suggests that two families of behavioral clues betray the lie—clues related to a liar's thinking, and clues related to a liar's feelings.[17] The former are typically found in the speech, and the latter in the face and voice tone. In addition, the body produces a mixture of both thinking and feeling clues. In the next section I discuss the signs that people display when thinking and feeling. Often people do not recognize these signs of genuineness in others, or they might misinterpret signs of disingenuousness. Those circumstances will be discussed later.

Thinking Clues

In order to deliberately mislead someone, a liar must create facts, describe events that did not happen or that he did not see, selectively present information (as when paltering; see Schauer and Zeckhauser, this volume), or suppress critical information. Moreover, the process of thinking about or creating this misinformation creates behavioral signs that additional *mental effort* is in action. These signs range from a hesitation in the speech, a misplaced word, or a contradictory statement to very vague accounts lacking logical structure.[18] These types of clues are particularly evident in situations in which the liar might be expected to know exactly what he or she is recounting, without having to think too much about it. A witness who claims to have been present at a crime scene, for example, should be able to tell the court without too much thought where she was standing when she witnessed the event. If the witness was not actually present at that scene, she would have to invent the details necessary to convince someone otherwise. This on-the-spot thinking, research has shown, often manifests itself in many speech hesitations, disfluencies, and errors and is often accompanied by fewer of the hand or facial gestures that typically illustrate speech.[19]

Not only are clues regarding misinformation driven by mental effort, but *naturalistic human memory processes* also leave clues as to when a memory is a real memory and when it is fabricated.[20] Originally called the Undeustch hypothesis after the researcher who first proclaimed it,[21] research in Criterion-Based Content Analysis has now gone beyond Undeutsch to articulate 24 criteria that separate true memories from those that have not actually been experienced. For example, in a real memory people can move back and forth ("spontaneous reproduction"), real memories are coherent, real memories are tied into the context of people's lives, and real memories involve more description of other people's states of mind.[22] Other researchers have noted other memory-based clues, such as: liars are less immediate; they use words that are more general and more simple to recall and generate; and they are less specific.[23] Of course, the most obvious verbal clue is when liars contradict their earlier statements, as they have the added task of remembering what they said to whom and when.

Feeling Clues

Not only do liars have to think out the lie and maintain a consistent story, but also emotions are often aroused within them that are associated with their lies. Emotions can enter into the lie process in one of two ways: either the person is lying about her feelings or emotions, or the act of lying produces feelings or emotions within the liar. Thus people may send out false signals as to what they are truly feeling by (1) hiding a truly felt emotion with a mask of neutrality, (2) hiding a truly felt emotion with a different, but false emotion, or (3) not feeling any emotion, but showing a false one. Examples of this include, respectively: feeling glee at a good poker hand but not displaying any emotion (a.k.a., maintaining a "poker face"), a disappointed runner-up smiling at the victor in a Miss America pageant, and smiling or laughing at a joke that one does not find humorous. Moreover, in some situations the lie itself can generate an emotion—as in the delight at "duping" someone, the guilt induced by telling a lie, or the fear of getting caught in a lie.[24] In most all of these instances, an individual is experiencing some emotion that he does not want the lie catcher to see.

Research has shown that when emotions are aroused, changes are unbidden and occur automatically. Subjectively, people report feeling that emotions *happen* to them, and not that they *choose* which emotions to feel (imagine what would happen to the psychological profession if the latter scenario were the case!). We know this through our own experience. For example, during times that we feel depressed, we may do things that we hope will make us feel better—go for a walk, eat some forbidden food, rent a comedy video—but the emergence of happiness as a result of those behaviors is never certain. Likewise, if we are walking down a dark alley and notice we are being followed by people dressed in gang clothing, we will typically feel fear, despite our efforts not to. These changes occur within a split second and are considered fundamental features of an emotional response.[25]

Part of this emotional response, besides changes in heart rate, blood pressure, and so forth,[26] is a facial expression of that emotion.[27] Research has shown that emotions such as anger, contempt, disgust, fear, happiness, sadness, and surprise appear on people's faces during an emotional experience, often despite their efforts to mask such emotions.[28] The reason for this resides in human neuroanatomy, and signs of these emotions are often missed by people who are assessing a signal's trustworthiness.

The Face as a Dual System

Researchers agree that most types of facial expressions are learned like language, that they are displayed under conscious control, and that the meanings of these expressions are culturally specific, requiring context for proper interpretation.[29] Thus the same lowered eyebrow expression that would convey "uncertainty" in North America might convey "no" in Borneo.[30]

On the other hand, a limited number of distinct facial expressions of emotion appear to be biologically wired, produced involuntarily, and similar in meaning across all cultures.[31] This idea—originally proposed by Darwin[32] and later elaborated by others[33]—was that these emotions exist to drive certain social behaviors, such as attack, satiation, distress, and danger, by reorganizing the body's physiological priorities to allow escape or attack. Social animals, such as humans, must communicate to others that the "action tendencies" that accompany these emotions, such as striking out in anger or fleeing in fear, are imminent, so that others can adjust their behaviors accordingly to permit smoother social interaction.[34] Therefore, groups that can communicate these states can capitalize on cooperation. For example, humans express the emotion of happiness by raising their lip corners and contracting the muscle that circles the eye; they express sadness or distress by lowering their lip corners and pulling their inner eyebrows upward.[35] Besides happiness and sadness, other emotions associated with specific facial expressions and that seem to be interpreted in similar ways across cultures include: anger, disgust, fear, and surprise, and to a lesser extent, contempt, embarrassment, interest, pain, and shame.[36] This "universal" production and perception of certain emotions across cultures implies genetic determination rather than social learning; further, such facial expressions are unbidden and are accompanied by a particular pattern of morphology and dynamic actions.[37] Moreover, a number of studies have documented the relationship between these facial expressions of emotion and the physiology of the emotional response.[38] Indeed, a recent review of the empirical evidence on the psychology of emotion leads to the unambiguous conclusion that the face is one of the key parts of an emotion.[39]

Neuroanatomical Foundation

Neuroanatomical research on the human face demonstrates that facial expressions can be both biologically driven, as in the case of some of the emotions, and socially learned, as in the case of all other facial expressions. There appear to be two distinct neural pathways that mediate facial expressions, each one originating in a different area of the brain. The pyramidal motor system drives the voluntary facial actions and originates in the cortical motor strip; in contrast, the extrapyramidal motor system drives the more involuntary, emotional facial actions and originates in the subcortical area of the brain.[40] The research documenting these differences[41] is reliable enough that, prior to modern technologies that allow researchers to see through tissue (such as CAT / PET scans), they served as the primary diagnostic criteria for certain brain lesions.[42]

Not only do voluntary and involuntary facial actions differ by neural pathway, but the actions mediated by these pathways also manifest themselves differently. In most people, voluntary pyramidal motor system–based movements are controlled solely by individual effort. Extrapyramidal motor system–based facial actions, in contrast, are characterized by synchronized, smooth, symmetrical, consistent, and reflex-like or ballistic-like actions on the part of the component facial muscles.[43] Relatively speaking, these actions appear to be less accessible to individuals' volitional control.

Distinguishing Involuntary Versus Voluntary Expressions

The research on these multiple pathways is best illustrated by findings on the smile. Darwin's colleague G. B. Duchenne first noticed a difference in appearance between smiles that are caused by an emotion of enjoyment and those that are posed but without any corresponding enjoyment.[44] Ekman and Friesen confirmed Duchenne's observation that genuine smiles—those driven by positive emotions—featured raised lip corners (*zygomatic major* muscle) along with action of the muscles around the eyes (lateral portions of the *orbicularis oculi* muscle, which cause the "crow's-feet" look), whereas posed, "artificial" smiles tended to have only raised lip corners.[45]

Based on facial neuroanatomy studies of movement, Duchenne's observation, and their own observations of a large data set, Ekman and Friesen[46] predicted that the raised lip corners with the crow's-feet[47] configuration observed by Duchenne (called the Duchenne marker) would be but one among several morphological and dynamic markers distinguishing smiles deriving from positive emotions ("enjoyment smiles") from those deriving from other motives ("nonenjoyment smiles"). Specifically, they predicted that enjoyment smiles, as opposed to other types, should be more symmetrical (*symmetry marker*); smoother in terms of onset, apex, offset, and overall lip corner raising (*smoothness marker*); relatively limited and consistent in overall duration of the lip corner raising across smiles, such that enjoyment smiles last between half a second and five seconds (*duration marker*); and synchronized, in that both the action of the lip corners and the crow's-feet reach the point of maximal contraction (apex) at approximately the same time (*synchrony marker*).

The most replicated and best documented marker, showing the most convergent validity across social groups and conditions, has been the marker first observed by Duchenne (raised lip corners with the accompanying formation of crow's-feet).[48] It is also the easiest to observe, most likely due to the fact that it can be captured by a single still image.[49] For example, laboratory research has shown that the number of smiles with the *Duchenne marker* increases when subjects watch films designed to elicit positive emotion, and decreases when subjects feign positive emotion while viewing films designed to elicit negative emotion,[50] including predicting which of two positive-emotion films subjects enjoyed more.[51] Duchenne-marked smiles also predict phenomena as diverse as the following: from the smile of an infant, researchers could predict whether the infant was being approached by its mother or by a stranger,[52] as well as whether the infant's mother was smiling at all.[53] It also predicts when people who lost their airline baggage began to feel less distress;[54] how much a person enjoys being smiled at;[55] whether a child has won or lost a game;[56] and whether one enjoys certain jokes and cartoons.[57] In clinical settings, smiles with the Duchenne marker also predict the following range of behaviors: whether a person will cope successfully with the death of his or her romantic partner;[58] whether a person is an abusive caregiver;[59] and whether a person is depressed,[60] schizophrenic,[61] recovering from an illness in general,[62] or likely to respond successfully to psychotherapy.[63]

The *symmetry marker* has been examined in a handful of studies looking at facial expression asymmetry.[64] The one study that looked at *spontaneous* smiles in reaction to jokes found the smiles much more symmetrical than the posed smiles elicited by experimenters.[65] This matched the observations of clinical neuroanatomists who noted that patients with hemifacial paralysis due to brain tumors on the contralateral cortical motor strip (which controls deliberate movements, facial or otherwise) were able to show symmetrical smiles when told jokes.[66]

In contrast to the work on the morphological markers above, very few studies have managed to examine the proposed dynamic qualities of enjoyment smiles versus nonenjoyment smiles, due entirely to the difficult and laborious process of gathering dynamic information.[67] For example, there are only six published studies on the three dynamic markers. Five of these examined the smoothness marker, and found that subjects who were hypnotized to feel happy showed smiles that had crow's-feet activity (the Duchenne marker), along with longer and smoother lip corner raising at the onset.[68] Another study showed that the smiles of abusive mothers toward their difficult children featured more abrupt offsets than the smiles of nonabusive mothers to their difficult children.[69] When the lip corner actions of individual smiles were broken down into separate components—onset duration, apex duration, and offset duration—researchers found that these three component durations correlated significantly in smiles that featured the crow's-feet Duchenne marker, but not in other smiles.[70] Likewise, frame-by-frame analyses of subjects smiling in two different contexts showed that the velocities of spontaneous emotion smiles were smoother in their onsets and offsets across different situations, suggesting they were more automatic behaviors.[71] Researchers also found that spontaneous smiles in general are smoother in their lip corner raising compared to posed smiles.[72]

The duration marker work showed that spontaneous smiles lasted between half a second and four seconds, whereas posed smiles were significantly shorter in duration.[73] Other research that compared the duration of a sample of smiles that contained the Duchenne marker versus a sample of smiles that did not show the Duchenne marker found no difference in mean duration between the types of smiles, but did find a significant difference in variability of the mean such that the smiles with the Duchenne marker were significantly less variable and therefore more consistent in their duration than other smiles.[74] Finally, to date there are no studies that directly examine the synchrony maker in smiling; this is because in nonenjoyment smiles, there are no muscle movements to compare to the crow's-feet and lip corner raising combination found in enjoyment smiles.

Taken together, although the smile has been the only facial expression of emotion to undergo such scrutiny, it is reasonable to predict that we should find similar patterns of morphological and dynamic markers that would distinguish between voluntary and involuntary expressions of anger, contempt, disgust, fear, sadness, and surprise. These of course would be specific to each emotion. However, to date no data exist that identify minute appearance or dynamic flow factors distinguishing voluntary and involuntary expressions of these other emotions.

When the Pathways Conflict

The study of the facial expressions produced when the voluntary and emotion-driven systems collide is of particular interest to us when assessing trustworthiness or the genuineness of an expression, as would appear to be the hallmark of a lie situation. For example, a person may feel inappropriate happiness at the misfortune of another; or a person may politely feign an expression of enjoyment about a foodstuff that he actually finds disgusting. In more serious criminal or terrorist situations, a liar may try to appear calm and reasonable when in fact she is feeling a strong emotion of fear. A suicidal patient may try to conceal his extreme sadness in order to obtain a quick release from a hospital to make a suicide attempt.

My colleagues Paul Ekman and Maureen O'Sullivan and I have been studying facial expressions in high-stakes deception situations under laboratory conditions. By high stakes, we are referring to lies in which there is a strong punishment for getting caught and a strong reward for getting away with the lie. Thus a lie about which photo one prefers, when there is no punishment for getting caught and no reward for getting away with it, is a low-stakes lie. However, if the same lie is told under the conditions that the liar will face electric shocks if caught, or receive a hundred dollars if not caught, would be a high-stakes lie. This is similar to (although for ethical reasons weaker than) a lie in a real law enforcement situation, in which a suspect who lies successfully can get away with the crime but who lies unsuccessfully may face jail. These stakes should have the effect of raising the emotional level of the subjects. Based on this reasoning and other observations, Ekman has identified four distinctive concepts that illuminate how emotion-driven expressions interact with voluntary facial displays:[75]

1. *Reliable action units.* These are related to facial muscles that are very difficult to produce deliberately when posing an expression, and also difficult to *suppress* when an emotion is present. The forehead is the main—but not sole—locus of such muscles. For example, research has shown that only 20 percent of people can deliberately control the

action of their orbicularis oculi (crow's-feet muscles),[76] which makes "enjoyment smiles" difficult to fake. Similarly, fewer than 15 percent of people tested could deliberately pull the inner corners of their eyebrows upward without interference from other facial muscles. This action is found in sadness and distress; and because this movement is hard to fake or suppress, it is a reliable indicator of sadness and distress.

2. *Temporal dynamics.* Expressions driven by felt emotion have a fast and smooth onset, are of a more circumscribed duration, and have synchronized components consistent with extrapyramidal-driven facial actions; in contrast, posed expressions tend to be slow and jerky in their onset, have irregular durations, and have actions that typically do not peak simultaneously.[77]

3. *Microexpressions.* Recent experimental research has shown that full-face or partial expressions of emotion—typically fear and distress, but also disgust, contempt, or even enjoyment—can occur compressed in time, lasting only a few video frames, so quick that they are only apparent to an untrained layperson using slow-motion video. These "micro-expressions" tend to occur under certain circumstances in which people have strong reasons to suppress a felt emotion.[78] For example, Ekman described how a suicidal psychiatric patient convinced a panel of doctors that she was feeling better and was ready to go home: when released, she committed suicide.[79] Upon review of a film of the interview, the only cue to her deception was a brief expression of despair in response to the question "What are your plans for the future?" which was visible only in frame-by-frame analysis and was quickly covered by a smile. Likewise, Frank and Ekman have found microexpressions of fear and distress in liars lasting as briefly as three videotape frames, or approximately one-tenth of a second.[80]

4. *Squelched expressions.* These are felt expressions that are interrupted, often covered to a controlled expression. They tend to last longer than microexpressions and the interruption itself may be noticeable.[81] My colleagues and I have been collecting data on these emotional expressions within the confines of a lie detection paradigm, where the volitional and involuntary can compete, and we have found that the expression of certain emotions can distinguish liars and truth tellers at rates of nearly 75 percent.[82] However, not all lie detection situations are as high stakes as the ones we studied; that is, telling a polite lie may not

reveal itself in this emotional way. However, *expressions* are genuine indicators of a felt emotion, and a person who knows this can better assess the trustworthiness of the signal, and hence the individual.

A Note on the Voice

The face is not the only vehicle for the physical expression of emotion. Although my work and that of my colleagues has been much more strongly centered on the face than on other regions of the body, research has shown that the voice can also generate a signal pattern that is universal for particular emotions. For example, particular patterns in fundamental frequency and amplitude distinguish anger from fear, and these emotions from others. There is some limited evidence that these vocal profiles for emotions are universal across cultures.[83] For example, in anger, the pitch gets lower and the volume gets louder, whereas in fear, the pitch gets higher and the volume gets softer. This higher pitch and softer tone are usually associated with lying.[84] However, results for accuracy in detecting deception from voice cues have been considerably lower (less than 62 percent accuracy) than results from the face.[85]

A Note on the Body

Unlike the face, body movements tend to be volitional. Exceptions to this include shivering and the shaking that occurs in extreme fear.[86] Research has shown that because of the social mythology of lying, people tend to concentrate on controlling their faces and words when lying. Yet the body will often "leak" discomfort and other clues that can contradict what a person is saying. Ekman and Friesen called this the "leakage hierarchy,"[87] and in later work they demonstrated some clues in body behavior that untrained observers could detect, which improved their accuracy at detecting lies from 50 to 60 percent.[88]

Three general categories of gestures can serve as behavioral clues: Ekman labels these manipulators, illustrators, and emblems.[89] *Manipulators* are grooming behaviors, usually involving the hands, in which an individual manipulates his or her hair, picks at his or her ears, or picks at lint; they can be also be seen as comforting or pacifying behaviors, such as when people rub their arms, touch their nose, bite their lips, and so on. Although these signals are often taught as "red flag indicators" of deception,[90] the available research does not lend as much weight to these clues.[91] This may be because manipulators increase in uncomfortable situations, but *also* increase in extremely comfortable situations.[92] The problem with much of the previous work on this topic is that the lie situations were not high stakes, and thus the participants' discomfort level may not have been strong enough to elicit manipulators. At its core, however, these behaviors are most closely associated with emotion.

The second class of gestures, called *illustrators*, accompany speech but do not mean anything outside of the speech context. Illustrators mainly occur in the hands but can also occur in the head or eyebrows. Illustrators serve many functions, including keeping the rhythm of speech (batons), identifying the direction of thought (diectics), emphasizing particular words or concepts (underliners), or showing spatial relations (spatials). Among liars, these illustrators tend to decrease,[93] apparently due to the cognitive overload experienced by the liar—particularly when there is ambivalence about what to do or say. However, when people are searching for words, illustrators tend to increase.[94] At its core, these behaviors are most closely associated with mental effort.

The third class of gestures, *emblems*, are word substitutes, such as "giving someone the finger," nodding to indicate yes or shaking the head to indicate no, shrugging (not sure), thumbs up (OK), and so forth. These emblems are really nonverbal language, and are culturally specific (that is, the same two-fingered palm-turned-in emblem means "peace" in the United States, whereas it means "screw you" in the United Kingdom and Australia). They are culturally specific enough that we believe they can be used to identify where a person grew up (for example, ask an American and an Italian to count to five on their hands, and the Italians will typically start counting on the thumb, whereas the American will start with the index finger). A Mediterranean person may indicate "no" with a sharp, short head bob upward. But more important, in the context of speech, these emblems—nonverbal language—can often contradict verbal language when people are lying.[95] For example, a person who shrugs while verbally expressing certainty about something is sending a mixed message, as is the person who nods subtly while saying "I did not take the money." At the core, these behaviors are nonverbal language indicating mental effort.

More generally, other categories of physical behavior may also be instructive. For example, there are several unsystematic real-world observations on body posture as an indicator of truthfulness,[96] although the laboratory research data do not support this assertion.[97] However, this has not been examined in high-stakes laboratory situations, thus researchers must be cautious about concluding that there is or is not information in the posture associated with deception.

Misperceptions of Genuineness and Trust

For the most part, there are markers that identify when a person has a genuine emotion and thought. People often misinterpret these signs, however. Reviews of the literature on what clues people believe are associated with deceit shows that only about half of those clues are actually supported by scientific research.[98] Thus, when assessing trust, people are already at a disadvantage, given that half of what they "know" is not true. Recent research shows that, in fact, specific regions of the brain respond to these particular facial expressions of emotion.[99] This means that people have the hardwiring to recognize and distinguish genuine emotions from fake ones, but that somewhere along the line they lose accuracy. O'Sullivan (this volume) identifies in greater detail why people lose accuracy. One reason is that politeness breeds out a lot of their perceptiveness, or that people receive improper feedback about the accuracy of their judgments, and so forth. In fact, if people are asked to judge liars and truth tellers without using those terms but instead substituting "is thinking hard" for the lie judgment, they improve on their accuracy.[100] Moreover, there are costs to being continually vigilant to false signals. It is effortful and exhausting, and it can interfere with interpersonal interactions. Thus it may be in people's interests to believe most others, to assume most signals are genuine, and to turn up their radar only when prompted by other circumstances in order to fully ascertain the genuineness of the signal and thus the trustworthiness of the individual. People will prefer to surround themselves with trustworthy people, knowing that a mutual, assured destruction may occur if they catch each other in a serious lie; that is, a lie would have long-term implications. This dovetails with Möllering's reasoning (this volume) on the suspension that occurs in trust—that individuals who are trusting are making a leap of faith, in which they treat uncertainty and vulnerability as unproblematic, while being entirely aware that this faith can be misplaced with bad potential consequences.

Cautions and Conclusions

Thinking and feeling clues are just that—*clues* that people are thinking, or *clues* that they are feeling or concealing some emotion, and not some "slam-dunk" giveaway that deception has or is occurring. To date, no one has been able to identify a human equivalent of a "Pinocchio response"—that is, a behavioral sign or constellation of signs that, across every person, in all situations, indicates that someone is lying. Thus, even if one observes the behavioral clues described above, one must always consider why a person would show guilt, or fear, or delight, or why a person would mull something over— there could be a variety of legitimate reasons, other than deception, that could produce these behaviors. In particular, two types of mistakes are commonly made when judging deception. The first Ekman called the "Othello error."[101] Like Shakespeare's tragic hero, lie detectors who *dis*believe truthful witnesses may make them appear anxious and fearful—and hence appear as if they are being deceptive. This means a lie catcher must decide whether the signs of fear that he believes he sees reflect the fear of a person caught lying or the fear of a truthful person who is afraid of being disbelieved. One can imagine this process occurring in the accounts of the Inka and Spaniards described by Urton (this volume); that is, the techniques of questioning by the Spaniards may have generated stress independent of any truth or lie, and these signs of stress or fear (such as the frequent swallowing of saliva) were erroneously interpreted as signs of deception. Once these believed signs of deception are noticed, the suspension of scrutiny described by Möllering (this volume) dissipates and trust is lost.

The second type of mistake Ekman called the "idiosyncrasy error."[102] This type of error is caused by a failure to observe a person's typical style of behavior. For example, research has shown that most people believe that liars do not make eye contact when they speak.[103] However, some people, either due to their shy nature or low self-esteem, never make eye contact in everyday conversation. To interpret a witness's lack of eye contact as evidence that the witness is lying, without knowing his or her typical behavioral style, would clearly make error more likely. Culture enters into this equation as well; for example, in some cultures it is considered a sign of respect not to look an authority figure in the eye.

This also means that attempts by law enforcement or others to simply look for these signs, without examining them in context, could potentially yield mistakes. However, if observers simply considered these clues as such—signs of thinking, signs of emotion—and used these behavioral "hot spots" to identify where in the conversation the person is uncomfortable in order to help the investigator formulate questions or pursue avenues of inquiry, then the cues can be very useful.[104] This approach suggests that the most effective way to detect deception from behavior is to look for changes in baseline behavior, such as when an expressive person suddenly becomes much less expressive on certain topics, or when verbal and nonverbal signals do not match—as when an individual displays signs of subtle or "micro" happiness when talking about a murder, fear when talking about an innocuous topic like lunch, or even microshrugging while making claims of certainty. Investigators trained to recognize these changes in baseline behavior could become more effective interviewers and more effective at identifying the genuineness of the behaviors they see.

When my colleagues and I interact with law enforcement, we discourage these investigators from making a judgment of "lie" when they see the changes mentioned or discrepant behaviors; instead, we encourage them to note the appearance of a "hot spot." As a bonus, identifying a "hot spot" encourages the investigator to keep gathering information, whereas we have noted in the past that investigators who label someone a "liar" early on tend to slack off in their subsequent information gathering in the belief that they have the right person—despite evidence showing that most people, including trained law enforcement officers, should exercise caution about their abilities to spot lies.[105]

This approach recognizes that an oppressive, pressured push toward a confession would not generate any behavior that is useful in identifying deception. Thus any examination of these behaviors must be performed in a rapport-building environment as a means toward helping the investigator gather information, and not as evidence in and of itself.[106] The only way to know with 100 percent certainty that someone is lying is to have unimpeachable corroborating evidence. That sort of evidence is only gained by a close examination of the physical evidence, and through a comparison of the stated account of the suspect / witness / informant to the physical evidence and other statements, in an environment in which individuals are made to feel as comfortable as possible.

Finally, law enforcement situations are the rare contexts in which trust is suspended—not ended, not requested, but simply suspended. This is not an obstacle to their establishing rapport, but my interactions with law enforcement suggest that those officers who can suspend their judgments as to whether the persons they are interviewing can be trusted or not seem to be better interviewers. Those who presume they cannot trust anyone tend to be poor interviewers and appear to be successful only because they work in a world where there is a high base rate for deception (that is, in an environment in which 80 percent of the people officers interview will lie, if officers assume that everyone they interview is a liar, they will be right 80 percent of the time).[107] Those who presume trust rather than suspend it are rare and are typically drummed out of law enforcement by the social pressure of their colleagues or their interview subjects. It is interesting that suspending trust seems to permit these officers to make clearer interpretations of the genuineness of behavioral signals, to cut through the fog of cultural norms, politeness, and other assumptions. However, we also find it to be a poor interpersonal interaction style for day-to-day life, as mistrust seems to suck the enjoyment out of all the little distortions that make our lives pleasurable.

4 Why Most People Parse Palters, Fibs, Lies, Whoppers, and Other Deceptions Poorly

Maureen O'Sullivan

> Now the serpent was more subtil than any beast of the field. And he said
> unto the woman, yea, hath God said ye shall not eat of every tree of the
> garden? And the woman said unto the serpent, we may eat of the fruit of
> the trees of the garden: but of the fruit of the tree which is in the midst of
> the garden, God hath said, ye shall not eat of it, neither shall ye touch it,
> lest ye die. And the serpent said unto the woman, ye shall not surely die
> for God doth know that in the day ye eat thereof, then your eyes shall be
> opened, and ye shall be as gods, knowing good and evil.
>
> *Genesis 3:1–5* [1]

In the previous chapter, Mark Frank reviewed how the disruptions in feeling and thinking caused by lying can result in observable clues that lie catchers could use to detect deceit. Quite surprisingly, few people seem to use these clues. A recent review of more than one hundred lie detection–accuracy studies found that average lie detection accuracy is just slightly greater than chance. But a few expert lie detectors (truth wizards) are able to discern the truth. As we will see, they are not bedeviled by the motivational and cognitive limitations that plague the social judgments of most people, including Eve, the mother of us all. [2]

MAUREEN O'SULLIVAN is professor of psychology at the University of San Francisco. She is interested in how one person understands another, which has led her to develop tests of social emotional intelligence and to study the lie detection abilities of a highly select group of expert lie detectors (truth wizards). She has also done research on romantic love, compassion, and courtesy.

Poor Eve! She was obviously not an expert lie detector. She fell for a con, the first but not the last person to do so. The passage from Genesis in which she stars contains many observations about lies and liars. The serpent is a "subtil" beast: a heavy hand is less convincing than an insinuated one. With his cunning, the serpent approaches the woman, not the man: not everyone is an equally gullible mark. And what is the temptation? Not only the fruit, but what the fruit imparts—the ability to become as gods—to know good and evil. To know something we do not know. And who is the liar? Not the serpent. True to his word, Adam and Eve did not die, and they did, indeed, learn about good and evil. Was God the liar? After all, Adam and Eve did not die a physical death, merely a sociological one, requiring a move to a less-desirable neighborhood, east of Eden. The definitional difficulties of what actually constitutes a lie are addressed by many of the contributors to this volume, but for our purposes, let's consider whether Eve lent the serpent a helping hand. Why did she believe the snake, rather than God? Did she really believe that God was deceptive? Did she really trust the snake? Or did she believe the snake because the fruit looked good, she was curious, and it might be interesting to be wise? Many lies succeed because we want the lie to be true.[3]

Consider con men who are simultaneously married to several women. Surely they are noteworthy in some regard, in order to enchant so many women. Yet they typically do not possess any outstanding personal characteristics; they are rarely rich, handsome, intelligent, or charming. They do, however, have other gifts, like the ability to spot those who want to believe their story. They feel no compunction in duping a dupe; they are unworried about minor inconsistencies in their stories and can revise stories to suit the particular vulnerabilities of each woman. Many con men are not particularly good liars, if one looks at them objectively. Women duped by such Don Juans later report that their family and friends tried to tell them that something was wrong, but they did not want to believe it. Were they too trusting, or was their motivation for romance or companionship too great to forestall the dupe?

Most of us collude in the minor deceptions required by the minuet of social life. When our friend looks terrible, we accept his protestations that he is fine. When a guest leaves a meal unfinished, we accept the explanation that the food is delicious, she just is not hungry. We accept many untruths as part of everyday courtesy; to do so keeps the social machine lubricated. But this ongoing acceptance of untruth may undermine our ability to detect important lies when they occur.

Art, Flirting, Faking It, and Other Contributors to the Common Good

Although P. T. Barnum is often quoted as saying "there's a sucker born every minute," what that legendary promoter probably said was "the people like to be humbugged"—a less-cynical, and perhaps, more true observation. But why do most people seem to enjoy being deluded at least some of the time? Why do most people seem to admire those canny tricksters who can dupe them and delight them? What is the adaptive value of being a willing audience, of having the capacity to suspend disbelief, and why do we seem to enjoy deceptions of certain sorts?[4]

As Kenneth Fields notes in Chapter 15, the coyote is a trickster featured in the tales of many cultures. An American version is the cartoon character, Wyle E. Coyote. We laugh at him because his tricks are so outlandish and because he usually gets his comeuppance. We teeter-totter between rooting for him and not rooting for him. This rapidly changing affective state may also be an aspect of the pleasure found in going to magic shows. People know they are being fooled, and they go, in part to be fooled and in part to see whether they can discover the trickery. Why do people wish to be fooled? Perhaps because they want to be surprised.

One of the basic emotions—along with anger, fear, joy, and disgust—is surprise. An emotion is basic if it is universal, biologically based, and serves an adaptive function for the species. Anger energizes behavior to stop someone from hurting us or obstructing us from achieving our goals; fear causes us to flee from harm; and joy moves us toward food, sex, family, and other elements of life maintenance. But what adaptive purpose does surprise—which can occur in response to both positive and negative events—serve? Recent research on education suggests that discrepant (that is, surprising) information is better learned and longer remembered than less-surprising information. From this it is not too far of a leap to suggest that being surprised helps us learn things—about the world and about ourselves, to remember the information longer and to form more sophisticated mental templates. So, those who are tricksters, who surprise us, keep us on our toes and cause us to exercise our minds and our emotional flexibility, the better to master the unknowns of both our intra- and interpersonal lives.[5]

In a chapter later in this volume, Tom Lutz describes fooling himself about what he was feeling, and falling in love with the woman who did not fall for his crocodile tears. He was surprised. He learned something about himself, and perhaps he could continue to learn something about himself from this woman. William Miller has described a related phenomenon—the self-consciousness of appreciating art in an art gallery—being aware of oneself appreciating the art and evaluating oneself as an art appreciator, but also being aware of possibly being observed by others in all of these roles.[6]

In romantic and sexual relationships, both inter- and intrapersonal deceptions are rampant. Such relationships often start with flirting, which can be an expression of desire and availability, but which might also be a seductive fiction created to establish desirability, to exercise control, or for other reasons unrelated to mating. As Phillips wrote: "Flirtation keeps things in play, and by doing so lets us get to know [potential lovers] in different ways. It allows us the fascination of what is unconvincing."[7]

Putting one's best foot forward in terms of dress, makeup, and behavior is a well-accepted and often-reported form of deception in the early stages of relationships. Jeffrey Hancock (this volume) provides data showing that women underreport their age and weight and men overreport their height in online personal ads. Many magazines and books encourage such deception as appropriate mating strategies. The idealized depiction of celebrities that Hany Farid illustrates in his chapter (this volume) also constitutes a kind of guidebook on how to construct a sexually desirable appearance.

Less well documented are the cognitive and emotional self-deceptions that may be involved in remaining "in love." The philosopher, Robert Solomon, made a convincing argument for considering romantic love as a deliberate cognitive achievement—an act of will fueled by sexual desire. Evidence for this view can be found in changes over time in the reported incidence of, and expectation for, romantic love as the basis for marriage. In previous generations, young people were more willing to marry a suitable partner, even if they were not in love. Solomon's argument is also supported by the wide variation among cultural groups in the acceptance of arranged marriages. Cultures generate different ideas about the importance of romantic love, depending on what the needs of the society are. Romantic love requires privacy, leisure time, and individualistic orientation. Not all societies can provide these resources, thus for them, romantic love is a foolish disruption.[8]

Why Only Some People Can Detect Deception

When the serpent tempted Eve, he told her that if she ate the fruit of the forbidden tree, she would be as a god, because she would then have the knowledge of good and evil. Why is it that only gods know about both good and evil? Perhaps the apprehension of duality involves an emotional cost that only a few can afford, an intelligence that only a few possess. As the novelist F. Scott Fitzgerald wrote: "The test of a first-rate intelligence is the ability to hold two opposing ideas in mind at the same time and still retain the ability to function. One should, for example, be able to see that things are hopeless yet be determined to make them otherwise."[9]

Most of us are not characterized by a first-rate intelligence, so defined. It is well documented that most people see themselves in a positively biased rather than a realistic way. Whether self-deception or positive illusion, people with unrealistic self-perceptions tend to report having a more positive mood, while those with less-positive self-assessment biases are more likely to be depressed.[10]

Let us consider some of the costs of the simultaneous knowledge of good and evil. Suppose a man suspects his wife of infidelity, what is he to do? Challenging her directly may cause a breach in the relationship, whether or not the suspicions are well founded. If the marriage might not survive the expression of such distrust, perhaps it is better not to know. Geoffrey Miller suggested that "there may be an adaptive binary switch from total trust to total mistrust, with no fitness payoff for being in an in-between state of semitrust."[11] Thus it may be easier for a spouse either to know all or to know nothing. Knowing both the good and the evil simultaneously makes it more difficult to know what the appropriate action is.

The difficulty that people have in acknowledging that others are lying is suggested by two studies in which observers made judgments about lying and truthful people based on only a part of their communications. Different versions of videotapes were prepared in which women discussed how they were feeling—half showed women who were lying, and half showed women who were telling the truth. One group of observers was shown only images of the face, without sound; another group was shown only the body, without sound;

a third group heard only vocal intonations; while a fourth group read transcripts of the interviews. Their judgments were compared with those made by a different group of observers, which watched the complete audiovisual record. The observers rated the honesty of the women in all of the conditions. Although the accuracy of these honesty judgments was not significantly different from chance, the observers used the information they received when watching honest people differently than they did when watching deceptive ones.

When the observers described individuals who were actually honest, they used all of the available channels in making the decision, since the ratings from all of the separate conditions (face, body, voice, and words) were positively correlated with the ratings based on the total audiovisual record. When the women were actually deceptive, however, observers tended to weight the words that the individuals used and to ignore the nonverbal channels. In other words, observers had different impression-formation strategies with honest and with deceptive people. Even though they were not accurate in distinguishing the women as honest or deceptive, they attended to different aspects of their behavior in forming an impression about them. This phenomenon illustrates the difficulty involved for most people in labeling others as deceptive.[12]

Bella DePaulo reported a similar finding. Observers also did not accurately distinguish truth tellers from liars, but when they were asked to rate people in terms of how comfortable they looked, these ratings were highly correlated with the speaker's actual honesty. Samantha Mann and Aldert Vrij found a similar result by asking people how hard liars and truth tellers were thinking. Observers rated the liars as thinking harder than the truth tellers, although their direct judgments of whether they were lying were inaccurate. Thus observers have no trouble labeling liars as less comfortable or as thinking harder than truth tellers, but when it comes to applying the term "liar," observers show a surprising amount of accusatory reluctance. This reluctance may stem from the unwillingness to take on the social burden of detecting deception: having the knowledge of good and evil and having to do something about it.[13]

In a related vein, Brooke Harrington (this volume) describes the reactions of stock market investors after they realize they have been swindled. Many of their responses suggest people's face-saving need to deny that deception has occurred. This denial, of course, may prevent them from learning from their mistakes.

Behavioral Impediments to Accurate Lie Detection

As a species, information processing is one of our few strengths, so it is perplexing that we are so poor at discerning the truth. Certainly we know that others wish to deceive us—gently, with fake compliments; more dangerously, in the theft of our identity or in the justifications for national policies. Yet people continue to be fooled, much like Charlie Brown perennially kicking Lucy's football. I have already touched on some of the motivations behind believing the unbelievable. Another reason that people are often fooled is the overlearning of social proprieties.

The demands of social life require an orchestration of impression-management strategies on the part of the actor, and the acceptance of such strategies on the part of the audience. Gary Fine (this volume) discusses the dialectic that occurs at a group level between rumor mongers and their audiences. He argues with respect to rumors that the issue is not whether the rumor is believed, but rather whether there is a belief about the primacy of conversation. That is, the audience acts as though what is more important is not the actual truth but the process of social interaction around a topic. A similar orchestration occurs at the individual level, where one person's impression-management strategies must be accepted, if not believed, by his or her conversational or relationship partner if the conversation or relationship is going to continue. Dale Carnegie graduates, people looking for love in the personal ads, and plastic surgery patients all share a desire to be seen as at least slightly better than they actually are. Observers of these efforts rarely say, "Who do you think you are kidding?!" Managing the impression we make and cooperating with the impression management of others involves social skills with a long evolutionary and cultural history.[14]

So the audience or target of the deception is essential to the adequately balanced teeter-tottering of palters, glosses, and wishful thinking. In ordinary social life, all but saints, sinners, and madmen not only collude with liars by believing them or at least not actively rejecting their stories, but they also interact with them in ways demanded by the social mores of the time. Such collusions are easily observed in the sharing of social courtesies concerning the delectability of a meal, the interestingness of the art show, the charming insouciance of the latest inappropriate partner.

Cognitive Impediments to Accurate Lie Detection

Both the desire to believe and the performance of expected social behavior erode our capacity to see things as they truly are. In addition, human thought is characterized by widespread cognitive heuristics, or thinking shortcuts, that provide adequate answers for most dilemmas, but which often lead us astray.[15]

In 1974 Amos Tversky and Daniel Kahneman described the kinds of consistent, predictable errors in logic that people make when they make decisions without complete information. They suggested that many of these errors exist because they provide shortcuts or heuristics that enable people to adapt to everyday life and to make quick decisions that are "good enough"—decisions that "satisfice." One of the more ubiquitous heuristics is *representativeness*, the tendency for people to make judgments in terms of how usual or representative a particular kind of occurrence is. If asked to judge whether a stranger is a child molester, most people would assume he is not, because most people are not child molesters.[16]

A recent, quite shocking instance of the role of representativeness bias in facilitating deception was reported in the *New York Times*. A 29-year-old convicted pedophile enrolled in several Arizona schools posing as a 12-year-old student. The adults who enrolled him claimed to be the imposter's grandfather or uncle. In actuality, they were also pedophiles with whom he was living, in their version of a "family." Neil H. Rodreick II was accepted as a 12-year-old at all but the last school he attended, partly because of his youthful appearance but also because of the sheer improbability of his ruse. Even those who had doubts about Rodreick's claims explained away their concerns with readily available explanations, telling themselves that he might have been held back a few grades, or that he was tall for his age.[17]

In detecting deception, a common representativeness error that occurs is the truthfulness bias. In psychological studies, in which observers are told that about half of the people they are to judge are lying, most people label significantly more than half as telling the truth. Although the frequency of palters, white lies, and other deceptions in social life is high, the percentage of truthful communications far outweighs that of deceptive ones. In an hour's conversation, two people may palter four or five times. This is a high frequency. But the conversation might include a thousand words or more. Even a hundred words devoted to paltering is a rather paltry percentage. Thus for most human behavior, the most representative behavior is truthful behavior. Given this base rate, it is more parsimonious to expect honesty, not deception. This may also serve well in ordinary social life, where the base rate of honesty is relatively high. If lies occur, however, this bias will lead to one's accepting lies as the truth.

Frederick Schauer and Richard Zeckhauser (this volume) describe a related phenomenon in their discussion of the impact of palters at a societal level. They argue that the presumption of honesty or dishonesty may be determined by the frequency of honesty within a group. Their view is consistent with a probability model of lie detection proposed by Hee Sun Park and Timothy Levine. One study testing that model demonstrated that average truthfulness bias increased with the actual percentage of honest samples in an array.[18]

People's average truthfulness bias will also be affected by their life experiences or their professions. For example, Paul Ekman reported that some police officers rated everyone whose truthfulness they were asked to judge as lying (that is, they had low truthfulness bias). Given the groups with which police officers deal, a deceptiveness bias is more consistent with their professional reality than a truthfulness bias would be. If one has a low truthfulness bias, a high accuracy in detecting deception is likely, since one will rarely miscategorize liars. On the other hand, errors in truth deception will increase, since even truth tellers will be categorized as liars, thereby decreasing overall lie detection accuracy. Although some people might argue that for police to err on the side of catching liars rather than disbelieving truth tellers is an acceptable risk, given the presumed checks and balances in the legal system, the raft of overturned convictions documented by the Innocence Project highlights the costs of this error.[19]

A related cognitive deficiency in parsing deception is the lack of corrective feedback. Most people do not have an available model to show them what a really good lie looks like. We think lies look like the poor-quality, easily detectable ones we have uncovered. Parents may say, "I can always tell when my daughter lies," but the template in their minds is how their daughter looked and acted in the lie they discovered. Obviously, they do not know what she looked like or sounded like in the lie she told that they believed.

Police officers, having interviewed hundreds, if not thousands, of suspects, can obtain corroborating evidence, either from witnesses or from recovered property. Those who are expert in lie detection may be more likely to attend to this confirming or disconfirming information. Similarly, therapists form hypotheses about patients, which can be confirmed by other information provided by patients or implied or suggested by other aspects of their lives. Therapists also have permission in the context of the therapy session to quiz their clients or patients about discontinuities between nonverbal expressions of emotion and the content of what they are saying. This is, in part, what they are paid to do. Expert therapists may be more willing and more able to seek the uncomfortable disconfirmation of their hypotheses than less-skilled therapists. Rules of courtesy and the parameters of social life do not permit most of us to query coworkers, teachers, or salespeople about discontinuities we might observe.[20]

A fourth type of heuristic is the *fundamental attribution error*, in which individuals ascribe others' behavior to enduring personal characteristics and incorrectly minimize the effect of situational factors. Put another way, the fundamental error in our assessment of others is to emphasize character at the expense of context. For example, we might attribute someone's homelessness to laziness or drug use and ignore economic factors beyond the person's control, such as a recession or a tight housing market. This attributional bias has been termed fundamental, because it is so well replicated in studies of social judgment.[21]

When the fundamental attribution error is applied to the lie detection situation, it may be termed the boy-who-cried-wolf effect. In Aesop's fable, the shepherd grew bored and ran to town, crying "Wolf! Wolf!" many times when there was no wolf. The townspeople came to see him as a liar. When the wolf actually came, they did not believe him. In research examining this phenomenon, participants made both trait (enduring) and state (transient) judgments of honesty. They were shown brief clips of ten men and asked to rate each of them on a number of enduring characteristics such as intelligence, trustworthiness, and likability. The enduring aspects of these characteristics were stressed in the instructions. After they had made trait judgments, the observers were then shown interviews with the same men in which some of them were lying and some were telling the truth. Once again, they were instructed that people who look honest may sometimes lie, and people who appear deceptive may actually be telling the truth. Nonetheless, the participants in this study were unable to decouple their ratings of enduring (trait) trustworthiness and transient (situational or state) honesty. If they thought a man was generally trustworthy from a brief view of his demeanor, they also judged him to be honest after watching and listening to him in a lengthier interview about his true beliefs. Furthermore, individuals who had made a decision that a man was untrustworthy to begin with had particular difficulty changing their opinion and discerning truthfulness accurately. In other words, if they think that someone is generally honest, people will tend not to see his deceptiveness. But there is some chance that with enough information, they will be able to catch him in a lie. Conversely, if people consider somebody to be a liar, it is unlikely that they will subsequently label her as honest, even when she is being truthful.[22]

This book abounds with examples of this social cognitive error. Two examples from literature and anthropology are provided by Kenneth Fields and Gary Urton (both in this volume). Fields describes how Pretty Jim's housemates erroneously assumed that his pleasant exterior was matched by an interior goodness, and so he was able to hoodwink them. Gary Urton describes how the Inkans represented the *khipu* keepers as constitutionally trustworthy, as being unable to lie, and having defined them in that way, no longer gave thought to their actual honesty as accountants. Whether they were really as honest as touted is less important than the impact of that belief on the unassailability of their accountings.

Another variant of the fundamental attribution error is found in the anchoring effect. This phenomenon was examined in the following manner. Observers were first shown a sample of behavior, without being told whether it was honest or deceptive. Perhaps because of the truthfulness bias, observers seemed to presume that the first sample showed honest behavior. If the first sample of behavior actually was honest, and the second sample was deceptive, then lie detection accuracy was significantly above chance. Observers saw that the second sample of behavior was different, and having presumed that the first sample was honest, they accurately judged the second sample as deceptive. The outcome was less desirable if the first sample of behavior was actually deceptive. In this case, the second sample, if honest, was perceived as different and therefore judged as deceptive, based on observers' assumptions that the first sample was honest. Lie detection accuracy, when the first sample was actually deceptive, was lower than chance.[23]

A fifth characteristic of social judgments that has relevance for the detection of deception is *cognitive laziness*. Susan Fiske and others have documented in scores of studies how people making judgments in social situations tend to take the easy way out, to ignore contradictions, and to stay with the first decision they reach.[24]

Sensory, Perceptual, and Intellectual Differences Among Lie Catchers

While a few humans are flawless liars, most liars betray themselves through subtle and / or rapid behavioral shifts. In the previous chapter, Mark Frank reviewed the many demeanor cues that are available and that can be used to differentiate honest from deceptive behavior, such as the difference between the smiles that occur in honest versus duplicitous discourse. Some are the genuine enjoyment smiles one sees when an Olympic competitor accepts a gold medal, while others are strained, such as the fake smiles sometimes shown by silver-medal winners—those who "coulda, shoulda" won, but did not. Although genuine and faked smiles employ different muscles, timing sequences, and apexes, most people ignore these differences. Thus when someone who enjoys "putting one over on you" smiles inappropriately—showing what Paul Ekman termed "duping delight"—most people ignore the contradiction between the smile and the content of what is being said. This ignorance can arise either from the nonperception of the differences among smiles or, for those who see that the smiles are different, a cognitive laziness in being unwilling to analyze the deviations further.[25]

Another highly informative class of behaviors is that of microexpressions, the rapidly occurring facial expressions of emotion that can happen when emotion is repressed or suppressed. Although people can be trained to recognize these microexpressions in real time, most do not see them. One reason that some people are poor at parsing deception, while others are accurate deception detectors, is a difference in powers of observation. Some people have better sensory acuity than others, particularly for interpersonal stimuli.[26]

Among humans, intellectual complexity is one mark of general intelligence. By analogy, people who are able to integrate many different sources of behavioral information would be expected to have a high level of what has been termed emotional intelligence. It has also been called social intelligence, interpersonal sensitivity, empathic accuracy, being a good judge of others, or any number of other terms. Underlying work in these areas is the presumption that, just as there are individual differences in abstract intelligence, which is reflected in the normal distribution of IQ scores, there is a normal or near-normal distribution of the intellectual capabilities involved in understanding other people. And detecting deception is one kind of social emotional intelligence.[27]

The Truth Wizards

As I have noted, most people are not very accurate lie detectors. But in the last 15 years, many different professional groups have been identified who, as groups, scored significantly above chance on standardized lie detection accuracy measures. Although most police groups do not do much better than college students, some law-related professionals are highly accurate. These include Secret Service agents, federal law enforcement agents chosen for their interviewing skills, forensic psychologists and psychiatrists, arbitrators, dispute mediators, and federal judges. Within each of these groups a few individuals scored extraordinarily high (90 or 100 percent). About ten years ago, my colleagues Paul Ekman, Mark Frank, and I started trying to find enough such highly expert individual lie detectors to study them. Because of the rarity of their abilities, I termed them "truth wizards."[28]

In order to be classified as a truth wizard, an individual had to achieve scores of 80 percent or better on at least two of three videotaped lie detection tests. The tests are difficult. Most people only score at chance—about 50 percent—thus scores of 80, 90, or 100 percent are uncommon. We have now tested more than ten thousand people and have identified 50 such truth wizards. Some of them were found in law-related groups such as those listed above. Others are therapists, artists, literature professors, and industrial designers. They range in age from 25 to 65, include both men and women, are located in all parts of the country, and represent a gamut of ethnicities and political and religious orientations.

The lie detection task used to identify the truth wizards is rather passive. They watched videos in which someone else interviewed liars and truth tellers about a high-stakes lie for about a minute. This experimental paradigm does not allow participants to use their interviewing skills or to observe the people they are judging for a significant period of time. Therefore, it is likely that the procedure produces many false negatives; that is, more expert lie detectors exist than those identified. It is unlikely, however, that the procedure produces many false positives.[29]

We were interested in how these exceptional lie detectors compared with others who were only average in their lie detection abilities, thus each truth wizard was matched with a nonexpert lie detector similar in age, geographic location, and social class. Usually this was a spouse. Sometimes, it was a coworker, friend, or neighbor. Everyone provided a life history and completed a "think-aloud" protocol. In the think-aloud process, the person is encouraged to say whatever comes to mind as he or she watched the lie detection videos for the second time. Verbatim transcripts were then analyzed with both word-count programs and content-coding systems to determine similarities among the truth wizards and between the truth wizards and their nonwizard controls.[30]

Although this analysis is still ongoing, let us consider the ways in which expert lie detectors are like most people and the ways in which they are different. The only characteristic that all expert lie detectors seem to share is a strong drive to know the truth and a willingness to expend energy to gain that knowledge. K. Anders Ericsson argues that whether the experts are grandmaster chess players, first violinists, extraordinary medical diagnosticians, or outstanding engineers, all reported intense, focused practice early in their career. He believes that expertise arises not from differences in basic intellectual talent (although one must have a rudimentary amount of such ability), but rather from focused practice. Many of the truth wizards were identified because they were part of a group attending courses in lie detection, interviewing, or nonverbal communication. They volunteered to participate in a study of lie detection, completed additional tests, and participated in life-history and think-aloud interviews that took many hours to complete. They wanted to know whether they got a lie detection item right, whereas their nonwizard matches rarely asked about particular items. For many of the controls, their interest in the project was fueled by acquiescence to the request of their spouse, friend, or coworker.[31]

So, while the social judgments of most people (such as the nonwizard controls) are characterized by cognitive laziness, this is not the case for the truth wizards. In the think-aloud procedure, the wizards regard even very brief segments of behavior from many different angles. They consider the behavior as a series of hypotheses, qualifying their interpretations with words like "could," "I think," and "perhaps." For example, a wizard might say:

> The flatness of his speech could mean that he is not invested in what he is saying. But it could also be just how he talks. Or perhaps he could have said this so many times that it is rote for him. On the other hand, I think he could have heard his family saying this. It is not that he doesn't believe it, but rather that he hasn't given it much thought. He is just repeating what he has heard his whole life. I need to listen to him some more before I make a decision.

A nonwizard might say, "That's it! He's a liar! Totally not believing what he's saying." Nonwizards tend to look for a single, definitive clue to end the task as soon as possible, to seek certainty. Nonwizards rarely continue to process information after they have made a decision, while the wizards almost always do. Wizards tend to look for a consistent pattern of behavior, to understand the person in totality, and then to determine whether this unusual behavior is an acceptable deviation within that totality or an outlier so extreme that it merits further consideration.

Other Cognitive Differences in Expert Lie Detection

The thinking of most human beings exhibits the kinds of cognitive heuristics described earlier. Those heuristics cause errors in thinking in all kinds of judgments made when information is unavailable or uncertain, as is the case in most lie detection situations. The truth wizards, by virtue of their professions or personal interests, seek feedback about the correctness of their decisions about truthfulness. This feedback serves to diminish the effects of heuristics such as representativeness and availability.

For example, certain occupations provide more access than others to information about deception: police officers can often obtain physical evidence confirming or disconfirming the reports of suspects and witnesses, and therapists who work with clients over time will uncover information that is consistent or inconsistent with the story their client tells them. Such professionals can obtain a more comprehensive view of certain types of lies. Their ideas about how representative certain kinds of stories or behavioral displays are in certain situations can enhance their accuracy when those kinds of truths or lies occur. In fact, among the truth wizards who were less accurate in one out of the three videos used to classify them, a common pattern was for therapists to be highly accurate on lies about feelings and less accurate about lies about crimes, whereas police personnel showed the opposite pattern. Among police who did well on two tests out of the three, they were more accurate at detecting deceptions concerning crimes than they were in discerning lies about feelings.[32]

The Miss Marple Effect

The representativeness heuristic seems less germane in lie detection for truth wizards for several reasons. In their personal lives, some truth wizards describe difficult early childhoods—emotional mothers, alcoholic fathers, social isolation, or similar challenges. These challenges are not in themselves a cause for the development of the social emotional intelligence needed for accurate lie detection. Rather, it is the truth wizards' efforts to understand their experiences and to deal with them that translates later in their life into the skills reflected in their high accuracy on several lie detection measures. Many of the nonwizard controls also reported early-life difficulties, but their way of dealing with these difficulties tended to be to downplay their importance or to deny their existence.

A second aspect of the personal lives of the wizards that may affect their lie detection accuracy is the tremendous variety of their personal and professional lives. Some police officers spend their entire careers walking a beat or riding in a patrol car. Many of the police wizards have worked undercover in narcotics, vice, or overseas assignments; they have headed murder investigations, founded interviewing schools, obtained advanced degrees, learned Vietnamese and Chinese, and established friendships with Chinese leaders. The truth wizards have a broad range of interpersonal experiences and scenarios to draw upon when they are evaluating the veracity of others.

These experiences, in which they have been exposed in an engaged and motivated fashion to a wide variety of people leads most of them to exhibit the "Miss Marple effect." Miss Marple is a fictional character in the stories of Agatha Christie. An elderly British woman, she solves crimes in part by noting the personality and behavioral similarities between the people involved in the crime and people she knew in her home town. Most of the wizards also seem to "take a read" on the people they seek to understand and to use this assessment in refining their interpretation of the behavioral discrepancies they note. Their sense of people, however, is highly idiosyncratic and wide ranging. They do not use psychiatric diagnoses or personality descriptions such as "extroverted" or "conscientious." They say things like, "He looks like a choirboy who has not been molested"; "He would as soon fight as spit"; "What a goofball! He thinks this whole setup is a crock"; "Look at that hair, every strand in place. That's how he speaks, too"; "Listen to how softly he said the word *money*. Money is important to him."

The Nimue Effect

While the truth wizards seem to suffer much less than most people from the cognitive heuristics involved in accurate lie detection, some of the motivational factors in poor lie detection, such as colluding with the liar, are so pervasive that even truth wizards sometimes fall prey. When a liar reminds a wizard of a loved one, or is sexually attractive, even the uncannily prescient wizards will be suckered. Let us call this the "Nimue effect," after the nymph in the King Arthur legend who was the wizard Merlin's protégée. She learned all of his spells, then seduced him into a cave, where she trapped him for eternity. Even truth wizards, particularly those in law enforcement, can be deceived sometimes. Wizards are able to control their emotional involvement when the task of judging someone else has relevance for their profession; they remain objective if they are merely observing another person. When they are emotionally involved, however, as in romantic or familial relationships, their accuracy diminishes. Thus for many of the truth wizards, their ability to understand others does not increase their success in matters of the heart.

A more benign version of the Nimue effect was observed in the think-aloud interviews. Occasionally, a wizard would err and would also report that the liar looked like a nephew or a friend. When the person in the video happened to be lying, fondness for the person he or she resembled would lead the wizard to judge the liar as honest.

Recapitulation

How humans form judgments when the information available to them is uncertain—unavailable, distorted, incomplete—has been the focus of research in cognitive psychology for decades. Deception is more likely to occur when the facts are unknown or uncertain. This essay examined how many of the cognitive heuristics (thinking shortcuts) that undermine logical thinking in other kinds of decisions affect decisions about deception, whether the deceits are the quibbles of prevarications or the blatancies of whoppers. The poor lie detection ability of most people can be understood, at least in part, as a by-product of these cognitive biases.

But kinks in the thinking process are only part of the problem. People's feelings and motivations are also involved in the ease with which they can be duped. On the positive side, the ability to suspend disbelief is part of the enjoyment of art and many leisure activities. In those contexts, too much cynicism may decrease pleasure. In our personal lives, we may also collude with liars who tell us what we want to believe or need to believe. In addition, we are often lazy and do not care whether something is really true or just true enough. All of these habits of perception and reaction contribute to the poor parsing of deception.

On the other hand, these limitations of thinking, feeling, and intention are not pandemic. Some people have a sagacity in judging others that allows them to achieve a high level of accuracy in lie detection. These truth wizards have developed methods for acknowledging and defusing the cognitive heuristics that undermine the judgment processes of most people. In addition, they show a noteworthy motivation to know the truth, particularly in their professional lives. In that context, repeated practice and the possibility of feedback allows their talent for understanding others to develop.

This perspective is consistent with arguments forwarded by other contributors to this volume and provides an understanding, from the perspective of the individual lie detector, of the group processes that many of them described. The ubiquity of many of the cognitive heuristics can also be seen in literature and anthropology from many historical periods. The current nuanced concern about deceptiveness is illustrated by Hany Farid (this volume), who contrasted the outrage over doctored war photos with the complaisant acceptance of celebrity photos that were obviously altered. "Truthiness" functions in some areas but not in others. People want celebrities to look like celebrities, whether that is young (Couric), slender (Winfrey), or upright (Lincoln). They will collude with portrayals that fit with their expectations, in areas that are not personally threatening. People seem to be less willing to collude with misrepresentations in more important areas, especially if the focus of their wrath is an unknown photographer or a distant news agency. If the deception comes from a political leader, then truthiness may slither back into the garden. People's desire to have truthful leaders may trump their desire to know the political facts.

Deception is dialectic. Telling your mirror that you own a Corvette, when you do not, is wishful thinking. Telling your girlfriend the same tale is a lie. Deception occurs when she believes you. Her acceptance of your story may not be total but may fall on a continuum that includes unquestioning belief, lack of interest, cynical acceptance, uninterested disbelief, and total disbelief without vocal dissent. Where she falls on that continuum, and how she responds to your story, will reflect her intellectual, perceptual, emotional, and motivational characteristics. This dialectic is an element of almost every kind of human deception reviewed in this book. A few wizards will not fall prey to these limitations if the lie is professionally relevant to them. But most of us, like Eve, will not be able to surmount these all-too-human limitations in our ability to detect deception.

II   DECEPTION AND TECHNOLOGY

5 Digital Doctoring

Can We Trust Photographs?

Hany Farid

W̶E MAY HAVE THE IMPRESSION that photography can no longer be trusted. From the tabloid magazines to the fashion industry, mainstream media outlets, political campaigns, and the photo hoaxes that land in our e-mail in-boxes, doctored photographs are appearing with growing frequency and sophistication. The truth is, however, that photography lost its innocence many years ago. The nearly iconic portrait of the U.S. president Abraham Lincoln (circa 1860), for example, was a fake and marked the beginning of a long history of photographic trickery. I will briefly explore this history as well as more modern examples of photographic tampering, and discuss recent technological advances that have the potential to return some trust to photography.

Abraham Lincoln and Winged Fairies

In the early part of his career, Southern politician John Calhoun was a strong supporter of slavery. It is ironic, therefore, that the famous portrait of Abraham Lincoln is a composite of Calhoun's body and Lincoln's head (see Figure 5.1). It is said that this was done because there was no sufficiently "heroic-style"

HANY FARID is the David T. McLaughlin Distinguished Professor of Computer Science and associate chair of Computer Science at Dartmouth College. He is also affiliated with the Institute for Security Technology Studies at Dartmouth. Hany is the recipient of an NSF CAREER award, a Sloan Fellowship, and a Guggenheim Fellowship.

FIGURE 5.1 Portrait of John Calhoun, from which the portrait of Abraham Lincoln was created; the Cottingley fairies and their creator; and Senator Millard Tydings (*right*) purportedly chatting with Communist party leader Earl Browder (*left*)

portrait of Lincoln available. While the creation of such an image required significant skill and effort at the time, it was by no means unique. In the early part of the 1900s, Stalin famously had his political enemies airbrushed out of official photographs. Between 1917 and 1920, two young girls in Cottingley, Yorkshire, created an international sensation when they released photographs purportedly showing tiny winged fairy creatures (see Figure 5.1). It was not until 1984 that some of the most spectacular photographs of World War I aerial combat first published in 1933 were exposed as fakes. The Brown Lady of Raynham, perhaps one of the most famous "ghost images," was a sensation when published in 1936 but was later discovered to have been created by superimposing two pictures on top of each other. It is believed that a doctored photograph contributed to Senator Millard Tydings's electoral defeat in 1950: the photo of Tydings conversing with Earl Browder, a leader of the American Communist party, was meant to suggest that Tydings had Communist sympathies (see Figure 5.1). And the list goes on—it seems that history is riddled with photographic tampering.

Oprah Winfrey and Brad Pitt

With the advent of powerful computers and sophisticated software, the creation of photographic frauds has become increasingly easier. Interestingly, the types of forgeries have not changed much: attaching a person's head to another person's body, for example, remains a popular digital deception strategy. Among the best-known examples of this technique was the August 1989 cover of *TV Guide*, which featured the head of popular daytime talk show host Oprah Winfrey composited onto the body of actress Ann-Margret (see Figure 5.2). And, in July 1992, the cover of *Texas Monthly* showed Texas governor Ann Richards astride a Harley-Davidson motorcycle, a picture created by splicing Richards's head onto the body of a model (see Figure 5.2); when asked if she objected to the image, Richards responded that since the model had such a nice body, she could hardly complain. The March 2005 cover of *Newsweek* featured a photograph of Martha Stewart with a headline that read, "After Prison She's Thinner, Wealthier & Ready for Prime Time." The photograph, however, was a composite, showing Stewart's head atop a (thin) model's body; its intent was apparently to illustrate what Stewart might look like when she was released from prison.

As with the Tydings fake, the use of compositing techniques to create the appearance of togetherness or relationship has also remained popular. In 1994, for example, *New York Newsday* published a composite of Olympic ice skaters Tanya Harding and Nancy Kerrigan in an improbable scene: practicing together at an ice rink shortly after Harding had an associate of her husband take Kerrigan out of competition with a blow to the leg. And in 2000, the University of Wisconsin at Madison—hoping to illustrate its diverse enrollment—doctored a brochure photograph by digitally inserting a black student into a crowd of white football fans (university officials said that they had spent the summer looking for pictures that would show the school's diversity—but had no luck). Reporters at the university's campus newspaper noticed lighting inconsistencies in the image and printed a story exposing the image as a fake.

FIGURE 5.2 Oprah Winfrey's head and Ann-Margret's body; Governor Ann Richard's head and a model's body; and digital composites of Senator John Kerry with antiwar activist Jane Fonda, and Brad Pitt with then-rumored sweetheart Angelina Jolie

University officials apologized, calling the decision to use the image an "error in judgment." In the political arena, as Senator John Kerry was campaigning for the 2004 Democratic presidential nomination, a doctored photo of Kerry sharing a stage with antiwar activist Jane Fonda was widely distributed (see Figure 5.2). Even after being revealed as a fake, the photograph did significant damage to Kerry's prospects by drawing attention to his controversial involvement in the antiwar movement following his service in Vietnam. With the headline "Caught Together!" the April 2005 cover of *Star* magazine featured a photo that appeared to show actors Brad Pitt and Angelina Jolie—who were rumored to have started a romantic relationship—walking on the beach together (see Figure 5.2). The *Star*'s readers were probably unaware that the picture was a composite of a photo of Pitt taken on a Caribbean island in 2005 and one of Jolie taken in Virginia a few years earlier.

Perhaps we have come to accept and even expect a certain amount of photographic trickery when it comes to Hollywood and politics. Regarding "hard news" such as wartime reporting, however, the expectations have proven to be decidedly different. In March 2003, a dramatic photograph of a British soldier in Basra, Iraq, urging Iraqi civilians to seek cover was published on the front page of the *Los Angeles Times* (see Figure 5.3). The photograph was discovered to be a digital composite of two other images, combined in order to "improve" the composition. In response, the outraged editors of the *Los Angeles Times* fired Brian Walski, a 20-year veteran news photographer. Similarly, in August 2006, the Reuters news agency published a photograph showing the remnants of an Israeli bombing of a Lebanese town—an image that, in the week that followed, was revealed by hundreds of bloggers and nearly every major news organization to have been doctored with the addition of more smoke (see Figure 5.4). The general response was one of outrage and anger: the photographer, Adnan Hajj, was accused of doctoring the image to exaggerate the impact of the Israeli shelling. An embarrassed Reuters retracted the photograph and removed from its archives nearly one thousand photographs contributed by Hajj.

While historically they may have been the exception, doctored photographs today are increasingly impacting nearly every aspect of our society. While the technology to distort and manipulate digital media is developing at breakneck speed, the technology to detect such alterations is lagging behind. To this end, I will describe some recent innovations for detecting digital tampering that have the potential to return some trust to photographs.

FIGURE 5.3 The published (*top*) and original (*bottom*) *LA Times* photographs showing a British soldier and Iraqi civilians

FIGURE 5.4 The published (*left*) and original (*right*) Reuters photographs showing the remnants of an Israeli bombing

Exposing Digital Forgeries

Given the variety of images and forms of tampering, the forensic analysis of images benefits from a variety of tools that can detect various forms of tampering. Over the past eight years my students, colleagues, and I have developed a suite of computational and mathematical techniques for detecting tampering in digital images. Our approach in developing each forensic tool is first to understand how a specific form of tampering disturbs certain statistical or geometric properties of an image, and then to develop computational techniques to detect these perturbations. Within this framework, I describe several such techniques.

Lighting

A close examination of the *Star* cover of Pitt and Jolie reveals surprisingly obvious traces of tampering (see Figure 5.5). The setting and shadows suggest that this photograph was taken outdoors on a sunny day. Several clues in this photograph indicate the location of the sun. Jolie's shadow cast onto the sand, the shadow under her chin, her evenly illuminated face, and the lighting gradient around her right leg all suggest that she is facing the sun. Given this position of the sun, we would expect the right side of Pitt's face to be illuminated. It is not. It is in shadow, which is impossible. It is clear that Pitt is facing the sun, which places the sun at a location at least 90 degrees away from the position of the sun illuminating Jolie. Were the lighting differences in this image more subtle, our manual analysis would most likely have been insufficient. We have, therefore, developed a computer program that automatically estimates the direction of an illuminating light source for each object or person in an image.[1]

By making some initial simplifying assumptions about the light and the surface being illuminated, we can mathematically express how much light a surface should receive as a function of its position relative to the light. A surface that is directly facing the light, for example, will be brighter than a surface that is turned away from the light. Once expressed in this form, standard techniques can be used to determine the direction to the light source for any object or person in an image. Any inconsistencies in lighting can then be used as evidence of tampering.

A photograph of the host and judges for the popular television show *American Idol* was scheduled for publication when it caught the attention of a photo editor (see Figure 5.5). Coming on the heels of several scandals that rocked major news organizations, the photo editor suspected that the image had been doctored. There was good reason to worry—the image was a composite of several photographs. A magnification of the host's and judges' eyes reveals inconsistencies in the shape of the specular highlight on the eyes, suggesting

FIGURE 5.5 Composite of Brad Pitt and then-rumored sweetheart Angelina Jolie (*top*); composite of the American Idol host and judges (courtesy of Fox News and the Associated Press) (*bottom*)

that the people were originally photographed under different lighting conditions. We have shown that the location of a specular highlight on the eye can be used to determine the direction to the light source.[2] Inconsistencies in the estimates from different eyes, as well as differences in the shape and color of the highlights, can therefore be used to reveal traces of digital tampering. In a related work, Nishino and Nayar describe a technique for reconstructing, from the reflection on an eye, the image of the world surrounding a person and what they were looking at.[3]

Cloning

In order to create more smoke in his photograph, Adnan Hajj cloned (duplicated) parts of the existing smoke using a standard tool in Photoshop, a popular photo-editing software. In this case, the duplication was fairly obvious because of the nearly identical repeating patterns in the smoke. When care is taken, however, it can be very difficult to visually detect this type of duplication. We have developed a computer program that can automatically detect image cloning.[4] A similar technique is described by Fridrich, Soukal, and Lukas.[5] A digital image is first partitioned into small blocks. The blocks are then reordered so that they are placed at a distance to each other that is proportional to the differences in their pixel colors. With identical and highly similar blocks neighboring each other in the reordered sequence, a region-growing algorithm combines any significant number of neighboring blocks that are consistent with the cloning of an image region. Because it is statistically unlikely to find identical and spatially coherent regions in an image, their presence can then be used as evidence of tampering.

In a similar but more serious incident, Professor Hwang Woo-Suk and colleagues published what appeared to be groundbreaking advances in stem cell research.[6] After its publication in *Science* in 2004, however, evidence began to emerge that the published results were manipulated and in places fabricated. After months of controversy, Hwang retracted the *Science* paper and resigned his position at Seoul National University.[7] An independent panel investigating the accusations of fraud found, in part, that at least nine of the eleven customized stem cell colonies that Hwang had claimed to have made were fakes. Much of the evidence for those nine colonies, the panel said, involved doctored photographs of two other, authentic colonies: the authors had digitally cloned their results. While the Hwang case garnered international coverage and outrage, it is by no means unique. In an increasingly competitive field, scientists are succumbing to the temptation to exaggerate or fabricate their results. Mike Rossner, the managing editor of *Journal of Cell Biology*, estimates that as many as 20 percent of accepted manuscripts to his journal contain at least one figure that has to be remade because of inappropriate image manipulation, and roughly 1 percent of figures are simply fraudulent.[8]

Retouching

While attending a meeting of the United Nations Security Council in September of 2005, U.S. president George W. Bush scribbled a note to Secretary of State Condoleezza Rice. The note, photographed by a Reuters correspondent, read "I think I may need a bathroom break. Is this possible?" (see Figure 5.6). Because the original image was overexposed, a Reuters processor selectively

FIGURE 5.6 A note written by Bush was retouched to improve readability, disrupting the color filter array correlations

adjusted the contrast of the notepad prior to publication. This form of photo retouching is quite common and can be used to alter a photograph in trivial or profound ways. We have developed a technique for detecting this form of tampering that exploits how a digital camera sensor records an image.[9] Virtually all digital cameras record only a subset of all the pixels needed for a full-resolution color image. These pixels are recorded by a color filter array (CFA) placed atop the digital sensor. The most frequently used CFA, the Bayer array, employs three color filters: red, green, and blue (see Figure 5.6). Because only a single color sample is recorded at each pixel location, the other two color samples must be estimated from the neighboring samples in order to obtain a three-channel color image. The estimation of the missing color samples is referred to as CFA interpolation, or demosaicking. In its simplest form, the missing pixels are filled in by spatially averaging the recorded values. Shown in Figure 5.6, for example, is the calculation of a red pixel from an average of its four recorded neighbors. Because the CFA is arranged in a periodic pattern, a periodic set of pixels will be precisely correlated to its neighbors according to the CFA interpolation algorithm. When an image is retouched, it is likely that these correlations will be destroyed. As such, the presence or lack of such correlations can be used to authenticate an image, or expose it as a forgery.

Ballistics

Firearm ballistics experts routinely analyze bullets and bullet impacts to determine the type and caliber of a firearm. In some cases, distinct grooves and scratches in the firearm barrel can be used to link a bullet to a specific weapon. In the field of camera ballistics, the goal is analogous: link an image to a specific camera, scanner, printer, and so on.

Because the JPEG image format has emerged as a virtual standard, most devices and software encode images in this format. This compression scheme allows for some flexibility in how much compression is achieved. Manufacturers typically configure their devices differently in order to balance compression and quality to their own needs and tastes. This choice is realized by adjusting the values in the JPEG quantization table, a set of 192 numbers. Smaller values yield less compression with higher quality, and larger values yield more compression with lower quality. Because camera manufacturers typically construct distinct tables, the JPEG quantization table can be used to identify the source of an image.[10] While this approach cannot distinguish between images taken with different cameras of the same make and model, it can be used to make a cruder distinction between different camera makes and models. In related work, Lukas and colleagues describe a more powerful technique to identify a specific camera based on the camera's pattern of noise.[11] This approach exploits the imperfections in a camera sensor that tend to be distinct. Having measured these imperfections from a camera, they can be matched against the same imperfections extracted from an image of unknown origin.

Real Versus Virtual

The child pornography charges filed against Police Chief David Harrison in 2006 shocked the small town of Wapakoneta, Ohio. At his trial, Harrison's lawyer argued that if the state could not prove that the seized images were real, then Harrison was within his rights in possessing the images. In 1996 the Child Pornography Prevention Act (CPPA) extended the existing federal criminal laws against child pornography to include certain types of "virtual porn." In 2002 the U.S. Supreme Court found that portions of the CPPA, being overly broad and restrictive, violated First Amendment rights. The court ruled that "virtual" or "computer-generated" (CG) images depicting a fictitious minor are constitutionally protected. In contrast, in the United Kingdom the possession or creation of such virtual images is illegal. The burden of proof in the Harrison case and countless others shifted to the state, which had to prove that the images were real and not computer generated.

Given the sophistication of computer-generated images (see Figure 5.7), several state and federal rulings have further found that juries should not be asked to make the determination between real and virtual. In 2006 at least one federal judge even questioned the ability of expert witnesses to make this determination. At the time, however, there were no data supporting the feasibility of making this distinction. To this end, my colleague Mary Bravo and I tested the ability of human observers to differentiate between CG and photographic images.[12] We collected 180 high-quality CG images with human, man-made, or natural content created over the previous six years. For each CG image, we found a photographic image that was matched as closely as possible in content. The 360 images were presented in random order to ten observers from an introductory psychology subject pool. Observers were given unlimited time to classify each image. Observers correctly classified 83 percent of the photographic images and 82 percent of the

FIGURE 5.7 A computer-generated (virtual) person
SOURCE: Created by Mihai Anghelescu.

CG images, inspecting each image for an average of 2.4 seconds. Among the CG images, those depicting humans were classified with the highest accuracy rate: 93 percent. The observer with the longest inspection time (3.5 seconds/image) correctly classified 90 percent of all photographic images and 96 percent of all CG images. This observer correctly classified 95 percent of CG images depicting humans. It seems that, at least for now, even with the great advances in computer graphics technology, the human visual system is still very good at distinguishing between computer-generated and photographic images.

As technology improves, it is likely that it will become increasingly more difficult to distinguish the real from the virtual. To this end, we have developed a computer program that can distinguish between CG and photographic images. Because CG images are created using idealized lighting, surface geometries, optics, and sensors, they tend to exhibit statistical regularities that are different from photographic images.[13] We have been able to quantify and measure these statistical differences and to use them to differentiate between photographic and CG images.

Photographs and Memories

Days before the 2004 U.S. presidential election, a voter was asked for whom he would vote. In reciting his reasons for why he would vote for George W. Bush, he mentioned that he could not get out of his mind the image of John Kerry and Jane Fonda at an antiwar rally. When reminded that the image was a fake, the voter responded, "I know, but I can't get the image out of my head."

Several studies have shown that doctored photographs can implant and alter childhood and adult memories.[14] In a study by Wade and colleagues, participants viewed doctored photographs of themselves and a family member taking a hot-air balloon ride, along with photographs of three real events from their childhood.[15] After as few as three interviews, 50 percent of participants reported remembering all or part of the hot-air balloon event. Similar results were reported by Garry and Wade, although the authors did find that images are not as powerful as narratives in stimulating false memories.[16] Adult memories seem to be equally influenced by doctored images. In a study by Sacchi and colleagues, participants were shown original and doctored photographs of memorable public events at which they were present (the 1989 Tiananmen Square protest in Beijing and the 2003 protest in Rome against the Iraq war).[17] The doctored images, showing either larger crowds or more violence, changed the way in which participants recalled the events. Images, real or fake, have a very real and lasting impact.

Photographs and Trust

Schauer and Zeckhauser (this volume) explore the nature of paltering, which they define as "the widespread practice of fudging, twisting, shading, bending, stretching, slanting, exaggerating, distorting, whitewashing, and selective reporting." While some forms of photographic tampering certainly rise to the level of fraud—such as Hwang's fraudulent scientific paper—many forms of photographic doctoring might be classified as paltering—such as Hajj's addition of smoke to a war photograph. Both forms of deception, however, are equally damaging to our trust in photographs. Each form of deception creates uncertainty in a medium that is becoming increasingly more malleable, so that no matter how minor the palter, trust is eroded. Perhaps this erosion of trust is inevitable in an increasingly digital age.

Hancock (this volume) explores how technology provides for new and sophisticated forms of deception in personal interactions over the Internet, such as online dating. In addition to underreporting their weight and overreporting their height and income, some date seekers have taken to posting digitally enhanced photographs. This erosion of trust will only increase with, for example, the next generation of cameras that automatically removes wrinkles (Panasonic) or ten pounds (Hewlett-Packard) at the push of a button.

The mushroom cloud from the nuclear explosion over Nagasaki; a young girl fleeing her village after being burned by napalm; prisoners being abused in Abu Ghraib prison in Iraq: these wartime photos have become ingrained in our collective memories and serve as powerful symbols of the horrors of war. Glenney (this volume) describes the potential for the use of doctored photographs in wartime to boost morale, demoralize or deceive the enemy, or justify military action. There is little doubt that these types of manipulations would raise serious ethical issues or that they add to a continued degradation of trust in photography.

Digital technology is allowing us to manipulate, distort, and alter reality in ways that were simply impossible 20 years ago. As the above examples illustrate, we are feeling the impact of this technology in nearly every corner of our lives. Tomorrow's technology will almost certainly allow us to manipulate digital media in ways that today seem unimaginable. As technology continues to evolve, it will become increasingly more important for us to understand its power, limitations, and implications, and to envision a different relationship with digital media. It is my hope, nevertheless, that the science of digital forensics will keep pace with these advances, and in so doing return some trust to this wonderful, and at times puzzling, digital age.

6 Digital Deception

The Practice of Lying in the Digital Age

Jeffrey T. Hancock

With this [Athena] touched him with her golden wand.
A fresh tunic and cloak replaced his rags,
And he was taller and younger, his skin tanned,
His jawline firm, and his beard glossy black.
Having worked her magic, the goddess left,
And Odysseus went back into the hut.

> Homer, *The Odyssey*

W HEN ODYSSEUS RETURNED TO ITHACA after his long absence, he returned in disguise as an old beggar. This was no ordinary disguise, but one conjured by the goddess Athena. She shriveled his skin, shrank his stature, took away the light hair from his head, dimmed his eyes, and added pounds of flesh. With the aid of Athena's disguise, Odysseus deceived almost everyone, including his wife and son (though his dog and nursemaid both recognized him). Odysseus used this deception to destroy his wife's false suitors and to test the loyalty of his subjects and the faithfulness of his wife and son. As described in the epigraph above, Athena removed the disguise after Odysseus defeated the suitors. His deception was forgiven, and Odysseus was reunited with his wife (for other wonderful examples of deception taken from literature, see Fields, this volume).

With the advent of modern information and communication technologies, most notably the Internet, we all have the power of the gods, at least with regard to deception. We can easily pretend online to be someone we are not

JEFFREY T. HANCOCK is an associate professor at Cornell University. He studies the nature of social interactions in online communication, with a particular interest in the practice and detection of deception.

by making up a new identity, appropriating someone else's, or just modifying our own. We can tell lies at a distance, and we can make it seem as though we are in one place when we are actually in another (for example, using a mobile phone to say, "Honey, I'm working late" while actually out with friends). These technologies can help us craft lies and perhaps make it more difficult for others to detect them.

This kind of deception, carried out with information and communication technology, is digital deception: *the intentional control of information in a technologically mediated message to create a false belief in the receiver of the message*. As Frank (this volume) notes in his discussion of the nature of lying and deception, a key element of any definition of lying is that it is a deliberate or intentional act. People who mistakenly provide incorrect information are not lying, they are just mistaken. A second key element is whether the attempt to deceive is authorized or expected by the target. When playing an online poker game, for example, players expect each other to attempt deception about what cards they are holding. They do not, however, expect the online poker service to rig the game. These properties also hold for digital deception, with the additional criterion that the deception takes place via some mediated form of communication, such as a telephone, e-mail, instant messaging, chat room, and so forth. For example, a common and important form of digital deception is the manipulation of photographs, both in the media and in online dating sites (see Farid, this volume). It is important to note that mediated communication is no longer limited to the desktop; we now communicate digitally on cell phones, and a tremendous range of services are emerging to move communication abilities off the desktop.

The digital world therefore is not a uniform place; information and communication technologies create a wide variety of online spaces, each with its own communication properties (such as cue availability and interactivity) and set of norms for deception.[1] Participants interacting in an adult chat room dedicated to fantasy sex, for example, hold very different expectations and beliefs about deception than participants involved in a message board dedicated to cancer survivors. As we will see, these expectations have important implications for digital deception.

This chapter examines three aspects of digital technologies that are adapted to the age-old practice of deception. The first section of the chapter considers how technology can *enable* various forms of digital deception by making it easier to lie or allowing us to lie in new ways. It is important to note, however, that the very technology that enables deception in one instance can, sometimes paradoxically, also promote honesty and self-disclosure. For instance, the "stranger on the train effect," in which strangers reveal highly intimate details about themselves, has been observed in a number of mediated communication spaces, including blogs, social support message boards, and computer-mediated therapy.[2] The question I address in the second part of the chapter regards which properties of technology affect how honest and self-disclosive we are, and why.

The final part of the chapter reviews recent research that examines our everyday lying practices in different digital media, including e-mail, instant messaging, the telephone, and online dating sites. As we will see, the aspects of technology that enable deception as well as the factors that promote honesty and self-disclosure both play a role in how and when we use technology to lie in our everyday lives.

This chapter does not examine deception in the field of computer security. Readers interested in this area should see Thompson (this volume) and his discussion of cognitive hacking (see also Schneider for deception related to information infrastructure).[3] It is important to note that Thompson's definition of cognitive hacking, which refers to the use of a computer system attack to alter human users' perceptions and behaviors, is generally consistent with the definition of digital deception. In the present discussion, however, the focus is on interpersonal forms of deception and communication.

Technology Enabling Deception

Communication technologies have several properties or affordances that potentially enable, support, or otherwise facilitate deception in several important ways. Key among these is the ability to represent and interact with others without being physically copresent.[4] That is, with technology we no longer need to be in the same physical space to communicate with others—our communication is *disembodied*. Of course, this is not unique to modern communication technologies; humans have devised a wide range of technologies for communicating at a distance or over time. For example, the Inka developed bundles of knotted strings, called *khipu*, to record information pertaining to the administration of the far-flung Inka empire (see Urton, this volume). As Urton describes, the Inka appear to have used the khipu to deceive their Spanish conquerors.

In addition to allowing for disembodied communication, digital communication technologies, such as the Internet and modern telephony, allow our messages to be exchanged in *real time* over any distance. A phone call, for example, can support synchronous conversation between two people in almost any place on earth (and with astronauts in orbit). Digital communication can involve single or multiple channels of information exchange, including verbal, visual, and audio information. Web pages, for example, can include textual descriptions, support visuals and graphics, and play music. Digital forms of communication also tend to be inexpensive, which allows a message producer to send messages to many people almost as easily and inexpensively as to one person.

Perhaps the best-known example of digital deception—spamming—takes advantage of the inexpensive nature of digital communication to reach millions of potential consumers and targets. Spamming refers to the use of digital messaging systems (e-mail, instant messaging, Usenet, and the like) to send unsolicited bulk messages, often to millions of recipients at a time. Spam messages are frequently duplicitous; a report prepared by the Federal Trade Commission for Congress revealed that approximately two-thirds of spam contained deception, either in its content, in the "subject" line, or in the "from" line.[5] Given the bulk nature of spamming, even if a very small percentage of receivers respond to the spam, the spammers can turn a profit. A related but more pernicious form of digital deception is the practice of "phishing." Phishing refers to attempts to steal sensitive information (such as bank account numbers and passwords) by directing users to a website pretending to be a trustworthy party (such as their bank) but that is actually controlled by the phisher. Successful phishing can lead to identity theft and financial loss, and recent research suggests that most users have a surprisingly difficult time detecting phishing deceptions.[6] For a more complete treatment of spam and phishing, see Thompson's chapter on cognitive hacking (this volume).

The affordances of digital communication technologies described above have also led to a wide range of "deception services" online. Alibi agencies, for example, provide alibis and excuses for clients by using technology to mask the agency's identity in order to appear to be whomever the client wishes. For example, one company, called Alibi Network, offers a virtual hotel service in which a client can use an agency phone number as a purported hotel number. When someone calls the "hotel," the "receptionist" will pretend to connect that person to the client's hotel room. In reality, the call is transferred to whatever number the client has provided. The ability of the alibi agency to credibly impersonate multiple businesses and to connect callers to clients in any location are all made possible by communication technology.

Similar forms of deception enablement are alibi and excuse clubs. These clubs are networks of individuals who help each other avoid work or people by means of text messages sent by members to the hundreds of people in the club. For example, a person can get out of a date with someone by asking one of the club members to pretend to be the liar's boss. The "boss" calls the date to say that the liar needs to stay late at work. Although humans have often relied on friends to provide false alibis and excuses, technology allows us to rely on strangers to accomplish the lie, which presumably reduces interpersonal complications such as guilt and potential blackmail.

With the tremendous popularity of online social networking sites such as MySpace and Facebook that focus on highlighting social connections, services have emerged that provide users with fake friends. For a period in 2006, the company FakeYourSpace offered to provide MySpace users with attractive, but fake, friends in an effort to help the user appear more popular (at a rate of $.99 per month per friend). The site closed after several media stories negatively covered the website.[7]

Perhaps the key technological affordance involved in each of the examples above is that they enable *identity deception*. Identity deception refers to the false manipulation or display of a person or organization's identity.[8] The deceiver can represent him- or herself without the constraints associated with the physical self. A great deal of research has focused on the disconnect between physical and virtual identities in online communication environments.[9] As the saying goes, "online, no one knows you're a dog." Turkle, for example, describes the Internet as a social laboratory for experimenting with identity.[10]

Donath provided one of the earliest theoretical treatments of how identity deception takes place online.[11] Donath used concepts described by Zahavi in his analysis of deception in biology in order to create a framework of identity deception online (see also Bergstrom, this volume).[12] This framework distinguishes between biologically expensive displays directly related to an organism's characteristics that are difficult to fake, called *assessment signals*, and low-cost displays that are only arbitrarily associated with a characteristic, called *conventional signals*. In online communication, conventional signals include most of the information that is exchanged in messages, including what we say ("I'm fit and athletic," for example) and the nicknames we use to identify ourselves (such as "hot-and-sexy"). Assessment signals may be more difficult to come by online, but they can include links to a person's "real-world" identity, such as a phone number or an e-mail address (for example, e-mails ending in .edu suggest that the person works at a school or university), or levels of knowledge that only an expert could display (such as highly technical information about a computer system). These conventional types of signals are related to the kinds of palters described by Schauer and Zeckhauser (this volume). Walther and Parks introduced a similar concept, *warranting*, which refers to links between a person's online persona and his or her true identity.[13] For example, if people let their friends know that they are engaged in online dating, a connection is established between their real-world life (their friends' knowledge) and their online life (their online dating activities).

Donath points out that conventional signals are an easy target for deceptive identity manipulation.[14] For example, category deception refers to manipulations of our perceptions of individuals as members of social groups, or categories—such as male vs. female, white vs. black, student vs. worker, or hockey player vs. squash player. Online, gender deception is perhaps the most commonly discussed example of category deception.[15] More subtle forms of deception include identity concealment, in which one omits or blurs important aspects of one's identity, such as using a pseudonym when posting in order to shield one's identity.

With the rise of digital cameras and online social networking sites that feature photographic user profiles, personal photographs have transformed online communication into a much more visual environment for identity presentation. In the context of Donath's conventional vs. assessment signal framework, photographs should operate as assessment signals because they link people to their real-world identity. But, as Farid (this volume) describes, digital photographs are easily manipulated in the service of deception, compromising their value as an assessment signal in digital contexts. Indeed, in a recent study of deception in online dating profiles, we found photographs to be the most deceptive element.[16]

The affordances of digital communication described above also have important implications for interpersonal communication, such as exchanging e-mail, instant messages, and phone calls with people we know (that is, those whose identity is known to us). For example, text-based forms of digital communication (such as e-mail, instant messaging, and text messaging) strip away many of the behavioral and demeanor cues associated with deception. As Frank (this volume) describes, two behavioral clues related to deception are *thinking clues* associated with the additional mental effort of lying, and *feeling clues* that reflect a liar's actual emotional state (whether lying about feelings or feeling guilty about lying). In the context of digital communication, feeling clues, which are typically exhibited in the face and voice, are *absent* in text-based environments such as e-mail and *reduced* in audio environments such as the telephone. Thinking clues, which are typically more verbal, should still be present in mediated communication, although they may be altered. For instance, because e-mail is asynchronous, a liar has more time to craft a lie, which should make thinking clues less likely to emerge.

Considered together, these observations suggest that digital communication should enable deception by reducing the number of clues available to catch the liar. For example, Keyes argues that "electronic mail is a godsend. With e-mail we needn't worry about so much as a quiver in our voice or a tremor in our pinkie when telling a lie. E-mail is a first rate deception-enabler."[17] But, as O'Sullivan (this volume) notes, for most people deception is extremely difficult to detect, even under face-to-face circumstances. Indeed, a recent meta-analysis reveals that people perform at chance levels when they have access to both verbal and nonverbal cues.[18] Consistent with this, when my research team compared deception detection in face-to-face and computer-mediated communication in an experiment, we found that participants in both conditions could detect deception only at chance levels, and that text-based detection was not worse than face-to-face detection.[19] As such, there may be little value to the liar in having nonverbal cues eliminated, given that such cues do not seem to be helpful when detecting lies. Other features of communication technology may also work against the liar, such as how recordable the medium is. We examine this issue in the next section.[20]

Technology Promoting Honesty and Self-Disclosure

One of the most surprising phenomena to emerge with digital communication is the amount and intensity of self-disclosure sometimes observed in online diaries, chat rooms, and news groups.[21] In online diaries, such as those posted at LiveJournal, users often open up about deeply intimate topics, from child abuse to secrets about love affairs to the commission of crimes. For example, one type of blog to emerge recently is dedicated to revealing how much financial debt one has. These users post all of their financial details, including current purchasing and saving behaviors. Some do this anonymously while others provide their identities. In another site called PostSecret, people mail postcards to a P.O. box that describe a secret they wish to reveal, from being raped to admitting to cheating in college. These postcards are scanned and posted online, where large audiences view the secrets each week. Other research has revealed that when people self-report about sensitive topics (like drug use and sexual activity), their answers tend to be more honest when they are communicating with or through a computer system than directly with a human.[22]

Why do people sometimes act so honestly and openly in digital communication? One common explanation is the psychological effect that communicating via technology can have on users. For instance, when people interact online, they experience increased *perceived anonymity*, which refers to the belief by users that they are unaccountable for their social actions within a specific medium. Perceived anonymity has been argued to increase disinhibition, leading people to engage in more risky and extreme behavior.[23] Anonymous Internet interactions resemble those identified in the "stranger on the train" phenomenon,[24] in which people sometimes reveal their most intimate thoughts to chance acquaintances on trains, planes, or other intimate travel circumstances.[25] The subjective experience of perceived anonymity promotes a focus on the self and reduces concerns about being accountable to others.

For example, in a clever series of experiments, Joinson demonstrated that people tend to disclose more personal information in text-based interactions than in face-to-face ones because their attention is directed more toward their own thoughts and feelings while being less concerned with how others may be viewing them or their actions.[26] This combination of increased self-awareness and decreased awareness of others' perceptions of self may be one reason that technology promotes self-disclosure and honesty.

Another important factor that reduces deception that is surprisingly easy to overlook is the nature of the communication medium.[27] Elsewhere, we have argued that at least three features of a medium can influence the decision to lie or not, including the degree to which a message is recordable, whether the medium supports real-time interaction, and whether the interlocutors are physically copresent or not.[28] The first and most obvious is whether a medium creates a record of the communication. The more recordable or permanent a message is, the less likely a person would choose to lie in that context. E-mail involves automatic records (copies are typically left on the liar's computer, intermediate servers, and the target's computer) and is perhaps the most durable interpersonal form of communication we have so far created. Many people have found this out the hard way, when their e-mails are subpoenaed as part of criminal and political investigations. E-mails, for example, played a key role in the Enron prosecution, and they have been the focus of attention in several recent congressional investigations (such as the Attorney General Gonzales scandal). Instant messaging can be easily recorded, although the exchanges are not automatically saved. Instant message records led to the downfall of former congressman Foley, who engaged in inappropriate sexual instant message conversations with congressional pages. Lying in these forms of digital communication carries important risks for the liar.

The second feature of a medium that affects lying behavior is whether interactions take place in real time (synchronously) or not (asynchronously). Lies in conversation tend to be spontaneous and often arise from situations in which a truthful response may be problematic.[29] For example, if Tarleton asks Jenna where she was at lunch, and she was planning his surprise birthday party, Jenna is compelled to lie. If Tarleton had asked via e-mail, Jenna could have simply ignored the e-mail or delayed her response until she could compose a believable palter. In other contexts, the time constraints of real-time interaction can also make it difficult to construct a response that is not an outright falsification but instead a more subtle distortion of the truth (such as equivocation).

The third feature to influence the decision to lie is physical copresence: interaction in a shared physical space, such as face-to-face interactions. As noted above, digital communication is disembodied and by definition not physically copresent. When we are not in the same physical space as the person to whom we are talking, we can lie about any number of things that we could not when copresent, including who we are with, what we are doing, where we are, what we are wearing, and so on.

Finally, our behaviors are always guided by relevant social norms, expectations, and conventions, including our online behaviors. A good deal of research has demonstrated that norms can be particularly important in determining how we behave in mediated contexts.[30] Norms associated with deception evolve within specific online domains, and the norms differ substantially from one domain to the next. Consider, for example, an adult online chat room. People are attracted to this kind of online space to take part in sexual conversations that they may not be able to have in their day-to-day lives. Participants in an adult chat room usually do not use their real names or identities when interacting online. As such, most people believe that the other people in the chat room are not actually who they say they are. In other words, the normative expectation here is one of joint pretense, in which participants are aware that each one is acting a role or playing a part.[31] But, obviously, in other online spaces deception is viewed as negatively as it is in face-to-face settings. Consider a cancer support newsgroup, which the members use as a safe place to reveal personal issues and fears and to seek advice from others. These groups work hard to build trust and give participants a place to feel safe when taking a trusting "leap of faith" (see Möllering, this volume). When a deception in this context is revealed, it can lead to intense outrage, feelings of violation, and heavy sanctions on the perpetrator of the deception.[32]

Practicing Deception in the Digital Age

As we have seen, digital communication can both enable deception and promote honesty, depending on the context and the social expectations. How do these factors come together to influence deception in our own everyday social interactions?

One approach to addressing this question is to ask people their beliefs about digital deception. For instance, Caspi and Gorsky found that three-quarters of the people in their sample of discussion group participants believed that "online deception is very widespread."[33] In online dating contexts, the majority of online daters believe that other users misrepresent their physical appearance.[34]

These beliefs suggest that digital deception is rampant. But empirical research comparing lying behaviors across different digital media suggest that the answer is not so straightforward. Consider a series of diary studies in which we asked people to record all of their social interactions and lies for seven days.[35] We also asked them to note which medium they were using in the social interactions they recorded. The data revealed that people tend to lie the most on the telephone, second most in face-to-face interactions and instant messaging, and least of all in e-mail. Consistent with the kinds of communicative factors described above, we concluded that people do not lie often in e-mail because it is a recordable and noninteractive medium. We also concluded that people lie frequently on the phone because it is not typically recordable, it is interactive, and interactants are not copresent. The evidence that lies occur the least in e-mail suggests that people's beliefs about deception online may be exaggerated.

The medium affected not only the frequency with which lies were told in our data set, but also the content of the lies. The telephone was used to lie about actions, such as where the liar was or who she was with. Lies related to one's feelings were told most often in face-to-face conversations. E-mail lies were most frequently explanation lies that provided reasons or excuses for some state of affairs. For example, students in our sample often reported telling explanation-type lies to professors ("my printer wasn't working"). Because e-mail is asynchronous and people can take their time to compose messages, it seems to be an excellent venue for crafting planned lies that are unlikely to be verified (that is, the professor is unlikely to check whether the printer was really broken).

Concerns about deception also seem exaggerated in online dating contexts. We asked online daters to come into the lab, where we measured their heights, weights, and ages in order to compare their actual characteristics against how they described themselves in their online profile.[36] Lies were certainly frequent: 81 percent of the participants lied about one of those characteristics. But the vast majority of the lies were minor. People lied about their weight by about five pounds (women lied more than men), they lied about their height by about half an inch (men lied more than women), and they lied about their age by about half a year (men and women did not differ). Most lies were so small they would be difficult to detect. Of course, there were a few whoppers (35 pounds, 3 inches, and 9 years were the biggest lies). Normative expectations seemed to guide some of the lying practices in this study. Participants uniformly reported that it was not socially acceptable to lie about one's relationship status, but that it was more socially acceptable to lie about hobbies and interests.

Taken together, these studies suggest that lying practices in interpersonal contexts can vary substantially across digital communication media, but that it is not the case that simply because behavior takes place online that more deception will be observed. Digital deception in more high-stakes domains, such as sexual predation and criminal activity, is a growing problem. For example, several investigations have revealed that sexual offenders (particularly pedophiles) use various online communication forums to lure potential victims.[37] In addition, criminal entities, such as organized crime and terrorist

organizations, increasingly rely on information technologies to communicate.[38] The military is also studying deceptive practices and developing potential countermeasures (see Glenney, this volume).

Conclusion

If digital communication gives us the power of the gods to deceive, then it
is quite clear from the deluge of spam and phishing e-mails that some mortals are taking advantage of it. Clearly, technology enables deception in many
ways. But the evidence so far suggests some hope that, just because we can lie
does not necessarily mean that we do. New communication and information
technologies may even encourage honesty and openness, and it seems that
many of us mortals are using our newfound powers rather carefully.

7 Cognitive Hacking

Detecting Deception on the Web

Paul Thompson

ANY OF THE CUES that in face-to-face communication would enable someone to detect deception are missing, or altered, in computer-mediated communication. *Cognitive hacking* refers to an attack on a computer or information system that relies on altering human users' perceptions and corresponding behaviors in order to be successful, in contrast to denial of service (DOS) and other kinds of attacks on information systems that operate solely within the computer and network infrastructure.[1] One example of cognitive hacking is website spoofing, in which a fake website is made to mimic a real one. For example, since 1999, a website has existed (www.gatt.org) that is a parody of the World Trade Organization site (www.wto.org).[2] The parody can be perceived fairly easily, but it nonetheless could mislead some viewers. In other cases, for example with phishing schemes, the website is fully intended to deceive the user. Phishing is "a form of social engineering in which an attacker, also known as a phisher, attempts to fraudulently retrieve legitimate users' confidential or sensitive credentials by mimicking electronic communications from a trustworthy or public organization in an automated fashion."[3]

With cognitive attacks, neither hardware nor software is necessarily corrupted; rather, the computer system is used to influence people's perceptions

PAUL THOMPSON is a research professor of computer science at Dartmouth College. He studies the detection of, and countermeasures for, disinformation in information networks such as the World Wide Web.

and behavior through disinformation. Cognitive attacks are not well addressed by the traditional definition of computer security, which calls for protection of the information system from three kinds of threats: unauthorized disclosure of information, unauthorized modification of information, and unauthorized withholding of information (denial of service). In this chapter the terms *cognitive attack, cognitive hacking,* and *semantic attack* will be used interchangeably.

A Cognitive Attack Example

Consider the following scenario. In 2000, a reader of press releases on the Internet may have come across the following misleading posting about Emulex:

> Friday morning, just as the trading day began, a shocking company press release from Emulex (Nasdaq: EMLX) hit the media waves. The release claimed that Emulex was suffering the corporate version of a nuclear holocaust. It stated that the most recent quarter's earnings would be revised from a $0.25 per share gain to a $0.15 loss in order to comply with Generally Accepted Accounting Principles (GAAP), and that net earnings from 1998 and 1999 would also be revised. It also said Emulex's CEO, Paul Folino, had resigned and that the company was under investigation by the Securities and Exchange Commission.[4]

Background

Identity theft and other computer-related crimes such as phishing have been recognized as the fastest-growing area of crime and increasingly as a problem to be addressed by computer security. *Social engineering* is a general term used in computer security describing the use of techniques adopted by con artists as applied to humans using computer systems.

Cybenko et al. defined cognitive hacking as a disinformation attack on the mind of the end user of a networked computer system, such as a computer connected to the Internet.[5] One example of a disinformation attack is a "pump and dump" scheme in which one or more people publish false or misleading information on the Internet about a publicly traded company in order to manipulate its stock price. If the disinformation causes the company to appear to be an attractive investment, its price on the stock market will rise. Once this happens, the people who published the disinformation about the company can sell their stock and make a large profit, as much as several hundred thousand dollars.

In another example of a disinformation attack, of the type now called phishing, customers of PayPal received the following e-mail: "We regret to inform you that your username and password have been lost in our database. To help resolve this matter, we request that you supply your login information at the following website." Many of these customers gave personal information about their PayPal account to the site linked to the message.[6] The alleged perpetrators apparently used their illicit access to PayPal accounts in order to purchase items on eBay.

Perception Management

As noted by many authors, perception management is pervasive in contemporary society (see Schauer and Zeckhauser, this volume).[7] Its manifestation on the Internet is one aspect of this broader phenomenon. Not all perception management is negative—for example, education is a form of perception management—nor is all use of perception management on the Internet cognitive hacking. Clearly, the line between commercial uses of the Internet (such as advertising, which would *not* be considered cognitive hacking) and manipulation of stock prices by the posting of disinformation in newsgroups (which *would* be considered cognitive hacking) is sometimes difficult to distinguish. Face-to-face interactions normally provide a context in which to evaluate the information being conveyed. Reliability is associated with information depending on who the speaker is and on what is known about the person. This context is not readily transferable to networked information systems such as the World Wide Web.[8]

Over the last 20 years, increasingly elaborate security approaches quickly became obsolete due to rapid changes in the computing environment, in particular the development of the World Wide Web. In recent years, dramatic and costly computer viruses, "denial of service" attacks, and concerns with the security of e-commerce have drawn the attention of computer security researchers. While these security breaches are a serious concern, semantic attacks deserve more attention, as well.

Cognitive Hacking Countermeasures

Preventing cognitive hacking involves either preventing unauthorized access to information assets in the first place, or detecting posted disinformation before user behavior is affected. The latter may not involve unauthorized access to information, as for instance in pump-and-dump schemes that use newsgroups and chat rooms.

It is sometimes possible to determine if information is actually disinformation, because multiple sources can be compared. First, however, consider situations in which only a single source of information exists, such as an authoritative corporate personnel database. One countermeasure, or *authentication of source,* involves using due diligence in authenticating the information source and ascertaining its reliability. In this spirit, Clifford Lynch, director of the Coalition for Networked Information,[9] describes a framework in which trust can be established for each individual user based on both the identity and the behavior of a source of information, such as could be determined through rating systems—for example, as used by e-commerce sites such as e-Bay.[10] Such an approach will take time and social cooperation to evolve.

Information "Trajectory" Modeling   This approach requires building a model of a source based on statistical historical data or analytic understanding of how the information relates to the real world. For example, weather data coming from a single source—such as a website or environmental sensors—could be calibrated against databases from previous years or against a predictive model, extrapolating from previous measurements.

As an interesting aside, consider the story lines of many well-scripted mystery novels or films. Arguably, the most satisfying and successful stories involve a sequence of small deviations from what is expected. Each twist in the story is believable, but when aggregated, the reader or viewer has reached a conclusion quite far from the truth. In the context of cognitive hacking, this is achieved by making a sequence of small deviations from the truth, not one of which fails a credibility test on it own. However, the accumulated deviations are significant, surprising the reader (or viewer) who was not paying much attention to the individual small deviations. However, a small number of major "leaps of faith" would be noticed, and such stories are typically not very satisfying. As Möllering (this volume) has pointed out, trust involves a leap of faith, which then provides a trustee, or deceiver, with increased opportunities to deceive the trustor. Here, because the deviations are individually small, the trustor does not even realize that a situation has been entered in which deception could be an issue. Modeling information sources is something that can be done on a case-by-case basis, as determined by the availability of historical data and the suitability of analytic modeling.

Genre Detection and Authority Analysis   A careful human reader of some types of disinformation—such as exaggerated pump-and-dump-scheme postings on the Web about a company's expected stock performance—can often detect the disinforming posting from legitimate ones, even if these legitimate postings also are written in a somewhat hyperbolic style. Since Mosteller and Wallace's seminal work on authorship attribution, statistical linguistic approaches have been used to recognize the style of different writings.[11] Mosteller and Wallace's stylistic analysis was done to determine the true author of anonymous Federalist Papers, where the authorship was disputed. Since then, Biber and other researchers have analyzed the genre of linguistic corpora using similar stylistic analysis.[12] A genre is a type of text, such as news or poetry. For example, a newspaper story answers the questions who, what, when, why, and how and uses a vocabulary and style of writing that is easily understood by someone with an eighth-grade education, while modern poetry uses very different language conventions. Kessler et al. have developed and tested algorithms based on this work to automatically detect the genre of text.[13]

The approach to genre analysis taken—for example, by Biber and by Kessler et al.—is within the framework of corpus linguistics; that is, it is based on a statistical analysis of general word usage in large bodies of text. The work on deception detection in psychology and communications is based on a more fine-grained analysis of linguistic features, or cues. Psychological experiments have been conducted to determine which cues are indicative of deception. O'Sullivan (this volume) and Frank (this volume) discuss a number of these cues. O'Sullivan describes "truth wizards"—experts at detecting deception in face-to-face communication—as people who are able to form a holistic impression of a potential liar based on all of the person's behavior and not only the seemingly unusual behaviors. Frank also notes that there is no single cue to detecting lies. He stresses the importance of the need to establish a baseline of normal, nonlying behavior for each individual, against which his or her lying behavior can be compared. The process of detecting lies, as described by O'Sullivan and Frank, suggests the difficulty in developing automated tools to detect deception. To date, software tools to automatically detect deception in computer-mediated communication have yet to be developed, but researchers see the development of these tools as a next step.[14] Hancock (this volume) describes some of the research on linguistic cues to deception in digital media and how these cues may enable the detection of digital deception.

If more than a single source of information about an event or subject is available, then possibly disinforming information can be compared to these. Several aspects of information dissemination through such digital and network media as the Internet and the World Wide Web make cognitive hacking relatively easy to perform. Enormous market pressures encourage the news media and newsgroups to quickly disseminate as much information as possible. As Farid (this volume) has discussed, with photo-editing tools now available, not only can a news photograph or a graphic depicting scientific results be doctored to better emphasize a point the creator of the image is trying to make, but the image can also be reworked to completely mislead the viewer. In the area of financial news, in particular, competing news services strive to be the first to give reliable news about breaking stories that impact the business environment. Such pressures are at odds with the time-consuming process of verifying accuracy. A compromise between the need to quickly disseminate information and the need to investigate its accuracy is not easy to achieve. Automated software tools could help people make decisions about the veracity of information they obtain from multiple networked information systems.

Source Reliability via Collaborative Filtering and Reliability Reporting   If multiple sources are available to verify possibly disinforming information, another cognitive hacking countermeasure is source reliability. The problem of detecting disinformation on the Internet is similar to detecting other forms of disinformation, for example, in printed news or verbal discussion. Reliability, redundancy, pedigree, and authenticity of the information being considered are key indicators of the overall "trustworthiness" of information. The technologies of collaborative filtering and reputation-reporting mechanisms have been receiving attention recently, especially in the area of online retail sales.[15] These technologies are commonly used by online price-comparison services to inform potential customers about vendor reliability. A reliability rating is computed from customer reports. A closely related technology is collaborative filtering. This can be useful in cognitive hacking situations that involve opinions rather than objective facts. Both approaches involve user feedback about information that the user receives from a particular information service, building up a community notion of the reliability and usefulness of a resource. The automation in this case is in the processing of user feedback, not the evaluation of the actual information itself.

Detection of Collusion by Information Sources   Collusion between multiple information sources can take several forms. In pump-and-dump schemes, several individuals may develop a scheme in which they agree to post misleading stories on different websites and newsgroups. Thus several postings will reflect common facts or opinions, typically in contradiction to the consensus. A countermeasure for this form of semantic attack would require automated natural language understanding (NLU) to extract the meaning of the content of the various available information sources. The statistical distributions of this extracted information would then be compared in some way. For example, in stock market discussion groups, a tool could be used to estimate the position of a poster, from "strong buy" to "strong sell" and a variety of gradations in between. Some averaging or weighting could be applied to the various positions to determine a "mean" or expected value, flagging large deviations from that expected value as being suspicious. Similarly, the tool could look for tightly clustered groups of messages, which would suggest some form of collusion. Such clustered messages might be posted by one person or by a group in collusion, having previously agreed to the form of semantic attack.

Although many statistical tests exist for detecting outliers, much less is known about detecting collusion that may be manifested not in outliers but in unlikely clusters that may not be outliers at all. For example, if too many eyewitnesses agree to very specific details of a suspect's appearance (height, weight, and so on), this might suggest collusion to an investigator. Automated software tools have not yet been developed that can perform natural language analysis of multiple documents, extract some quantitative representation of a "position" based on that document, and then perform a statistical analysis of the representations, although they remain a future possibility.

Authorship Attribution

Authorship attribution, or stylometry, is a field of study within statistics and computational linguistics with a long history going back to Mosteller and Wallace's work mentioned above. More recently, Rao and Rohatgi have shown that stylometry can be employed even more successfully with text taken from the Internet.[16] Forensic linguistics has become a recognized research discipline, with professional societies including the International Association of Forensic Linguists and professional journals such as *Forensic Linguistics*.[17] Contemporary experts such as Foster have assisted law enforcement with investigations on the Unabomber and the murder of JonBenet Ramsey, for example.[18]

Although there are general linguistic text-analysis software packages, such as *LIWC2001*, forensic linguistic tools specifically tailored for authorship attribution do not exist.[19] A recent account of research on authorship attribution is given by Love.[20]

The News Verifier

A reader taking the story about Emulex mentioned at the beginning of this chapter at face value would want to quickly sell any Emulex stock he or she held. Although this news item might be reliable, it might instead be disinformation being fed to unwary readers by a cognitive hacker as part of a pump-and-dump scheme to spread false or misleading information about the company, involving the hacker's subsequent selling—or shorting—of the stock as the price of its shares rise or fall due to the disinformation. The reader would like to act quickly to optimize his or her gains but could pay a heavy price if this quick action is taken based on disinformation.

A prototype cognitive hacking countermeasure was built that allows a Web user to effectively retrieve and analyze documents from the Web that are similar to the original news item. First, a set of similar documents is retrieved by the Google News clustering algorithm. The Google News ranking of the clustered documents is generic, not necessarily optimized as a countermeasure for cognitive attacks. A combination process is being developed through which several different search engines are used to provide alternative rankings of documents initially retrieved by Google News. The ranked lists from each of these search engines, along with the original ranking from Google News, are combined using the Combination of Expert Opinion algorithm, which provides a more optimal ranking for purposes of detecting deception.[21] Relevance feedback judgments from the user are used to train the search engines. It is expected that this combination and training process will yield a better ranking than the initial Google News ranking. This is an important feature in a countermeasure for cognitive hacking, because a victim of cognitive hacking will want to detect disinformation as soon as possible in real time.

Detecting Deception

Detection of deception in interpersonal communication has long been a topic of study in the fields of psychology and communications (also see Frank, Hancock, and O'Sullivan, this volume).[22] The majority of interpersonal communications are found to have involved some level of deception. Psychology and communications researchers have identified many cues that are characteristic of deceptive interpersonal communication. Most of this research has focused on the rich communication medium of face-to-face interactions, but more recently other forms have been studied, such as telephone and computer-mediated communication.[23] A large study has trained people to detect deception in communication.[24] Some of this training is computer based. Most recently, a study has begun to determine whether psychological cues indicative of deception can be automatically detected in computer-mediated communication such as e-mail, so that an automated deception-detection tool might be built.[25]

Intelligence and Security Informatics

In 2003, the U.S. National Science Foundation and the National Institute of Justice held the first of what has become an annual series of conferences on Intelligence and Security Informatics.[26] The motivation for these conferences is that a new science of intelligence and security informatics is needed that is analogous, say, to bioinformatics. It will be important to provide this new science with an analysis environment supporting mixed-initiative interaction with both raw and aggregated data sets.[27] This environment should include a tool kit of countermeasures against semantic attacks. For example, if faced with a potentially deceptive news item from the Foreign Broadcast Information Service (FBIS), a tool such as the News Verifier, discussed above, might provide an alert.

Military Deception: Inferring an Adversary's Intent

Bell and Whaley, in their book *Cheating and Deception*, provide a taxonomy of deception that has been adapted by many researchers.[28] The six types of deception shown in Table 7.1 fall under two main headings: dissimulation and simulation.

This taxonomy was recently used in a project on adversary intent inferencing in which a model was developed of the Chinese intervention in the Korean War in 1950. When opposing sides face each other in a military conflict, neither side knows what the other's intentions are. However, each side can try to infer the opponent's intent by observing the opponent's actions. Each side also has some preconceived idea of the other side's goals and beliefs. In this conflict, the U.S. forces' model of their adversaries, the Chinese

TABLE 7.1 A taxonomy of deception

Dissimulation—Hiding the Real	Simulation—Showing the False
Masking: concealing one's charcs	Mimicking: copying another's charcs
Repackaging: adding new charcs, or subtracting old charcs	Inventing: creating new charcs
Dazzling: obscuring old or adding alternative charcs	Decoying: creating alternative charcs

NOTE: "Charcs" is shorthand for "characteristics," or the observations made by the person who would be deceived.
SOURCE: Adapted from J. Bowyer Bell and Barton Whaley, *Cheating and Deception* (New Brunswick, NJ: Transaction, 1991).

forces, was based on their understanding of the goals and beliefs of the Chinese. This model, combined with observations of Chinese actions, allowed the U.S. forces to attempt to infer the intentions of the Chinese, including the intent to deceive. Although the Chinese intervention in the Korean War was a surprise to the U.S. forces, the surprise was due less to deception on the part of the Chinese than to the strong assumption by the United States that the Chinese would not intervene. On the other hand, as the intervention proceeded, examples of deception became apparent. The Chinese sought to give the impression that the intervention was a small-scale activity of some volunteers, rather than the massive intervention that it in fact was. In support of this goal of deceiving the United States into believing that the intervention was small scale, Chinese soldiers wore uniforms that belied the size of their military units. Using Bell and Whaley's taxonomy, this is an example of "repackaging."

Adversarial Information Retrieval on the Web

Since the early days of Web search engines, an adversarial relationship has existed between the operators of the search engines, on the one hand, and other parties who seek to influence the rankings of documents produced by the search engines. There has long been a community of marketers, called search engine optimizers, who have made their services of manipulating Web search engine rankings available to their clients. When certain search terms are used by Web searchers using the major Web search engines, their clients' Web pages can achieve a higher ranking. The type of deception engaged in by optimizers in order to further this aim is the type that Libicki wrote about in his original report on semantic attacks.[29] The target of the deception is not a human, but rather a decision process in the computer system: the algorithm used by the search engine to rank documents.

Many deceptive techniques have been used by optimizers over the years, while search engine designers have rewritten their algorithms in order to thwart the optimizers. For example, one common practice is to print website text in the same color as the background of the Web page. The human viewer of the Web page will not see anything, but the search engine will react to the text by ranking the document higher. If, say, there are many searches made for a particular popular movie star of the moment, an optimizer might invisibly repeat the name of the star many times in the Web page. Another often-used technique is to insert many "popular" words in metadata fields of the Web page. These fields are not seen by the human viewer of a Web page but can be picked up by search engines. However, many search engines no longer use these metadata fields because they have so often been misused by optimizers. These early, relatively unsophisticated deceptive techniques have been augmented by many new techniques. More recent concerns include click fraud and link farms.[30]

The Insider Threat

Trusted insiders who have historically caused the most damage to national security were caught only after prolonged counterintelligence operations. These individuals, who held positions in an intelligence organization on which they spied for an adversary intelligence organization, are also known as moles. In some cases, they carried out their illegal activities for many years without raising suspicion. Even when it was evident that an insider was misusing information, and even when attention began to focus on the insider in question as a suspect, it took years more before the insider was caught. Perhaps the most well-known and damaging examples of moles in recent years were Aldrich Ames, a CIA counterintelligence officer, and Robert Hanssen, an FBI counterintelligence officer.

Traditionally, apprehension of trusted insiders has been possible only after events in the outside world led to an analysis that eventually focused on the insider—such as a high rate of double agents being apprehended and executed. Once it was clear that a problem with insider misuse of information was likely, it was eventually possible to determine the identity of the insider by considering who had access to the information as well as other factors such as the results of polygraph tests.

The insider threat is much more pervasive, however, than a small number of high-profile national security cases. It has been estimated that the majority of all computer security breaches are due to insider attacks, rather than to external hacking.[31] As organizations move to more and more automated information-processing environments, it becomes potentially possible to detect signs of insider misuse much earlier than has previously been possible. Information systems can be instrumented to record all uses of the system, down to the monitoring of individual keystrokes and mouse movements. Commercial organizations have made use of such "clickstream mining," as well as of analysis of transactions, to build profiles of individual users. Credit card companies build models of individuals' purchase patterns to detect fraudulent usage. Companies such as Amazon.com analyze purchase behavior of individual users to make recommendations for the purchase of additional products that are likely to match the individual user's profile.

A technologically adept insider, however, may be aware of countermeasures deployed against him or her, and thus operate in such a way as to neutralize the countermeasures. In other words, an insider can engage in cognitive hacking against the network and system administrators. A similar situation arises with Web search engines, in what has been referred to as a "cold war" between the search engines and the search engine optimizers—marketers who manipulate Web search engine rankings on behalf of their clients, as discussed above.

Models of insider threats can be built based on (1) known past examples of insider misbehavior, (2) the insider's work role in the organization, (3) the insider's transactions with the information system, and (4) the content of the insider's work product. This approach to the analysis of the behavior of the insider is analogous to that suggested for analyzing the behavior of software programs by Munson and Wimer.[32] One aspect of this approach is to look for known signatures of insider misuse, or for anomalies in each of the behavioral models individually. Another aspect is to look for discrepancies among the models. For example, if an insider is disguising the true intent of his or her transactions by making deceptive transactions, then this cognitive hacking might be uncovered, for example, by comparing the transactions to the insider's work product.

Security Evaluations

The participants in a recent workshop on detecting deception in language in security evaluations—such as background investigations, interviews, and interrogations—concluded that while multiple types of deception are involved in verbal and written behavior, such as lies of commission, omission, partial truths, paltering (Schauer and Zeckhauser, this volume), and identity fraud, it is nonetheless unclear how well various linguistic techniques can detect such deception and the extent to which linguistic styles may vary depending on social situations, personality, and psychological states. It was noted that, despite the many well-controlled laboratory studies and field research related to deception detection based on linguistic cues, relatively few of the thousands of speech elements and acoustic features have been explored in this context. One conclusion of the workshop was that it is urgent to develop a large, shared corpus of empirically validated truthful and untruthful messages drawn from a variety of situations, including both laboratory and real-world settings, with samples in multiple languages drawn from blogs, e-mails, natural conversations, interviews, phone calls, telephone text messages, instant messages, chat rooms, written and spoken confessions, letters, criminal statements, hostage notes, and target group manifestos.[33] Among some of the promising technical approaches that may provide unique and valuable opportunities to assess deception are the development of new technologies for exploring word, phrase, and narrative use across a wide range of contexts and languages, including real-time or near real-time text analyses, and computer-mediated communication such as e-mail, chat room conversations, and instant messaging.

Conclusion

The information age—with its reliance on increasingly networked computers that will soon be ubiquitous not only in the developed world but increasingly throughout the world—is an age in which understanding and detecting deception becomes increasingly important. As business processes become automated, the supply chains and the infrastructures on which these automated systems depend become more vulnerable to semantic attacks.[34] This volume shows the wide range of perspectives that can be brought to bear on deception. The Semantic Hacking Project suggested several countermeasures for deception in the form of semantic attacks on information systems. The information infrastructure is constantly and rapidly evolving. Some of these specific suggestions for countermeasures may become obsolete, but the framework can still be applied. Specific new countermeasures are needed to address the new semantic attack technique of phishing, but the same general principles apply.[35] For example, linguistic genre analysis similar to that proposed above to distinguish deceptive postings about companies, as part of a pump-and-dump scheme, from legitimate postings, might be used to distinguish fraudulent phishing websites from legitimate websites.

The Internet and other information infrastructures such as the World Wide Web were built by technologists. Except in certain environments, such as military message-handling systems or financial systems, even physical and syntactic security was given little attention. Semantic attacks have been largely ignored until recently. In everyday life, deception involving face-to-face interactions and communication has been well studied. Deception can be said to be the analogue to semantic attacks on the information infrastructure, which is also primarily a communication medium. The semantic attacks prevalent in this medium must be understood and effective countermeasures developed.

The focus of the Semantic Hacking Project was on detecting deception on the Web, in particular on detecting pump-and-dump schemes. While detecting such computer crimes remains important and while newer computer crimes such as phishing have drawn much attention, detecting other types of semantic attacks on information systems is perhaps of even greater importance. The Enron and Arthur Andersen debacles, for example, showed that financial fraud in the information infrastructure can be committed on a scale beyond the level of phishing schemes. Furthermore, many nations are preparing for offensive and defensive cyber-warfare. Developing tools to detect deception in this context is a vital national security concern.

III TRUST AND DECEPTION

8 Leaps and Lapses of Faith

Exploring the Relationship Between Trust and Deception

Guido Möllering

I N TIMES WHEN PHRASES LIKE "weapons of mass deception"[1] evoke cynicism and anger around the world, we may easily believe that contemporary politicians, journalists, managers, scientists, lovers, and others are particularly deceptive, but the prevalence of deception is hard to compare historically in empirical terms.[2] We do not know if we are deceived more frequently or extensively than before. Arguably, the occurrence of deception as such is often less noteworthy than the meaning and implications of deception in specific cases.

We need only look around us to identify the most recent incidents of deception, but some cases from antiquity are at least as exciting: for example, Zeus, who was both deceived and seduced by Hera, his own wife in disguise. This example from Greek mythology and countless other stories of sexual masquerades and amorous identity games over the centuries bring out basic questions about the skills and, more important, the motives of both the deceiver and the deceived. How is deception achieved? How can it be recognized? Why is it committed? And why is it uncovered, or not?

Deception can occur for better or worse, knowingly or unknowingly, with relief or with regret. Whether it is seen as harmless or disastrous, commendable or outrageous depends on the relationship between the deceiver and the

GUIDO MÖLLERING is a researcher at the Max Planck Institute for the Study of Societies in Cologne, Germany. He studies the internal and external relationships of organizations. His book on *Trust: Reason, Routine, Reflexivity* was published by Elsevier in 2006.

deceived, the nature of their mutual trust, and their places in society. It is nonetheless a key characteristic of human agency and vulnerability that one person can mislead another.

Hence, deception is always topical and interesting, touching on very basic social foundations, temptations, and emotions. It involves some of the strongest experiences in social life for the deceiver, the deceived, and their social networks. For example, imagine the emotional turmoil that is common for all parties involved in cases of infidelity. Note also the anger in public reactions to manipulated war photographs as described in Hany Farid's chapter on digital doctoring (this volume). Generally, every case of suspected or detected deception can trigger more than just a bit of disappointment and may become a threat to the whole relationship between the deceiver and the deceived.

We can all imagine how the mere suggestion of deception can disturb trust and trustworthiness, especially when the act of deception is seen as a betrayal of the trustor's positive expectations and willingness to be vulnerable. Yet, I am surprised how little is known about the relationship between trust and deception. About a hundred years ago, one of the German founding fathers of sociology, Georg Simmel, pointed out that "modern life is based to a much larger extent than is usually realized upon the faith in the honesty of the other" and that, under modern conditions, the lie becomes particularly devastating as "something which questions the very foundations of our life."[3] While this is an early recognition of the fact that deception destroys trust, a number of authors such as Erving Goffman and Paul Ekman have noted another common insight, namely that trust makes us prone to being duped and misled.[4] This suggests that trust invites the very deception that will destroy it. If this is the case, we should be alarmed. We need to take a closer look at the relationship between trust and deception, as is the purpose of this chapter.

It appears intuitively that trust is "good" and deception is "bad." This intuition matches the primary moral connotations of trust and deception, but we have to be careful to distinguish between acts, intentions, and outcomes. The normative content lies mainly in the intentions and outcomes, while acts of trusting (accepting evidence) and deceiving (faking evidence) per se are relatively neutral operations. It is possible that deception is socially desirable—a well-intentioned recognized skill or even an entertaining pleasure. And, if there is a bright side to deception, there is also a dark side to trust and its motives and consequences. The positive bias of trust and the negative bias of deception are really just biases, and the attributes "harmful" and "beneficial" can be attached to both trust and deception. This is why it is interesting to analyze the relationship between the two concepts and to ask how far trust and deception enable or prevent each other. Is deception invited or avoided through trust? Is trust destroyed by deception or is there an element of deception in all trust?

In this chapter, I will address these questions and explore the characteristics of the relationship between trust and deception. After outlining some conceptual foundations so that we know when it makes sense to use the terms trust and deception, I first discuss how trustors can be deceived about the trustworthiness of others. I then argue that trust always involves a leap of faith, which increases the opportunities for the trustee to deceive the trustor. However, because this leap implies moral obligations, trust may reduce the threat of deception by the trustee. I then turn to the trustor and discuss the *self*-deception involved in all forms of trusting, which, as I note subsequently, does not mean that trust is irreversible or unconditional. At the end of the chapter, it will be clear that trust and deception simultaneously enable and prevent each other. This sheds a new light on the cases of deception and broken trust that we observe around us.

Conceptual Foundations: What Are We Talking About?

We can already learn a lot about trust and deception by clarifying what we mean by those words. A widely supported definition of *trust* describes it as "a psychological state comprising the intention to accept vulnerability based upon positive expectations of the intentions or behavior of another."[5] The carrier of trust is an actor who can have expectations and refer to them in action. The trustor expects favorable intentions and actions on the part of the object of trust—another actor referred to as the trustee. In short, we need to be able to identify trustors and trustees in order to speak of trust. And these actors need to be able to form expectations of each other.

The general problem of trust arises due to the principal vulnerability and uncertainty of the trustor toward the trustee. The trustee can harm the trustor, who cannot be absolutely sure whether this will happen, but who can be aware of and influence the extent to which he or she is vulnerable to harm. The actions of the trustor and the trustee are therefore interdependent.

Moreover, the social vulnerability and uncertainty underlying the problem of trust reflect the agency of both trustor and trustee, who are autonomous in that their states of mind and actions are not fully determined. Neither trust as a state of mind nor genuinely trustworthy behavior can ultimately be forced or guaranteed. Trustors and trustees have a choice. Otherwise, we would not need the concept of trust. Hence, trust is "risky" in the general sense of the word, but it is irreducible to calculation. Therefore, as I discuss below, trust is more than a probabilistic investment decision.

It is also important to note exactly how vulnerability is understood in the context of trust. Vulnerability is a precondition for trust; that is, the trustor can always be harmed in principle, but in reaching a state of trust, the trustor no longer expects to be harmed. This is sometimes misunderstood. The willingness to be vulnerable does not imply a willingness to be hurt. Rather, trust captures the highly optimistic expectation that vulnerability is not a problem and that no harm will be done. Trust is not about avoiding or eliminating vulnerability, or resigning to it, but about positively accepting it.

Often, trusting and being trustworthy are not even conscious decisions. Instead, they are taken for granted and routine. In many contexts it is normal to trust, in the sense of relying on others to respect the rules and play their roles. It is only when actors deviate from this normality that trust—or rather distrust—becomes an explicit issue. Vulnerability is always present, however, and it depends on the circumstances whether actors will routinely tend to trust or whether they will routinely assume that others generally cannot be trusted.

It follows that it is also important to recognize that the trustor and the trustee are embedded in a social context that influences how they can define themselves as actors and enact their agency. Networks of social relationships and institutionalized rules are particularly important in setting the context for trust. Trust, in practice, is never a purely dyadic phenomenon between isolated actors; there is always a context, a history, and the influence of other actors.

In sum, without actors, expectations, vulnerability, uncertainty, agency, and embeddedness, the problem of trust does not arise. Overall, trust is an ongoing process of building on reason, routine, and reflexivity, suspending irreducible social vulnerability and uncertainty *as if* they were favorably resolved, and thereby maintaining a state of favorable expectation toward the actions and intentions of more or less specific others.[6] In comparison to other works on trust, this definition emphasizes that trust is not static and that it requires leaps of faith.

The notion of deception certainly warrants a detailed discussion in itself, and many chapters in this volume contribute clarifications on how deception can be defined. For the purposes of this chapter, I propose to apply the same conditions to the concept of deception that I have outlined for the notion of trust above: at least two actors are required, one of whom can deceive the other and both of whom play their parts in whether deception occurs. Deception also requires standards of truth and honesty from which a deceiver deviates. This deviation has to make a difference; it must have the potential to cause (or prevent) damage to a vulnerable other. The precondition of uncertainty—especially in the sense of asymmetric information—enters the picture because deception would not be an issue if all actors possessed the same knowledge and were able to know with certainty who will (try to) deceive whom, when, where, and how. Moreover, actors have to have a choice as to whether they deceive the other party in a dyadic relationship, as well as whether to trust the other party or suspect deception. Finally, it is hard to imagine deception in a context-free environment: the context (such as institutions and networks) will always have an influence on the meaning and form of deception and its consequences. At a minimum, the deceiver's reputation may be at stake, and this is a concern that actors take into account.

I define deception as the deliberate misrepresentation of an actor's identity, intentions, or behaviors as well as the distortion of any facts relevant to the relationship between actors. This captures the gist of other definitions, but with less emphasis on the element of opportunism and guile, because the deceiver's motives may well be laudable. Tom Lutz (this volume) asks to what extent it is necessary that deception be deliberate, but we would probably agree that completely accidental or unintended misrepresentations do not constitute deception.[7] Hence, the deceived is not simply given wrong information but is also kept deceived about the actual knowledge and intentions of the deceiver. This sets deception apart from obvious irony or parody.[8] When we look at deception in a somewhat more competitive light, it can be seen as an attempt to gain the upper hand and to move the deceived parties to act in ways that contradict their best interests.

Whatever definition is applied, however, the act of misleading should not be confounded with its intentions and consequences. Moreover, we should not frame deception only as a matter of deviance from truth. Erving Goffman's dramaturgical perspective gives an unusual view of "misrepresentations" by demonstrating that people always present but a part of themselves, that they have to manage the impressions they give, and that in most encounters what is true or false is less important than what is appropriate and acceptable role behavior.[9] Hence, we may already feel deceived just because somebody did not behave as expected, even if this did not involve any lies or broken promises.

Signals and Other (Deceptive) Bases of Trust

It is a useful starting point for this exploration of the relationship between trust and deception to consider the following question: How can the trustor recognize a trustworthy trustee? Conversely, how can the trustor identify an untrustworthy trustee and, more dramatically, avoid a trustee who only pretends to be trustworthy and wants to deceive the trustor? The most straightforward answer to this question is that a trustee is trustworthy when it is not in his or her interest to be untrustworthy toward the trustor. In other words, trustworthiness depends on the payoffs in a given trust game. This implies that, if necessary, a trustee can be *made* trustworthy by modifying the payoffs, ideally in such a way that, by exploiting trust, the trustee will harm him- or herself. Similarly, the incentives for deception decrease severely when actors share goals, such as increased efficiency from coordination. However, this approach hinges on the trustor's ability to reliably estimate net payoffs, which makes this a dubious heuristic in reality. Trustors can be deceived by trustees and other parties about the true payoff structure of the game, which exacerbates the danger of trusting on the basis of this kind of analysis.

Nevertheless, this approach is very common and it can be refined further by introducing a probabilistic element, whereby it is assumed that a trustee is sometimes trustworthy and sometimes untrustworthy or, more precisely, that a certain number of trustees in a given population are trustworthy while the rest are untrustworthy.[10] If the probability of meeting either type is known, the trustor can apply it to the payoff structure of a given trust game and determine whether trusting has a positive expected value, or not. As much as this approach with its numerous further refinements has to offer, it cannot resolve the problems of (self-)deception in the generation of reliable estimates for payoffs, probabilities, and other assumptions.

The same applies to the approach suggesting that trustors look for indicators of trustworthiness that are not primarily a matter of payoff and probability in a particular situation, but that capture relatively stable characteristics of a trustee. For example, taxi drivers use a number of criteria in order to discriminate between trustworthy and untrustworthy passengers.[11] Pretty Jim's blue eyes, in the poem recounted by Kenneth Fields in the final chapter of this volume, indicated his trustworthiness but evidently misled the other visitors at Thom Gunn's house.

In a more abstract model, Roger Mayer and his colleagues propose ability, benevolence, and integrity as the main indicators of trustworthiness.[12] Despite some variation on the labels, such indicators are widely accepted and used to explain why people trust. The indicators may be commonsensical, but so is the possibility that they may be misinterpreted by the trustor or deliberately faked by the trustee. According to Michael Bacharach and Diego Gambetta, the only reliable signals of trustworthiness are those that would be too costly for an inherently untrustworthy trustee to fake: "No poisoner seeks to demonstrate his honesty by drinking from the poisoned chalice."[13]

Specifically, while an inherently untrustworthy trustee has an even bigger incentive to send fake signals of trustworthiness than the inherently trustworthy trustee—which means that the signals would be useless per se—it may take substantially more effort to mimic a signal than to send it naturally. The greater this difference is, the more reliable the signal is, but it still holds that the bigger the payoff from deceiving a trustor, the more likely it is that an untrustworthy trustee will incur the costs of mimicking the signal.

Beyond the question of which signals of trustworthiness are reliable, actors should also pay attention to signals of deceit. There is a further signaling game—this time about masking signals of deception—that a deceiver will be willing to play if the incentives are attractive. Moreover, as the chapters by Mark Frank and Maureen O'Sullivan (this volume) make clear, actors are generally not very good at detecting deception. Hence, although signaling theory introduces the notion that deception may be costly—which is an important insight—it still boils down to estimates of net payoffs and probabilities that are hard to ascertain in practice due to limitations on the trustor's part and the semiotic chaos and ambiguity in most real-life situations. As Mark Frank puts it in his chapter, there is no "Pinocchio response" in the sense of a single, unambiguous clue to deception.

However, the core problem with looking for indicators of trustworthiness is not simply that this quest is futile, but, more seriously, that it misses the point that trust occurs when the trustor makes a leap of faith, takes the trustworthiness of others for granted, and does not keep on looking for evidence and safeguards. In other words, when we talk about trust bases, we are still in the realm of decisions under risk, subsuming the risk of deception, but we are not yet considering the essence of trust, which sets trust apart from mere risk assessment. In exploring the relationship between trust and deception, I argue that it is less interesting to analyze how trustors can be (or avoid being) deceived about bases for their trust than it is to discuss how trust in itself both increases and decreases the threat of deception, and how trust and deception both enable and destroy each other.

The Leap of Faith: Suspension of Doubt and Suspicion

Trust goes beyond simply predicting that the future will be like the past, because the conviction that the future can be known has to be produced as well. I follow Georg Simmel and argue that trust is both less and more than knowledge and presumes a leap of faith.[14] The leap of faith connotes agency without suggesting perfect control or certainty. I suggest that we can also use the term "suspension" to capture the underlying process that enables actors to make a leap of faith.[15] To say that trust involves the suspension of uncertainty and vulnerability implies an "as if" attitude on the part of the trustor who neutralizes certain dangers that cannot be removed.

However—and this is perhaps the most important point to note since it is easily misunderstood—suspension is used in the Hegelian sense of *aufheben*, which means that vulnerability, doubt, and uncertainty are not eliminated.[16] Hence, when actors achieve suspension for trust, they treat uncertainty and vulnerability as unproblematic, even if it could still turn out that they are problematic. Leaps of faith enable trust to take place, but this does not rule out lapses of faith later on.

For the discussion about deception, this has the following implications. First, we might say that someone who begins to trust stops worrying about deception (and other things that would jeopardize positive expectations). For example, when people use digital media and communicate using technologically mediated messages as described in the chapter by Jeff Hancock (this volume), they can frequently reach a point where their wariness about deception leads to paralysis and certainly not to the desired in-person date or to further digital exchanges. Only when they trust *beyond* the potentially false information on their screen are they able to interact—for better or worse. More clearly, people who still worry about deception are not really trusting, because they have not achieved suspension yet. They may be willing to take a risk and cooperate nevertheless, but they do not really trust.

Second, when trust is reached and the danger of deception is suspended, this actually opens the door to deception. Kevin Mitnick, the notorious (ex-) hacker, calls trust "the key to deception,"[17] because it makes the con artist's job so much easier when the mark lowers the guard in trust. In Erving Goffman's terms, when an audience accepts cues on faith, "this sign-accepting tendency puts the audience in a position to be duped and misled."[18] In a theater this is the basis of much entertainment, but in real-life performances it is more of a threat. Placing trust creates an enhanced opportunity for malfeasance on the part of the trustee. The trustee could deceive the trustor and display trust-honoring behavior while actually exploiting the trust behind the trustor's back. The trustor, having positive, trusting expectations, would not monitor the trustee to the same extent as a distrusting actor would. Again, we can imagine very well how information given truthfully and trustfully can be abused by a recipient or, in return, how deliberately incorrect information can mislead a trusting recipient for better or worse.

When actors trust they accept the possibility of being deceived and the impossibility of completely avoiding deception and its desirable or harmful outcomes. Acceptance does not mean denial or capitulation, nor does it rule out that trust is withdrawn later on when positive expectations are disappointed. However, like Thom Gunn's visitors who were not wary of Pretty Jim (see Kenneth Field's chapter again), trustors do not anticipate deception, which is why the trustee is able to carry it out unnoticed by the trustor. To make matters worse, one act of unnoticed deception often triggers further such acts and possibly an escalation of deception, because the deceiver wants to conceal the initial deception or has self-reinforcing incentives to exploit the situation further and further.[19] Well-intentioned deception can spiral out of control, too, as in the German movie *Good-bye, Lenin!* in which, a few months after the fall of the Berlin Wall, the East German character Alex has a difficult time pretending to his sick mother (a devoted socialist) that nothing has changed in the German Democratic Republic.

Overall, if trust opens the door to potentially harmful deception, this makes trust appear foolish and dangerous. Should we not be very careful whom we trust and perhaps prefer to cooperate without trust? Should we not be more alert and informed, arming ourselves with techniques and technologies that discourage and detect deception? However, this kind of thinking misses the crucial point that it is the leap of faith in trust that enables positive social interaction with great potential benefits to take place instead of falling into a paralyzing paranoia of opportunism. Trustors are, by definition, vulnerable to deception, but I suggest this could be the root of a norm of special protection for trustors. If trust as the willingness to be vulnerable is desirable, should not those who trust and make themselves vulnerable enjoy the social support of others in the same way that children are saved from harm? Should not malevolently deceiving someone who trusted be punished much more severely than deceiving someone who distrusted or merely gambled? If this logic is accepted, then conveying trust could actually reduce the threat of harmful deception.

Trust's Compulsory Power Against Harmful Deception

The moral connotations of trust and deception can hardly be ignored. Georg Simmel attributes an "almost compulsory power" to trust and claims that "to betray it requires thoroughly positive meanness."[20] Betrayals of trust can cause damage—and outrage—beyond the ordinary losses of resources and opportunities, because trust is a moral value within societies.[21] This raises questions about how strong the moral value of trust is in different social circles at different times and in different places. The moral power of trust is also limited by the somewhat tautological requirement that trust must not be given blindly or lightly. Moreover, there are many gray areas where it is difficult to establish whether deception has actually occurred and whether moral consequences should follow. Nevertheless, within limits, those who make themselves more vulnerable by trusting might also expect a higher level of protection, and those who deceive might expect more severe punishment, because (and as long as) trust is seen as a public good protected by moral norms within a given community.

With specific reference to deception, we can therefore recognize the possibility that trust opens the door to deception, but, inasmuch as deception implies the harmful betrayal of trust, the door is not just open but has a highly visible "Friends only!" sign above it. This may be a more effective strategy for preventing deception than to keep the door closed or even locked with a "Keep out!" sign attached. Once more, think about Pretty Jim (in Kenneth Field's chapter) who abused the openness of Thom Gunn's house and apparently did not feel morally bound by the bohemian community. He even appears to have enjoyed his deception and thievery, but we do not know if he also felt guilty later on. Did he destroy the trustful openness within the community, or did his deviance reinforce trust among the others? The poem does not say. However, we know that deception surrounding infidelity, for example, usually triggers highly negative moral and emotional reactions on the part of the deceiver and the deceived and within their social networks, too. Shame, guilt, and fear usually keep us from abusing trust.

At any rate, when trust is highly valued and the deception of trustors is strongly condemned, the overall effect of trust may well be a reduction in the actual occurrence of deception. This is not the first strategy that comes to mind when we think about reducing deception. It is also a strategy with severe boundary conditions, but it is not completely unrealistic. After all, we all trust lots of other people every day, and usually we believe, more or less explicitly, that our trust induces others to be trustworthy. It does not always work, since trust can always be disappointed. And trust may not always be welcome by the trustee, because of the obligations it entails, which might become a burden or simply be unwanted and untenable for the trustee. Nevertheless, trust always presents deception in a different light by framing the moral context in which deception occurs.

Living as if the Future Were Known: Trust as (Self-)Deception?

In the previous sections, I have looked at how trust enables and prevents deception. However, we need to ask whether, in return, deception might also both sustain and destroy trust. Let us take a closer look at the trustor and his or her leap of faith. If trust means that people have positive expectations despite some irreducible uncertainty, are they not deceiving themselves in their trust? David Lewis and Andrew Weigert express this most clearly when they state that "to trust is to live *as if* certain rationally possible futures will not occur" and that "to trust is to act as if the uncertain future actions of others were indeed certain."[22] The power, but also the fragility, of the "as if" must not be underestimated. Trust does not rest on objective certainty but on a kind of illusion. It rests on the fiction of a reality in which social uncertainty and vulnerability are unproblematic. This matches findings in deception research: for example, Robert Mitchell's observation that "a victim's wanting to believe in the deception comes up repeatedly in deception scenarios,"[23] as well as Maureen O'Sullivan's comments (this volume) on "collusion with the liar" and "accusatory reluctance."

The fiction of trust needs to be achieved and sustained psychologically by the individual, but this fiction of trust is also a socially constructed fiction of trust, produced intersubjectively through interaction with others and through institutionalized practices. It is striking that, because social uncertainty and vulnerability are only *suspended* in trust, the actors can remain aware that they are deceiving themselves, for better or worse, as long as the fiction of trust and trustworthiness is upheld.

The notion of self-deception raises difficult philosophical and psychological questions about multiple selves as well as the relationship between cognition and affect. However, the problem is mitigated in the case of trust because trustors are not assumed to make themselves believe something that they know to be wrong. They (merely) reach positive expectations by suspending the doubts that they might still have. Hence, the main inconsistency trustors bear is that trust risks defining the future, although trustors know that the future is ultimately unknowable.

How do actors create the fiction that enables them to trust? As a first attempt at answering this question, let us consider the concept of "overdrawn information" introduced by Niklas Luhmann.[24] When actors "overdraw" information they make inferences beyond what the underlying information can actually support. In the face of a deficit of information, according to Luhmann, actors deliberately overinterpret whatever information is available to serve as a springboard into uncertainty. We are reminded of the search for indicators of trustworthiness discussed earlier in this chapter, the signals perceived by taxi drivers, and the cues to deception that some people are better at detecting than others (see the chapters by Mark Frank and Maureen O'Sullivan, this volume). However, while "overdrawn information" is a plausible idea that confirms the need for at least some kind of basis for trust, we still need to be able to specify the conditions under which actors come to not only accept but also go beyond a given level of information and construct a fictional version of reality that allows them to trust.

The trustee plays a very important part in creating the trustor's fiction. The trustee offers a definition of him- or herself as well as a definition of the situation and does so with empathy for the trustor's needs, creating the impression of trustworthiness. This is more easily said than done and goes beyond mechanistic signaling games. The trustee's performative acts require impression management, self-confidence, ontological security, and an active engagement in social relations: "Whoever wants to win trust must take part in social life and be in a position to build the expectations of others into his own self-presentation."[25]

We can see a very vivid example of the complexity and ambiguity in the interaction between trustee and trustor, deceiver and deceived, in the account given in Tom Lutz's chapter (this volume) of his crying for the first time in front of his new partner (and future wife). Also, the Shakespearean lovers referenced by Kenneth Fields (this volume) collude knowingly in maintaining their fiction of youth and mutual devotion, which they prefer over the unflattering reality of aging and infidelity. Trustors and trustees build and maintain their positive fiction together in a process akin to the coproduction of rumors by narrators and their audiences (see the chapter by Gary Fine, this volume). In deception research, Robert Mitchell calls this "a shared delusional system."[26]

In sum, trustors rely to a great extent on trustees when constructing an image of those trustees as being worthy of trust or not. Nevertheless, the fiction coproduced by trustor and trustee remains a fiction, potentially a dangerous sham, and it is still up to the trustor to suspend uncertainty and vulnerability. The trustee's performative (potentially deceptive) acts and a high level of (potentially self-deceiving) familiarity with the situation merely assist the trustor in making the leap of faith. Countless daily activities and interactions rely on fictions and only become possible because people act as if they were possible.

"As if" can have a number of different meanings. First, in the sense of a "natural attitude" it refers to the action-enabling qualities of taken-for-grantedness and continuity.[27] Second, "as if" can also refer to the more performative "taking something for something" or "defining something as something." For example, by addressing somebody as if he or she were a friend, that person becomes a friend. We may take somebody for a trustworthy person and in so doing *make* him or her a trustworthy person, because trust exerts an almost compulsory power, as outlined above. Third, "as if" can also refer to the construction of unrealistic but nevertheless helpful idealizations. For example, the image of an ideal institution, organization, person, or practice as being trustful and trustworthy may never be realized fully in reality; yet, by actors behaving as if it were reality or, at least, as if the ideal were being seriously pursued, trust is facilitated.

It is worth exploring this interesting conjunction and peculiar linguistic trick of "as if" further. I propose that it enables us to understand the relationship between trust and deception better, because it suggests that trust and deception do not always work against each other but can complement each other in creating and maintaining a common understanding of social reality. This is not a value in itself, however, if it allows some to prosper and causes others to suffer. Trust and deception will be revised in the light of their outcomes.

Lapses of Faith:
Trust Is No License to Deceive

While trust opens the door to deception and involves a kind of self-deception by the trustor, the positive expectations at the heart of trust must be realized in order for trust to endure over time. Trustors who make a leap of faith still monitor the outcomes of their trust and usually notice when their expectations are disappointed. To be sure, trustees may enjoy the benefit of the doubt, and trust is not easily broken; on the contrary, it can be quite robust, because trustors seek to confirm their positive expectations. Numerous empirical studies in psychology illustrate this confirmation bias, and anecdotal examples abound of the strength of self-deception: for example, people are frightened after watching a horror movie, although they (should) know that it was only a movie; or television viewers grieve over the death of Lassie, although they (should) know that the dog playing the role is actually fine in reality; or parents refuse to believe that their "good son" is actually a criminal, despite the facts presented to them.[28]

Continued self-deception in the form of denial or accusatory reluctance, as a first response to suspected or detected deception, gives the deceived time to come to terms with the deception itself as well as with the imminent loss, emotional turmoil, and social costs that uncovering deception triggers. However, when the evidence is irrefutable, self-deception will end. As David Shapiro writes, "there are limits to self-deception in the specific sense that it is never completely successful . . . genuine belief remains present, only for the time being out of reach."[29] When things go unmistakably wrong in trust relationships, trustors feel betrayed and the leap of faith will quickly turn into a lapse of faith.

After all, trust is an idiosyncratic achievement on the part of the trustor, which ultimately cannot be requested, but must come from within, and cannot be sustained if the trustor's faith is lost. This brings us to Niklas

Luhmann's observation that trust is an "operation of the will" in which "the actor willingly surmounts this deficit of information."[30] Trust transcends that which can be justified by the actor in any terms, but the actor exercises agency through his or her will either to suspend uncertainty and vulnerability or not. Luhmann's reference to "will" in the context of trust and suspension inspires a closer look at William James's essay on "The Will to Believe." In this essay, James defends the actor's right to believe—in religious matters, but also generally; for instance, in social relations—even when there is no conclusive evidence. Such a belief would be called faith: "We have the right to believe at our own risk any hypothesis that is live enough to tempt our will."[31] Note that by introducing the condition that the hypothesis has to be "live enough," James points out that belief is not random; it has to feel true to the believer. Faith as a part of trust has to resonate with the actor's experience.

It follows that trust rests on a kind of "will to trust," but trust cannot be willed against the trustor's very personal and private sentiments. This means that lapses of faith will occur when the trustor has clear evidence of deception or betrayal. In sum, to say that trust entails a leap of faith is not to say that trust is irreversible or unconditional. Trust is not trust if it cannot be broken or withdrawn. Hence, practices of deception that exploit trust and harm the trustor are only sustainable as long as the trustor believes (or can be misled to believe) that no harm is done.

In a certain sense, the maxim "trust but verify," often attributed to Lenin (and now also to former U.S. president Ronald Reagan), applies in practice as long as it is understood that trusting means to reduce verification, monitoring, and control to a minimum. Hence, it is not paradoxical that the Inka *khipukamayuqs* described in the chapter by Gary Urton (this volume) were considered to be simultaneously truthful and accountable, because trust and control constitute a duality.[32] However, I can imagine very well that the Spaniards—who were unable to read *khipus*—had a problem when they found that they could neither trust nor control the Inkas.

The Ambivalent Relationship Between Trust and Deception

Taking the above considerations together, I propose five main points for further discussion on the relationship between trust and deception: (1) Trustors can be deceived when interpreting signals of trustworthiness, but some signals are more reliable than others because they cannot easily be faked. (2) Trust always involves a leap of faith, and hence goes beyond "good reasons," which opens the door to deception. (3) Trust bestows a moral obligation on the trustee, which reduces the threat of deception. (4) Trust requires some degree of self-deception on the part of the trustor, who creates an "as if" scenario, a kind of fiction that vulnerability and uncertainty are unproblematic. (5) Trust is not irreversible or unconditional; the leap of faith turns into a lapse of faith when the trustor recognizes deception and unfulfilled expectations.

Overall, this means that trust and deception both enable and prevent one another, and that this ambivalent relationship is due to the leaps and lapses of faith that characterize trust and distrust. This has important implications, for example, for the question of how trust can be repaired after it has been broken.[33] Deception is a special form of breach of trust, and we need to ask how repairing trust following deception differs from repairing trust after simple disappointments or mere trouble. We need to distinguish between different forms of deception and how actors respond to them, as well as between different forms of trust, yielding a matrix of numerous and more precise trust-deception relationships.

What is the benefit of considering trust and deception together instead of separately, given their ambivalent relationship? For example, we can refer to deception as an explanation not only for why trust is withdrawn but also for why it endures. And the ambivalent nature of the trust-deception relationship should lead us to be careful with general normative statements about trust and deception. Recognizing the relevance of trust extends the analysis of deception from very technical concerns about acts of deception to the social contexts in which deception occurs. As I have argued, trust relationships can explain not only why deception is possible—and sometimes necessary—but also why actors choose not to deceive or why trustors collude with the deceiver. In a dramaturgical perspective, we see a collective effort at maintaining an "as if" scenario for trust that allows for, and requires, a certain amount of deception. Hence, deception will be seen not so much in terms of what is true or false, but rather in terms of the benefit or harm it produces for social relationships.

Let us consider two examples. First, trust in food production is a hot and recurrent topic rife with cases of unethical producers deceiving consumers by selling adulterated wines and mislabeled meat.[34] There is no doubt that these are harmful, criminal acts. Their implications clearly reach beyond individual incidents, destroying much of the consumer's trust in wine and meat producers and regulatory systems more generally. At the same time, consumers have to ask themselves why they trusted in the first place and whether it is not all too convenient to believe in the safety of (suspiciously cheap) food. Overall, modern life seems impossible without trust in food produced by others, which makes deception possible, but the consequences of exposed deception and a loss of trust are so severe that most producers will abstain from opportunism and invest in their reputation—and they will assist consumers in maintaining the fiction that food is safe.

Second, deception by politicians is the object of so much public outrage that it is surprising that people still trust them at all. If trust means living as if the future were bright and certain, then politicians deliver just that: promises that they know what is good for us, that we will be better off, and that our soldiers will only engage in clean, justified acts of war. People are more than willing to accept these convenient but unrealistic promises until the outcomes are undeniably poor or even catastrophic. Hence, trust in politicians not only enables deception but even calls for it. This does not make deception morally acceptable, however, which is why politicians have to hide their deceptions and get used to eventually losing people's trust, only to regain it by making new, convenient promises that people are happy to accept. In the relationships between politicians and voters—and within political coalitions—many strange episodes are stories of how trust and deception both enable and prevent one another.

A further example is the U.S. subprime mortgage crisis that started in 2006 and led to financial and economic chaos around the world. We will never be sure whether it was caused by too much deception or too much trust. It is clear, however, that too many borrowers, bankers, raters, and regulators wanted to believe in the illusion of eliminating risk by inventing new financial products. This belief broke down dramatically, but the reconstruction of a more secure financial system was started immediately. Like old Baron Münchausen, teller of the tallest of tales, we set out to pull ourselves out of the swamp by our own hair once again.[35]

Thus the trust-deception ambivalence that has been explored conceptually in this chapter has practical relevance for making better sense of cases of deception in private and public life against the background of trust relationships that enable, prevent, require, and prohibit deception—all at the same time.

9 Tying the Truth in Knots

Trustworthiness and Accountability in the Inka Khipu

Gary Urton

HOW CAN WE TELL not only whether people living in an ancient society lied to and deceived each other (which most of us presume they must have done), but also whether—and why—they might have set out purposefully to create permanent records that would deceive us, the people of the future? More to the point for our interest here, how can we know when a lie was told by people living more than five hundred years ago, who—despite not having a written language—created administrative records in a notational system that we can only partially decipher today? And finally, how can we know whether statements made about these same "nonwriting" people by their conquerors were in fact truthful? These are some of the problems I will address in this chapter.

Telling Truth and Lies in the Past

We are confronted daily by the problem of determining whether the people we encounter are being truthful with us in the statements they make about themselves and about the world around us. In face-to-face cases, however, we have

---

GARY URTON is Dumbarton Oaks Professor of Pre-Columbian Studies in the Department of Anthropology, Harvard University. He is the author of numerous articles and books on Inka civilization and colonial and contemporary Andean / Quechua cultures and societies, including *At the Crossroads of the Earth and the Sky* (1981), *The History of a Myth* (1990), *The Social Life of Numbers* (1997), *Inca Myths* (1999), and *Signs of the Inka Khipu* (2003). He is director of the Khipu Database Project at Harvard University.

access to all manner of clues and signals that we can rely on to help us gauge the trustworthiness of our present-day interlocutors. These truth-seeking methods, some more reliable than others, include scrutiny of subtle cues such as tone of voice, posture, and the steadiness (or lack thereof) of the gaze of people as they speak to us (see the chapters by Schauer and Zeckhauser and by Frank in this volume). But how can we evaluate the truthfulness of statements made in the distant past, at a remove of considerable time and perhaps space as well, when we do not have access to the emotive, acting bodies of interlocutors to interact with—to look at, listen to, and (more impressionistically) to give reign to our intuitive powers—in seeking signs of truthfulness?

The questions leading off this chapter put the problems we will be concerned with here in the starkest and most poignant terms possible. How, indeed, might we ever hope to know whether a long-dead people lied to each other, to their neighbors, and to us, their historical interlocutors? Unfortunately, I have no magical retrospective truth serum, nor even a novel method for ferreting out lies within musty chronicles and notarial records from the past (although Kathryn Burns does a fine job on this score[1]). My objective here is not to test the veracity of statements made by peoples in the ancient world. Rather, I will explore a pair of historical landscapes in which veracity and deceptiveness were paramount features in shaping the social relations and political encounters between two groups of people of notably differing, and contesting, pedigrees. In each setting, one of the competing groups exercised accounting and power of control vis-à-vis the other.

Leaving aside the quest to ever know what is true and what is a lie when examining historical documents, the question that will direct our investigation is how questions of trustworthiness and deception shaped the interactions and power struggles between different groups of people in the past. The two principal settings in which I will examine these dynamics and relations of veridicality are, first, in the record-keeping practices by means of *quipu* (khipu; Quechua for "knot") in the Inka empire of the pre-Columbian Andes; and second, in the long struggle between native Andeans and their European conquerors and colonial administrators following the Spanish conquest of the Inkas in 1532.

Accounting and Accountability in the Khipus

The defeat of the great army of one of two pretenders to the Inka throne, Atawalpa—which was followed by his capture and execution in 1532–33 by

Francisco Pizarro in the highland Andean town of Cajamarca—set in motion a process of transformation in the Andean world that has reverberated through the centuries down to the present day. At the time of his confrontation with Pizarro in Cajamarca, Atawalpa was involved in a fierce struggle with his half-brother, Waskar, over who would succeed their father, Wayna Kapaq, to the throne of the largest state of the pre-Columbian New World, the Inka empire. At the time of the entry of Francisco Pizarro into what is now the nation of Peru, the Inka empire stretched almost five thousand kilometers along the spine of the Andes mountains, from the border between present-day Ecuador and Colombia southward through Peru, Bolivia, northwest Argentina, and down to a couple of hundred kilometers south of the present-day city of Santiago de Chile.

The archaeological record that attests to the rise and expansion of the Inka state suggests that the Inkas emerged as a dominant force in the Andean world only a century or two before the arrival of Pizarro and his troops. In the short span of 150–200 years, the Inkas were able to establish control, often highly contested, over a myriad of peoples across a wide swath of territory in the Andes. From their capital in Cuzco, the Inkas established and oversaw numerous military and administrative installations throughout the Andes. These centers housed Inka troops and service workers whose energies were directed at the accomplishment of state projects ranging from warfare and conquest to agricultural production.

Inka control also took the more subtle form of a network of state officials whose administrative oversight and coordination of state affairs bound together a population of several million people into what appears, from the archaeological and early colonial historical records, to have been a unified imperial administration. One remarkable aspect of this administration is that, in lieu of written documents, its records took the form of bundles of knotted strings, called *khipus* (see Figure 9.1). The khipus were produced, stored in archives, and "read"—in some manner that we do not entirely understand at present— by state officials known collectively as *khipukamayuqs* (knot makers / keepers). In the course of this study, we will see that the khipu keepers continued to record information in the knotted strings for several decades after the Spanish conquest—and a few have continued to be used down to the present day.[2]

The Spanish chroniclers who investigated Inka record keeping in the years following the European invasion inform us that every village in the empire had no fewer than four khipu keepers who retained in their khipus informa-

FIGURE 9.1 Khipu
SOURCE: Ethnographic Museum, Göteborg, Sweden. Photo by G. Urton.

tion of interest to state administrators pertaining to their respective villages. The information recorded on khipus included census data; records of tribute obligations and performance; counts of the numbers and types of animals in state camelid herds; measures of state, priestly, and commoner agricultural landholdings; and information on a great variety of other raw, processed, and manufactured goods that were of interest to, or were the property of, the state. Local khipu keepers in settlements scattered throughout the provinces in every corner of the empire were overseen by governors (*tukriquq*, or overseer; see Figure 9.2), who made inspection tours into the countryside from the provincial administrative centers. Higher-level khipu keepers were responsible for synthesizing the information that came in from the surrounding communities, or the dispersed settlements of clanlike groupings known as *ayllus*. As we read in an account of one of the earliest Spanish chroniclers, Cieza de León, from 1551:

> In each provincial capital they had accountants who were called *quiposcamayos*, and by their knots they kept the records and accounting of what the people in that province owed in the way of tribute, including the silver, gold, clothing and

FIGURE 9.2 Provincial administrator with pair of khipus

SOURCE: Felipe Guaman Poma de Ayala, *El Primer Nueva Corónica y Buen Gobierno* [1615], critical edition by John V. Murra and Rolena Adorno; translation and textual analysis by Jorge L. Urioste, 3 vols. (Mexico City: Siglo Veintiuno, 1980), 320, 343.

livestock, even to the firewood and other lesser things, and by these same *quipos* at the end of one year, or 10 or 20, they kept records so well that not even a pair of sandals would be lost.[3]

After collecting and collating the information that came from numerous different sources, the governors were responsible for forwarding the information on to higher-level officials.[4] The information from the 80 or so provinces throughout the empire eventually reached the four *Apus*—the lords of the Four Quarters—who served the Inka as the highest officials of the quarters of the Inka empire in the capital city, Cuzco.

A word should be said here about the nature of the information available to us for studying khipu accounting and the truthfulness of these knotted-string records. The central problem that khipu researchers face today—the consequences of which will concern us throughout this study—is that, being limited to reading only the numerical values recorded on the khipus, we are forced to rely on transcriptions of the contents of these accounts (that is, the identities of the objects enumerated) that were made by Spanish scribes and administrators during the colonial period. Given the fact that the native record keepers and their Spanish overlords often had very different interests in, and interpretations of, the social and political realities of the world they shared, our reliance on Spanish accounts means that we must continually evaluate the qualitative features of khipu accounts—concerning agency, intentionality, and even their perceived truthfulness—as seen from the Andean point of view.

Researchers working on the khipu information system today are generally in agreement that, as different levels of record keepers interacted with each other in the hierarchy of administrative officials—ranging from lower-level record keepers in local communities up to those in the imperial capital—the system must have been grounded, at least in its mid-to-upper levels, in a body of conventionalized signing and recording values, principles, and practices.[5] Such mutual intelligibility of recording values and procedures at these levels would have been essential in order for the administrative officials to achieve some minimal degree of coordination of the information coming from a great variety of local record keepers who spoke a myriad of languages and who, according to one chronicler, produced khipus in a variety of forms.[6] Although many references in the Spanish documents attest to the trustworthiness of the native accountants, the Inka accounting system itself included multiple levels and forms of checks and balances.[7] These procedures were presumably put in place and maintained for the purpose of ensuring the trustworthiness of khipu records and the truthfulness of record keepers at all administrative levels. But here we encounter a problem: If it was true, as native informants insisted to their Spanish colonial interlocutors, that the khipu keepers "always" recorded and told the truth, why was their system of checks and balances necessary?[8]

The Dialectic of Trustworthiness and Accountability

The assumption of the innate truthfulness of the khipu keepers and the simultaneous maintenance of checks and balances sat uneasily together as foundational principles of khipu record keeping in the Inka empire. Maintaining the presumption of trustworthiness while employing strict procedures of accountability might appear to signal contradictory sensibilities and thus constitute a paradox. Yet recent research and commentary on the relationship between truth and verifiability see this sentiment-procedural pair of trust juxtaposed with control as complementary and inextricably linked to each other. This latter perspective recognizes that accounting systems that contain stringent accountability procedures usually operate on a presumption of the inherent trustworthiness of the record keepers, or accountants (we are all now well aware of the consequences of an excessive reliance on the latter in the almost complete absence of the former from recent events in the U.S. and global financial and banking industries; see Harrington, this volume). According to this view, trust and control are structurally, psychologically, and (in terms of the agency of those concerned) strategically inseparable.

In his insightful and cogent writings on this topic, Guido Möllering proposes that trust and control are linked in what he terms a "duality," suggesting that they "refer to each other and create each other, but remain irreducible to each other."[9] Möllering argues that in the best of circumstances—for example, when relationships and institutions work smoothly and all concerned have confidence that people will act honorably—trust and control will both be operative:

> I propose that an analytical framework for control and trust can be devised that translates the duality of structure and agency specifically to the basic problem of the formation of positive expectations of others: when an actor rests positive expectations on structural influences on the embedded other, we speak of

control . . . When an actor rests positive expectations on an assumption of benevolent agency on the part of the other, we speak of *trust*.[10]

Möllering also discusses a fascinating case study involving a negotiation
between a potential author and a German publishing house that went badly
awry, largely on the basis of a disconnect between the two parties with respect
to their perceptions and understandings of the degree of accountability and
the benevolence of the actors involved in that negotiation.[11] These differences
eventually led to the collapse of the deal and to resentment by both parties
toward their interlocutor in the bargain.

Misunderstandings deriving from different perceptions and expectations
of implicit trust and explicit controls overseeing negotiations—especially
when the parties to the (potential) agreement are of radically different back-
grounds and represent contesting interests—are precisely the kinds of situations I address in this chapter. I focus on two circumstances of trust / control
relationships that existed in the Andes during two different (but contiguous)
time periods. The first concerns the relationship in the pre-Columbian era
between khipu record keepers and the commoners whose records they kept.
The second relationship is the one that emerged during the years following
the Spanish conquest of the Andes, between native record keepers and Spanish administrative officials. The trust / control issues that arose in these two
settings concerned the degree to which benevolence between the two parties
in each relationship was assumed in symmetrical terms and accepted by both
parties, and whether the parties involved in these relationships assumed that
certain structures were in place that would have a controlling influence on the
other side, thus preventing both sides from acting in an exploitative manner.

We will see as we proceed the scarcity of data providing an unbiased, objective understanding on the question of how commoners in the empire actually viewed the Inka record keepers (and vice versa) with respect to issues
of trust and control. On the other hand, abundant data from the colonial
period make it clear that the trust-control relationship between native record
keepers and Spanish administrative officials became poisoned after only a few
decades of Spanish rule. Once the relationship between natives and colonial
officials was undermined by a lack of confidence that each side was acting
benevolently toward the other—which coincided with the mutual loss of confidence in the efficacy of structures of control—people on both sides became
convinced that interactions between the two groups were suffused with lies

and deception. We will see later how this conviction expressed itself on both sides of an increasingly dysfunctional trust-control duality.

In the following section, I will first examine how the related principles of innate trustworthiness and proper accountability intersected in Inka record-keeping practices before the time of the Spanish conquest. I will then turn to the question of how native notions about khipu veracity and the maintenance of procedures ensuring proper accountability fared as khipu record keeping continued to be practiced in the early years following the establishment of the Spanish colonial state in the Andes. Before addressing these issues and problems, it may be helpful, especially for readers who are unfamiliar with the remarkable knotted-string khipu, to begin with an overview of the basic features of these devices and a brief account of how information was registered on them.

The Khipu and Its Methods of Information Registry

According to my own inventory, there are some 750+/− khipu samples in museums and private collections in Europe, North America, and South America. While many samples are too fragile to permit their study, about 350 samples have been studied closely.[12]

Khipus are knotted-string devices made of spun and plied cotton or camelid fibers (see Figure 9.3). The colors displayed in khipus reflect the natural colors of cotton fiber and camelid hair or the dyeing of these materials with natural dyes. The "backbone" of a khipu is the so-called primary cord, approximately 0.5 cm in diameter, to which are attached a variable number of thinner strings, called pendant cords. Khipus contain from as few as one up to as many as 1,500 pendants (the average is 84 cords). Top cords are pendant-like strings that leave the primary cord opposite the pendants, often after being passed through the attachments of a group of pendant strings. Top cords often contain the sum of values knotted on the set of pendant cords to which they are attached. About one quarter of all pendant cords have second-order cords attached to them; these are called subsidiaries. Subsidiaries may themselves have subsidiaries, and examples exist of khipus that contain pendant cords with as many as six levels of subsidiaries, making the khipu a highly efficient device for the display of hierarchically organized information.[13]

The majority of khipus have knots tied into their pendant, subsidiary, and top strings.[14] The most common knots are of three different types, which are

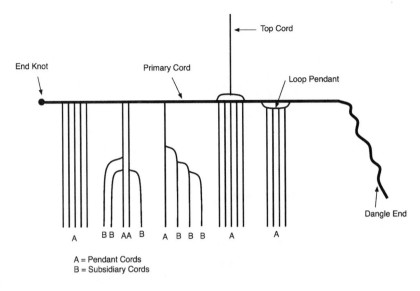

FIGURE 9.3 Khipu structures
SOURCE: Drawing by Carrie J. Brezine.

usually tied in clusters on the cords at different levels to indicate decimal numerical values. The first study to demonstrate that many of the khipus encoded numerical values in a base ten system of number registry was L. Leland Locke's, *The Ancient Quipu, or Peruvian Knot Record.*[15] The most thorough treatment to date of the numerical, arithmetic, and mathematical properties of the khipus is Ascher and Ascher's, *Mathematics of the Incas: Code of the Quipus.*[16] The Aschers have shown that the arithmetic and mathematical operations used by Inka accountants included, at a minimum, addition, subtraction, multiplication, and division; division into unequal fractional parts and into proportional parts; and multiplication of integers by fractions.[17]

What kinds of information were registered on the khipus? According to numerous Spanish accounts, records were kept of censuses, tribute assessment and performance, goods stored in the Inka storehouses, astronomical periodicities and calendrical calculations, royal genealogies, historical events, and so on.[18] The overriding interest in the manipulation of numbers in the recording of this wide range of types of information was achieving balance, or rectitude, in the calculations. This meant balancing what was added here with something subtracted there, and what was divided in this instance with something multiplied in another instance; and other such account-balancing procedures. These kinds of rectitude-seeking calculations, practiced in Quechua arithmetic operations in communities today, would presumably have held as well for the manipulation of numerical data by the Quechua-speaking khipu keepers in Inka times.[19]

With this basic overview of khipus and the general types of records they retained as background for what follows, we now move to a consideration of the question of the presumed truthfulness of khipu accounts.

The Veracity of Khipu Records and Their Keepers

In talking about the procedures connected with visits by Inka administrative officials from the capital, Cuzco, to provincial centers for what we could term administrative oversight and reconnoitering, the early traveler and astute observer of Inka cultural practices, Cieza de León, noted that "when they come from the city of Cuzco to take the accounts, or when such are sent to Cuzco, these same khipu accountants with their khipus . . . were unable to commit fraud [*no podía haber fraude*] because all of them were upright [*cabal*]."[20] The ideal of the innate truthfulness of khipu keepers and their accounts is also presented as one of the central, presumptive qualities of the Inka administrators by the Jesuit chronicler, José de Acosta. Writing in 1590, Acosta noted: "Appointed to possess these *quipus*, or memorials, were officials who today are called *quipucamayos*, and these men were obliged to render an account of each thing, like public notaries here in Spain, and hence *they had to be believed absolutely*."[21]

It is interesting to note the degree to which, in their simple naming of and references to the khipu devices themselves, the Spanish accounts incorporate a presumption of the veracity of the records retained therein. For example, a passage from a 16th-century *visita* (administrative visit) from the Lake Titicaca area notes that, while the khipu keeper from a certain town (Acora) had died, the record keeper of the nearby town of Chucuito kept an account of the records of all the province. The latter khipu is referred to in the document as *el quipo cierto y verdadero de toda la provincia* (the certain and true khipu of all the province).[22] It is unclear whether such characterizations in the documents are a reflection of the Spaniards' own beliefs about the veracity of the native records at the time, or if they merely reflect assertions from the testimony of native informants that worked their way into the written testimony in an unconscious manner.

There are, then, numerous instances in which Spaniards referred to khipu keeping before the time of the conquest that indicate the innate truthfulness of both the records and their keepers. Perhaps an important motivation of Spaniards for these generally unequivocally positive statements was related to the fact that, as much of the information concerning censuses, tribute, and even history contained in early Spanish accounts came originally from native readings of the khipus, claims of the truthfulness of the native accounts were a way of asserting the validity of the Spanish written records themselves. In any case, such explicit characterizations of the trustworthiness of the khipus represented one of the ways that presumptions about the veracity of the knotted-string accounts became embedded in the minds and discourse of the Spaniards and in the colonial textual tradition.

One important context in which the Spaniards encouraged the use of khipus, and attested thereby to their value, was in the telling of confessions (see Figure 9.4). Pérez Bocanegra, a priest who served in the parish of Andahuaylillas, near Cuzco, wrote a manual advising priests on strategies for encouraging natives to record their sins on khipus.[23] In his description, Pérez Bocanegra indicated that the confessants consulted the knots and colors of the khipus, each color being associated with a specific sin.[24] From the point of view of the clergy, recording confessions on khipus was considered to be a good and efficient way of focusing the attention of confessants on the variety of actions that might need to be atoned for in the confessional. The natives no doubt kept the confessional khipus because they were strongly encouraged to do so, but also because of the intense interrogations on their actions and motives to which they were subjected by the priests. As a consequence of this scrutiny, village elders developed elaborate strategies for coaching members of their communities in remembering and recording sins—some of which the Spaniards came to suspect were as much (if not more) to hide sins than to expose them, as the Friar Martín de Murúa noted concerning this practice in the 1610s:

> Going about, a few years ago, the Indians [men and women] had trained confessors, experienced in confessing by these strings and *khipu*, hearing their general confessions based on the Commandments, and then each time they confess, they bring out their *khipu*, and by it they recite their sins, which has certainly been a marvelous medium and most effective in ensuring they make their confessions more complete and convincing.[25]

FIGURE 9.4 Indian confessing to a priest

SOURCE: Felipe Guaman Poma de Ayala, *El Primer Nueva Corónica y Buen Gobierno* [1615], critical edition by John V. Murra and Rolena Adorno; translation and textual analysis by Jorge L. Urioste, 3 vols. (Mexico City: Siglo Veintiuno, 1980), 584, 615.

In another context, assertions about the veracity of khipu administrative accounts and of the native officials themselves were made repeatedly in court testimony concerning a variety of legal proceedings. For example, in 1579, the khipu keeper Alonso Yanxi, from the province of Sacaca in present-day central Bolivia, stated in court testimony: "They appoint as *quipo*-keepers in the said *repartimientos* [accounting districts] the most credible Indians that there are in them by reason of which the said *quipos* were trustworthy and for this reason *there is no fraud in them nor are there any lies.*"[26]

The above passage derives from testimony from one of several native khipu keepers in a proceeding that centered around contested claims of the payment of tribute during the 1580s. As such, we have already in this passage left the relatively "innocent" realm of characterizations of khipu trustworthiness pertaining to historical constructions for pre-Hispanic recording practices and have entered the highly contested realm of colonial confrontations between natives and Spaniards in the colonial Andes. I will take up this matter in a later section; for the moment, I wish only to establish that at least a rhetorical and discursive tradition emerged in the early colonial literatures (legal, administrative, and ecclesiastical) in which khipus and their keepers were presumed to be truthful and trustworthy virtually beyond question. This characterization is implied in the following passage from José de Acosta from the 1590s:

> [N]owadays in Peru every two or three years, when a Spanish governor is subjected to a trial of residency, the Indians come forward with their small woven reckonings [their khipus], saying that in a certain town they gave him six eggs and he did not pay for them, and in such and such a house a hen, and in another place two bundles of hay for his horses, and that he paid only so and so many *tomines* [coins] and still owes so and so many; and *all of this is accurately proved with a quantity of knots and bundles of strands, which they consider to be witnesses and authentic writing.*[27]

From the previous passage, we become aware of a potential problem that would, in fact, soon come out into the open and grow to crisis proportions; that is, what if the ex-governor contested the testimony of the Indians, the latter of which was made from their "small woven reckonings?" What if he in fact kept his own accounts in written form in a medium that, unlike the khipus, could be read by a judge? Such confrontations of accounting practices and record-keeping systems emerged with greater frequency and intensity toward the end of the 16th century and spelled the end of official khipu record keeping. What all these cases point to, aside from the virtual inevitability of conflicts of interest between Spaniards and native Andeans, is that one-half of the trust-control duality was absent from this relationship; that is, as the Spaniards never mastered the reading of khipus, any check on the accuracy of a disputed khipu account had to be performed by a khipu keeper. When, as occurred increasingly in the waning years of the 16th century, trust between the two sides began to deteriorate, there was no way for Spaniards to assure themselves of the veracity of khipu testimony presented at trial, for instance. This is not to suggest that Spaniards were the only aggrieved party in this relationship, as they, the conquerors, had betrayed the trust of the Andean people beginning with their very first encounter with the Inkas. Most notably, the initial—and decisive—battle between the two forces, in the highland town of Cajamarca, ended with the capture, ransom, and ultimately the betrayal and execution of the Inka Atahualpa.[28]

In short, disputes and confrontations increasingly arose between natives and Spaniards over record keeping throughout the 16th century. I will take up these issues more directly below. However, let us return to the pre-Hispanic period in order to investigate the Inka insistence on accountability, or checks and balances—practices that appear to have been intimately linked to the supposed innate trustworthiness of khipu accounts, thereby forming a duality of trust and accountability in native record keeping.

Accounting for Truthfulness

Numerous statements in the Spanish chronicles attest to the existence of checks and balances in khipu accounting. For instance, Garcilaso de la Vega noted in 1609:

> Although the quipucamayus were as accurate and honest as we have said, their number in each village was in proportion to its population, and however small, it had at least four and so upwards to twenty or thirty. *They all kept the same records*, and although one accountant or scribe was all that would have been necessary to keep them, the Incas preferred to have plenty in each village and for each sort of calculation, so as to avoid faults that might occur if there were few.[29]

Other commentary speaks more directly to the matter of one accountant checking up on another (see Figure 9.5). For instance, in communities divided into halves, or moieties—*hanan* (upper) and *hurin* (lower)—each had

FIGURE 9.5 *Collcacamayoq*—khipu keeper of storehouse, reporting to an overseer

SOURCE: Felipe Guaman Poma de Ayala, *El Primer Nueva Corónica y Buen Gobierno* [1615], critical edition by John V. Murra and Rolena Adorno; translation and textual analysis by Jorge L. Urioste, 3 vols. (Mexico City: Siglo Veintiuno, 1980), 309, 335.

its khipu keeper for various interests, or resources, and it was assumed that the records of the pairs of khipu keepers would contain identical information.[30] As for khipu accounting at the provincial level, Garcilaso de la Vega noted that "the Inca governor of each province was required by law to keep a copy of the accounts in his possession so that no deception could be practiced by either the Indian tribute payers or the official collectors."[31]

Checks and balances also existed within individual khipu accounts themselves. We read of such an accounting method in what is the earliest surviving testimony about khipu record keeping. In this account, Hernando Pizarro, the brother of Francisco Pizarro, tells us that on one occasion, in 1533, he and his soldiers took certain items—firewood, "sheep" [probably llamas], corn, and *chicha* [corn beer]—from an Inca storehouse along the royal highway. H. Pizarro went on to note that the accountants—*quipucamayoqs*—"untied some of the knots which they had in the deposits section [of the *quipu*], and they [re]tied them in another section [of the *quipu*]."[32] Curiously, this is one of the few accounts we have from Spanish testimony of an actual event of "balancing the books" in a khipu transaction.

When we turn to the extant khipus housed in museum collections today and ask the question of whether any structural features or numerical patterning in the surviving samples might support the reported existence of checks and balances in the khipus, we in fact find a fair amount of evidence. One of the most interesting bodies of evidence to take note of in this regard involves what appear to be copies of accounts, or what I have referred to as duplicate, or "matching" khipus.[33] Such khipus occur in three different forms. First, we have examples in which the numerical values of a sequence of strings on one sample are repeated exactly on a different khipu. In some paired samples exhibiting these qualities, we find that, while the two khipus bear the same knot values, the string colors vary.[34] Second, we have instances in which two khipus contain similar but not exactly matching information. I have referred to such pairs of khipus as "close matches." Close matches perhaps resulted from paired (moiety based) khipu keepers using different methods of accounting, or of counting and recording information on similar circumstances at different times and, therefore, ending up with slightly different data (see Table 9.1). Finally, we have examples in which data recorded on one part of a khipu are repeated exactly, or closely, on another part of that same khipu. In sum, I think that duplicate, or in a few cases even triplicate, copies of khipus provide solid evidence for the existence of a system of checks and balances in khipu accounting as attested to later in the chronicles.[35]

TABLE 9.1 Data from two closely matching khipus—
Puruchuco, central coast of Peru

KHIPU UR064 / 1000263			KHIPU UR068 / 1000262		
Cord Number	Color	Value	Cord Number	Color	Value
1	AB	1	1	AB	1
2	W		2	GG	
3	MB		3	W	
4	GG		4	AB	
5	CB:W		5	KB:W	
6	W		6	W	
7	MB		7	AB	
8	GG	1	8	GG	1
9	CB:W		9	KB:W	
10	W	1	10	W	1
11	AB		11	AB	
12	GG		12	GG	
13	CB:W		13	KB:W	
14	W	3	14	W	3
15	MB		15	AB	
16	GG		16	GG	
17	CB:W		17	KB:W	
18	W	7	18	W	8
18s1	W	1	19	AB	2
19	AB	2	20	GG	1
20	GG	1	21	KB:W	
21	CB:W		22	W	8
22	W	8	23	AB	1
23	MB	1	24	GG	3
24	GG		25	KB:W	1
25	CB:W	1	26	W	56
26	W	56	27	AB	5
27	MB	5	28	GG	4
28	GG		29	KB:W	1
29	CB:W	1	30	W	1,213
30	W	1,212	31	AB	43
31	AB	43	32	GG	64
32	GG	64	33	KB:W	17
33	CB:W	16	34	W	2
33s1	W	1	35	AB	
34	W	2	36	GG	1
35	AB		37	GG:W	
36	GG	1	38	W	8
37	W	8	39	AB	1
38	MB	1	40	GG:AB	
39	GG:AB:W		41	KB:W	
40	CB:W		42	W	8
41	W	8	43	AB	1
42	AB	1	44	GG	3
43	GG	3	45	KB:W	1

We have now looked briefly at the two features of khipu record keeping in the pre-Columbian Andes that, I argue, represent an Andean manifestation of the trust/control duality. I return to the general theoretical issues raised in the introduction in order to now reflect on their potential applicability to Inka khipu accounting. In parting from the prevailing view on the trust/control relationship, which sees the two as separable and not necessarily linked in terms of structure and agency, Möllering began by asking the question: "How can actors form positive expectations of the behavior of other actors by whom they may be positively or negatively affected, i.e., to whom they are vulnerable?"[36] This question is relevant to khipu record keeping in Inka times in two ways. First, how could the commoners whose data (census, tribute owed/paid, and so on) were collected by local khipu keepers have confidence not only that the information was being collected and recorded correctly but also that the correct data pertaining to their community/ayllu were being passed up the administrative hierarchy? And, on the other side, how could local record keepers have confidence in the information they collected? Had people hidden members of their households at the time of censuses? More important, with regard to the latter recording circumstances, how could higher-level administrative authorities have confidence that the correct information had been forwarded to them from the local record keepers? Had the lower-level, local record keepers under-reported the numbers of people present in their respective communities? These questions all go to the heart of the trust/control relationship in Inka record keeping.

In addressing such questions in theoretical terms, Möllering theorized several behavioral and institutional structural features of interactions between actors in circumstances when both sides needed, or sought, confidence in each other's intentions and in the effectiveness of existing security procedures, or controls. One notion that becomes crucial here is that of "embedded agency." This is a notion that seeks to address the fundamental question that is raised in any given social setting requiring mutual confidence in interactions involving two or more parties. In such settings, should/can an actor base his or her expectations of the other on structural influences, or controls, operating on the other or on the apparent intentions of the other? In confronting this question, Möllering follows various agency and structuration theorists in adopting the notion of embedded agency,[37] whereby actors are understood to be constituted and constrained by social structures but at the same time are understood to be the originators and carriers of structure through their contingent and purposeful action.[38]

Möllering goes on to add to the notion of embedded agency the concept of "suspension," which he likens to a "leap of faith." This concept emerges when an actor recognizes that his or her positive expectations of others might be disappointed. Suspension does not eliminate the doubt that arises in such circumstances, but rather it brackets it, making the situation livable for the time being (see also Möllering's chapter, this volume, for a more extensive discussion of the leap of faith in trust assessment).[39]

In sum, an actor reaches positive expectations of other actors by referring to a "trust/control duality and by suspending remaining uncertainty, too. Positive expectations of others are not possible, if the actor fails to understand in a favorable way the embedded agency of those others and the uncertainty it entails."[40]

I propose that all of these calculations and presuppositions, including the grand leap of faith, would have to have been operative in order for us to claim that the Inka administrative system functioned in pre-Columbian times, as it is represented as having done in the Spanish chronicles. It is critical to note in this regard that the great, synthesizing works of Inka/Andean "history" that are referred to as the Spanish chronicles were all products of the testimony of informants in Cuzco, the former capital city of the empire. As such, their testimony, particularly as it regards the efficacy of Inka policies in the provinces and the attitudes of subjects toward Inka domination, must be considered suspect. Certainly, a great deal of information is found in the local documents (as opposed to the Spanish chronicles) that points to local resistance, contestation, and outright rebellion against Inka rule by peoples throughout the Andes.[41] We can thus conclude that, despite the existence of pockets or areas of cooperation between subjects of the empire and local and provincial administrative officials, this was by no means an uncomplicated relationship. Undoubtedly, the presumptions of embedded agency and suspension were fully effective in some settings, and in those instances a trust/control duality between subjects and record keepers would have been fully operative. However, in other settings and circumstances little or no confidence between the two sides was apparent, and a leap of faith on the part of either party regarding the intentions of the other or the efficacy of control mechanisms was far from the norm. These are the settings in which the state would have been required to exercise coercive control, foregoing the preferred hegemonic relationship with provincials.

The preceding conclusion leaves us with the problem of explaining why the accounts on these matters contained in the Spanish chronicles are so over-whelmingly positive in their evaluations, not only of commoner compliance with state projects and policies but also of the inherent trustworthiness of the khipus and the inherent veracity of the khipu keepers. I suggest that the con-tradictions that become evident on these matters when we look more closely at the ethnohistorical evidence are, in fact, a product of contested relations and contradictory forces and perspectives that emerged within the colonial setting itself. I will explore the evidence that supports this interpretation in what follows.

Colonial Conflicts over Khipu Accounts

It is important to note at this point that, as far as we are aware from colo-nial records, no Spaniard succeeded in learning to read the khipu accounts with sufficient precision and detail to allow us to use that information to read extant khipus in museums today.[42] In fact, the mestizo Jesuit priest, Blas Valera, upbraided the Spaniards for failing to learn to read the khipus, as the natives themselves had learned to read Spanish script: "We moreover are slower in understanding their books than they in following ours; for we have been dealing with them for more than seventy years without ever learning the theory and rules of their knots and accounts, whereas they have very soon picked up not only our writing but also our figures, which is a proof of their great skill."[43]

The Spaniards' inability to read and therefore to verify the renderings of khipu produced by native accountants, rendered them dependent on native readings of these records. Thus one-half of the "trust but verify" duality was absent in this setting. In some cases, the data recorded on khipus had been collected in preconquest times; in other cases, as the record keepers contin-ued to record census, tribute, and other potentially highly sensitive informa-tion on the khipus, the conditions increasingly emerged for conflicts to arise between native khipu keepers and colonial administrative record keepers. Records from the 1570–80s indicate that such cases often ended up in court trials. These contests involved census and tribute accounting as well as the reciting of confessions. What we will find in the testimony regarding these matters below is that, while the Spaniards initially accepted native testimony read from khipus, they increasingly came to suspect the verity of that testimony in all settings in which it was produced. A few examples will suffice to expose the problems that emerged in these areas of colonial life.

I have noted that, at least in the early years following the conquest, Spanish administrators accepted khipu keepers' readings of the knotted-string records, even entering such readings in court testimony.[44] However, as Spanish written testimony increasingly came into conflict with testimony from the khipus, the Spaniards became suspicious of the native accounts. One perspective from a Spaniard on these matters comes to us from Solórzano y Pereyra, who not only called khipu testimony into question but who also clearly intended in doing so to undermine confidence in the integrity and veracity of the khipu keepers (and, in fact, of all natives) in the following statement from 1629–39:

> I would not venture to give any or such great faith and authority to the *quipos*, because I have heard it said ... that the manner of making and explaining them is uncertain, deceitful, and convoluted; and furthermore, I do not know how it can be affirmed that the *quipo* keepers are selected with the authority of the general public for this post ... *When all is said and done, they are Indians, whose faith vacillates, and thus also, they will equivocate in the explication they give of their quipos.*[45]

The sentiments in these lines run strongly counter to earlier statements by Spaniards expressing confidence in the khipu keepers and their records. It appears that at least this one Spanish official had decidedly turned against making the kinds of presumptions and adopting the attitudes—including taking the necessary leap of faith—that were necessary to remaining engaged in a productive trust/control relationship with the native record keepers.

Similar sentiments, pointing to what some Spaniards took to be the native people's growing habit of dissembling in their record keeping, particularly when it involved claims on what Spaniards owed to local people, appear in the following quote from Martín de Murúa, from the early 17th century:

> In these *quipus* they tend to put down when the *corregidor* [governor] or priest or others don't pay them for all the food and other things they demand, and later they demand payment in the officials' residence or during official *visitas* [inspections], and even ask for more than what is owed them so as not to fall short, for their slyness has grown beyond what it was, and as they see that such requests always lead to compromises and deductions, they generally put down more than what they are owed, so that with the deduction they can get back everything they gave.[46]

Further expressions of cynicism in other contexts in which Andean peoples employed khipus emerged over time; one such example concerns confessions. We saw earlier that the Spanish priests at first encouraged the use of khipus for the recording of sins and the reading of confessions. However, native uses of khipus in this domain of religious practice soon became suspect, as well, as the clergy realized that the Indians were making "confessional khipus," which were passed from one confessant to another. The priest Pérez Bocanegra noted in 1631 that "they loan them [the khipus] out, and they hand them off to those who come to confess another time, whether it's young boys or young girls, old men or old women: warning them exactly which sins they were to say for each color, or knot, and they carry them to another confessor, because he doesn't know them."[47]

The above conundrum led to the development of techniques for interrogating confessants in order to verify whether they were telling the truth. For instance, one priest noted that if the Indians always claim they committed sins repeatedly in round numbers of ten (for example, I got drunk ten times, or I failed to hear mass ten times), the priest should try to trip them up by asking how many times they committed the act one week, then how many times the following week, and so on.[48] The priest was presumably supposed to total up the number of episodes and confront the confessant if the sum was not a multiple of ten! The techniques of interrogation became increasingly subtle, reaching the point at which priests were instructed to observe the body movements and gestures of the confessant:

> And if it seem to the priest that the male Indian or the female Indian gets quiet or hides whatever sin, cajole him or her with loving, nonthreatening words, helping them and encouraging them to say all their sins: especially those which (for their reasons) they want to hide, sins that are easily seen by the frequent swallowing of saliva, and not kneeling calmly, coughing, looking at one spot and then another, and other signs, which God has them show, when they want to commit this sacrilege.[49]

This, what almost reads like a manual for detecting lies and deceit in the native confessants, echoes through the centuries of encounters between actors of good and bad intentions and officials charged with detecting deceitful intent in facial expressions, body gestures, and other such behaviors. But the insights from present-day techniques for ferreting out liars, in which one individual is charged with observing the behavior of a subject/suspect, also give us caution with regard to inappropriate presumptions that might inform such procedures. For instance, Mark Frank (this volume) discusses a form of misinterpretation of intentions known as the "idiosyncrasy error":

> This type of error is caused by a failure to observe a person's typical style of behavior. For example, research has shown that most people believe that liars do not make eye contact when they speak. However, some people, either due to their shy nature or low self-esteem, never make eye contact in everyday conversation. . . . Culture enters into this equation as well; for example, in some cultures it is considered a sign of respect not to look an authority figure in the eye.

Thus the issues that emerge concerning truth and deception in the confrontation between natives and Spaniards in early colonial Peru are more complicated and culturally nuanced than the ways they are portrayed in the—inevitably one-sided—accounts recorded by Spanish priests and administrators. The critical point is that, by the time relations and presumptions of truthfulness or deception between two parties reach the point evoked in the various testimonials reported above, there will be little or no inclination by the members of either party to take a leap of faith in assuming good intentions on the part of the other.

The above is the state of affairs that emerged after the first few decades following the conquest and that set the stage for a complete breakdown of relations and the undermining of sentiments of trust and structures of control in the colonial Andes. Undoubtedly, no single act or event accounted for the complete lack of trust that came to characterize relations between Andeans and Spaniards. Rather, many acts committed by members on both sides, from the fudging of tribute records[50] to the abuse of native peoples by the Spanish *encomenderos*, governors, and priests.[51] The complaints would have escalated over time, with acts of betrayal or deception reinforcing the feelings of injury by those first on one side and then the other. This became a war in which each side sought advantages over the other in an increasingly confrontational relationship. Every misunderstanding would be read as an intentional act of deceit—and active deception became increasingly common. As Guido Möllering observes (this volume), "one act of unnoticed deception often triggers further such acts and possibly an escalation of deception, because the deceiver wants to conceal the initial deception or has self-reinforcing incentives to exploit the situation further and further."

Textual Truth and the Spanish Administrators

While the written record of acts of duplicity in the trust / control relation-ship outlined above overwhelming implicates the native Andeans as the ones responsible for undermining the trust that (we are led to believe) earlier char-acterized their relationship with Spanish officials, nonetheless, accusations also pointed in the other direction. These countervoices were the few that have filtered through the almost impenetrable barrier erected by colonial ad-ministrators who were in control of official record keeping in the colony. In the rarest of cases, these voices came from Andean peoples; however, more commonly they came from the Spaniards themselves.

We may turn briefly to the remarkable written and pictorial testimony provided by the native Andean chronicler, Guaman Poma de Ayala.[52] Poma wrote a long (approximately a thousand-page) letter to the Spanish king, Philip II, protesting the destruction of Andean life and civilization at the hands of the Spanish conquistadors, the clergy, and the emerging class of *mestizos* (mixed bloods) in the colony. Poma reported a litany of evil and dis-honest acts performed by the Spaniards in their interactions with Andeans, and he protested Spanish duplicity and its negative effects on Andean social life. In one image (see Figure 9.6), Poma depicts a native Andean person beset on all sides by a host of ferocious animals, each identified as one or another of the rapacious and mendacious officials in the colonial administration.[53] The text that accompanies this image details the myriad ways the colonial officials acted in corrupt, rapacious, or deceitful ways in their dealings with their Andean subjects.

For an example of commentary by Spanish officials themselves that pointed to a lack of forthrightness and truthfulness in public affairs on the part of officials in the Andean colony, we can turn to the fascinating study of colonial notaries recently published by Kathryn Burns.[54] Burns focuses our attention on notaries because these were the people who were responsible for setting down in writing the myriad transactions that people brought to the state to see, judge, and adjudicate. Notarial records—as dull, mundane, and formulaic as they tend to be—are also the most abundant documents that remain from the colonial era. As Burns notes:

> Manuals with specific itineraries of [notarial] meaning were used in Europe and the colonial Americas to guide these men in straightening the endless di-versity of people's actions and language into the approved formulae. Notaries

FIGURE 9.6 Colonial and church officials threatening a native Andean

SOURCE: Felipe Guaman Poma de Ayala, *El Primer Nueva Corónica y Buen Gobierno* [1615], critical edition by John V. Murra and Rolena Adorno; translation and textual analysis by Jorge L. Urioste, 3 vols. (Mexico City: Siglo Veintiuno, 1980), 655, 694.

were thus truth's alchemists, mixing the singular into the formulaic in accordance with prescribed recipes to produce the written, duly witnessed, and certified truth. Their truth was recognizable not by its singularity but by its very regularity. It was truth by template.[55]

In her detailed study of the notarial documents from Cuzco, Burns finds that the "truth" written into the records of notaries was, more often than not, the product of whatever version could be sold to the highest bidder. Rather than upright bearers of truth, notaries are often portrayed in the colonial literature as stock figures of corruption and greed, "eager to produce the best truth money would buy."[56] From the earliest years following the conquest of Peru, the Spanish monarchy was aware of what Burns calls "notarial indiscipline" in the Americas. As early as 1564, Philip II became concerned with slippage in the production of notarial truth. He noted reports indicating that unqualified people were often named as notaries:

> [This] has resulted in documents and inquiries with notable errors, and [the people in question] should be trained and capable, as is fitting for the exercise of their office, and verifiable through examination, since the security and good form of their records and registers, which they do not keep with the necessary care, is so important. And from this [failure to keep good records] follows confusion, and variance in the facts of the truth, because sometimes petitions and documents are lost, and with them an accurate account.[57]

Thus the picture that emerges is one of a general loss of trust —on the one side, from the native Andeans with respect to the officials of the colonial administration and, on the other, from the administrators with regard to the native subjects of the colonial state.

To bring this discussion full circle, returning to issues discussed in our treatment of the relationship between khipu record keepers and commoners in the empire in preconquest times, Burns raises the question of the degree to which indigenous notaries—the khipu keepers—had in fact served as faithful mirrors of their communities' wishes. While recognizing (as we have seen here) that the data do not exist that would allow us to speak authoritatively on this matter for pre-Columbian times, she suggests that, as native record keepers began to practice their trade in the colonial context, the evidence suggests that their interests began to diverge markedly from those of the people whose records they kept and that working in their own interest increasingly came at the expense of the community they were designated to serve.[58]

Conclusion

I conclude this overview of truth and falsehood in the khipus by pointing to the need to draw a clear distinction between, on the one hand, the (unrecorded) ideas about and administrative practices relating to these matters as they pertain to pre-Hispanic record-keeping practices and, on the other hand, the representations and characterizations that appear in Spanish documents in the decades following the conquest and colonization of the Andes. I would argue, in the first place, that the well-honed practices of accounting checks and balances, evident both in the written testimony and in the khipus themselves (given the existence of matching and closely matching khipus), testify to the Inka administrative understanding that all accounts must be checked and verified. Secondly, I argue that claims about the innate veracity of khipu keepers and the trustworthiness of the khipus first emerged in the context of nostalgic representations of the preconquest past made by native Andeans (or sympathetic Spaniards) in formal inquests into Inka history. Such representations were later reinforced and made with greater resolution in the context of the highly contested and conflictual relations that came increasingly to typify native-Spanish relations in the colony. The latter claims emerged as the Spaniards bore down on the native population ever more forcefully in terms of controlling their energies and movements in the service of colonial state interests (such as the raising of tribute revenues, the increase in mining production, or the saving of native souls). Under such pressures, the natives became increasingly assertive of their own interests, which included (in addition to running away and escaping the strictures of colonial surveillance and governance) standing squarely behind the veracity and the inherent truthfulness of the records that had been produced by local khipu accountants before the imposition of Spanish record keeping. This was increasingly a war not only of wills but also of words—and of records, both quantitative and narrative.[59]

As tensions and conflict heightened, the solution that became most desirable from the perspective of the Spanish administrators was the destruction of the khipu accounts. And this was one of the determinations of the Third Council of Lima (Chapter 37), in 1583: "since among the Indians, who are ignorant of letters, there were instead of books certain signs made of different strings, which they called khipus, and from these come many testimonies of ancient superstitions in which they keep the secrets of their rituals, ceremonies, and iniquitous laws, let the Bishops completely destroy all these pernicious instruments."[60]

In the end, the final solution was the attempt to silence the native records by ordering their destruction. But in this case, a supreme irony prevails, as the khipus were only ever spoken of in the written records emerging from one side of the contesting parties—that of the Spaniards who translated khipu accounts and copied them into the written (Spanish) documents.

One of the great uncertainties that surrounds the study of the khipus today is whether, in the pre-Hispanic world, both sides—the khipu-toting Inka administrators and their local subjects—understood, equally participated in, and shared trust in the information collected and recorded on these devices. If not, then perhaps the contest that emerged in the colonial Andes described in the second half of this chapter was merely a continuation, in the European records, of a long (pre)history of the failure to maintain the structures and relations essential to ensuring both truthfulness and accountability in khipu record keeping. In the end, I would concur with Möllering when he stresses that the most important factor in what he terms the trust/control duality is how it is *enacted*.[61] For there is, indeed, no way to reach confident conclusions about people's intentions and sentiments, or about the structural controls that ideally ensured truthful and proper accounting, when the only records that remain for us to examine from those claims and exchanges are bundles of knotted cords.

10 Does Rumor Lie?

Narrators, Trust, and the Framing of Unsecured Information

Gary Alan Fine

N APRIL 1991 fliers appeared throughout African American communities in New York City claiming that Tropical Fantasy, a recently introduced and increasingly popular low-priced soft drink, was adulterated with a mysterious chemical that sterilized those men who consumed it. The company, so the story went, was owned by the Ku Klux Klan and wished to emasculate black men, in effect performing an act of genocide. The story was treated as plausible because the primary outlets for the drink were convenience stores in New York's working-class African American communities. Many whites and middle-class blacks were unfamiliar with the soft drink. Some New Yorkers claimed that the alleged ill effects of the drink had been exposed on ABC's news magazine *20/20*.[1] Sales of Tropical Fantasy plummeted in its inner-city target market, and it was reported that some distributors had been threatened with baseball bats and that bottles were thrown at drivers of delivery trucks.

Of course, the story was false. Brooklyn Bottling, the family-owned company that had once specialized in seltzer, counterattacked, asking the FDA to test the drink and had then-mayor David Dinkins, himself African American, consume a bottle of it on television. Some people, including the owners of

GARY ALAN FINE is John Evans Professor of Sociology at Northwestern University. He has authored numerous books and articles on rumor, gossip, and contemporary legend, including *Rumor and Gossip: The Social Psychology of Hearsay* (with Ralph Rosnow), *Manufacturing Tales: Sex and Money in Contemporary Legends*, *Whispers on the Color Line: Rumor and Race in America* (with Patricia Turner), and *Rumor Mills: The Social Impact of Rumor and Legend* (edited with Chip Heath and Veronique Campion-Vincent). He is currently completing an analysis of rumors about terrorism, migration, and international trade, entitled *Whispers on the Border Line: Rumor and Global Politics* (with William Ellis).

Tropical Fantasy, believed that the rumor was spread by larger beverage companies or disgruntled former employees, while others suggested that competing truck drivers were instrumental in spreading the story. However derived, the claim was swaddled in falsehoods.

.   .   .

Lying is a challenging concept for a social scientist. It assumes that individuals are knowingly—maliciously—providing false information to audiences, relying on their audience's predisposition to trust. It assumes the conscious rejection of consensual moral values in favor of what is, presumably, self-interest. In our hope to protect ourselves from ethical stain, we establish the category of "white lies" to distinguish those falsehoods that we justify because of an allegedly greater good from those that lack such justification. White lies preserve our purity. Sometimes, as Schauer and Zeckhauser note (this volume), we edge further from lying, engaging in paltering, directing attention in ways that deceive without, precisely, deceiving. We believe that we are preserving our purity by choosing to mislead without explicitly conveying false information. However, when knowingly false claims cannot be justified through assertions of benefits to others—or when we convince ourselves that we are technically accurate, albeit not in the way we believe that the claim will be understood—we find ourselves in the dark reaches of the human soul. Knowingly spreading false information to benefit oneself at the expense of others is not a wholesome activity, but it is all too often a reality.

The line between rumor and lying is faint. Rumor is defined as unsecured or unverified information, a truth claim that has not been legitimated by the imprimatur of recognized social institutions or by confident assertions of personal knowledge.[2] As a statement of fact, rumor lacks recognized backers, yet it does not simply appear from the ether. Rumors are verbal or written texts that are spread by a person or group and received by another person or a group, representing an intersection of speakers and audiences. Often enough, the source or details of a rumor are forgotten or transformed in memory, and this provides some license for imprecision or alteration. Because of our inability to confirm their accuracy, rumors are situated within a sociology of localism; the trust that we place in these claims is a function of the context in which they are spread: the who, what, where, how, and why of diffusion. At times we may plead with others to accept the validity of what we are proposing, as Tom Lutz (this volume) describes.

For a rumor to be a lie, the information must be not only unsecured but also contrasted to a claim that the presenter believes better reflects reality. For the audience, the existence of alternative knowledge undercuts the trust that is typically given to a speaker's assertions and to the speaker's motivation. The speaker must be aware that the information is wrong but still willing to make this claim to an audience. Personal knowledge is part of the politics of deception. This returns us to the problem of the malevolent rivals of Tropical Fantasy and to many other examples of mercantile rumors. It is often believed—sometimes with a basis in reality—that employees of rival companies deliberately spread rumors aimed at competing products and services. Given a folk view of corporate capitalism—economics red in tooth and claw—consumers find it plausible that McDonald's would be gunning for Wendy's, Wendy's for Burger King, and Burger King for McDonald's. The existence of a culture of deception in the marketplace seems plausible for many, because self-interest is perceived as trumping ethics. As a result, lying is often treated as a primary motivation for rumor. While such motivation cannot be dismissed casually and may apply in particular cases, we err if we proclaim that a bright line divides an uncertain claim from certain knowledge. More often, people rely on the comforting ambiguity of rumor. They spread claims that seem implausible without actually being lies, thus preserving their moral integrity. Not knowing "for sure" the veracity of a rumor can be a tonic for expressing one's beliefs, permitting elaborate and heartfelt narratives. Speakers hold different standards of how plausible a claim should be and how credible a source they require before they will spread information. To appreciate the space between rumors and lies, we must consider how convictions about the plausibility of a claim and the credibility of a claims-maker are manipulated by those who choose to transmit accounts.

The Politics of Plausibility and Credibility

For rumor to serve as communal knowledge, it must be perceived as reflecting something that might reasonably have happened or will soon occur. A claim that is outside of one's primary framework of experience is often framed as humor, a put-on, teasing, deception, or some other realm that is not to be judged as empirical truth.[3] This does not mean that rumors need to be considered as "true." We willingly accept stories about which we are not certain. Belief does not demand certainty.[4] This does not mean that people embrace stories that they know to be wrong, but often they will not inquire too closely about accounts that are "too good to be false."

As Guido Möllering (this volume) emphasizes, truth and falsity are often unknowable, but some decision must be made about how much trust to extend to a claim. No one wishes to be taken in by a lie, but few wish to be so suspicious as to be skeptical of all claims. With regard to truth, there are Type I and Type II errors: naiveté and cynicism, undeserved conviction and undeserved distrust. Understanding rumor as reflecting "unsecured," "unverified," or "suspect" information reveals the dilemma inherent in treating rumor as either being true or false. A more appropriate question is, who has the authority to describe a particular set of truth claims as definitive or as unsecured? Put another way, what person, group, organization, or institution has the right or power to determine the legitimacy of a truth claim, not just in its accuracy and its usability, but in whether it should be treated as rumor? Such a focus involves asking when and how rumors are accepted as claims to be believed and spread. In a world that is awash in information, what criteria will knowledge communities rely on to make distinctions?

This process constitutes the politics of plausibility and the politics of credibility. By the first, I refer to the conditions of verbal or written bodies of speech, or texts, that lead audiences to provisional acceptance of a proffered claim and the possibility of further transmission or action. The politics of credibility connects to our evaluation of the source: whether we award credibility and whether the fact that a particular individual is the source of the claim will be incorporated into the body of information when it is further transmitted, substantiating its believability. Credibility is a characteristic of interaction and of relationships. As noted, in making these choices people rarely transmit information that they know to be false, but they can choose to avoid knowing. They can avert their eyes from examining the means by which assertions are to be judged. As reputations are often linked to the information that is spread, narrators attempt to avoid the label of liar, deceiver, or unreliable source. When uncertain information is being transmitted, communicators strategically establish distance between self and story.

The Challenge of the Uncertain Narrator

Narrators often discover that they are married to their tellings. A narrator that a community considers to be trustworthy and as unlikely to deceive will find that this characteristic rubs off on the narrations that he or she presents.

The reputation of the narrator in a local information field affects how information is judged. Certain individuals, by virtue of their position within a communication network, are expected to have legitimate access to knowledge and are expected to be "honest brokers" in their reportage. To be sure, this does not always apply, but that is our expectation. Our awarding of authoritativeness to a set of social actors is linked to their connection to facts and to our assumption of their willingness to provide those facts without deliberate deception. Trust is essential to the stability of an information realm, creating a connection between trustor and trustee, audience and narrator.

Audiences have opportunities to impute motives to a speaker that provide for a challenge to credibility, opening the possibility for questioning or re-evaluating the plausibility of a verbal or written text. Trust is always in play in local social systems. To appraise the credibility of a source, audiences evaluate a narrator's remove and motive.

Remove   Audiences typically assign weight to truth claims that are from individuals who are defined as being in a position to know. They are not socially removed from the events on which they are reporting. Government spokespersons are often granted this assumption of closeness, particularly as regards their statements of fact, as opposed to claims of motivation. It is legitimate to question a press secretary as to why the president acted in a particular way, whereas it would be odd—and perhaps offensive—to question whether the president acted. The press secretary has the authority to know because of her placement in an information field. These actors are believed to be able to ascertain truth, and audiences often treat this information as "fact," releasing it from the demands of personal evaluation. In contrast, motivation, as an internal state, can be readily disguised and linked to strategies of deception, thus claims that present an actor's motivation are treated as problematic.

Audiences routinely decide whether a speaker is likely to have acquired information from trustworthy sources, and they judge the degree to which the information seems plausible by virtue of the process by which it was obtained. As a result—and ironically—personal gossip may be treated as being more likely to be true than are claims from the same sources about the larger social system. Narrators are deemed more likely to know about their personal lifeworld than about the institutional order. Local knowledge carries great weight. A narrator's claim of having received information from the media or from friends of friends, often a salient part of truth claims, is an attempt to bolster one's trustworthiness, given one's remove from the reported fact.

Motive   Motive is the worm in the apple of belief. Does the narrator have a reason to deceive, to palter, or to shade information? The assumed motivation of a speaker influences how audiences will interpret his or her message. This is connected to what J. L. Austin speaks of as the "illocutionary force" of an utterance.[5] What is the person attempting to do in making the claim? What kind of statement is it by virtue of its likely motivation? Recognizing this, speakers shape the assumptions of their audiences by presenting "motive talk" and by providing accounts, giving their own assessment of their motivation.[6]

Audience judgments of motivation relate to interest and history, both connected to social trust and the assessment of deception. Most audiences are predisposed to accept the claims of others, unless compelling reasons suggest caution. In evaluating a speaker, we ask whether she has something to gain or hide, or whether he has provided poor information in the past. Political commentators, lovers, and parents know that they must interpret with care the claims of those who attempt to persuade them. In some cases, such as the presentation of many rumors, the narrator does not have much invested in the audience's belief, and the stories are told from a desire to entertain or to gain confirmation of an uncertain claim. In these cases, doubt as to the plausibility of the claim can be entertained without questioning the honor of the speaker.

The importance of history or narrator reputation is well known to those authoritative spokespersons, swains, and children who, in presenting information that is once deemed false, find that their later sincere utterances are questioned. They have cried wolf once too often. Deception can become part of an established reputation. Each text affects the response to those that come after: these judgments resonate with narrator credibility. Those who acquire reputations as malicious gossipers or rumormongers discover that their later statements are discounted.

The Context of Credibility

In practice, information is variably linked to its source, as the circumstances and settings of communication affect interpretation. In most instances an audience evaluates the narrator, while also evaluating what is narrated. On some occasions, demands for knowledge swamp the characteristics or the character of a narrator.

When information spread in the aftermath of the assassination of President John F. Kennedy, few questioned the identity of the source, particularly when media confirmation quickly followed. These sources were empty nodes in a social network and could have been filled by anyone. Contrary to much information transfer on mundane occasions, a significant amount of information was spread by strangers on that November afternoon. Gaining information was so important that it was assumed that narrators had no motivation to express anything other than the truth as they knew it.

Similar patterns of diffusion occur in the wake of sudden and cataclysmic disasters, such as the aftermath of the South Asian tsunami or Hurricane Katrina. Such occasions have the potential for diffusing information that is subsequently learned to be inaccurate. Wild claims may be accepted as plausible because of public consensus and because of the assumption that no one is motivated to deceive. Yet it is precisely for this reason that a set of secondary truth claims can be entertained as plausible without considering the characteristics of the narrator. Put differently, there is little need to challenge the information given. Often the local context and the striving for information of any kind outweigh the evaluation of the narrator.

Tamotsu Shibutani emphasizes this feature of rumor in his classic study of rumor, *Improvised News*, stressing: "In disasters one of the first things that men seek, after saving themselves, is news. Sometimes they become so desperate for such information that they get careless about its source."[7] The care that one takes over confirmability depends greatly on circumstances, particularly in light of the rumor's immediacy and importance. Accounts that are either immediately relevant or unimportant are least likely to be questioned. Rumors of disaster have great immediacy and importance, creating a demand for action, whereas contemporary legends tend to have the opposite characteristics—little immediacy and little importance—and are narrated in circumstances of good fellowship without pressure to act. Both types of rumors are accepted at face value without a heavy critique. The assumption is that nothing is to be gained by deception. Truth claims that are consequential but do not require immediate action are the ones that audiences are most likely to doubt. It is here that audiences can imagine narrators with personal interests, which leads them to question the claim's plausibility.

The physical location of narration also shapes its evaluation. Some contexts, encouraging a demand for action or for sociability, promote credibility. Credibility operates differently at a cocktail party than at a seminar. One can get away with broader truth claims in informal situations before being called to account. Perhaps the need for sociability is so insistent that questioning the honesty of one's source in a setting such as a cocktail party might imply rejection of the person and the event. In contrast, the narrower and seemingly more proven claims made at a professional seminar might be trusted with less-overt criticism, because the speaker's seriousness of purpose is assumed. Occasions that provoke assertions by those with vested interests, such as speeches at political rallies, lead to suspicion.

How a truth claim is presented also influences its reception. Performance styles convey those genres in which speakers desire their remarks to be placed. While style has numerous dimensions, one of the most important in the examination of informal communication concerns the communicator's desire to distance him- or herself from the information and its plausibility. In these cases, the narrator does not demand total belief and may doubt the accuracy of the proposed truth claim. Much informal communication is narrated with ironic detachment. Conversational markers, such as tone, gestures, and paraverbal cues, suggest to an audience how the material is to be treated. Some statements claim the mantle of facts, others disdain this claim, and still others are agnostic about how they are to be judged. Narrators of rumor—particularly narrators of statements that claim to be rumor—tend not to be heavily invested or fastidious about the truth of their accounts; instead, they maintain role distance, encouraging discussion about the information's validity and allowing audiences to select their levels of belief.[8]

The Dynamics of Audience

Students of rumor have undertheorized the role of the audience. Audiences can be analytically divided into those that are present and those that are implied. The latter category includes audiences that are not recipients of personal verbal communication, as described by Jeffrey Hancock (this volume). Those who compose their words for a present audience can, in the course of presentation, determine the extent to which their truth claims require proof, incorporate deception, or elide certainty. Likewise narrators on television, film, video, tape, radio, or the Internet find themselves talking to empty others; they must assume how their audiences will respond. Those talking on the telephone or those visually impaired have a somewhat reduced version of the same problem, although these narrators depend on the verbal or paraverbal responses of their audiences. The more feedback available, the more an account can be shaped to make it plausible.

Audiences also differ in their emotional tenor and their evaluative stance—their willingness to embrace claims—in part a function of the context of performance and in part a consequence of the characteristics of the audience and its relation to the speaker. Some audiences are critical, whereas others are accepting or gullible. Critical ability is tethered to the topic but is also characteristic of the audience.[9] Business executives may be motivated to examine the hidden, hostile motivation of the narrator of a mercantile legend, whereas those who mistrust the structures of late capitalism might find the same story plausible, accepting it at face value.[10] Systems that depend on cynicism and conflict for their sociopolitical organization may be more accepting of such "manufacturing tales" that support this worldview than societies that depend on consensus.

The audience generates a politics of plausibility and credibility in addition to that created by the context and the narrator. The identical body of information can be treated as certain truth by one person, as a plausible account by another, as a wild speculation by a third, and as a deliberate fabrication by a fourth.

Audiences have a moral and communal responsibility to make talk flow smoothly.[11] Good talkers need good audiences, and, in some measure, good audiences generate good talkers. In informal discourse, being a good listener does not mean that one is respectfully silent while an authority talks. Conversation is not a lecture. In contrast, a narrative is often a collaborative performance.[12] This especially characterizes rumor, for which audience confirmation may be desired. A narrative may be, in effect, a question more than an answer, and in such cases a good audience is an actively involved, questioning participant. Deception may be less problematic than is uncertainty under such circumstances.

A further characteristic of a good audience is that it supports the speaker's intentions and contributes to the achievement of the speaker's goals, whether or not audience members accept those goals as their own. Audience members need not believe the claim, but they must recognize it as a truth claim. Smooth interaction, one of the bases on which a civil society depends, must be negotiated. Rumors do not depend on a suspension of disbelief, but rather on a belief in the primacy of conversation. In this, what goes on in the head is of less significance than what goes on via body language and spoken utterances.

Cultures of Judgment

Rumors are spread and judged within communities. Information and its evaluation are socially located and are not merely the result of individual decisions. Although rumor researchers properly examine the characteristics of audiences and their critical ability to judge rumor, these approaches downplay how communal judgments create shared response. Rumors are evaluated within cultures of judgment. This is akin to distinguishing between personal memory and collective memory. While memories belong to individuals, they are shaped and become useful when they transcend individuals to take on a social reality. Rumor belongs to a Durkheimian framework that treats collective representations as determining action. These communities operate both on the level of interaction and through analytically separate processes of institutionalization, where belief systems are more than a collection of believing selves.

An audience must determine whether it should trust the proffered claim. While individuals rely on personal assessments, few individuals are in the position to judge truth for themselves, although they routinely accept working hypotheses. As Eviatar Zerubavel emphasizes in his discussion of cognitive sociology, cognition is a social phenomenon.[13] What we believe has much to do with our location in the interaction order, that is, what groups and social networks shape our experience. We judge statements and persons based on shared standards for evaluation. We reside in communities of judgment. These communities provide the basis by which we embrace the evaluations of others, sharing our autonomy with those whose word we count on.

The community of judgment permits rumor to be translated into trust or to forswear that trust. As a result, this generates protection against deception. The community establishes the relationship between rumor and trust, and this social engagement affects the extent and vibrancy of rumor in a community.

Trust and Rumor Intensity

The extent of rumor within a social system varies widely, but how are these differences linked to the presence or absence of trust within a social system?[14] While I describe several critical dimensions, a smoothly functioning civil society requires a moderate level of rumor, both in its frequency and diffusion. Up to a point, rumor bolsters the social order. Societies characterized by distrust and those characterized by fear or apathetic acceptance are likely to have more and less rumor, respectively, than those with an active public sphere. In this analysis, I address five dimensions through which patterns of rumor can be distinguished as related to trust: frequency, diffusion, boundaries, divisiveness, and stability. Each reflects the form that trust takes as revealed through the distribution of unsecured communication.

Frequency

A first question that arises about rumor is how much is present. This is a difficult question to answer in that the boundaries of what constitutes rumor are unclear, and no adequate methodology can determine the precise amount of rumor being spread. In practice, one can inquire about the number of distinct rumors that are active and about the frequency of rumor transmission. In other words, social systems may be characterized by many rumors or by a small set of rumors that are widely spread (or, of course, by many widely spread rumors). In each case, the existence of rumor reveals uncertain public confidence in the adequacy of a social system in providing information. In cases where information is not crucial, rumor is entertainment, but when information is suppressed, transmission of rumors becomes resistance.

A society in which much rumor spreads (particularly those claims that address consequential social issues) is characterized by institutional breakdown: either institutions are not communicating, or they are not believed to be providing accurate, fair, or necessary information. Authoritarian states are the classic instances in which rumor frequency has been linked to system failure.[15] In these cases, the public rejects official information. Informal communication channels provide alternative knowledge streams, avoiding manipulative sources. While the state may attempt to suppress oppositional public knowledge, complete control over talk is impossible. State workers may share extraofficial claims with those in their personal circle. Rumors in democratic states with traditions of free speech may be less robust or consequential than those in societies in which an Orwellian-style government forcefully attempts to stifle what citizens can know. Authoritarianism justifies the spread of rumor, serving as counterhegemonic political discourse or as the basis for revolutionary change.

The extreme expression of this is totalitarianism, differing from authoritarianism by the degree of surveillance and political control over citizens' lifeworlds. The cases of Nazi Germany (in contrast to Fascist Italy) and Stalinist Russia during the purges (in contrast to Communist Hungary) exemplify these systems. In such regimes, speakers and audiences can be sanctioned for participating in alternative knowledge systems. Because of the importance of the communication, rumor will continue to spread, but its frequency will be dampened or locations circumscribed because the state steadily increases the transaction costs of rumoring. It is an empirical question as to how repression decreases rumor (or shifts its location), although systematic research is impossible. In this case, the information revealed through rumor becomes more valuable as it becomes scarcer. Trust in the system, tied to internalization of official values and identification with authority, is replaced by pressured conformity.[16] Under conditions of repression, the speaker must trust audience members not to reveal the source of their knowledge.

More rumors with political implications are expected in systems that lack institutional trust, provided the costs of diffusion are not perceived as excessive. In turn, the existence of competing claims and explanations—presenting alternative truth realms—should decrease the degree of trust that citizens award to the system. Thus the amount of political rumor and trust in a system operates in a recursive fashion.

Diffusion

Distinct from the number of rumors circulating within a social system is the extent of rumor diffusion. Here, two dimensions are relevant: how rapidly and how far a rumor will spread. A rumor can spread with white-hot speed while reaching only a corner of the society; or, in contrast, it may spread steadily but slowly and achieve wide dispersion. In considering patterns of diffusion, the forms of communicative technologies used are crucial. In the light of recent technological changes, the Internet has proven a major shaper of the diffusion of rumor.[17] However, this medium is only the most recent example of a similar phenomenon, as evidenced by the effects of telephone, television, radio, telegraph, fax, and print. Technology shapes transmission patterns, creating the temporal organization of communication and lines of trust, depending on how the technology is seen as encouraging or discouraging honest and knowledgeable talk.

Technologies have temporal structures. Because of the low cost of diffusion, rumor in cyberspace spreads rapidly and can then quickly collapse in the face of contradiction or doubt. Internet communication represents an archetypal example of minimal trust invested in anonymous diffusers. The Internet, with its anonymous or uncertain communicators, is often scorned as an information bazaar that institutionalizes a philosophy of caveat emptor, but in reality there are fewer buyers than renters among the audiences.

Other methods of rumor dispersion, including word of mouth, have different patterns of diffusion, and are trusted differently. The politics of credibility are linked to the form of diffusion. Information systems are treated in terms of the political structure of the social system in which they are embedded. The openness and cost of participation differentiate technologies, along with the possibility of surveillance, a feature that affects the extent to which citizens trust the security of private or counterinstitutional claims.

Information technologies operate at different speeds and with different ranges. The mass media make information available in a different fashion than does face-to-face communication. Electronic media can rapidly communicate (and retract) information, reaching diverse populations, whereas direct, interpersonal communication depends on lengthy strands of contacts, typically those who have much in common. Rumor that spreads through word of mouth typically has a longer lag time between the rumor origin and the slowing of diffusion; the decay of memory is slower as well. Each medium has a potential audience that shapes the extent of diffusion, as some technologies do not reach all populations.

Trust differs in these conditions. Face-to-face communication depends on the local negotiation of trust in which the audience can make an informed and immediate assessment as to how much trust to award. In contrast, in mediated communication the previously established reputation of the source becomes the basis for trust, less subject to negotiation. Deception is possible in both domains, but in the case of face-to-face communication, the trustee has the challenge of controlling the various forms of nonverbal communication from leakage (Frank, this volume) in the face of those who might discern the deception (O'Sullivan, this volume).

Boundaries

Related to diffusion are boundaries of information preserves. Imagine two societies in which a rumor reaches half the population. In one society, communication is random, a function of who on a given evening happens to be listening to a radio broadcast popular among all citizens. In the second society, radio listening is linked to gender. All women hear the rumor, but no men do. While the extent of diffusion is identical, the dynamics of rumor differ greatly. In the second case, what appears to be a single society turns out to be—in terms of its informational boundary—two nonintersecting societies sharing a geographical space.

The most dramatic contemporary instance of the power of demographic boundaries to shape communication networks and trust involves racial divides. Black Americans and white Americans are said to have distinctive racialized pools of knowledge.[18] Sadly, and too often, one race is unaware of the beliefs of the other. Being dominant, white Americans are particularly liable to be unaware of the knowledge claims of African Americans, having little direct access to black media and perhaps feeling no reason to be concerned about these beliefs. Rumors in the white community tend to be better known, if only because white-dominated media are more accessible to a multiracial public.

African American rumors, tied to local claims of how society operates, often suggest the presence of broad institutional conspiracies. A notable example is the belief in "The Plan," an assertion that white elites systematically discredit or murder any black leader who effectively articulates the grievances of the community.[19] The report that the HIV virus was developed in a government laboratory as a form of biological warfare is similarly largely spread within the black community.

Rumors in white communities have different content. These claims typically suggest that blacks—individuals or small groups—have committed or are planning a horrific crime. Rumors about cannibalism in the aftermath of Hurricane Katrina take on this form, as do claims that aspiring members to black gangs were required to rape blonde virgins in order to be initiated. Unlike rumors in the African American community, these rumors do not assume systemic malice; instead, they presume that idiosyncratic events (that often never occurred) are characteristic. They assume moral depravity, rather than structural malevolence.

When divergent beliefs are discovered, the assumption of community and its underlying trust is shaken. Communities become divided and distant. White Americans privately assert that black Americans are paranoid in their fears of a continuing policy of racial animus or genocide, whereas blacks assert that the rumors that are spread in white communities reveal covert racism. The willingness to accept rumors that others dismiss depends on the politics of plausibility, tied to historical consciousness. Within a community, rumors represent the updating of collective memory in light of current understandings.

The default belief is that all people have similar understandings. To be sure, the existence of stories that depict wickedness reveal that equality is not taken for granted, but at least it is assumed that all citizens share a body of knowledge. When that assumption is challenged or even negated, trust in the equality of social participation is challenged. Societies in which informational boundaries are most salient are those that must confront issues of cross-community trust most explicitly.

Divisiveness

The content of rumor is closely linked to social boundaries. Does the content bind groups together in a common cause or does the content prove divisive? The classic rumor research of Robert Knapp distinguished among fear-based rumors, wish-fulfillment rumors, and wedge-driving rumors, the last a salient category in times of war and ethnic strain.[20] Divisive rumors fall into the category of wedge-driving rumors, both bolstering and responding to the boundaries of informational divides.

Rumors can separate groups either demographically or institutionally. They can generate suspicion and a breakdown of trust. The "Lights Out" rumor of the early 1990s asserted that African American gang members drove their cars with their headlights off. When courteous (white) drivers flashed a warning, these Samaritans would be murdered. This claim exacerbated mistrust toward young black male drivers, at least temporarily. Similarly, rumors detailing attacks of male sexual predators divide men and women.

Divisive rumors also undercut trust in the legitimacy of authority. Véronique Campion-Vincent argues compellingly that the public increasingly embraces rumors that uncover elite conspiracies.[21] Suspicion of outsider groups is now joined by mistrust of social institutions. While this is not a new phenomenon (suspicions of bankers and politicians have a lengthy pedigree), such claims entered mainstream discourse over the past several decades. Many rumors doubt official, institutional truth and give more weight to unsecured knowledge, critiquing social policy.[22] Rumors that assert that the Federal Bureau of Investigation is targeting dissidents or that the Federal Communications Commission will soon ban religious programming transform policy disputes into questions about the legitimacy of the institutional order. Rumors within African American communities proclaiming that authorities deliberately target communities of color not only reveal the boundaries of diffusion but also emphasize that worldviews can be divisive.

Plausibility judgments not only cause, but are embedded in, preexisting social divisions. Demographic and institutional malaise breed rumor. In societies in which mistrust exists about the actions of demographic groups or political institutions, rumors are easier to start, they seem more plausible, and they enter into memory as reflecting the divided lifeworlds of citizens.

Stability

The final category relevant to the relationship between trust and rumor concerns the degree to which information is stable over time, long a topic of rumor research. Rumors vary in how rapidly they change. Early research from Allport and Postman, relying on Bartlett, examined the dynamics of memory. They asked what processes alter the content of rumor, suggesting forgetting (leveling), emphasis (sharpening), and cognitive consistency (assimilation).[23] The spread of rumor is likened to the game of telephone, in which children whisper a phrase through a chain of participants. What is reported at the end bears little resemblance to the original message. The recognition that information can be garbled is a source of great amusement for children, but for adults it is more troubling. In practice, however, rumor does not alter quite as wildly as misheard phrases in a children's game, but the idea that communication can be systematically distorted has been central to rumor scholarship.

While it is generally assumed that rumor texts become truncated as they are transmitted (as in laboratory simulations of real-world rumor chains), some evidence exists that under favorable conditions, such as with community excitement, rumors can be elaborated.[24] When narration is status enhancing and when audiences plead for more information, imaginative details may be woven into an embellished account.

Stability can be conceptualized either as temporal stability or as content stability. The former addresses whether the same rumors are recalled over time or whether they will fade from memory and become latent, with the possibility of reemerging later. Content stability refers to whether the details that are narrated remain constant. When examining a corpus of rumors, instances of temporal instability are easily recognizable. Many rumors are forgotten or are no longer actively spread. Content instability occurs when the targets of rumors change (from Jews to Asians, K-Mart to Wal-Mart, or Phil Donahue to Oprah).

Stability is linked to the dynamics of trust in that unstable rumors suggest a society pressured by social change. However, a lack of stability may be interpreted in two alternate ways: it may suggest a society that is open to change—incorporating new content and processing emerging concerns—or it may indicate that new fears threaten to overwhelm social order. Rumor scholars have not yet developed techniques to test these hypotheses, in part because of the difficulty of gathering rumor texts systematically. Until these methodological problems are confronted, rumor research will be little more than insightful hunches and informed guesswork.

Credible Witness

Rumor stands at some distance from certainty. This permits it to be used by those who hope to deceive without precisely deceiving, relying on a strong desire to trust. While investigations of rumor do not suggest that lying is very common in the web of unsecured information, deception does happen and—more significantly—is believed to happen. Most people do not feel comfortable in deliberately presenting falsehoods and reject considering themselves as liars. As a result, they structure their communication to skirt these labels while still communicating what they wish and need to say through phrases such as "I heard . . ." or "Could it be true?" These rumors connect to the discussions of paltering in other chapters in this volume. In this desire to appear to play straight, as much self-deception as public deception takes place. The frames of interpretation that Erving Goffman has spoken of—play, put-ons, fabrications, testing—help to transform lying to something else that is at least marginally more innocuous.[25]

Responses to rumor are a function of plausibility (features of the statement) and credibility (features of the teller). Both plausibility and credibility are filtered through the assumptions and desires of audience members. Rumor is embedded in a community—a knowing and trusting group—and the structure and culture of the group affects individual interpretations.

Rather than treating rumor as a characteristic of a communication, it is fruitful to regard it as tied to a local social structure. Rumor is fundamentally relational and symbolic: it is linked to information that speakers and audiences consider plausible, given their worldview; that is transmitted by credible sources; and that conveyers announce in appropriate circumstances. In turn, the credibility of the conveyers of information depends on how they present their identities and how those identities are received.

To understand informal communication as a sense-making enterprise demands that we focus on the orientations of the parties to talk. This complex minuet of comprehension occurs without most hearing the music. Rumor reveals standards of evaluation by which both social scientists and the public judge claims about the reality of our shared world. As we trust and as we are sometimes deceived, we must select which truth claims deserve the label of lie, which of truth, and which of rumor.

11 Crocodile Tears, or, Method Acting in Everyday Life

Tom Lutz

C ARL BERGSTROM'S Indo-Malayan octopus (or fish, or sea snake, or anemone—for, which is it?—the thing presents itself, somewhat deceptively, as all of them) is the kind of natural phenomenon that can make a lay person like me, someone with only the most woefully incomplete collection of scientific knowledge, ask stupid questions: Does it know what it is doing? How can it be so smart? Has it studied these other life-forms and practiced its mimicry in some kind of mirror? The octopus, which can flatten itself out and perfectly impersonate a flatfish, stretch itself out to look like an eel or snake, or wave its tentacles in the air to suggest an anemone, all based on perceived threats or feeding opportunities, is one of the several animals Bergstrom mentions that masquerade as others to gain an advantage (Bergstrom, this volume).

The ability to deceive has obvious evolutionary advantages, he suggests; but within species, information sharing is necessary, and therefore a certain level of what might be called honest dealing. Thus the evolutionary conundrum is this: how does a species balance the necessity for cooperation with the strategic advantage an individual might gain from deception? How does any species manage to square trust and fraud, since both have individual and

TOM LUTZ has taught at Stanford University, the Universities of Iowa and Copenhagen, CalArts, and now the University of California, Riverside. He is the author of *Doing Nothing* (2006), *Cosmopolitan Vistas* (2004), *Crying* (1999), and other books. He is at work on a limited series for television about the Teapot Dome scandal and a book about attention.

collective advantages and disadvantages? Bergstrom offers a systemic answer, having to do with redundancy, distributed control, and other factors, but even this leaves me asking the silly question, again: What does the octopus know and when does he know it?

Having no stake in octopus biology, I am only interested in the question for how it might shed light on human deception. Investigators have tried to pin down the nature of that deception in a number of ways, including developing a taxonomy, dividing deceptive acts into paltering, impersonation, self-deception, distortion, rumor, misdirection, and, of course, outright, intentional, motivated verbal deception. This last category, which is the one that has the most vibrant social and juridical life and perhaps the most extreme costs, turns out to be the least interesting as a conceptual category, and the in-between cases, those in which deception shades into its less obvious—and less obviously culpable—variants, are where the quest for understanding deception seems most fruitful.

My question about the octopus's intentions, for instance, was itself a mild form of deception. I represented myself as a naïve anthropomorphizer, someone who can only think of animal behavior in terms of human understanding, and this is not true. I paltered for a reason: I wanted my audience to do the thought experiment with me, to imagine the octopus with a human brain, and I did this for a specific purpose. I knew I would be asking, eventually, for readers to imagine human beings with octopus brains, that is, to imagine what our interpersonal deceptions would look like if we take conscious reflection, intention, ethical decisions, and the other aspects we consider part of human deception out of the equation. I wanted to ask my audience to consider our mutual deceptions as part of an interactive system in which the question of ethics never appears (for in most discussions of deception, ethical questions are seldom far away), just as we would never ask the octopus, "How can you be so disingenuous, so fraudulent, so underhanded?" The deceptive octopus is, after all, simply being the best octopus it can be. My essay here is about human deception that is as *impersonal*, one might say, as the morphing of the octopus: deception at its most sincere, most honest, most fully human; deceit we might even go so far as calling necessary, normal, and, finally, a kind of trustworthiness. Or at least I like to think of it that way.

What follows is a personal story that gets at some fundamental issues about deception in everyday life, but one that I know is also a somewhat peculiar tale, an anecdote that even I can see needs a sympathetic audience. Thus I probably should not have started this reader-writer relationship with a slightly deceptive rhetorical flourish, and for that I apologize. (Of course, my apology is itself a kind of paltering, since if I was really sorry I would edit it out; my apology was simply another attempt at disarming the reader by admitting, right up front, my failings.) The story features me as an emotional antihero, at a certain point dissolving into tears, and not being, by most standards, particularly honest. Why would I choose to tell such a story to an audience of strangers? Why tell you all that I am a man who has wept in an attempt to get his way—how embarrassing! (This, too, naturally, is a dishonest question, since I think I know why. It is just a ruse meant, somewhat counterintuitively, to develop trust, to suggest that, since I am readily willing to admit that I stretch the truth sometimes, I am a trustworthy narrator. In other words, perhaps I lie so that you will trust me. I tell this story because I am, as all untrustworthy narrators eventually declare of themselves, an honest man.)

So here, then, is the story.

Once upon a time, about a dozen years ago, I met a woman, a successful journalist, a writer for the major newspapers and magazines. Like a lot of people who experienced that low moment in the prestige of the humanities, I was itching to write for a "larger audience," and she and I talked about a number of ideas I had, none of which had obvious appeal for the fashion magazine where she was a contributing editor. Because of my work in the history of nervous diseases, she suggested I might do something on shoe fetishes—women's shoe fetishes, the whole question of why a woman with dozens and dozens of pairs of shoes would feel an overpowering urge to drop hundreds of dollars on yet another pair. I never got very far with that project, perhaps because, finally, I simply did not understand women.

I thought I did. Early in this budding relationship, when we were telling our first batch of self-defining stories to each other, I bumped, somewhat accidentally, into how wrong I was about that, and at the same time into the problem of crying and deception. As we lay together in bed one night, I told the tale of my traumatic youth, my own heroic origin myth, and by the end of it my eyes had welled up; nay, they were brimming with tears, so affecting, at least to me, was my story. I looked into her eyes and was a bit taken aback, frankly, to see that hers were dry as a bone. She looked, in fact, what I can only call standoffish. Vaguely disconcerted, I let a tear fall.

Now, to some people, this action may already seem not particularly manly or romantic, but, I came to find out in subsequent years, such weepiness has a long history. Ancient cultures are full of stories of lovers' tears. Ovid, for instance, counseled young men to seduce women with tears, and women who could not cry naturally, he wrote, should learn to fake it. The medieval saints all considered tears the true mark of their love for God. As late as the 18th and early 19th centuries, tears were seen as a normal part of sexual and other forms of intimacy—Thomas Jefferson claimed (to a married woman he was seducing, thus proving, if proof were needed, that the duplicity of adultery is not a recently evolved presidential trait) that there existed no more "sublime delight than to mingle tears with one whom the hand of heaven has smitten!"[1] The 18th- and 19th-century poets and novelists all wept and represented weeping men. During the 20th century's concerted effort to get men to stop displaying "feminine" emotions, such intimate crying became largely women's province; but even then, Spencer Tracy, Humphrey Bogart, and the rest of our cultural models for masculinity occasionally let a tear drop in their romantic exploits. In the late 20th century, under pressure from various feminisms, with men getting back in touch with their feelings, the weeping male lover become more prevalent yet again, and there is nary a major male movie star today who has not wept on screen for love—any more than there are male presidential candidates who will not drop a tear, or at least well up at the appropriate moment, on the stump.

Still, weeping remains primarily coded as feminine. When I was in my twenties, I mingled tears with a few lovers, and the first time I cried always caused me a great crisis of confidence, a fear that my unmanly weakness would be ridiculed rather than comforted, that I would find incomprehension rather than empathy. As the seventies turned into the eighties, I began to realize that not only were my tears unlikely to be repulsed, they were regarded as a sign of my emotional maturity, my sensitivity, and my general state of enlightenment about things intimate. Although I never fully articulated these things to myself or others, I clearly had begun to understand myself as a minor feminist hero, and I had begun to take a certain amount of pride in my own openness and fearlessness in the face of conventional vulnerabilities. I also had begun to take for granted (at least in retrospect; none of this was entirely conscious) my lovers' respectful and enthusiastic response to the marvelous, deep qualities evidenced by my tears.

But this woman was conspicuously unmoved, while eyeing me skeptically. My first response, although it is a bit embarrassing to admit, was to let myself go a little more.

Now I say this as if it were a conscious decision—it was not, really, at all. Nonetheless, I let another tear drop, and then one more.

Her suspicion increased rather than subsided. It was only at that moment, really, that I became conscious of what I was doing and realized that tears were falling from my eyes. When I realized this, they stopped.

And only then did I start to have some inkling about how insincere this performance of my own deep feeling could seem and, indeed, might have become. This woman was not snowed by it. She said, in fact, that she had come to mistrust crying men, especially men of my ilk, who had learned the lessons or at least the various etiquettes of feminism. "Look," she said, "I've been around the block. I've been cried to before." It seemed to her that some men, rather than delving honestly into their own souls, had learned to use crying as a bit of cover whenever the necessity of true self-disclosure presented itself. I wiped my eyes, blinked, stared at her, and felt a bit sheepish.

As we talked, she made it clear that she was pleased that I was not afraid to cry, and pleased that I felt the desire to be as intimate with her as my couple of tears implied. She just did not think I deserved any particular accolades for the performance and did not assume that those tears proved, once and for all, my sincerity. Of course, she was right: however sincere my tears might have been at one level, they represented a performance that had meanings well beyond any that I consciously intended. They could mean that I was either sincere or insincere, a neurotic wuss or a romantic hero, enlightened or benighted, all or none of the above.

My tears could mean, for instance, that I was just trying to be some kind of New Age Thomas Jefferson, using tears as part of the process of seduction. I remember a conversation in the early 1990s, when a woman in her thirties told a friend and me that she had never seen her husband cry during their three years of marriage. My friend, a bit of a lothario, was shocked. "After three years!" he said, laughing. "Wow. I cry on the first date!"

Now, I do not think I was really an emotional Machiavellian, trying to maximize my advantage through the combined flattery and coercion of tears, and my wife-to-be was not accusing me of that. I had some vague sense of the allure of tears, but my tears were not merely produced as tools for seduction. I was sincerely articulating deep emotion. I was, even if she was not, moved by my own story. This meant that, among other things, I was honestly offering for view what I thought of as my truest and realest self *and* trying to appear a certain way, the way I had concluded, through some subconscious calculus, that would make her fall in love with me. Like a form of existential method acting, my tears were the result of real feeling manufactured for a purpose—both a simulation of the real emotions I wanted acknowledged and a mask designed to represent the person I understood myself, at least ideally, to be.

And I have since realized in thinking this scene through that something else was at work. My tears, like an infant's tears, were the honest expression of another, albeit related, desire. That sincere wish was, as is often the case with an infant, simply a desire to be cradled and comforted. Groping after sanctuary, my tears were meant to initiate a warm bath of shared emotion with which to ward off my fears and doubts; fears and doubts about, among other things, this relationship I was entering. I sincerely wanted that kind of comfort and, I believe, not in an entirely selfish way. I knew that such intimacy—however crisscrossed by multiple motives, projections, and misconceptions (and, seen from certain angles, deceptions)—had rewards and pleasures for both of the actors in the drama. I had experienced such pleasure from the other side, comforting my lovers as they cried and providing cover in their storms of self-doubt and self-disclosure. I knew that there was a potential for mutual pleasure and that I was asking for and offering one of the mutually compensatory sensations that romantic lovers can provide for each other. This is one of the reasons that in the 18th century mingling tears was thought to be the most intense form of pleasure and among the loftiest forms of human interaction. It is a way we create, at least for the nonce, a sense of confidences proffered and accepted, prayers answered, affection reciprocated, a way for both egos to be stroked, with the dyad awash in manufactured trust.

And yet on that night, as my future wife suggested, something else was going on, as well, something that may be, as Sartre suggested, fundamental to emotional experience.[2] Tears can be a sign of intense, intimate engagement, but they can also be a means of escape. As we weep, we can turn our attention away from the world and direct it at the sensations of our own bodies, which in turn can give us respite from whatever thoughts, concerns, anxieties, or demands that might, in fact, have brought us to tears. Emotions can be substitute satisfactions, magical thinking that remakes the world into one that is closer to our desires. Like Alice, floating away on a river of her own tears, weeping can move us away from the current moment, whatever that happens to be.

Tears are engagement, tears are escape. And more: tears also sometimes signal neither intimacy nor oblivion, but submission. Children learn early to cry as a way to ward off parental anger or punishment. Tears can be a way to say "you win, I quit," the human equivalent of a dog putting its tail between its legs. Perhaps I was trying to present myself as submissive, as someone who was willing to lay himself bare, open to emotional attack—my tears were a way of saying, "Here, as I tell this story, I can go no further down the road of vulnerability than this; I have preagreed to your judgment, you can stop making it." My partner was too wise to fall for this beta dog act. She knew she could yet get bitten.

Although this was not the first time I had wept in front of a lover, it was the first time I had, goaded by her distrust, examined my motives. Examination, of course, tends to kill feelings. Seeing a bear in the woods, for example, causes a rush of adrenaline. We run, we reach the car, we drive away. All of a sudden, now in safety, we feel our heart beating at close to its maximum rate. Sometimes this is enough to send us into a panic again, realizing how close we came. Sometimes, however, we put two fingers to our throat and look at our watch, timing the beats. We are no longer afraid, we feel the bodily effects waning. We think: "Wow, I was scared. That was a lot of adrenaline. Wow, I don't think I ever ran that fast. I could have died!" We are feeling things, but we are no longer full of fear.

Under my lover's scrutiny, and thus my own, my enchantment with my own tearful state was waning; she did not want to play, at least not that game, not yet. Tennis anyone? No? We put the racket down. Crying, as it is from the very beginning of human life, can be a demand, and however unclear the demands of wailing or the more tentative requests of a whimper might be to their audiences—however less clear than a verbal demand, perhaps—tears nonetheless sometimes have their own eloquence. We all learn early on—at the breast, as it were—the power that crying has to communicate our desires. But when the persuasiveness of the rhetoric of tears is ineffective, when the demand is not met, stopping is the only option. Severely neglected infants, in fact, stop producing tears. And only a fool keeps asking for what is categorically denied. In this case, I had not quite realized that I was making some kind of demand until my lover said, in effect, "no."

In *Adam's Rib* (1949), the classic screwball comedy, Katharine Hepburn and Spencer Tracy play a wife and husband who are lawyers on opposite sides—she defending, he prosecuting a woman accused of attempting to murder her philandering husband. During the day they argue the case in court, and at home at night they go through a series of fights and reconciliations, both convinced that they have justice and reason on their side. During one fight, Hepburn begins to cry, and Tracy throws up his hands. "Here we go again!" he says. "The old juice! Guaranteed he-man melter: a few female tears, stronger than any acid. But this time it won't work. You can cry from now until the jury comes in but it won't make you right." Weeks later, when they are on the verge of divorce, he begins to cry, truly saddened at the pass they have come to. She sees it and is moved. He sees it has an effect on her, and cries some more. She joins him in tears and they decide to stay together. Later, he claims that he had faked the tears to keep her from leaving, but she refuses to believe it. "Those tears were real," she insists, and he agrees. "Of course they were," he says. "But I can turn 'em on anytime I want. Us boys can do it too, only we never think to."

The fact is that neither Hepburn's nor Tracy's characters turn them on artificially, and his claim to be able to control his tears is a bit of classic male bluster. He is also, self-evidently, exaggerating when he claims that men never think to cry, since he obviously has. My wife, who in no other way resembles Spencer Tracy, was also not going to be duped by tears. I was, in fact, as she suspected, asking her to believe, with the story I had just told, that we had just reached the innermost sanctum of my feelings, that I was standing before her in complete and uninhibited emotional nakedness. This she was shrewd enough to discount as false bravado, as exaggeration, as premature. We had known each other only a month or so, after all. But that does not mean that I was being intentionally deceptive. My tears were true and untrue, sincere and insincere, duplicitous and honest, manipulative and honestly communicative, intentional and unintentional, all at the same time.

The fact that my wife partially rejected my communicative gambit, likewise, does not mean that she was simply uncovering the truth beneath some falsehood. She was also performing a role, a role that was both sincere and somewhat less so, suggesting to me that she was a tough customer, not easily swayed. By refusing to mirror my emotions, she was, among other things, doing a bit of self-presentation as well, offering me one of her notions of herself, which is that of the compleat skeptic, the "it means nothing until you have two independent sources" investigator, the been-around-the-block, hard-nosed reporter. Maureen O'Sullivan (this volume) discusses the "accusatory reluctance" that often allows deception to go unchallenged, and it is precisely part of my wife's tough-cookie persona to pointedly have no such reluctance. This is a deep part of her character, so she was not completely faking it, but at the same time, I came to learn, she also can weep unrestrainedly at a

Broadway musical, as sappy a form, short of emo, that exists. She had to leave halfway through the remake of *Lassie* because she was sobbing. Her refusal to mingle tears was due to both more and less than she let on. She *was* the unsentimental woman-about-town she purported to be, but she was also a bundle of other, conflicted, overdetermined motives and desires. She was being self-protective, she was acting out of a fear of the very intimacy being offered, she was hiding behind the dry-eyed facade. And, truth be told, she was being a bit of a control freak, unwilling to let her guard down. As a hardboiled tough gal she was literally playing a role, one that revealed and concealed what she was thinking and feeling. I was doing the same thing, of course.

Again, it is impossible to determine with any clarity whether at such moments we are being deceptive, whether we are, in Gary Fine's words (this volume), in those "dark reaches of the human soul," where we knowingly make false claims to manipulate people to our own ends. Most of the time, I would contend, we are in some much murkier zone. What he calls the "complex minuet of comprehension" can only be at best partially understood, and only as a mess of tangled intentions and understandings that work as much against as with each other. Both people in an intimate encounter are trustors and trustees (in Guido Möllering's sense of the terms, this volume), with all the contingency, vulnerability, and self-deception that this requires.

Möllering proposes that we understand such scenes as the one I've just laid out as attempts at the leap of faith required for mutual trust. I was using tears as signs that cannot easily be faked in order to establish my trustworthiness. He understands that there is something deeply fictional about such transactions, that we at some point need to act "as if" we could trust another person in order to have trust. Eventually my wife-to-be and I came to understand that we were both being somewhat deceptive and somewhat honest, both of us a bit sincere and a bit insincere, and that we were going to accept a certain level of trust and lack of trust as endemic and go ahead and get married. We liked whatever odd dance we were doing that night and decided to continue throwing these manufactured self-images at each other to see what would stick.

Perhaps what we mean by "trust" comprehends the full complexity of such moments: the constantly shifting interactions and expectations; the fluidity of both honesty and deception; and the fact that what honesty and deception and trust and distrust mean in any particular instance are constantly, moment by moment, under revision, the question of their validity constantly deferred. Thus it makes sense when the lovers in Shakespeare's sonnet that

Kenneth Fields (this volume) reminds us of, lie to each other as a form of simple, everyday flattery, or when Lennon and Ono define love as a double fantasy. What does it mean to tell someone he or she is the most beautiful person in the world? What are the chances that such a statement might be true? One in three hundred million. And yet it is said in complete honesty by millions of people each hour. Does it matter that the speaker might, under torture, for instance, admit that he did not really believe it to be true? Or that she only believed it to be true "in a manner of speaking"? Möllering (this volume) suggests that deception can be defined as "deliberate misrepresentation of an actor's identity, intentions, or behaviors as well as the distortion of any facts relevant to the relationship between" two people. But how deliberate? What percentage deliberate? And is there ever any love without it?

If my lover and I had ended in some nasty bout of mutual recrimination, though, our dishonesty with each other at that moment would mean something entirely different. If we had each ended up simply as minor actors in the other's catalogue of dating gone bad, the whole scene would appear, necessarily, infinitely more sordid, we might easily go down in each other's chronicles as duplicitous, as unforthcoming, as unsympathetic, as jerks. But the interaction and the overlay of motives would have been the same. It is also worth noting that, whatever honesty we mustered at that moment means something now, almost fifteen years later, that it simply could not possibly have meant an hour, a day, or a month after it happened.

What this all suggests, I hope, is that the binary thinking we are pushed toward in all of our considerations of trust and deception, all of our attempts to understand truthfulness and deceit, necessarily fails to account for the endlessly recursive variety of motives and understandings informing any intimate encounter. To examine duplicity is to watch it quickly disappear into multiplicity. When my wife and I began to talk that evening about what had just passed between us, we moved quickly through a number of topics, including tears in fiction and film, our own family histories in relation to tears, theories of emotion from psychology, philosophies of emotional expression, and the ways children learn to use, abuse, and control their emotions. Here we were doing something else again, displaying our intellectual and cultural abilities and attainments, showing off a little, testing each other, measuring each other, monitoring our effect on the other, and so on. I do not remember a specific instance, but I will bet very good money that each of us, at one point or another, suggested (tonally, gesturally, or verbally) that we knew a little more about some aspect of what we were talking about than we actually did. We were, at that moment, trying to deceive the other into thinking that each was smarter or better read or more astute than either one of us truly was. We were presenting ourselves as the people that, if push came to shove, we were willing to try to actually be in order to win each other's esteem.

Do we not generally "trust" that people exaggerate their good qualities somewhat, however, and factor that tendency in? Do we not assume the deep waters, the system of mirrors, the endlessly peeling onion? If we do, if such an understanding of human complexity governs our decoding of each other's statements, are not our minor deceptions themselves a form of ritualized truth telling? Who knows what tipped off my wife—she is a very good poker player— perhaps some small tic of mine, some "microexpression" (see Frank, this volume) or "leakage cues" (Hancock, this volume) made my performance fail in its primary mission. But if she had accepted my tears at face value (as it were), would there have been, in retrospect, more deception or less?

The talk we had that day had one other consequence: at one point during the discussion she said, "That's it. You should write a book about crying." Reader, I did. I made a study of crocodile tears and the rest of the weeping bestiary, reviewed the social scientific and physiological literature, sifted the literary and artistic record for lamentations of all kinds, and wrote a book.

All of this study had one very interesting effect for me. I cry less. I no longer trust tears. Or, I suppose it is more accurate to say I now habitually distrust tears, my own and others. And I suspect (in fact I assume) ulterior motives. I assume deception. I have become my wife. I suppose that happens, too. Is it paltering to say so? Perhaps it is more accurate to say that, like Carl Bergstrom's octopus, and similarly unconsciously, I have learned to impersonate her, at least some of the time.

IV DECEPTION AND INSTITUTIONS

12 Deception and Trust in Health Crises

Ford Rowan

MISLEADING STATEMENTS by public officials can erode public trust in government and hinder efforts to cope with emergencies. Three public health threats in North America in the first decade of the 21st century—the anthrax attacks of 2001, the SARS outbreak in 2003, and the aftermath of Hurricane Katrina in 2005—are instructive. Taken together they show how misleading statements, exaggerated assurances, and efforts to blame others can undermine confidence that the government will act in a competent, trustworthy manner. As will be described below, outright deception is only one of the ways trust can be forfeited; even the *perception* that officials have deceived the public can significantly confound the public health response. For instance, two months after the worst bioterror incident in U.S. history, the anthrax attacks, the American public felt so misled by federal officials that nearly twice as many people said they would trust their local officials rather than federal leaders to advise them what to do in an anthrax attack.[1]

The anthrax episode is one example of how, in a time of extreme danger, with a newly apprehended risk, the suspicion that leaders are not telling the truth could compound the disaster. Trust is fragile. But trust is a crucial element during an emergency when people need information on how to protect themselves, their families, and their communities. In a terrorist attack,

FORD ROWAN is professorial lecturer in organizational sciences at George Washington University. He chairs the National Center for Critical Incident Analysis and has served on the board of the Santa Fe Institute.

particularly a bioterror attack, or a naturally occurring pandemic, trust may be the key to whether society can cope with the physical and psychosocial consequences of mass casualties. The case studies demonstrate that trust would be crucial to the successful transmission of lifesaving advice about a newly apprehended health risk, such as a pandemic.

The political context is not favorable for trust in American officials. Over the past four decades, skepticism about the trustworthiness of officials has been prompted by such controversies as the Vietnam War, the Watergate scandal, Iran-Contra, the Clinton impeachment, and now, the dispute over the war in Iraq. After the attacks of 9/11, Americans responded favorably to strong leadership and put their faith in public officials to combat al-Qaeda. But five years later many felt misled about the conflict in Iraq and took vengeance on Republican leadership at the polls. It is important to note that deception does not have to be established beyond a reasonable doubt for trust to crumble. "Leaps of faith enable trust to take place," Guido Möllering states (this volume), but when expectations are not met, those who trusted others feel betrayed "and the leap of faith will quickly turn into a lapse of faith." He notes that simple disappointment from unfulfilled expectations can escalate to intense frustration and anger.

Dashed expectations may not be the product of purposeful deception. We can be misled in countless ways: mistaken statements by officials, flawed strategy, botched execution, hype and exaggeration, and naïve hopefulness by the public. Almost by definition, poor leadership misleads. When expectations are trounced, particularly in life-threatening situations, the public may respond as if it had been deliberately misled. Several authors in this volume (including Maureen O'Sullivan and Mark Frank) have noted how difficult it is for most people to accurately detect when they have been deceived—often their detection skills are worse than random chance. The flip side of this phenomenon is that people may erroneously conclude they have been deceived even if more benign explanations can account for dashed expectations. Either way, trust is lost. And with it, official leadership can be crippled in a crisis.

This chapter explores ways that public trust was lost in prior crises and how it can be earned by officials. The credibility of officials depends upon (1) the honesty and accuracy of what they say, (2) the ethical character of their decisions and (3) the reasonableness of actions that they do (or fail to do). The lessons from the anthrax attack, SARS, and Katrina suggest ways that the government can build healthy trust and avoid some of the downside risks of losing the confidence of the public or of using deceptive means to generate blind trust.

The Public Health Challenge in a Crisis

Public health measures to cope with a contagious disease outbreak can include mandatory interventions and stringent prohibitions on the activities of people infected with, or potentially affected by, an emergent disease. Examples from past outbreaks include quarantines, vaccination or treatment, physical examination or diagnostic testing, travel restrictions, epidemiological investigations, and breaches of patient privacy. Such interventions would interfere with rights and freedoms that people believe are protected under the U.S. Constitution. These measures can generate tension between the public and government officials and have in the past been the focus of public unrest during disease outbreaks. Because civil liberties are at stake, the suspicion that officials are acting deceptively can poison public acceptance of such mandates.

If such interventions were to be invoked during a pandemic, it is likely that social disruption and potential violence will be a major concern. During a period of increased public unrest we are faced with the prospect that personnel that could be used for enforcement of the public health measures will have to be drawn from a wider pool than local and state law enforcement officials, as many of these will be suffering from influenza. National Guard forces may play a key role in augmenting law enforcement personnel. The use of troops may increase the tension between a scared public and those trying to restore order.[2]

Officials may be tempted to minimize the risks, give false assurances, exaggerate their own actions, and manipulate public opinion. The anthrax attacks, the SARS outbreak, and the Katrina aftermath in New Orleans catapulted beyond health crises and were characterized by law enforcement challenges, allegations of racism, and fear mongering by the news media.

In case of a pandemic, any actions to minimize the negative reactions of the public and generate behaviors that can benefit the impacted communities will be of great value. In a worldwide pandemic, the assumption that people will feel "we're all in this together" may prove erroneous. Those ill with the disease and those who belong to what are feared to be the main carrier groups can be stigmatized. This can include avoidance, segregation, and abuse and may even lead to acts of violence. All kinds of disparate but corrosive effects may occur: friends, family, and neighbors may be feared—and strangers above all; the sick may be left uncared for; those felt to be carriers may be shunned or abused. People often overlook medical concepts of disease in favor of long-standing folk explanations based on ethnic or social stereotypes, as Nelkin and Gilman note:

> We still use disease to protect our social boundaries or to maintain our political
> ideals. And, at a time when control over disease is limited, we still blame others
> as a way to protect ourselves. By drawing firm boundaries, that is, by placing
> blame on other groups or on deviant behavior, we try to avoid the randomness
> of disease and dying, to escape from our inherent sense of vulnerability, and to
> exorcise the mortality inherent in the human condition.[3]

During the SARS outbreak in Toronto, some individuals became fearful of all people who looked Asian, regardless of their nationality or actual risk factors for SARS, and wanted them to be quarantined. Fear of being socially marginalized and stigmatized as a result of a disease outbreak may cause people to deny early clinical symptoms and may contribute to their failure to seek timely medical care. It has also been noted that stigmatization associated with discrimination often has social and economic ramifications that intensify internalized stigmatization and feelings of fear.

Unlike the SARS example, the wide geographical spread of a pandemic disease would move quickly beyond any one ethnic group and encompass most of the world's population. Therefore, although it may not be possible to blame specific ethnic groups for the spread of disease or for representing a higher risk from infection, it is possible that people who work in high-risk vocations may be stigmatized. Workers in professions that come in contact with infected persons may be perceived as representing a higher risk of transmitting the disease and result in their being targets of stigmatizing or discriminatory actions by other people. During the 2003 SARS outbreak, health care workers and their families were among the groups identified as experiencing significant episodes of stigmatization and discrimination. The fact that these people were risking their lives to treat disease sufferers did not protect them from the negative reactions of persons intent on avoiding direct contact with anyone who could possibly transmit the disease.

Newly apprehended risks—such as avian flu and bioterrorism—create new challenges for ordinary people. They create unprecedented choices about how individuals can protect themselves and their families, as Baruch Fischhoff has stated:

> As citizens, they must decide which policies best serve the nation's desire for physical safety, economic vitality, civil liberties, and social cohesion. Without good information, people may find themselves living with choices that they do not understand or want. Feeling that they have been denied critical information further complicates an already difficult situation. If things go badly, having misunderstood the risks can intensify the attendant pain and regret.[4]

The common good may conflict with the values of civil liberties, posing important and critical choices for the average person. Americans consider their freedom of movement to be a basic right. Imagine the problems that restrictions on travel and quarantine might trigger. And as citizens are told what they cannot do, they will watch in vain for the government to find a quick medical cure to stop the spread of the disease, particularly in the early stages. The limited resources to combat influenza will likely cause confusion and increased anxiety based on the perception that "not everything is being done to help us." Medical services would almost certainly be reserved for those who are government officials, emergency personnel, and health care workers. Triage would be necessary, but how would someone who is unsure of the criteria feel if his or her sick child were to be left untreated?

Dysfunctional psychological and behavioral health responses to a disease outbreak can impede response efforts. For example, psychological and psychosomatic distress responses (grief, anger, fear, depression, and psychosomatic illness) and behavioral changes (such as ignoring public service announcements about hand washing) may decrease an individual's ability to adhere to public health measures that minimize personal exposure and minimize disease transmission in the community. Maladaptive emotional and behavioral responses can disrupt the economy, overtax the health care system, and provoke efforts to take protective actions that backfire.[5] The consequences can include the following, according to Reissman and her colleagues:

- Psychological distress
- Fear and suspicion
- Psychiatric illness
- Multiple unexplained physical symptoms
- Stigmatization and discrimination

- Altered behaviors (such as the use of alcohol and drugs)
- Altered perceptions about safety and danger.[6]

Accounts of the 1918 pandemic flu are filled with descriptions of a disease that exhibits frightening characteristics. As the outbreak occurred during the First World War, officials were secretive and did not accurately reveal the enormity of the death toll. Misleading information and false assurances would be the kiss of death for public trust in a future pandemic. To effectively manage the outbreak and decrease the psychological damage that results from a pandemic, the managers of any incident must seek to institute measures that:

- Maximize public trust and effectiveness of communication
- Maximize adaptive behavior change
- Reduce social and emotional deterioration while improving adherence and prosocial functioning
- Maximize professional performance and personal resilience for key personnel in critical infrastructure.[7]

Trust as a Crucial Element in Risk Communication

The potential for an influenza pandemic creates new challenges for communicating risk. Much has been learned from dealing with environmental and public health controversies over the past three decades, particularly in situations when the public felt deceived by corporate or government statements. These lessons can be applied in a disease outbreak. Undoubtedly, timely and accurate communication will be critical to ensuring public cooperation and understanding during a pandemic. Better communication has been advocated by Covello and Sandman as a way to deal with such things as fear, frustration, helplessness, outrage, anxiety, and distrust.[8] Four ways to improve risk communication are targeted:

- Agencies must avoid errors in decisions and messages.
- Officials must maintain public trust in sources of information.
- News organizations need to avoid amplification of risk.
- Officials must encourage individuals, communities, and families to use coping mechanisms, particularly protective steps.

For more than 30 years, risk communication has evolved from a scientific focus (quantifying the probabilities of hazards) to one that also considers the cultural and social factors influencing risk perception. The National Academy of Sciences stated in 1989 that risk communication is "an interactive process" involving "multiple messages," including some "not strictly about risk" such as "opinions" and reactions to legal issues and institutional management. The academy's recommended approach is to treat people as partners in a dialogue with the leadership of interested groups to ascertain their concerns, fears, ideas, and demands and to agree on ways to address these issues.[9] Over the years of dealing with environmental health controversies, it was realized that quantification of risk takes a backseat to quality of life and other value issues during such crises.[10]

The New Orleans hurricane experience is relevant: lessons can be learned from the way people were forced into shelters without adequate provisions. Promises of assistance proved to be deceptive in some instances. In the case of a pandemic, it is not difficult to imagine that people trapped in inner cities and told they cannot leave their homes might feel abandoned and discriminated against. Allegations of racism and unfair treatment of the poor surfaced in New Orleans due to the mishandling of a flood. Consider a national health crisis in which state and local governments attempt to restrict the movement of millions of people. Risk communication efforts can be greatly compromised if the news media focus attention on the plight of outraged victims.

Authorities usually want to do the talking, to portray themselves in the best possible light as leaders, rather than engage in dialogue with the public. Communication can be defined in three ways: what I say, what they hear, and what we learn. Many people never move beyond the I-oriented view of communication to consider the impact of their messages on their audiences. The decision of what to say is very important, but speakers should focus on what the audience hears, remembers, and ultimately acts upon. Communication is a two-way street and an essential conduit of learning for individuals and society. The purposes for communicating range from informing to educating, from persuading to motivating, and from manipulating to coercing.[11] Many Americans become unsettled when a communicator moves from offering choices to forcing actions. Deception is a way to obscure a manipulative or coercive goal.

When people are informed about risks, they want an unambiguous answer to the question: Is it safe for me and my family? The public is not interested in scientific theories in the immediacy of a potential crisis. People want to know what should be done about the risk.[12] Yet clear and definitive answers are rarely possible, and dealing with uncertainty is a difficult but essential part of risk management. Although authorities may be tempted to keep people in the dark about risks (why scare them?), organizations that hide information risk ruining their credibility when the problem is exposed. Any suspicion of a cover-up can hinder subsequent efforts to communicate risks and cause the public to feel powerless, fearful, and even outraged upon hearing about a newly disclosed threat to public health. People's main motivation is to protect themselves and their families, thus feelings of powerlessness are especially problematic. Risk communication is about *more than* just technical hazards and probabilities of harm. It is intimately related to peoples' values; thus psychological, social, and cultural explanations must interact with the risks in ways that can heighten public perception and affect positive behavior.[13]

Risk communication is also about the prospect of loss. Complex technical health information is difficult to comprehend in a time of stress. People process risk information in the context of their ability to control the risks.[14] Voluntary risks are perceived as less risky than coerced risks. Risks that an individual has direct control over seem less risky than uncontrolled ones. Risks that are familiar appear to be less risky than unfamiliar risks. Risks that are judged to be fair seem less risky than unfair ones. Additionally, risks that provide direct benefit seem less risky than ones with no payoff. Such factors—familiarity, controllability, voluntariness, fairness, and benefit—affect who knows, who decides, who pays, and who gets what. In sum, they are all about power. Life seems very risky, indeed, when people feel powerless. The downside of risk perception involves people feeling left in the dark, deprived of choice, coerced into accepting uncontrolled risks, and feeling overrun by the system.[15] Such feelings of political impotence trigger outrage and lead people to reject the advice of experts. What many people want is not to be told by officials what the scientific risks are, but rather to force the system to listen to and address their concerns.

Successful risk communication aims to empower people to choose the best alternative to reduce the risk to themselves and their families. Slovic attributes shortcomings in this communication to lack of trust in the sources of information. If the risk manager is trusted, communication is relatively simple, but if the level of trust is low, then communication cannot bridge the gap. Slovic noted the following difficulties for those who want to be trusted:

- Trust is easier to destroy than create.
- Negative events that diminish trust are more noticeable than trust-building efforts.

- Trust-destroying events carry greater weight with the public than positive events.
- Bad news is seen as more believable than good news.
- Distrust, once initiated, reinforces and perpetuates distrust.
- Distrust colors interpretations of events, reinforcing prior belief.
- Once trust is lost, it may take a long time to regain it.[16]

Trust appears to be correlated with the way people perceive risk and accept or reject advice from experts.[17] In some cases, people may trust an expert but still reject his or her advice about risk because they may recognize that not enough is really known about the risk.[18] The credibility of the source of information is one of the most important determinants of effective risk communication.[19] There is some debate over how specific the expertise of the leader must be for effective communication with the public about a particular hazard.[20] Clearly, the more the source of information is perceived as an expert about the specific threat, the more likely trust will influence how well the information is received by the public.

Various teams of social scientists have tried to measure the attributes that constitute trust. In addition to expertise and competence, they include caring and empathy, openness and honesty, fairness, commitment, and dedication to duty.[21] Motivation seems as important as competence because the receivers of information are vulnerable. People "prefer to trust rather than be suspicious," Paul Ekman states.[22] But if they discover they have been lied to, the psychological impact is that the victim of the lie has to face his or her own mistake in having been taken in.[23] Elsewhere in this volume, O'Sullivan notes the reluctance to detect deception because the consequences are great. "Lying is a very basic exercise of power," according to Michael Lynch. The liar's gain in power results in the victim's loss.[24] The psychological and power costs are why trust once lost is so hard to regain.

Lessons from the Anthrax Attacks: The Need for Accuracy

The anthrax episode was an unprecedented event in the United States, one that was fraught with uncertainty. In September 2001, *B anthracis* spores were sent via the U.S. Postal Service to several locations in the nation. The letters were addressed to political leaders and news media organizations. Twenty-two confirmed or suspected cases of anthrax infection were tallied, and five persons died. The fear that spread was out of proportion to the death toll. After the first case surfaced, the extent of the danger posed by unopened mail was slow to emerge. Concern first centered on Congressional staff members who worked in buildings where tainted mail was opened. Awareness about the danger to postal workers came more slowly. It took weeks for a dawning recognition of the extent of the risk, first to people who opened letters containing anthrax spores, then to those who worked in adjacent rooms, then to those who processed the mail, and then to those who received a letter that had been comingled with a contaminated envelope. Although anthrax is not contagious, the fear spread as it became clear that the risk extended far beyond the addressee of a letter from the perpetrator.

Immediately prior to the first diagnosis of an anthrax case, the government was trying to reassure the country shocked by the 9/11 attacks. Health and Human Services Secretary Tommy Thompson appeared on CBS's *60 Minutes* on September 29, 2001, and proclaimed that the United States was prepared for biological attacks and urged people not to be concerned. Officials who had worked on preparedness issues at his department, including Margaret Hamburg, recalled being "apprehensive because we knew that simply wasn't true." She dismissed his upbeat comments about preparedness as "wishful thinking."[25] Within a week, Thompson's predictions were shown to be too optimistic. False assurances failed utterly.

When he disclosed the first case of anthrax on October 4, Secretary Thompson reassured the public that this was an isolated case, that the infection might have occurred naturally by drinking water from a stream, and that it was not a case of terrorism. As he spoke, Dr. Larry M. Bush, the doctor who had diagnosed inhalation anthrax in Robert Stevens, the first victim, knew that Thompson's statements were all incorrect. The federal government decided to centralize all official statements from one spokesperson, a political appointee, and Thompson ordered his public health officials not to speak to the media. This decision resulted in the initial exclusion of knowledgeable experts from the airwaves and newspapers such as those at the Centers for Disease Control (CDC), the Federal Food and Drug Administration, and the National Institutes of Health. Only later would they be called upon to speak on the technical issues that eluded the more senior, political appointees.

With the confusing and contradictory statements emerging from Washington, DC, skepticism grew about the technical advice being provided. The anthrax episode coincided with people's already wary views of technical explanations for risk. As Pat Caplan stated before the anthrax attack, "The faith of a previous generation in the ability of science to provide answers has turned to doubt, partly because scientists themselves are not in agreement, partly because the answers science now gives are much more complex and contingent, and partly because 'they' are always changing their mind."[26] This assessment proved right in the anthrax case, in which botched explanations from ill-informed spokespersons set the stage for misunderstanding and mistrust.

The government was off to a slow start in communicating with the medical community as well as other public health specialists. It was not until October 12, one week after the first anthrax-related death, that CDC issued its findings on the computerized *Morbidity and Mortality Weekly Report* (MMWR) website. The former editor of the MMWR, Lawrence Altman, was then working as a correspondent for the *New York Times*, in which he wrote on October 16 that "the bulletin that doctors and health workers look to for information about communicable diseases, devoted only two paragraphs to the anthrax situation, providing only sketchy details of the first two cases and a description of anthrax symptoms." Altman added, "As a former editor of the report, I know that it can quickly transmit needed health information." But the bulletin's current editor, Dr. John W. Ward, called the report "out of the loop." CDC spokespersons, by then freed to comment to the press, seemed not to have access to information about cases in Florida and New York, Altman stated. They issued "puzzling statements," and in response to a query from news reporter Altman, "they asked me to explain the science, saying they did not understand it or had not been informed."[27] Dr. Julie Gerberding, who headed the CDC's National Center for Infectious Diseases at the time of the anthrax attack (and who would later become director of the CDC) recalled that few persons, including doctors or municipal health officials, could get information from CDC.[28] Existing data was not always correctly interpreted or applied by health officials, the media, or the public. For example, it was incorrectly stated that a person needed to inhale ten thousand anthrax spores to become infected. The CDC did not recognize the importance of a Canadian Defence Forces study released in September 2001 about how fast and far an anthrax stimulant powder contained in envelopes could spread in a room. There was no process for identifying and dealing with the novel scientific questions that arose.

Scientific uncertainty caused confusion at CDC, according to Elin Gursky and her colleagues.[29] They conclude that poor communication among health officials, the media, and the public compounded the problem: "The lack of a consistent, credible message emanating from CDC in the early days after the anthrax attack has yet to be fully explained."[30] Senator Bill Frist noted how conflicting messages about risk, about who should be taking antibiotics, and about how the mail ought to be handled led to distrust, confusion, and fear, "sometimes bordering on panic." Frist said that gaps in the public health system became "glaringly apparent."[31] For example, when the CDC sent an alert on bioterrorism to all state health departments after 9/11, word did not reach local hospital emergency rooms for days or weeks. One-fifth of public health offices did not have e-mail. Disease surveillance and coordination require updated communications technology. "As we witnessed during the anthrax scare last fall, we must improve and streamline our methods of communicating with the public," Frist said.[32]

The errors and inconsistencies that surfaced during the anthrax episode include the following items:

- On September 30, Secretary Thompson stated that the nation is prepared for bioterrorism.
- On October 4, Thompson said that the first case is likely due to naturally occurring anthrax.
- From the beginning, reassurances were given about the safety of the mail.
- On October 18, Brentwood (DC) postal workers were assured of workplace safety.
- CDC initially believed that anthrax spores could not escape a sealed envelope.
- CDC initially advised postal workers not to take antibiotics.
- Even after it was learned that one Trenton, NJ, postal worker had developed an anthrax lesion, workers there and at the Brentwood facility were reassured that they were safe.
- The Bush Administration initially silenced health experts at CDC.
- Conflicting messages were broadcast about "weaponized" anthrax spores.
- Inconsistent information was given regarding how many spores were needed to cause infection.
- Postal authorities failed to quickly close contaminated postal facilities.

- Disparate treatment was apparent regarding precautions for the (mostly white) congressional staffers and the (mostly black) postal workers.
- Information about the benefits of different antibiotics used for congressional staffers and postal workers was incomplete.
- The failure to act quickly caused the deaths of two postal workers.
- The risks and benefits of postexposure vaccination were not adequately explained.

This last item—inadequate information about vaccination—is a sad postscript to the efforts to prevent disease among the postal workers. In mid-December, Secretary Thompson decided to make a vaccine available to ten thousand persons who had been taking antibiotics as an added precaution against the possibility that spores remained in their bodies. The anthrax vaccine in question had been approved only for preventing the disease before exposure to anthrax spores. Now, it was being recommended for postexposure, an unapproved use that required patients to sign consent forms acknowledging that they understood the risks. This caused a storm of controversy among postal workers, who said they were being asked to enter into an experiment. Of those ten thousand eligible, only 130 persons decided to be vaccinated.[33] The federal government's credibility had hit bottom.

From the onset of the anthrax episode, the national news media was critical of the federal government's response. The handling was criticized as "badly coordinated"[34] and as stressing on the public's nerves.[35] The *National Journal* stated on November 11, 2001, that the public health response amounted to "contagious confusion." On January 6, 2002, the *New York Times* criticized the government's actions as "missteps." *Time* magazine chimed in on January 12, proclaiming it "clumsy handling." Of course, news headlines alone do not prove that the federal government performed as poorly as alleged, but scores of stories in major publications raised doubts about what was being done to protect the public. The repeated criticism had an impact.

A comprehensive opinion poll showed the public's reaction to all the news about anthrax. It was conducted within two months of the disclosure of the first outbreak of anthrax by the Harvard School of Public Health and funded by the Robert Wood Johnson Foundation. The study found that Americans were not panicking over anthrax but were beginning to take precautions, including handling the mail with care. The poll of more than one thousand people had a margin of error of +/−3.74 percent. About one-fourth of persons surveyed were very or somewhat worried that they could contract anthrax from opening mail at work or at home. The most dramatic finding, according to Robert Blendon, who directed the project, was that "no national figure emerged as a source of reliable information" during the anthrax outbreak.[36] Americans were more likely to trust public health officials than political leaders and more likely to trust local officials than national figures. Asked whom they trusted, respondents gave the following answers:

- Director of the federal CDC: 48 percent
- U.S. Surgeon General: 44 percent
- Local or state health director: 52 percent
- Director of the FBI: 33 percent
- Local police chief: 53 percent
- Director of Homeland Security: 33 percent
- Local fire chief: 61 percent
- Personal physician: 77 percent.[37]

In every case, local and state officials were judged as more trusted than federal officials. One surprise is that the local fire chief was more trusted as a source of information about a disease than the federal officials in charge of protecting public health. While fire chiefs had credibility, it is unlikely they had as much expert knowledge as the head of the CDC or the surgeon general.

To the credit of the CDC and the Department of Health and Human Services, these officials have made a concerted effort to learn from the errors of their handling of the anthrax attacks and to provide accurate information in any future health emergency. These improvements have occurred as these agencies considered how to prepare for a possible pandemic.

Lessons from SARS: The Need for Ethics

The recent experience of Severe Acute Respiratory Syndrome (SARS) illuminates the importance of ethics in public health actions. The efforts by Canadian officials to stop the spread of the disease in Toronto are instructive; they help to bring ethical issues to the surface and to cast light on their resolution. The perception in Canada that officials acted with sound ethical guidelines increased public trust in their actions, even when they took steps that increased public fear of the disease. Most important, Canadian officials did not copy their foreign public health colleagues who had suppressed information that the disease had been detected in other countries, creating problems as SARS spread across the globe.

Of particular relevance is the experience with isolation of ill persons and efforts to quarantine others. Isolation is the separation and confinement of individuals known or believed to be infected with a contagious disease to prevent them from transmitting disease to others. Quarantine is the compulsory separation and restriction of movement of persons who may have been exposed to a disease in order to segregate them in specific areas to prevent the spread of disease.[38] Quarantine is a controversial option in an outbreak of illness, and its consideration has been made more urgent by the threat of bioterrorism. The Canadian experience with SARS can inform U.S. planning for a response to a pandemic or bioterrorist attack. If we face a contagious disease outbreak, Tara O'Toole warns, "[we] do not want to be figuring out at the last moment whether [we] should institute a quarantine, or clap somebody into mandatory isolation, or implement an immunization program by force. [We] really need to think these things through long before [we're] in the middle of a disaster."[39]

Thinking things through requires looking at how decisions were made in the middle of an urgent situation, such as the one faced by Canadian officials in the SARS outbreak of 2003. Useful lessons can be gained from a retrospective study conducted by a working group at the Joint Center for Bioethics at the University of Toronto under the direction of Peter Singer, which looked at the ethical issues that surfaced during the SARS outbreak.[40] A number of competing ethical theories exist, including utilitarianism (which looks at consequences), deontology (which seeks to identify duties), and a variety of approaches based on value orientations. The latter include traditional virtues, values based on relationships, values expressed in actions and precedents in cases, and professional principles.[41] The last, principlism, is the current mainstream approach in biomedical ethics. It focuses on four main principles: (1) the autonomy of the individual (to make choices about his or her health care), (2) beneficence (to care for the ill), (3) nonmalificence ("first, do no harm . . ."), and (4) justice (in the distribution of care).[42]

For medical practitioners, the patient's individual autonomy has become the primary value in making decisions. This may be completely proper in dealing with individual cases, but it has limitations when considering populations whose health is at risk. Individual autonomy is not a realistic guiding principle in dealing with threats to the community. While autonomy may be a brake on decision making, it cannot be the driving force in public health. Society encroaches on personal autonomy when it restricts the freedom of those who create a risk to the community.[43] Debate on where to draw the line between personal autonomy in medical cases and protecting the community from risk can raise legitimate differences of opinion.[44] Public health experts may be uncomfortable with the implications of the idea that government should override individual health choices when such decisions could have an impact on society. If mandatory quarantine or vaccination are imposed, it will be controversial. In Canada the imposition of quarantine increased public fear of disease.[45] Such difficult questions are best considered beforehand, when no emergency looms, rather than in the heat of a crisis. The consideration should be a broad one, with participation invited from a wide segment of society. Such dialogue could strengthen public health and public trust and is consistent with emerging ethical principles of 21st-century health care and bioethics.[46] Addressing these ethical challenges is a crucial element in preserving trust in public officials.

In Canada, the Singer working group noted several "lessons learned":

- Under the ethical value of proportionality, authorities have the right to impose quarantine and isolation, but it is preferable, as was the case in Toronto, to use voluntary measures first. When people are fully informed, and see that they are being treated as fairly as possible, it is likely that voluntarism will prevail in times of emergency. In fact, most people in Toronto cooperated with restrictions. More coercive measures (such as detention orders or surveillance technology) should be reserved for those cases where noncompliance is documented and potential harm to others is anticipated.

- Under the ethical value of reciprocity, people placed in quarantine and isolation should be assisted to overcome the hardships imposed. This will also facilitate compliance.

- There is also a need for transparency, honesty and good communications on health issues.[47]

The working paper concluded with a call for a "new global health ethic based on solidarity." It defined solidarity as "feeling that one has common cause with others who are less powerful, wealthy or healthy."[48]

Lessons from Katrina: The Need for Action

The experience of Hurricane Katrina in New Orleans demonstrates how a natural disaster can be compounded by media attention to human error (delays in responding), technical failure (levee breaks), and systems dysfunction (particularly in intergovernmental relations and the chain of command). These problems were amplified by round-the-clock news coverage in the aftermath of Hurricane Katrina. These lessons are particularly important because the federal agency widely blamed for botching the response, the Federal Emergency Management Agency (FEMA), is in charge of the nonmedical response in the event of a pandemic. The nonmedical aspects include economic impacts, law enforcement, provision of food for people confined to their homes, and a host of emergency services.

Conclusions about the Katrina debacle have been well recounted in the news media:

- The city of New Orleans was not well prepared, despite the clear risk of hurricane-driven flooding.
- The U.S. Corps of Engineers knew of the inadequacy of the levees but had not taken steps to strengthen the flood control system.
- City officials, state officials, and officials in nearby parishes (counties) disagreed on evacuation requirements.
- Evacuation advisories were inconsistent and late.
- Some highways were rendered impassable after the storm because bridges were destroyed; at least one highway was closed by officials from a neighboring parish to prevent refugees from New Orleans from entering.
- Graphic news coverage showed the impact of inadequate preparation and inept response.
- Federal officials seemed to be unaware of the extent of death and despair and responded slowly to the crisis.
- Promises of federal assistance proved to be false.
- Widespread looting, shootings, and attacks on hospitals occurred.
- The media focused on the plight of the poor, elderly, and blacks.
- Crisis-related hospital deaths and allegations of euthanasia were reported.

- The cleanup and rebuilding efforts have moved very slowly.
- Almost all involved have played the blame game.

The public health situation in New Orleans after Katrina shared the following common elements with both the anthrax attacks and the SARS issue:

- Lack of clarity on the rules and procedures prevailed prior to the crisis.
- Responses were slow to be organized and implemented.
- Second-guessing of government decisions was common.
- Ethical controversies surfaced over who would receive medical care.
- Law enforcement was a loose cannon.
- Allegations arose of mistreatment of minorities and the poor.
- Decisions at all levels of government seemed to be made at the spur of the moment.
- Involvement of news media personnel as victims may have affected news coverage of these episodes.
- Trust and credibility issues abounded.

Deception hampered the responses in all three of the cases outlined. In Katrina, as in the anthrax episode, inaccurate and deceptive assurances backfired. In the SARS situation, the deception occurred abroad, as foreign officials lied about or downplayed the number of cases of disease. In New Orleans, promised actions did not materialize. Officials forfeited the trust the public had placed in them. The impact has been to further traumatize the people who are struggling to rebuild in New Orleans. One can sympathize with officials who *wished* to do the right thing but promised more than they could ever hope to deliver. That is the sort of paltering that Fred Schauer and Richard Zeckhauser (this volume) condemn for conjuring an incorrect perception of reality. Conjuring is not an appropriate response to a natural disaster.

What can we learn from one natural disaster and apply to planning for a different kind of natural disaster? I thought about this as I drove away from New Orleans with my parents one day prior to Katrina, and again, nine days later when I went back to retrieve belongings from the city where I grew up. The destruction I saw on that trip was enormous. On repeated trips home I have seen little progress. The overwhelming impression is that action was needed before the storm and after the flooding, and that it either did not happen or was slow in being implemented. I was able to drive my parents out of New Orleans to Texas the day before the storm because we had always evacuated when a hurricane loomed. My parents—both in their eighties—were lucky, but we had done this dozens of times before, whenever hurricanes threatened, over a 30-year period. We had a family evacuation plan, we had executed it many times, and it worked in the big one. There is almost no argument with the idea that the hurricane plans of federal, state, and local officials failed miserably during Katrina. As I surveyed the damage I reflected how officials had—by inaction—forfeited public trust. While officials at all three levels were blaming each other, the problem was more than a failure of leadership. The system failed.

The Dark Side of Trust

The aftermath of Hurricane Katrina, like the response to the anthrax attacks and the SARS outbreak, proved to be confounded by the dishonesty of public officials who provided false assurances, downplayed risks, or made promises they did not keep. Deception was an additional impediment to recovery in a health crisis. But another aspect cries out for examination in the wake of the anthrax episode of 2001 and the sad outcome of Katrina. The decline of public trust after officials misstated the risks or overpromised assistance was entirely justified. Although it confounded the response, the decline in public trust was a healthy response when the public recognized that it had been misled. It mattered little whether the deception was well intentioned, inadvertent, or wishful thinking. People reacted to the untruths by withdrawing trust. In the anthrax episode, for example, a national poll indicated that people were much more likely to trust local officials, even if they might be "out of the loop," to inform them about anthrax, rather than trust federal officials who were perceived to have misstated the facts.

This decline in public trust in the anthrax episode indicates that people can discern when they have been misled and may be able to avoid what Guido Möllering calls "a dark side to trust." Möllering (this volume) warns that once someone has made a leap of faith and put his or her trust in another person, that trust can facilitate an increase in the occurrence of harmful deception. Trust might facilitate self-deception, as the receiver of the false information accepts it on the basis of his or her trust in the speaker. The anthrax episode is one example in which such deception did not persist for long and was in fact recognized by the public at large within two months.

There is little question that traumatic events of the sort examined here—bioterrorism, contagious disease, and enormous destruction—can affect the psychological health of victims and spectators. The psychiatrist Vamik Volkan has warned that shared trauma can forge attitudes in large groups. Volkan stated that the relationship between a political leader and the public is like a busy street: "In normal times, the traffic—information and political decision-making as well as other means of influence—flows smoothly in both directions between the leader's influence and the public's awareness. . . . During times of crisis and terror, there is more focus on the 'traffic' traveling from the leader/government to the public, since the public seeks a 'savior' to protect them and their personal and large-group identities."[49] When people have endured trauma together, they may regress to more infantile behavior, Volkan states, as leaders manipulate followers and exaggerate the culpability of enemies to blame. Blind trust in a leader can undermine the basic trust that humans have for one another; it can become a destructive force leading to a perversion of trust. The examples he cites are ethnic conflict, genocide, and, more relevant to this discussion, the reaction to 9/11 in the United States. The American reaction, particularly toward Iraq, failed to separate the real threats from fantasy, in Volkan's view.[50]

Humans seek meaning in their suffering, and that means finding someone or something to blame as the cause of the troubles. That may seem to be illogical when the disaster is an "act of God" such as a hurricane or disease. But we humans are stubborn about wanting to hold someone accountable, if not for the initial event, at least for the inadequacy of a response. The blame game is an open invitation to fantasizing. The risk of self-deception lurks in the stigmatization of the alleged guilty parties. As a society, we all share to varying degrees in the shortcomings of preparation, the slowness of response, and the pain of recovery. It is better to study such crises with the aim of improving our performance in the future rather than of punishing the villains of the past. Robust preparedness costs money; true resilience means tolerating inefficient slack. There are no easy options.

The cases studied show the need for restraint in political leadership during crisis situations. The lessons are threefold and match the advice that Aristotle gave in speeches that have been collected in the book *On Rhetoric*. To be persuasive, Aristotle said that the speaker must articulate good reasons (which he called *logos*), a clear sense of ethical responsibility (which he called *ethos*), and an understanding of the feelings and concerns of the audience (which he termed *pathos*).[51] In the anthrax response, the logos got twisted. In the SARS case, the ethos was essential. In the Katrina response, the pathos was ignored as government dithered.

Public trust—healthy basic trust—is not blind. It is founded on these ideals of accuracy, ethical standards, and reasonable action to address the pathos of those who suffer. Put another way, to be persuasive, these three horsemen of the Acropolis—logos, ethos, and pathos—must align. When my actions show my ethical commitment to address your concerns, for example, only then do I have a shot at winning you over. What poisons the process is when I try to deceive or, more precisely, when you suspect that I have.

In a future health crisis these lessons may prove essential. Honest, accurate, timely communication can help people take protective steps, mitigate risk, facilitate the delivery of medical care and essential supplies, maintain community, and expedite recovery.

13 Responding to Deception

The Case of Fraud in Financial Markets

Brooke Harrington

I took such pains not to keep my money in the house, but to put it out of
the reach of burglars by buying stock, and had no guess that I was putting
it into the hands of those very burglars now grown wiser and standing
dressed as Railway Directors.

Ralph Waldo Emerson, 1857[1]

THE ECONOMIC HISTORY of the 21st century reads like a litany
of Biblical plagues: instead of locusts, frogs, and boils, we have
Enron, WorldCom, and Tyco, followed by the options-backdating scandal and
now the subprime mortgage meltdown. It is perhaps even more dishearten-
ing to realize that American investors are still in much the same position as
Emerson was over 150 years ago: dismayed to find themselves on the receiving
end of deceptive corporate practices. *BusinessWeek* summed up this crisis in
financial markets with the headline: "Can You Trust Anybody Anymore?"[2]

What happens when deception on such a massive scale is uncovered? How
do social beings cope when they discover they have been duped? As it turns
out, one of the biggest gaps in our knowledge about deception concerns the experience of those who have been deceived; as fragmented as research has been
on deceivers, we know far more about them than we do about their targets.
This chapter addresses itself to that lacuna by examining the responses of U.S.
retail investors to deception by the companies in which they invested, as well as
by the auditors and institutions that maintained trust in the financial system.

BROOKE HARRINGTON is the Alexander von Humboldt research fellow at the Max Planck
Institute for the Study of Societies in Cologne, Germany. Her research examines the social un-
derpinnings of financial markets. Her book on retail investors, *Pop Finance: Investment Clubs
and the New Investor Populism*, was published by Princeton University Press in 2008, and she is
now conducting a study of dynastic wealth and offshore banking.

While other chapters have explored definitions of deception, its ethical status, and the pragmatics of its execution—from minute movements of facial muscles (see Frank, this volume) to photographic forgeries (see Farid, this volume) and cognitive hacking (see Thompson, this volume)—this chapter will focus on deception's aftermath: the repair work "dupes" must undertake in order to participate again in social life, including economic activity. The eminent sociologist Erving Goffman termed this process "adaptation to failure." Writing about con artists and their "marks," Goffman noted that among the consequences of deception for those on the receiving end, losing money was less distressing than losing an idea of themselves as competent, intelligent individuals.[3] As a result, people who have been fleeced by con artists rarely go to the authorities for legal redress, because to do so means public exposure (and humiliation) as dupes. Instead, the dupes often turn to private means of identity repair, such as seeing a psychiatrist or accepting the ministrations of the con artist's "cooler"—a person charged with consoling the mark and patching up the identity damage done to him or her.

Unfortunately, Goffman's analysis stops short before offering a more comprehensive analysis of "adaptations to failure." Since his theories posited *action* (rather than beliefs) as the basis of social life, his primary interest was in the puzzling *inaction* of those who had been deceived by con artists: why they did not go to the police, for example. My goal is to build on the foundation Goffman laid by examining in more detail what the deceived do to repair the damage done to their social identities by the discovery of a deception. If they are not going to the authorities, what *are* they doing?

To this end, I will propose a model of responses to deception, illustrated with anecdotes from my own field research among U.S. retail investors: individuals whose contributions to the stock market fuelled the prosperity of the 1990s, and who lost significantly when the dot-com bubble burst and the revelations of corporate fraud began to unfold. My findings build on and expand Goffman's model by illustrating a set of responses stemming from a possibility he did not consider: marks sometimes refuse to acknowledge that they have been conned. This is closely tied to the phenomenon of self-deception described in Lutz's chapter (this volume).

My findings, detailed below, show two framing devices (another theoretical contribution of Goffman's) that marks use to deny that they were conned. One approach acknowledges the con, but not the individual's role as a mark; rather, the individual asserts him- or herself as a knowing accomplice of the con artist. While this creates a burden of culpability for the individual, he or she also avoids the loss of status associated with being identified as a victim. The second method means denying that the con ever took place, instead framing losses as a temporary setback in a fundamentally sound endeavor. Both strategies allow the deceived parties to continue their participation in the con—of course, in a different kind of game than the one-time, hit-and-run cons that Goffman's theory envisaged. Instead, this chapter, along with several others in the volume (see Rowan, for example), supports what might be called the "P. T. Barnum hypothesis": that some cons can be both chronic and systemic, with deception built into certain institutions as an enduring feature of their operation. But the stock market, unlike the circus, does not require a sucker to be born every minute: rather, marks manage their own sustained participation in a corrupt and deceptive financial system.

My interest here is not so much *why* individuals participate in these frauds, which may include motives such as financial necessity, greed, naïveté, a desire for risk as entertainment,[4] or even misguided love (see O'Sullivan, this volume, on the ways in which even truth wizards can be blinded by affection). Rather, I want to examine *how* actors engage in these practices, making themselves knowingly complicit with those who wish to defraud them. Through what means do individuals accommodate themselves to corrupt arrangements and then "move on" in the aftermath? These processes form an essential part of what Goffman called "a very basic social story": that of the seduction, deception, and consolation of marks by con artists.[5]

Adaptation to Failure

Unlike previous generations who fled the stock market following major downturns (most notably the cohort who could recall the crash of 1929 and the Great Depression that followed), the retail investors of the 1990s have largely stayed put: the proportion of Americans who own investments in the stock market has remained relatively stable since 1999, at a little over 50 percent, and their input continues to buoy stock prices. This is noteworthy for a number of reasons. First, it suggests why we need a better model of responses to deception. The repertoire of "adaptations to failure"—in this case, failure to anticipate the bursting of the dot-com bubble and to expose the corruption that underpinned it—appears to be broader than the withdrawal and wound licking that Goffman posited.

Second, the persistence of retail investors defies economic expectations as well as sociological ones. While caveat emptor may be the rule in individual transactions, even conservative economists agree that public trust in markets as a whole—including the belief that cheating will be caught and punished, by prices if not by regulation—is a necessity in order for modern capitalist economies to function.[6] Indeed, modern economics views the financial markets not just as a mechanism for conducting transactions and generating profits, but as a means of social coordination: a system of governance and a basis for social order unto itself.[7] Thus when markets break down, the whole social system is endangered.

Alan Greenspan—then-chairman of the Federal Reserve Board—summed up the problem in a 1999 commencement address at Harvard College: "Trust is at the root of any economic system based on mutually beneficial exchange. In virtually all transactions, we rely on the word of those with whom we do business . . . If a significant number of business people violated the trust upon which our interactions are based, our court system and our economy would be swamped into immobility."[8] While the years immediately following Greenspan's speech were filled with revelations of the ways in which "a significant number of business people violated the trust upon which our interactions are based," his predictions of an immobilized economic and legal system did not come to pass until recently, when U.S. banks stopped lending to one another. Remarkably, though, the millions of amateur investors who were expected to lose faith and take their money out of the stock market have not done so. Their savings and retirement funds have remained largely unchanged since before the credit crunch, despite the risks presented by institutional insolvency and plummeting stock prices.

This begs the question: How is such robustness and resilience possible, particularly among people whose whole net worth may be at stake? At a practical level, how do investors continue participating in a market system that has shown itself to be corrupt at many levels? While this may be due in part to regulation designed to restore faith in the system—such as the Sarbanes-Oxley bill—recent evidence suggests that such measures have been largely ineffective and may actually have increased incidents of financial fraud. For example, a 2007 economic study of regulatory measures taken following the Enron and WorldCom cases found that "tougher regulation may sometimes have unintended consequences; in particular, making disclosure of firm results more precise can actually increase incentives to commit fraud."[9]

And while we can make some educated guesses as to the reasons *why* Americans continue to invest in a market system that has violated their trust—reasons such as the economic necessity imposed by an inadequate social safety net—we know almost nothing about *how* they do it. How, for example, do people overcome the distrust that Greenspan and many others have posited as fatal to the market, and continue entrusting their money to corporate entities within a system that has proven itself to be rife with deception? What "adaptations to failure" have these individuals developed?

Examining these questions about contemporary American investors can shed light on a much broader puzzle in social life: how individuals sustain their participation in systems they know to be corrupt or fraudulent. This theme crops up throughout the chapters in this volume, as when Fine describes how some people willingly spread rumors they know or suspect to be false, or when Möllering writes of the suspension of disbelief that makes both trust and deception possible. Both imply a troubling complicity between deceivers and their targets, one that raises further questions about the ethical status of deception, such as: Do some people, sometimes, want or need to be deceived? Perhaps, as T. S. Eliot wrote in *Four Quartets*, the problem is that "Human kind cannot bear very much reality."[10] If so, then what happens when we are confronted with the disillusioning reality that we have been duped? How do we make ourselves whole again?

"Irrational Exuberance" and the New Investor Class

In hindsight, it is easy to point out signs that some sort of fraud underlay the U.S. stock market boom of the 1990s. As economist and historian John Kenneth Galbraith once wrote, all of the great swindles—from the South Sea Bubble of 1720 to the Ponzi schemes of the 1920s—have been driven by the "mass escape from sanity by people in pursuit of profit."[11] As if to illustrate his point, just months before the dot-com bubble burst, U.S. publishers brought out three books (by three different authors) vying to make the most optimistic claims about the trajectory of the bull market: the publication of *Dow 36,000* in May 1999 was followed in June by *Dow 40,000*, and in September by *Dow 100,000*. Though we might now wish to shelve these books in the science-fiction section of the library, at the time their ideas were treated quite seriously and discussed earnestly in almost every public news forum.

However implausible it might seem in the morning-after light of the early

21st century, these books simply reflected the astonishing upsurge in the stock market just prior to their publications. For example, on March 29, 1999, the Dow Jones Industrial Average—an index of the stocks issued by 30 industrial firms that has long been used as a barometer of the U.S. stock market as a whole—closed above 10,000 for the first time in its history, having doubled its value since 1995; just five weeks later, the index climbed another thousand points to close over 11,000—the fastest run-up in its history. This frenzy of economic optimism culminated on January 14, 2000, when the Dow closed at what was then an all-time high of 11,722.98, followed by a descent almost as swift as its rise, with the index dropping almost three thousand points over the next few months.

Among the most notable legacies of this extraordinary period was a shift in what could be called the "investor class." Once limited to a tiny elite among America's wealthiest families—the 1 percent of adults who owned stocks in 1900, which by 1952 had risen to just 4 percent—investing in stocks became a mass activity, involving over half the U.S. adult population by the end of the 20th century.[12] Much of this growth in "market populism" occurred during the 1990s. For example, at the beginning of that decade, about 21 percent of American adults owned stocks; seven years later, the percentage had more than doubled, rising to 43 percent; by 1999, the figure was 53 percent, where it has held steady despite the market downturn.[13]

Investment clubs were a major source of this growth in the investing population; as do-it-yourself mutual funds, they made it easy for first-timers to start buying stocks and learning about the market. The clubs typically involve 10 to 15 people who contribute an average of $35 each—the mean cost of a single share on the New York Stock Exchange[14]—at monthly meetings; the group then allocates this investment capital to a portfolio of stocks the members own in common. In this respect, the designation "club" is somewhat misleading: while investment clubs are voluntary associations, their ownership of stocks subjects them to legal, accounting, and taxation requirements much like any small business. Perhaps more important, the clubs have significant economic clout: by the late 1990s, an estimated 11 percent of American investors—about 20 million people—belonged to an investment club, pouring hundreds of millions of dollars into U.S. stocks every month.[15] Since "firms commit fraud in order to get funds from investors," all this new capital flooding the market through investment clubs presented a tempting target for corporate deception.[16]

Retail investors do not deserve blame for being conned. In fact, as recent economic research concludes, "It is pointless to blame investors for the abuses

[of corporate corruption] by arguing that they were careless or naïve when making their decisions. . . . it may have been fully rational for them to trust publicly
available information in many cases, instead of carefully monitoring firms that
requested funds."[17] Rather, from a sociological viewpoint, studying U.S. retail
investors and their experiences in the late 20th and early 21st centuries presents
a rare opportunity to examine fraud from the perspective of the mark.

Goffman argued that individuals who have been conned shun attention
afterwards, preferring to repair the damage they have sustained in private.
But my investigation of the repair work done by defrauded investors suggests
that, rather than retreating from social life, they used *small-group interaction*
to cope with their predicaments.[18] Their identity-rebuilding project employed
the same kind of group processes, including call-and-response mechanisms,
posited by Goffman in his work on the construction of self.[19] And while many
of the investors I studied defined their experiences in terms of being defrauded
by deceptive corporate practices, they nonetheless continued investing in U.S.
stocks. This behavior was due in part to structural reasons I describe in greater
detail elsewhere[20]—most notably to the lack of secure retirement funding
from either public or private sector organizations—and was consistent with
the national trend. Even by 2003, well after the dot-com bubble burst, investment clubs still owned $125 billion worth of U.S. stocks—including significant
stakes in Fortune 100 firms like General Electric and Intel—and were pump-
ing in new investment dollars at the rate of $190 million per month.[21]

Because they were still actively engaged in the stock market following revelations of deception by many major firms, the investors I interviewed had
adapted to their situation in ways that permitted them to continue participating in the system rather than withdrawing. These adaptations were my
primary interest, as the existing scholarly literature had little to say about how
people recover from such significant breaches of trust. Rather than the post-
deception withdrawal posited by Goffman (and by economic theory), I found
investors using other strategies to make the seemingly impossible possible: to
continue investing without trust or faith in financial institutions.

Responses to Deception

Before discussing the adaptations in use by the retail investors I studied, it
may be helpful to review the little that is known about responses to deception.
As Goffman notes, marks assume a series of common postures following their

discovery that they have been duped. These include despair, denial, and of course anger, leading to the need to "cool out" the mark. The process typically happens in private and culminates in withdrawal—not just from the scene of the con but also from social life more generally. Being conned, Goffman wrote, destroys the self symbolically, rendering victims "socially dead."[22] This may help explain why many of the adaptive mechanisms observed among the deceived resemble those seen in individuals grieving the death of a loved one, such as denial and lethargy.[23]

Goffman's interest lay in the production of *inaction*: the docile or lethargic state of the mark that protects the con artist from exposure and punishment. Thus Goffman focused on the role of the "cooler," the con artist's accomplice who comes in after the deception is complete to offer "words of consolation and redirection" to the mark.[24] Coolers encourage marks to define their positions in such a way that their responses do not threaten future con operations.

When the bull market of the 1990s collapsed, financial and government institutions deployed similar mechanisms to "cool out" the millions of investors who discovered that they had been defrauded following the collapse of the boom market. The effort deployed by the coolers in this case was formidable, from the public officials who consoled retail investors by assuring them that their sufferings would be avenged in the courts, to policymakers who lowered interest rates and encouraged investors to redirect their attention toward real estate, and finally to the finance-industry journalists and pundits who encouraged retail investors to turn their anger inward, blaming themselves as accomplices in the market's collapse.

Retail Investors: The Interview Participants

The investors I interviewed in 2004 were members of a sample group originally chosen at random in 1997 from a list of investment clubs in the San Francisco Bay Area, where I was conducting research for the large, multimethod study that became *Pop Finance*. All 50 interview participants—28 men, 22 women—belonged to one of the seven investment clubs whose monthly meetings I observed between late 1997 and early 1999. Since not all of the clubs I had followed in the 1990s survived the market downturn, I was not able to interview all 83 members of the original clubs I had studied in the earlier part of my research; many had left the Bay Area and were out of touch with other club members, so I was unable to trace them. However, by the time of my 2004 follow-up study, four clubs were still in operation with a largely unchanged cohort of members, and I ultimately managed to find and interview over half of the members of the three clubs that had disbanded. When I reconnected with them, my questions focused on whether and how their investing behavior had changed following the revelations of financial deception in American companies over the previous three years.

In this regard, it was useful to begin the interviews with one of the most difficult questions: How much money did you lose when the dot-com bubble burst in mid-2000? Of the four clubs that remained intact, all had lost substantial sums of money compared to their cash outlay—most estimated the loss at between one-third and one-half of the club's precrash portfolio value. Perhaps tellingly, few of them kept detailed enough records for me to confirm these figures independently; maybe not knowing exactly how much they lost was part of what enabled them to survive. Among the three clubs that had disbanded, the members I interviewed were also vehement that money had nothing to do with their decision to split up, citing other factors—such as fragile relationships among members—instead.

Table 13.1 summarizes the financial status of the seven clubs at the time of the follow-up study. For the groups that remained intact, I was able to use their current records to calculate their annualized internal rate of return, a standard performance measure used in the finance industry as well as by many investment clubs. For disbanded clubs, I spoke to the treasurers and

TABLE 13.1 Postboom performance of investment clubs

Club	Still Together?	Compound Annual Return from Inception Through February 2004, or Date Disbanded
Portfolio Associates	Yes	24%
Valley Gay Men's Investment Club	Yes	16%
Ladies With Leverage	Yes	3%
California Investors	Yes	−2%
Bulls & Bears	No	30%
Asset Accumulators	No	22%
Educating Singles Against Poverty	No	9%

either obtained the last accounting statement or used the treasurer's best estimate of the group's returns. While these estimates are obviously less reliable than the accounting statements, my goal was not to document rates of return with precision, but rather to establish a context for the adaptation strategies the interview participants had developed. To put these figures in broader perspective, investment clubs across the United States earned an average 12.6 percent annual rate of return on their portfolios during the 1990s—somewhat above the average for U.S. stocks over the past century, but well below the annual return rates of those stocks during the 1990s, which sometimes exceeded 30 percent.

While it would be unwise to rely too heavily on these figures, there does appear to be a surprisingly weak relationship between profits and investment club participation. That is, clubs that were doing poorly (such as California Investors) did not necessarily disband, and those that were doing better financially (such as Bulls & Bears) did not necessarily stay together. This "loose coupling" between financial payoffs and perseverance in investing may have provided participants with some valuable flexibility in reframing their experiences on the receiving end of corporate deception, allowing them to adapt rather than withdraw from the market as previous generations had done.[25] Also, as studies of organizations in complex environments have shown, the more instability and rapid change that surrounds it, the more an organization has to adopt a "chameleon strategy," remaking its identity and self-presentation in order to adapt and survive.[26] For groups investing in the stock market—one of the most volatile organizational environments imaginable—reframing their identities in an adaptive way allowed them to continue participating in the financial system even after its deceptive practices were revealed. So, rather than withdrawing, as predicted by Goffman's theoretical model, these marks who were targeted as a group also responded in groups. In the language of Goffman's theories about identity, retail investors were able to maintain their lines of action via their identity-related *inter*actions.

Findings

Paralysis: Frozen in the Headlights of History

Like the marks in Goffman's study of con artists, most of the investors I interviewed experienced a period of shock and paralysis upon learning that they had been deceived. Many said that they "froze" when the news broke about

Enron, WorldCom, and other financial frauds: unsure what the declines in stock valuations meant, or how long they would last, the majority of participants in this study just stopped buying or selling stocks. Some participants were still in that state of suspended animation when I interviewed them in February 2004. As Carla of the disbanded mixed-gender club ESP put it: "I don't know whom to trust. I'm not sure if [our] system is wrong, but [it] assumes that you can trust firms' financial statements, and I have no idea what to do now that we know you can't trust anything firms tell you." Like Carla, other participants in my study expressed resignation upon learning of the frauds perpetrated on them, even as recognition grew as to the pervasiveness of corruption in the stock market. Neither angered nor energized by the crisis, most still claimed to be frightened, both by the losses they had already experienced and those that the future might hold. Yet their fear did not motivate action: these investors just sat on their portfolios and did nothing. While they lacked the generalized, impersonal trust in the "system" that economic theory suggests is necessary for the capitalist economy to function, they kept their money in the stock market rather than "cashing out."

These investors reached stasis in part by construing their situation as offering no alternatives to remaining invested in the stock market. This interactive framing process, which—like their investment decisions—occurred through group discussion, closed off options that were objectively available to them, such as FDIC-insured savings accounts or certificates of deposit. As a result, these participants acted "as if" they had no choice about where to put their money. Troy of Valley Gay Men's Investment Club summed up this point of view by asking: "Where else are we going to put our money? In the mattress?" This phrase recurred, verbatim, in interviews with men and women from other clubs I had studied, almost as if it had become a mantra for the survivors of the dot-com crash. Repetition of this phrase was like a magic spell immobilizing those who used it, leading directly to their (in)actions.

On the one hand, the financial losses these clubs and individuals experienced as a result of corporate fraud and the subsequent collapse of the bull market make it surprising to see a rationale like "where else are we going to put our money?" invoked. After all, if their money had been stashed in a mattress, at least they would not have lost it as they did in the stock market. And yet Susan of Ladies with Leverage, echoing the sentiments of many of the interview participants, said, "I can't afford to leave [the market] . . . I have to make back my money." Since her club still owned 62 shares of WorldCom—by then delisted and almost valueless—and had lost everything it had invested in the TriTeal IPO (a firm described by Motley Fool as one of the "worst investments of the 1990s"), the prospect of making the money back with new investments seemed a little far-fetched. But her trust seemed to be grounded in the interactions of the investment club proper, rather than in the market as an institution whose untrustworthiness she acknowledged. "We did not lose money because we made bad decisions," she said. "We lost money because the market was sinking under its own corruption." The men of Portfolio Associates gave a similar account of their reasons for continuing to invest as part of the club, despite the shock and disappointment of their losses in the previous three years. When I asked them why they kept investing together, several of the men responded in quick succession:

Charles: Inertia.

Dave: Habit.

Kevin: We're joined at the hip.

Arnold: We needed someone to commiserate with about the market.

All four answers foregrounded the role of the group as a coping mechanism rather than the profit-generating entity that it once was. In a sense, this was a textbook example of the "chameleon strategy," shifting from one identity to another as the market environment required. All the clubs that remained intact performed this kind of adaptive maneuver, which probably contributed to their survival. Members of the clubs that did not effect this identity reconstruction had to do it themselves—not alone, but in small groups other than their investment clubs—in order to continue investing (see the following two sections for details on the processes of denying the con and identifying as an accomplice).

Among the clubs that were still investing together in 2004, interaction patterns remained very similar to those I had observed five years previously. The members of Portfolio Associates continued to bicker amicably after amassing over a million dollars in stock holdings; similarly, I found that Ladies with Leverage still relied on members' consumer experience as its primary means of evaluating stocks. Valley Gay Men's Investment Club had experienced some turnover, but five of the original members remained, six new ones had joined, and most of the stock purchases the club had made since its inception six years earlier were still in the group portfolio, including Dollar General, Amgen, Lear, and Medtronic. The other all-male group, California Investors, was largely unchanged in membership and investment strategies; its portfolio had changed only because the club members continued to employ costly and counterproductive stop-loss orders to automate the sale of stocks they owned when the share values dipped below a specified limit.

In other words, these four clubs seem to have weathered the discovery of widespread fraud in the U.S. stock market by ignoring or minimizing it. To the extent that the participants made changes in their investing strategies, they were relatively minor. While some had begun investing in real estate because it seemed less prone to the kind of "book cooking" frauds exposed in the Enron and WorldCom cases, most participants made smaller moves, like choosing firms that paid cash dividends or seeking information from individuals they knew and trusted, rather than the mass media or other arms'-length sources. As Stan of California Investors put it, "I love cash dividends; you can't fudge a cash dividend." This "show me the money" response was echoed by the members of Valley Gay Men's Investment Club as well as those of the defunct club Bulls & Bears, whose members continued to invest on their own. Some participants also began seeking advice from finance professionals, but only those with whom they had long-term, face-to-face relationships. For example, Janet of ESP turned her portfolio over to her nephew, a professional money manager; similarly, Greg of Bulls & Bears said he "only trades now based on the recommendations of people I know personally." Both of these responses are essentially tactical adaptations rather than withdrawals or active strategy changes, and their consequence was to maintain the status quo and keep these individuals invested in the stock market.

Denial as Adaptation

Some investors adapted by simply refusing to acknowledge the con: they claimed no deception had occurred. Social psychologists who have observed similar phenomena within cults and other insular groups call this response "escalation of commitment."[27] Perhaps the most eloquent expression of this quasi-religious faith in the market was provided by Stan of California Investors. When I asked the group when members knew the bull market of the 1990s was over, Stan rejected the premise of the question:

> I don't agree that the bull market ended. I don't believe there ever was a bear market. The bull just slowed down for a few years. I believe in the optimism of the people—people are going to create things and want things for themselves

and their children, and that's going to keep the big wheel turning. And if you think it's over, you're making a big mistake.

Several other participants indicated similar leanings by minimizing the impact of the ongoing financial scandals and shifting their focus to a notional "bright side." Tara, of the disbanded all-women's group Asset Accumulators suggested that it was only a matter of time before stock prices recovered and vindicated her commitment to remain invested in the market:

> My husband wanted to sell everything when the market went down, but I convinced him to hold onto our stocks. And he trusted me because I'd been meeting with Asset Accumulators for ten years and he thought I must know something! He would have sold everything if I hadn't convinced him otherwise; and now the stocks are going up again.

While not as extreme as Stan's position, Tara's framing of her experience suggests a similarly intense and unshakeable faith in the ideology of capitalism. In fact, many participants spoke of their experiences in the market downturn using terms that would be familiar in any tale of sin and redemption: "I'm still a fundamentalist," said Berry of Asset Accumulators; "We never lost faith," said Skip of Portfolio Associates. By construing the news from Enron, WorldCom, and similar cases as something other than evidence of pervasive deception in the stock market, these investors were able to continue participating in the system, even if they simply remained in stasis.

Self-Blame: The Individual Investor as Knowing Accomplice

Another group of investors I interviewed took a position of self-blame vis-à-vis the revelations of corporate fraud—a perspective heartily encouraged by finance professionals and corporate media. As one investment adviser wrote to his clients, "The seeds of the current crop of corporate scandals were planted not by corrupt executives but by greedy investors and their Wall Street cheerleaders."[28] As WorldCom prepared to file the largest bankruptcy claim in U.S. history, the New York Times rallied sympathy for the firm by noting that its crimes included falsifying accounting statements to avoid earnings shortfalls of 1/100th of one cent—WorldCom's executives were reportedly trying to avoid the economic punishment meted out to companies that missed earnings expectations, with miniscule underperformance often resulting in losses of 10 percent of the firm's market value.[29] In this variation of the "I blame society" defense, corporations like WorldCom managed to shift the focus from their illegal activities to the alleged unreasonableness of investors and regulators.

Surprisingly, many of the participants in my study were quite willing to accept the blame. Many spoke of a sense of complicity in the decline of the bull market, as though their actions contributed to falsified accounting statements or to corrupt auditing and governance practices. While the problems in these areas were clearly systemic, involving dozens of firms and hundreds (if not thousands) of finance professionals, the only anger the participants in this study expressed was directed at themselves. Several used the word "delusional" to describe their thinking during the bull market, while others used phrases that hinted at a sort of temporary insanity: "We thought we were brilliant," one said. "We were living in a fool's paradise," said another. Still others judged themselves in terms reminiscent of an old-time revival meeting. Cate of Bulls & Bears said, "We got greedy—it was too easy for us. We forgot the basic principles." Frank of Valley Gay Men's Investment Club put it even more bluntly: "We were money whores back then—we would buy anything that would make us a buck."

And in the classic mode of redemption narratives, these confessions of error and decadence were followed by a recommitment to the fundamentals—the Old Tyme religion of investing in undervalued firms and expecting modest profits in return. In this light, the financial losses that the participants experienced, both in their club portfolios and personal investments, were interpreted as just punishment for straying from the path of fundamentalism. Frank of Valley Gay Men's Investment Club said that when the group was confronted with facts or reliable data on the stocks they owned or were considering for purchase, "we would discount the data and manipulate it to fit our needs." Similarly, Dan of California Investors summed up the attitude of his group toward analysis during the 1990s as: "Don't confuse us with the facts because we already have our minds made up."

This self-blame coexisted with a surprisingly tolerant attitude toward corporate corruption. While one or two expressed shock at the revelations uncovered by the Enron trial, the majority treated the news as—literally—business as usual. Many expressed some version of the perspective voiced by Karen of the all-women's group Ladies with Leverage:

> My experience in the work world taught me that business people cheat all the time, so the scandals didn't come as a surprise. But in the 1990s, people weren't looking that closely at the veracity of the numbers, either, because it was all good news. That's just human nature—why look a gift horse in the mouth?

Similarly, Greg—former president of the disbanded club Bulls & Bears—argued not only that he should have known better than to trust in the financial markets, but that he *did* know better, and participated nonetheless:

> I knew it was a sham back then. I was just riding it as long as I could. I remember being so surprised that a startup like Iomega was valued more highly than General Motors; there's no way a startup could be worth more than GM on the first day of trading. I knew there was cheating going on in the whole market, how some people got in on IPOs and some did not, and I knew I was only a two-bit player, because I had to buy stock on the open market. I knew there was favoritism among boards of directors. It was all a sham when people said "It's a new era, things are different now." I never believed it. And the scandals haven't damaged my trust in the system because I never trusted it to begin with. So some people got special deals from mutual fund managers—so what? I work at [a major defense contractor]: we see special deals all the time!

His former colleague Cate responded in a strikingly similar way, albeit independently of Greg, in a separate interview. On the one hand, she claimed to have gone into the market with her eyes open to the corruption: "We sort of knew the books were cooked; I kind of saw it coming." In the next breath, however, she reaffirmed her faith in the system in the abstract: "I never considered getting out of the market; I still believe in the business models, even though the top management is corrupt." This is reminiscent of the profession of faith made by some believers who disdain the corruption of clerical leadership while remaining loyal to religious institutions in principle. The analogy is fitting, since—as economic anthropologist Keith Hart points out—"economics has become the religion of our secular scientific civilization."[30]

Discussion and Implications

In studying investor behavior following the exposure of pervasive deception within the U.S. stock market, I was surprised to find that none of the participants in my study had made the usual "adaptations to failure" posited by Goffman: instead of cashing out their investments and withdrawing, as previous generations had done in the wake of stock market frauds, they were all still engaged in the system. Moreover, they maintained their positions despite often-significant financial losses. And instead of finding the anger and sense of betrayal I expected, my interviews uncovered a mix of resignation, denial, and self-blame, all of which enabled the people interviewed to continue participating in a market system that had proven itself corrupt. To achieve this feat, the marks reframed their collective identities within their investing groups, either casting themselves as knowing accomplices to the con, or denying that a con ever took place.

This is quite different from what Goffman predicted in his model of responses to deception and, as such, contributes an expanded understanding of deception as a social interaction. While the majority of research has focused on deceivers, this chapter has used Goffman's own work on social identity, combined with interview data from 50 American retail investors, to show how people who have been deceived can do more than withdraw or allow themselves to be "cooled out." While such passivity remains an option, the individuals in my study were far more active in responding to the con they had just experienced. Whether they took blame on themselves or reframed the events as a "temporary setback" in a basically sound financial system, they did not retreat from investing.

In addition to the expanded model of responses to deception, this chapter offers another implication for future research, as well as for policymakers: cons are not always one-time events but can be enduring and systemic as well. In terms of financial institutions, history suggests that deception is not an anomaly in investment markets, but rather a chronic condition. This suggests another reason to expand our model of deception by including responses that allow interaction to continue even after a fraud comes to light. A willingness to serve as a target of ongoing deception might be driven by necessity (as I suggest elsewhere), by self-delusion (see Lutz, this volume), or by technological innovations (see Thompson and Hancock, both in this volume). Or it may be as simple as the overwhelming pervasiveness of deception in social life (see O'Sullivan, this volume) causing investors to say to themselves, essentially, "if you can't beat 'em, join 'em."

For policymakers, the implications are somewhat different. The evidence suggests that widely held beliefs about the need for public trust in financial markets may be unfounded. For example, although Alan Greenspan posited that the functioning of such markets is based on trust vested in business people, the individual investors in my study repeatedly affirmed that their faith lay elsewhere, in something far more abstract that they did not always articulate but that could perhaps be identified as capitalism or the American Dream. Their beliefs might be wishful thinking, but it is clear in any case that trust in individuals has little to do with these investors' ongoing participation in the stock market. Second, although Greenspan, along with other policymakers and economists, predicted that widespread violations of trust would result in the breakdown of the economic system, all of the evidence is poignantly to the contrary: despite being collectively defrauded of billions, individual investors have continued to pour their money into a market system they know to be corrupt. Banks may be putting the brakes on lending, but in the face of structural exigencies imposed by public policies and the rewriting of the social contract between management and labor, individuals in the United States have little choice but to keep investing, even if it means spinning pie-in-the-sky tales of "prosperity just around the corner," or adopting the weary resignation of marks who know they *will* get fooled again.

14 Military Deception in the Information Age

Scale Matters

William Glenney IV

Although to use deceit in every action is detestable, none the less in the managing of a war it is a laudable and glorious thing; and that man is equally lauded who overcomes the enemy by deceit, as is he who overcomes them by force.

Niccolo Machiavelli[1]

Moral considerations have validity only in civilian life and should not interfere with preparations for war.

General Waldemar Erfurth[2]

MILITARY DECEPTION is fundamentally different from deception in any other context and different from what is normally understood when talking about deceiving or lying. This difference is derived from the recognition by most societies that war itself is fundamentally different from any other human or societal interaction.[3] As quoted above, Machiavelli stated in *The Discourses Upon the First Ten (Books) of Titus Livy*, deception in warfare is an acceptable individual and group behavior. Therefore, military deception should be considered a valuable skill, not a character flaw. As will be discussed in this chapter, the social acceptability of military deception is borne out in history and in current world events.

Despite a consistent historical validation of the value of military deception, the understanding of and perceptions about deception, and its role within the U.S. military, often cause strategic deception to fall short of its potential value.

WILLIAM GLENNEY IV is deputy director of the Chief of Naval Operations' Strategic Studies Group tasked with generation of revolutionary warfighting concepts for 30–50 years in the future.

Contributing to this shortfall are principles of U.S. military deception that are deeply based on the experience of World War II. These principles are not reflective of the warfighting environment of the early 21st century. In addition, U.S. military deception remains too heavily reliant on the ability to influence the perceptions of a single leader while neglecting the role of organizations. Current thinking fails to recognize that military deception is a time-sensitive "competition" in which nuance, subtlety, and time have grown in importance over the past 60 years. Current principles underestimate the breadth of temporal, organizational, informational, cognitive, and technical factors that characterize the environment where deception must occur. The interdependence of relationships across the strategic, operational, and tactical levels of war and the coupling of the three levels demand new methods for the understanding of, planning for, and execution of deception at every level of war. In today's environment, neglecting effects of deception at any level imperils the effectiveness of deception at the other two levels.

Further complicating the human dimension of deception is the military fact that the adversary may be geographically dispersed and functionally distributed, changing the nature of the battlespace and environment in fundamental ways not accounted for in existing military deception doctrine. The experience of World War II, while useful for understanding the sophistication of deception and its relationship to strategic and operational warfare, is not an effective model to use against modern adversaries in an environment where time scales range from fractions of a second to years—all of which must be accounted for simultaneously.

All aspects of military deception need to be part of mainstream U.S. military thinking and practice, and done in a manner that accounts for the scale and context of the deception at all levels of war.

Military Deception Defined

Military deception "is a conscious and rational effort deliberately to mislead an opponent."[4] Current military doctrine regarding deception is based on the ability to influence the perceptions of a single leader in an attempt to cause a desired emergent behavior by a single unitary enemy.

Contrary to current doctrine, military deception should be more appropriately considered in terms of setting or controlling conditions that lead one or more adversaries to perceive or misperceive a situation, come to an erroneous conclusion about it, and then act accordingly—all in a manner consistent with the deceiver's objectives.

Military deception should be viewed as a competition of information vying for the attention of people's minds. In this competition, one side uses people and technology to deceive, while the other side uses people and technology to detect deception or to carry out its own deception. The same human strengths that enable imaginative deception also make one susceptible to being deceived. Equally, as discussed by Hany Farid (this volume), the technology that offers the possibility to produce false images to deceive also offers the methods to detect those forgeries.

Although military deception is generally an acceptable behavior, common Western rules do place some limitations on the use of deception in warfare. The applicable body of international law and related military practice is often referred to as the law of warfare, the law of armed conflict, or the Geneva Conventions. This body of law prohibits certain methods of military deception referred to as "perfidy." Perfidy draws on a false belief by the target that he is being given safe haven or sanctuary when in reality the deceiver's intent is to betray that belief. Positioning military forces in hospitals or religious buildings, using protected symbols such as the Red Cross or Red Crescent for military cover, and military forces donning civilian clothes during combat are examples of perfidy. Perfidy aside, there are few, if any, additional prohibitions on methods of military deception employed at the operational or strategic levels of war.

Nation-states, either by virtue of membership in the United Nations or accession to other international treaties, have agreed to abide by norms established under the Geneva Conventions. A fundamental assumption of the Geneva Conventions is that all participants in a conflict will abide by these norms. However, terrorists, insurgents, freedom fighters, criminals, and the like may not comply with these constraints. They may consider perfidy not only acceptable but an advantage to be exploited, as demonstrated in the conflicts in the Middle East and Sub-Saharan Africa. They will use whatever means they deem appropriate to achieve their goal. Assuming the U.S. military complies with the existing international law, its approaches to military deception must account for and be prepared to counter adversaries who do not.

Too often in a technology-driven world, people forget that war, and by corollary, military deception are human endeavors. All of the factors that affect individual, group, and organizational behavior (such as emotion, motivation, leadership, trust, influence, and fear) have roles in military deception and warrant careful consideration. Body language (see O'Sullivan, this volume), assumed trustworthiness (see Urton, this volume), and online relationships (see Hancock, this volume) are all at play in military deception—whether they are used to deceive or to uncover deception.

Unlike most other social interactions and relationships, there is no explicit expectation of trust between protagonists in war. An implicit level of trust may develop as adversaries "get to know each other," but the relationship is inherently adversarial and any trust may be baseless. Opponents may even convince themselves that they know each other so well that there can be no deception. The German invasion of the Soviet Union in June 1941 was facilitated, in part, by an unfounded level of trust that Stalin drew from the German-Soviet Nonaggression Pact of 1939 with Hitler.

Military deception is a proactive concept; the deceiver takes action to produce the deception. Unlike surprise, which may or may not be planned, military deception is premeditated. Surprise may result from deception or it may be the result of luck or coincidence. As will be discussed further below, the surprise associated with the timing and location of the Allied invasion of France in World War II was the product of a careful and elaborate deception plan. On the other hand, the Germans' surprise counterattack at the Battle of the Bulge was the proximate result of Clausewitz's "fog" of war. The art and science of military deception and of military surprise share some common principles, but there are also principles unique to each. While surprise on the battlefield may be the result of a deception, deception and surprise are not the same.

Finally, military deception *is not* a matter of ethics or morals; *is not* about individual lies or deceit that must be told to protect a strategic or operational level deception; *is not* about what is commonly referred to as strategic communications based on the truth that are generally focused on nonmilitary people and large populations; and *is not* about political deception—although if political leaders are deceived the result may play out militarily.

Levels of War

A detailed discussion of what the military refers to as "levels of war" is well beyond the scope of this chapter. Any discussion would fill volumes because of the central role that the levels of war play in national security and the use of the military tool of statecraft.[5] Yet, in order to understand deception in a military context, one must have a basic appreciation for the three levels of war: strategic, operational, and tactical. These levels provide a framework to discuss, plan, and carry out military operations. The levels of war can generally be characterized based on the perspective applied, the intent of military operations, and the effect sought from them.

Strategic level of war deals with actions by nations, multinational entities, or similar organizations in the development and execution of grand visions and objectives, including the employment of military force. World War II provides a useful illustration in that at the strategic level, the Allies employed an overall worldwide perspective intended to defeat the Axis powers. Roosevelt, Churchill, Stalin, and their immediate staffs considered the world as their environment, the effects of their actions in terms of years, and time constants of change measured in months to years.

Operational level of war deals with actions by large military commands or large numbers of commands in the conduct of a campaign. Eisenhower and his immediate subordinates, such as Bradley, Patton, and Montgomery, functioned at the operational level of war with a regional theater perspective carrying out campaigns in North Africa, then in Europe, and assessing the effects of their action in terms of weeks to months.

Tactical level of war deals with actions by smaller commands and small groupings of soldiers that make up part of a campaign. It is addressed by a variety of people, from subordinate division commanders down to individual riflemen, who operate in geographic areas measured in square yards and square miles, and time durations measured in minutes, hours, and days.

At the most basic level, an understanding of the levels of war and their interrelationships can be gained by considering geographic areas of regard, duration of activities, time scales of change in the environment, and numbers of troops, as summarized in Table 14.1.

Despite the differences between them, all three levels of war exist in and are considered within a single common environment. Tactical activities have an effect on the environment, as do operational and strategic activities. But tactical activities are not the same as, and do not become, strategic activities because of that relationship. It is the nature of this common environment that has dramatically changed since World War II and caused great changes with regard to military deception.

Each level of war involves a number of aspects including conceptualization, problem solving, perception, creativity, imagination, humanity, and

TABLE 14.1   Basic comparison of levels of war

Level of War	Geographic Area of Regard	Duration of Activities	Time Scale of Changes in Environment	Numbers of Troops
Strategic	Regional to global	Years to decades	Months to years	Hundreds of thousands to millions
Operational	Hundreds to thousands of square miles	Weeks to years	Days to months	Thousands to hundreds of thousands
Tactical	Square feet to tens of square miles	Minutes to months	Seconds to weeks	Individuals to tens of thousands

morals. Each of these aspects can provide the opportunity and means to deceive, as well as a means to be deceived. A blend of art and science is inherent in each level of war, requiring "an understanding, even mastery, of the medium—war and nature—over which the artist must perform."[6] Military deception must account for the roles of humans *and* technology, and there is no clear indication of which makes deception harder or easier.

Further complicating military deception is that the levels of war do not aggregate up or disaggregate down. In other words, the operational level of war is not simply the aggregation of tactical activities; nor is the strategic level of war an aggregation of operational actions. Similarly, a strategy cannot be broken down into a mere collection of tactical activities. Strategic deception is not simply a tactical deception carried out against millions of soldiers. A strategic deception might have no detectable influence on tactical activities.

For the remainder of this chapter, the term "military deception" will mean deception conducted at the strategic or operational levels of war.[7] Deception at these levels is intended to prevent war, to facilitate warfighting should it be required, to attempt to control escalation of warfighting, and to succeed at the operational and strategic levels of war.[8]

Historical Examples of Military Deception

Military deception is affected by the human and technical considerations discussed throughout this book, but these considerations, either singularly or in aggregate, are not sufficient to fully understand military deception. Some historical examples illustrate successful military deceptions, and insights from these examples will also show why military deception must change to meet today's environment.

One of the most studied military deceptions, code-named Operation Bodyguard, surrounded the Allied invasion of Normandy in 1944. The historical record of Bodyguard is rich and detailed, making it an excellent case study of military deception and the roles of the human and technical considerations presented throughout this book. Among other things, Bodyguard illustrates the value of military deception, the difficulty of conducting deception at the operational and strategic levels of war, and the sophisticated planning and execution required for military deception to be successful. Bodyguard represents the zenith of the American belief in the importance and utility of military deception, a belief that was not easily arrived at. According to Michael Dewar, "Even the Americans, who had initially regarded deception as an unnecessary subtlety in view of their superior mobility, firepower and material resources, had come round to the idea."[9] The complexity, scale, and importance of Operation Bodyguard required five coordinated subsidiary plans: Fortitude North, Fortitude South, Zeppelin, Vendetta, and Ironside.[10]

Fortitude North portrayed a fictitious invasion of Norway in order to bring Sweden to the side of the Allies, thereby setting the conditions to invade Germany from the north through Denmark. The deception succeeded, causing the Germans to retain two hundred thousand troops in Norway, and out of central Europe, in anticipation of a diversionary invasion that never occurred.

Fortitude South posed a fictitious invasion of Pas de Calais; its credibility was enhanced by publicly making General George Patton the commander of the fictitious army group that would carry out the invasion. Fortitude South was so successful that the German forces near Pas de Calais remained in place until well after the actual invasion at Normandy and the firm establishment of Allied forces in France.

Zeppelin exaggerated the size of Allied forces in the eastern and central Mediterranean Sea in order to keep German forces from being moved out of the region to reinforce central Europe. The deception successfully convinced the Germans that there were 71 Allied divisions in the Mediterranean when in fact there were only 38.

Vendetta planned for a fictitious invasion into southern France. This operation required significant strategic nuance. The perceived size of the invasion force had to be large enough to keep German forces in southern France and

Italy from moving north toward Normandy. At the same time, the threat had to be perceived as small enough to avoid attracting additional German forces into France from outside the region.

Ironside involved another fictitious invasion into France along the Bay of Biscay, with the intention of keeping local German forces from being repositioned to the north. Limitations on Allied capabilities and resources constrained the effectiveness of Ironside. In addition, the Germans never really considered the Bay of Biscay as a serious invasion route, removing a condition for successful deception.

The fundamental premise of Operation Bodyguard and the most important environmental condition for its success was the knowledge that Hitler and his key military leaders had already concluded, based on sound military principles, that the main Allied invasion would occur at the narrowest part of the English Channel near Pas de Calais. The German leaders assumed that landings anywhere else in Europe were diversions from the main Allied strategic effort. Each of the subsidiary plans reinforced this preconceived notion, masked Allied actions, reduced ambiguity in German perceptions, and increased ambiguity about Allied intentions. Had soldiers on the Western front been the target of the deception, Operation Bodyguard would have been a tactical deception. The fact that the German leaders responsible for setting the course for that nation were the ones deceived, in part, made Bodyguard a strategic and operational deception instead.

Other illustrative historical examples of strategic and operational deception include:

German rearmament after World War I[11]—The German government played on the popular international perception that Germany was a weak nation while executing a systematic approach of cheating, lying, covert actions, and concealment to rearm prior to World War II.

Arms buildup by the Soviet Union during the Cold War[12]—Throughout the Cold War, the Soviets aggressively improved their intercontinental ballistic missile capabilities under a cover story that fostered perceptions on the international stage that missile superiority was not their aim. At times, they even resorted to strategic actions intended to convince the world that the Soviet Union wanted to stop the arms race and even disarm.

Chinese troop movements during the Korean War[13]—During the Korean War, the Communist Chinese carried out an operational deception by marching their army nearly three hundred miles over a period of 18 days, moving only at night and resting under concealment during the day. This deception was successfully carried out despite the Allies' technical superiority and the presence of supposedly infallible Allied air surveillance.

The Arab-Israeli wars[14]—Prior to 1970, Israelis and the world perceived Israel as the weaker power, resulting in Israel's aggressive employment of deception at all levels to establish every possible military advantage against the surrounding Arab nations. By 1973, after repeated victories against the Arabs, the Israelis came to view themselves as the stronger power and abandoned deception as part of their military strategy. At the same time, the Arabs embraced military deception. The results of these changes played out in the 1973 war with significant Israeli defeats before outside support from the United States helped Israel to stop the Arab invasion.

U.S. Military Deception Doctrine

The principles, referred to as "doctrine," for U.S. warfighting are published by the Department of Defense in a library of documents called Joint Publications and may be supplemented by service-specific publications. The doctrine for U.S. military deception is summarized as follows:

Military deception affects the quality of information of the target—the object of the deception—by (1) degrading its accuracy; (2) providing a false sense of its completeness; or (3) causing misjudgment about its relevance.

Strategic deception "attempts to influence adversary strategic decision makers' capability to successfully oppose U.S. national interests and goals. . . . [and] to undermine adversary national leaders and senior military commanders' ability to make accurate decisions . . . [resulting in] adversary strategic objectives, policies and operations that favor [U.S.] interests."

Operational deception "seeks to influence adversary operational-level decision makers' ability to successfully conduct military operations. . . . [and] to undermine adversary operational commanders' ability to make decisions and conduct campaigns and major operations . . . [influencing decisions] before, during and after battle so that tactical outcomes can be exploited at the operational level."

The objective of military deception is to "focus actions and resources to cause an adversary to take (or not to take) specific actions, *not just to believe certain things*" [my emphasis].

Methods for military deception include: masking activity, shaping perceptions, reinforcing preconceived notions, distracting attention, overloading systems and people, creating illusions, desensitizing through patterns of behavior, confusing, and reducing the ability to perceive.

Military deception is a component of what the U.S. military refers to as information operations.

Military deception differs from psychological operations in terms of the intended target. Psychological operations, which may or may not coincide with military deceptions, "normally targets groups while [military deception] targets specific individuals."[15]

In short, U.S. military deception is directed at an individual decision maker and is intended to cause specific actions, while neglecting the role of organizations in conducting deception and the equally vital task of unmasking deception. The current doctrine also fails to recognize value in changing an adversary's beliefs or causing inaction through confusion.

The success of Operation Bodyguard was the outcome of using the principles for military deception: (1) meticulous preparation; (2) a credible premise—one made more so by reinforcing an adversary's preconceived notions; (3) well-executed timing, duration, and coordination with specific events; (4) the use of all possible means to communicate the deception and receive feedback on its effectiveness; (5) highly centralized control; (6) the use of flexibility and expendability to preserve operational security and mask real intentions; (7) keeping knowledge of the deception closely held to prevent discovery; and (8) careful coordination among the appropriate military staffs.[16] Both the human and technical dimensions of deception were critical to the detailed planning and execution of Bodyguard. Both were also critical to preventing the failure of the deception or its discovery by the enemy.

Clausewitz or Sun Tzu?

Sun Tzu and Clausewitz are frequently credited as the sources of the intellectual foundation of U.S. military thinking and doctrine. Carl von Clausewitz was a Prussian general, historian, and military theorist whose seminal book, *On War,* was based on his experience in and observations about warfare from the 1790s to the 1810s. Clausewitz has played and continues to hold the preeminent role in American military training, education, doctrine, and strategic principles.

In chapters 9 and 10 of Book Three of *On War,* Clausewitz discussed surprise and cunning, respectively. He acknowledged that every action based on surprise had at least a partial basis in deceit. But cunning based only on deceit "has nothing in common with methods of persuasion, of self-interest, or of force."[17] Clausewitz concluded that cunning and deception had not played significant roles in warfare over the course of history. Deception had so little strategic value, and then only when a coincidental situation arose making it effective, that Clausewitz declared it lacked practical value. The level of effort and expenditure of resources required to conduct a deception were excessive and well out of proportion to the strategic or operational value achieved, and the same results could be realized by applying those efforts and resources to warfighting. "Strategy is exclusively concerned with engagements and with the directions relating to them. . . . [the] strategist's chessmen do not have the kind of mobility that is essential for stratagem and cunning. . . . accurate and penetrating understanding is a more useful and essential asset for the commander than any gift for cunning."[18] Clausewitz's dismissal of deception has caused the U.S. military to inappropriately minimize, or even neglect, military deception.

Sun Tzu had a different view regarding military deception:

All warfare is based on deception. Therefore, when capable, feign incapacity; when active, inactivity. When near, make it appear that you are far away; when far away, that you are near. Offer the enemy a bait to lure him; feign disorder and strike him. . . . Anger his general and confuse him. Pretend inferiority and encourage his arrogance. Attack where he is unprepared; sally out when he does not expect you. These are the strategist's keys to victory.[19]

Unlike Clausewitz, Sun Tzu concluded that cunning and deception played a central role in warfare. He also emphasized deception that focused on the mind of the enemy, especially its leader. Warfare in China around 500 B.C. led Sun Tzu to conclude that the successful leader must be equally facile with the use of force and the use of deception.

Sun Tzu has played a minor role in U.S. and Western military thinking, resulting in only limited consideration of deception in strategic or operational planning. In contrast, his message was embraced by Communist Chinese leader Mao Zedong and by the leader of the North Vietnamese Army, General Vo Nguyen Giap. The writing of Sun Tzu is central to the thinking of many terrorists and guerillas. Although strongly relevant to the military environment today, Sun Tzu remains neglected by the U.S. military.

Both Clausewitz and Sun Tzu acknowledged that deception requires an investment of significant time and resources. While neither theorist explicitly addressed the human dimension of resources, they would probably agree with Frank (this volume) and O'Sullivan (this volume). On an individual level, deception requires significantly greater cognitive capacity and personal attention than remaining truthful. Clausewitz and Sun Tzu would also agree that planning, executing, and maintaining deception places similarly heavy demands on the intellectual resources of an organization. Greatly complicating these individual and organizational challenges is the requirement that the U.S. military must be able to deceive an adversary while simultaneously being "scrupulously honest and credible" to the American public.[20]

Current U.S. Military Culture and Deception

Existing American military culture has made military deception a lost art. Routinely neglecting the human aspect of warfare, the current culture embraces technology as the solution to military challenges of all types. Many military theorists argue that advances in technology make deception prohibitively difficult, if not impossible. The high-cost equipment and systems that characterize much of today's modern military have pushed lower-cost, less-tangible activities such as deception into the background.[21] This gravitation toward expensive systems reflects an American tendency to believe that if something costs more, it must be better and thus more valuable. The American military's belief in the value of overwhelming military capability argues against applying effort, resources, and planning to military deception, favoring instead the reliance on unmatched firepower, precision, and speed. Yet, as discussed elsewhere in this book relative to deception, technology is a double-edged sword and may not always provide the benefit desired or intended.

Like Clausewitz, U.S. military commanders are reluctant to devote scarce resources and time to activities that are considered less important or less certain than technologically based tactics or that may have only limited value in combat. Military deception also suffers from the fact that it is unique to every situation and cannot be mass produced, requiring skill and imagination on a case-by-case basis. Few Americans are proficient in its planning and execution.

Finally, within the U.S. military, deception is perceived as a "Third World technique," or action beneath the dignity of a first-rate military power.[22] The employment of deception is viewed as an admission of weakness, when it should be treated as a complement to agility at the strategic and operational levels of war.

The American dismissal of military deception is particularly disconcerting in the face of strong evidence that the Soviet Union employed aggressive deception throughout the Cold War, as al-Qaeda and other adversaries do today.[23] As a result, the U.S. military suffers in its ability to understand, recognize, and counter deception by its potential adversaries. By neglecting military deception, the U.S. military has hindered its ability to compete in the information domain where deception occurs.

Unique to the U.S. military is the constraint on the conditions under which military personnel, on an individual level, and the Department of Defense (DOD), on an organizational level, can carry out deception. While the DOD may use military deception as part of military operations, the American public has made it clear that deception by the DOD off the battlefield is not acceptable behavior. The short existence of the DOD Office of Strategic Influence illustrates this point. In late 2001, the Office of Strategic Influence pursued its assigned mission to secretly conduct psychological operations and propaganda using foreign media, the Internet, and covert operations in order to influence sentiment and policy in both unfriendly and friendly countries.[24] In compliance with U.S. domestic law, and to keep a clear distinction between military deception and conveying information to the public, the U.S. military has traditionally used a function called the Public Affairs Office (PAO). The success of a PAO is directly connected to the trust established between PAO officers and their audiences. In general, military commanders do not involve PAOs in any military deception efforts whatsoever, in order to prevent jeopardizing that trust.[25] The mission and activities of the Office of Strategic Influence broke that trust, and with it, the DOD violated an American constraint on military deception. In response to American public pressure, the Office of Strategic Influence was quickly disbanded.

In summary, U.S. doctrine and military culture regarding military deception currently accord it little or no value in warfare; argue that it is not worth the necessary time and resources; allow it to be trumped by high-technology weapon systems and raw firepower; discredit it as only used by an inferior military force; assume that all sides conduct military deception in full compliance of international law and norms of warfare; require it to be conducted simultaneously with complete honesty regarding other military activities; assume that it is conducted in a relatively static, stable environment reflective of World War II; mistakenly apply a "one size fits all" approach; target only an individual adversary decision maker; and validate deception effectiveness strictly in terms of observable action by the adversary.

The Environment for Military Deception Today

Today, military deception must be conducted in an environment with time, scale, intensity, speed, and adaptability factors that is vastly different from that of the past. Military deception occurs within a broader competition of ideas that requires continuous, consistent, and sustained effort to prevail against opposing ideas. Military deception, much like other deception, is an interactive social process that occurs on multiple levels and on multiple scales. First, military deception is a problem of detection: in order for the deception to occur, the target must detect the signaling. Second, the target must recognize the situation, at least implicitly: seeing a picture or hearing the sounds generated by a deceptive tactic does not guarantee that the target recognizes the deception. Implicit recognition may be sufficient if the deceiver is trying to display a status quo as a cover for changes. In contrast, explicit recognition is necessary when the deceiver seeks changes in the environment in order to change the target's perceptions. Third, military deception requires cooperation from the target, individually and organizationally, in its ability and willingness to "take the bait." Finally, military deception requires action by the target, with the expectation that the action will be useful to the deceiver. Action in a manner different from that desired by the deceiver can be problematic, causing the deception to fail or inducing other undesirable actions.[26]

The environment is characterized by complexity. There is a dramatic difference between changing the behavior of a single individual and changing the behavior of a group of individuals. Predicting what will happen in a short time frame (minutes to days) may be reasonably achievable, but predicting what will happen in a medium or long time frame (weeks, months, or longer) may not be possible with any degree of certainty. Cause-and-effect relationships are often highly nonlinear and typically not straightforward. Success or failure of military deception hinges on understanding these aspects of a complex adaptive system.

Americans tend to view warfare as primarily a nation-state–to–nation-state matter. Furthermore, they view the other nation-state and its military as a homogenous entity with clear interests led by a single leader. Too often, the United States either starts from this single, unified, Rational Actor model or quickly devolves to that perspective. Current U.S. military deception doctrine suffers from this specific shortcoming. While desires for simplicity may drive U.S. efforts to focus on a single actor, the reality demands an approach that goes beyond a single actor to recognize nonstate organizations within a nation-state, as well as groups that may have no relationship with any existing nation-state.

Current U.S. military doctrine requires action in order for a deception to be considered successful. The absence of action or the delay in a decision is not considered a valid objective for deception by the U.S. military, despite the fact that, in a time-sensitive environment, delay may be exactly what is needed to gain an advantage or establish the desired conditions. Further complicating this matter is the reality that the speed and reach of information has increased dramatically in the past 10–20 years. Arguably, time zones may be more important than territorial boundaries. Consider, for example, an anecdotal case in which information provided to a local leader in an underdeveloped nation is on the front page of the Los Angeles Times within 48 hours. All of this occurred without any sense that the information was intended to deceive the local leader, but it quickly became part of U.S. domestic reporting.

The matters of scale and context are second nature to biology and the social sciences. In addition to the levels of war discussed earlier, military deception in the 21st century warrants an equally sophisticated approach with due consideration for (1) the human aspect, (2) the duration and time constant of change, (3) information availability and movement, and (4) technology.

Human Consideration

The human consideration in today's environment for military deception must address individuals, organizations, and networks. Existing U.S. doctrine remains focused on the adversary commander as the target to be deceived. Discussions about perceptions are tied to the specific individual's view of reality and "who will perform the act (a threat commander with the power to act)."[27] In reality, the conduct of military deception and the target's reaction to being deceived must play out on the targeted individuals and their organizations, simultaneously. The ubiquity of information movements and the organizational arrangements that characterize the battlespace today further shift the balance away from one individual and toward the organization within which decisions are made. Principles of military deception that focus on the individual leader are not sufficient.

A detailed discussion of the cognitive factors and organizational influences related to decision making are beyond the scope of this chapter. Graham Allison and Philip Zelikow present three useful frameworks for considering the balance between the individual and the organization in the process of military deception. Military deception, much like decision making in foreign affairs, is a mix of "art," focused on uniqueness and nuance, and "science," with a drive to discover generalities and rigor.[28] The theory and practice of U.S. military deception is predicated primarily on a belief in the Rational Actor model. This perspective neglects the organization and the surrounding government that have a direct role in being deceived, in fostering any decisions, and in carrying out the action that results from the deception.

Further complicating the human scale is the military fact that the adversary may be geographically dispersed and functionally distributed, which changes the nature of the battlespace and environment in fundamental ways not accounted for in existing military deception doctrine.[29] Unlike World War II, the adversary may no longer be geographically localized or reasonably well behaved (in terms of compliance with the Geneva Conventions or in terms of following traditional habits).

Time Consideration
Time accounts for such temporal factors as duration of activity (for example, how long does the activity persist?) and the time constant of changes in the environment (for example, how rapidly does the environment change?). Military deception must operate in an environment that is sensitive to time scales ranging simultaneously from fractions of a second to years or decades. At the strategic level, some opportunities for military deception may be protracted in nature; others may be fleeting. Regardless of the duration of the deception, it must remain sensitive to events that can occur in seconds or minutes. Just as significant, deceptions made in response to fleeting opportunities may persist beyond their intended duration. Consider the persistence on the Internet of what are referred to as "urban legends." Despite invalidation, many urban legends persist in the competitive domain of ideas having to be disproved over

and over again. There is no clear pattern regarding the temporal dynamics of the Internet and other technologies, or of their role in deception. While one must account for time scales of months or years—highlighted so often in the history of military deception—deception must also be able to be carried out in seconds, minutes, and hours.

In addition to the complexities of the overall environment, the limiting factor in conducting military deception (or in being susceptible to an enemy's deception) may be the ability of an organization to gather, synthesize, and disseminate the necessary information to decision makers; for those decision makers to make a decision; and, finally, for the organization to implement the directed actions. An organization that requires hours or days to sense and react to a situation may be oblivious to deceptive actions carried out in seconds or minutes. Similarly, an organization that senses and acts in minutes or hours may well lose sight of a deception that is carried out over months or years.

Information Availability and Movement Consideration

Information availability and movement addresses the factors related to information, such as availability, plausibility, credibility, latency, and perishability, which are at the heart of all deception. Of particular interest to practitioners of military deception are the number and variety of channels to send and receive information, and the implications that surround the sheer volume of information. Selecting the right channel to communicate with the target audience has become critical to the process. Information in the mainstream newspapers or in commercial television may be unrecognized by an organization that lives in the blogs and wikis of the Internet.

The plausibility of the information and credibility of the source are both important for determining its truthfulness. These factors must be evaluated in the context of the appropriate social framework, as discussed by Fine (this volume). Military deception may act on plausibility and credibility to generate a false sense of trust, or it may act to undermine an existing trust. Both actions may have a significant negative effect on social networks by causing them to fracture, by offering an advantage to potential insurgents, or by alienating loose coalitions of like-minded nations.

In addition, Urton (this volume) concludes that strongly hierarchical organizations and controlled information flow are two conditions that make deception more easily accomplished. When coupled with an underlying belief that certain people are truthful, deception becomes still easier and detection of deception more difficult. As the perceived trustworthiness of the information source increases, the more likely the deception is to succeed and to escape discovery. The challenge becomes recognizing the limits over control of information that exist today and determining the effect those limits have on plausibility and credibility.

Today, the information domain has become marked by a faster competition of ideas. Ideas have varying degrees of persistence; they cannot be killed like a person or sunk like a ship. Practicing deception, preventing deception, and countering active deception reflect vigorous competition in which one idea is replaced by another that seems more credible or more compelling. Metaphors inspired by biology—such as viral marketing, infectivity, and flocking—describe how ideas can flow through a group, with resultant effects on the behavior of the group.[30] Military deception must consider this information fluidity and its effects on group behavior.

In the past, the objective of getting an individual decision maker to decide *and act* as the result of deception provided some reasonable bounds for information availability and persistence. Taking the view that military deception is a time-sensitive competition of ideas, any delay or inaction caused by doubt or distraction of the decision maker may be an effective outcome for a strategic deception.

Technology Consideration

Technology is a two-edged sword; it can help carry out, prevent, detect, react to, or counter deception. Often neglected and equally relevant is the fact that technology may also cause the deceiver to be misled. Technology can be empowering, but it must be approached with caution. The deceiver must be able to recognize, admit, and adapt to the possibility that the technology may not perform in the manner expected, or that it may cause unexpected human or organizational actions. This potential self-deception is driven by the common belief that modern technology is always good and correct, and by people's tendency to default to some excuse ("Well, the computer said . . ."). Technology can deceive the user. Military deception requires an agile and informed combination of technology and humanity, with full recognition of the strengths and weaknesses of both.

Technical methods, such as the alteration of digital photography (Hancock, this volume), present a significant challenge to military deception due to the lack of clear patterns or rules. Current military deception doctrine does not recognize the significance of "technologically mediated message[s]." Hancock focuses on the individual agent level, where nuance, context, method, and other seemingly unimportant factors become important to both deceiving and detecting deception. Farid (this volume) discusses how technical means have been used to start and maintain deceptions at all levels. The presence of digitally produced visual imagery has become central to communications. As a balance to the use of technology for deception, Farid states that the counter to digital forgeries may lay in "the science of digital forensics." Hancock and Farid address some technical aspects of the competition of ideas in military deception, and Thompson (this volume) expands on this theme by probing the use of the Internet. Yet none of these authors indicate that technology provides an advantage to the deceiver or the target.

U.S. military deception must change from its current staid condition to a doctrine and culture in which:

- Deception becomes part of a compelling competition of ideas that must be engaged.
- Deception would require significant intellectual capital, resources, and time to maximize the probability of success.
- Deception would be routinely considered as part of the overall military planning at the strategic and operational levels of war.
- Deception would be enhanced by modern technology.
- Deception would be assumed to be part of the strategy of all adversaries.
- Deception would be conducted by the United States in full compliance with international law and the norms of warfare, with the recognition that an adversary may not be comparably constrained.
- Deception by U.S. forces that is conducted simultaneously with other military activities would be subject to complete honesty, with the recognition that an adversary may not be comparably constrained.
- Deception would be conducted in a dynamic, complex environment.
- Deception would be accounted for as a human endeavor.
- Deception would be targeted at both adversary decision makers and relevant organizations.
- Deception would be considered successful if it causes the action, inaction, delay, or confusion on the part of the adversary, as appropriate for the strategic and operational intentions.

Conclusion

> It will be better to offer certain considerations for reflection, rather than
> make sweeping dogmatic assertions.
> *Alfred Thayer Mahan*[31]

Clearly, the environment within which military deception occurs has changed dramatically since the end of World War II. Yet existing U.S. doctrine for military deception remains essentially unchanged since 1945. Modern adversaries appear to recognize the dichotomy between existing U.S. doctrine and the environment, and they are using it to their decisive strategic and operational advantage.

Simply stated, the environment, scale, time frame, and relationships—in essence the context—within which military deception is conducted has changed significantly, making general conclusions difficult to draw and precluding unsophisticated or "one size fits all" approaches. At the same time, the failure or inability of the U.S. military to understand today's cognitive battlespace for military deception—a highly competitive, time-sensitive, information-filled domain—hinders U.S. ability to carry out successful military deceptions.

Military deception is intended to induce behavior from a target by influencing the target's perceptions. Accordingly, to be most effective the deceiver must match the scale and complexity of the deception to that of the target much the way biologists and social scientists address scale and context in their work. Military deception requires an equally sophisticated approach.

The effectiveness of a single action taken to deceive one person or a small number of people may be diminished through inconsistency with all other actions—either intentionally or unintentionally. The importance of the individual decision maker as the target of deception may be less important when much of what is sensed, perceived, consolidated, and acted upon—the battlespace—is accessible to and occupied by millions of people. The evolution of military command arrangements *from* centralized command, control, and execution *toward* decentralized collaboration, control, and execution—across a network of people surrounding the military commander—further challenges the validity of deception principles based on a single decision maker.

Military deception must shift away from deceiving the national leader or military commander and toward deceiving the collective organization—the social, organizational, and technical networks—within which the leader functions, decisions are made, and actions are carried out. The deception surrounding the Allied invasion of France in World War II, for example, focused heavily on deceiving Hitler and a few of his key generals, and current U.S. military deception doctrine still embraces this approach. While deception of key leaders remains important, al-Qaeda's deceptions, for example, are less about deceiving President Bush, the Secretary of Defense, or the U.S. regional military commander than they are about deceiving the world, the larger U.S. national security community, and the American people. al-Qaeda's deceptions are less concerned about the abilities of its individual leaders to deceive and more concerned about its ability as an organization to plan and carry out a deception at the strategic, operational, and tactical levels of war, simultaneously.

The professionals responsible for military deception must be *intellectually* agile and adaptive, and any adopted doctrine or plan must be *operationally* agile and adaptive. At any point in the planning and execution of military deception, the environment may change in unexpected ways. Military deception must be robust in order to absorb an attack or actions taken to foil the deception, while still being able to prevent deception by adversaries.

Over the past three hundred years, the nature of the battlespace has changed. The geographic scale of forces and the commander's area of regard have increased from visual range (hundreds of yards) to global ranges (thousands of miles). The time domain of warfare has expanded from a range of hours to months to a range of nanoseconds to decades.

Some argue that technology has made everything in the battlefield "seeable," driving the situation back to the early 1800s. The same line of reasoning implies that technology has made deception even more difficult.[32] Nothing could be further from the truth. In reality, modern military deception is neither easier nor harder than in the past—it is just different. Relying exclusively on past techniques and understandings is not sufficient for understanding deception today. It is time for military deception to become central to U.S. strategic thinking and military operations, and for the practice of military deception to adapt to the 21st century.

15 The Pleasures of Lying

Kenneth Fields

> The Greeks have bequeathed to us two figures whose real or mythical
> lives conform to these two notions—Plato and Ulysses. The one shares
> Reason with the Gods, the other shares it with the foxes. . . . the history of
> the practical Reason must be traced back into the animal life from which
> mankind emerged. Its span is measured in terms of millions of years,
> [whereas] the history of the speculative Reason is altogether shorter. It
> belongs to the history of civilization, and its span is about six thousand years.
>
> *Alfred North Whitehead, The Function of Reason*[1]

W HEN I TOLD A COLLEAGUE I was going to a conference on
lying and he asked, "Are you for or against?" I realized that
only a fool would be against. What would the world be without lies? Sometimes we expect a delicious lie, in a bar for example, with the Bellamy Brothers
on the box: "I'm a doctor, I'm a lawyer, I'm a movie star / I'm an astronaut,
and I own this bar, / And I'd lie to you for your love. And that's the truth."
Self-confessed lies are especially delicious, as in Lord Charles Beresford's tele-
gram to the Prince of Wales: "Very sorry can't come. Lie follows by post."
Liars require "lie-ees," an audience, and their relation is a kind of contract,
as in this line from the poet Edgar Bowers: "Deceit was the desire to be deceived."[2] In Shakespeare's sonnet 138, both lovers are lying and want to believe
their lies: "When my love swears that she is made of truth / I do believe her,
though I know she lies."

A classic example is the urban legend. What should we think of someone
who begins a story by swearing that it is not a lie but the truth, and that he or
she has witnesses—never a friend, but a friend of a friend? (Folklorists call

---

KENNETH FIELDS is professor of English and creative writing at Stanford University. His
books of poetry include *The Odysseus Manuscripts* (1981) and *Classic Rough News* (2005). He is
completing a book of essays, "On the Loose."

this attribution a FOAF.) Unless we are professional debunkers, we ignore the standard markers of a lie; we want these marvelous fictions to be true. And, like Miniver Cheevy, we have reasons.

Folklorists have noted the persistence of stories about a famous actor admitted to the Cedars-Sinai Hospital emergency room for the removal of what has been called the colorectal rodent.

Let us say the story gives the teller a sense of superiority, or, let us say, of dominance. Gary Alan Fine, in *Manufacturing Tales*, argues that corporations such as McDonald's, KFC, and Coca-Cola are the targets of urban tales because of an American anxiety about capitalist dominance.[3] Perhaps our movie stars represent another sort of dominance, another sort of anxiety. What interests me is that, whereas some of the racist legends get repeated with more current athletes or other stars, the rodent in the homoprurient legend has remained lodged in the now white-haired but still handsome costar of *Pretty Woman*. This leads me to suspect that for straight men the story may not be homophobic, but heterophobic. Men can tell it to women, suggesting that although they might think this prepossessing man is a stud, they do not know about his inner submissive sex life; and men can tell it to each other, slyly hinting that he could be our bitch. These stories pass easily from the improbable to the impossible, and yet we want to believe them.

People who fill our in-boxes with stories and grave warnings resent being directed to snopes.com. For complicated reasons related to the structures of our social anxieties, as Fine has shown us, we want those rats to stay where they are—in the pretty boy and the KFC fry basket—and we resent any facts that dim the pleasures of these deceptions. On the other hand, when Gary Alan Fine shows that mice *have* been found in Coca-Cola bottles, does it not speak to our complex relation to these stories that some of us are actually disappointed?

The poet Thom Gunn's house in San Francisco was open until his death in 2004, a survival of bohemian hippie culture, with many visitors. One was a young man they called Pretty Jim, who during the time he was there did not say a word to anyone until one day when he uttered a single astonishing sentence, "Trust is an intimate conspiracy." That is all he said. The next day this trickster ripped off the house and disappeared, surviving now only in the world of poetry.[4]

> I see him
> picking through their things
> at his leisure, with

a quiet secret smile
choosing and taking,
having first discovered
and set up his phrase to
scramble
that message of
enveloping trust.

The mention of the supreme trickster-transformer of many Indian tribes, Coyote, sets off a complicated set of expectations, according to Barre Toelken and Tacheeni Scott. Coyote conjures a world made of stories—we might translate, a world of fiction or poetry:

> The stories act like "surface structure" in language: by their articulation they touch off a Navajo's deeper accumulated sense of reality; they excite perspectives on truth by bringing together a "critical mass" made up of ethical opposites (one thinks of the Zen koan here); they provide culturally enjoyable correlatives to a body of thought so complicated and profound that vicarious experience in it through entertainment is one of the only access points available to most people.[5]

Children often begin to giggle at the start of a story because they know they will hear about Coyote's impulsiveness; Archie Phinney, the Nez Perce anthropologist, translates this characterization as "You inveterate doer of this kind of thing!"[6] If Coyote is commanded not to open a box, the children laugh because he will not be able to control himself. He will open the box. In many of the stories, Coyote himself ends up being deceived—the fooling fool fooled, to use Karl Kroeber's trope. Liar, buffoon, shrewd knower, this trickster is a powerful deity, we might say, a divine fuckup, present from the creation, before people came into the world; his unwitting function is to prepare the world for us, to transform it.

Yellowman tells Barre Toelken, "Through the stories everything is made possible." This is Coyote's role as transformer. Although he nearly always brings death into the world, he is unaware of consequences—that is for us to know. What does he authorize or make possible? Well, lying, deception—but also the possibility of perceiving deception and of learning from one's mistakes. Toelken says of his informant, "For whatever it is worth, Yellowman sees Coyote as an important entity in his religious views precisely because he is not ordered. He, unlike all others, experiences everything; he is, in brief, the exponent of all possibilities"—perhaps the agent of multiplicity that Murray Gell-Mann might admire.[7]

Even his motives are complex beyond categorization. When he tells the Quail mother that he loves her babies and would like a topknot like theirs, of course he wants to eat them, but it is his nature to genuinely like them, too. Like Odysseus, curiosity is one of his traits. Quail tells him to do what she did to them: find a cedar wedge and drive it into the top of his head with a rock. He does and dies, but when he comes back (he is always in motion) they say he is smarter, with that bump of knowledge on the top of his head. Similarly, he is fooled, dies, and comes back with good eyes, teeth, nose, and those distinctive markings on his side. Quail, Deer, and his other adversaries are right to deceive this deceiver, who comes back "wise in conditions," to take a phrase from the poet Alan Stephens, whose rattlesnake, purveyor of death, is wise in conditions.[8]

One of Coyote's conditions is excrement. I recall one story, perhaps from California, in which Coyote allows himself to be recorded by an anthropologist who discovers, on returning home, that the tape recorder is stuffed with Coyote's turds. And in the Oregon stories, he frequently consults his excrements (this is the part children love), which talk back to him, giving him advice—reversing the tagline of *The X Files*, "the truth is out there." For Coyote, the truth is within him. To recall Yeats, he embodies the truth even if he cannot know it.

Much of Coyote's impulsiveness and subsequent shrewdness are captured in the transition from the first to the second pair of phrases in this Pima song from southern Arizona, recorded by Frank Russell near the end of the 19th century.[9] There are two different bunches of quail, and you should watch me recite it:

The gray quails were bunched together,
Coyote ran to look upon them.
The blue quails were bunched together;
Coyote looked sidewise at them.

As charming as many of the trickster stories are, it is important to know that tricksters are not human, although they may seem to be. Sometimes they are horrifying. In a famous Clackamas Chinook story from Oregon, "Seal and Her Younger Brother Lived There," Seal's brother brings home a wife.[10] The only suspicious person is Seal's daughter, a young girl, who complains to her mother that when her uncle's wife goes out to urinate she sounds like a man. Her mother shushes her. Throughout, bodily functions are described in euphemisms. The story has been amply commented on by many scholars, most notably Dell Hymes: the euphemisms (indicated in translation by quotation marks) include "goes out" for urinates, "lying" and "going" for intercourse, and so on. The girl, whose bed is below her uncle's, feels something drop on her face and tells her mother, who says, "Hmmmm. Shush. Those two are 'going.'" The girl hears something dripping down, "t'u'qt'u'q," and her mother silences her the same way. Finally, the girl gets up, lights the fire, holds up a torch, and sees that her uncle's throat has been cut, admonishes her mother's euphemisms, as opposed to her own direct sensory perceptions, and weeps real tears, while her mother speaks of her brother's wealth and social station. My summary cannot give the full sense of this story, but for our purposes it is important to note that social conventions (euphemism, traditional deference to the male family member, wealth, and station) have abetted this fatal deception. Many of us are accustomed to thinking of native or first cultures as being bound rigidly to convention, but this story points otherwise. Convention may be a deceiver. The girl—her functional trope here is "youngest, smartest"—sees directly; she is "wise in conditions." She also weeps, producing moisture from her own body in a story about urine, semen, and blood, and so it becomes a story about a girl reaching sexual maturity and talking back to her mother.

Hymes is persuasive when he rejects the idea that the story is about a homocidal transvestite. Rather, he says the "wife" is in reality a trickster, probably Raven, close here to being an ogre, who needs no motivation for deceiving and killing a human. Here, deception puts us on guard about a number of blinding cultural conditions. Tricky Dick told us, "I am not a crook." Another legendary figure of malevolence, Chain Dickey, was not drinking when he shot his friend in the face. His nominal boss, Grubby Shrub, would not have taken his kingdom to war without good legal cause, and so on. These fictional figures ought to sharpen our perception of lying. Ought to.

My other story comes from the great Nez Perce linguist, anthropologist, and student of Franz Boas, Archie Phinney, who learned these stories from his mother. It is called "Red Willow."[11] Although it is not a trickster story, it has dark and deep implications about deception, perhaps with a more comforting presentation of the tacit public voice. The fiancée of a young boy tells him she is going away on her vision quest. She then says—and it is not clear whether she speaks to him or only to herself or whether he overhears her or intuits it—"I am going for ten days, and if I do not return, then you will know that something has killed me." The boy follows her and kills her and hides the arrow in a clump of willows. He comes back and grieves. His little brother imitates him, singing "my fiancée," over and over again and shooting targets with arrows. His mother watches the little brother's mime and tells her husband that it is likely that their son has killed his fiancée. The girl's mother is looking toward the mountains, weeping, when a fly goes straight into her mouth; when the old woman bites down on it, it is fetid. She says immediately, "My daughter is dead," and calls a search party. They find the daughter's body but not the arrow, thus they cannot discover who the murderer is. And that is how the willow became red, the story ends, by maiden's blood.

Karl Kroeber says the story deals with matters he has not found in any ethnography, but which must have occurred; furthermore, he says—in a brilliant suggestive moment—that *we* know what the story is about (others may say privately what I said: "We do?"): "We do understand the young man's motivations, but we are hesitant to identify them"—which surely plunges us into mystery, into meditation.

From another essay by Kroeber, we learn that Nez Perce boys and girls went alone in search of their spirit guardian between the ages of five and ten—they were children.[12] Moreover, failure to have a vision was considered a disgrace. The child returning told no one, but acted it out in a dance, and the adults guessed its nature and judged whether it was real or not. (Think of the boy's mother observing the younger brother imitating him, singing "My fiancée, my fiancée.") Moreover, such a murder, if proved, demanded blood revenge. The story, according to Kroeber, embodies the anxieties and dangers of the vision quest. Did the girl want to die if she did not have a vision? Did the boy kill her because of this? Or because he was jealous of her vision? Was her vision that he would kill her? Or, most shocking, was *his* vision to kill her? However we meditate on this story, it displays what Kroeber, discussing American Indian literature, calls its "ramifying intricacy of ambivalences," and it ought to give us pause before seeing the issue of deception in terms of black and white.

The adults do not want to kill another child, but the little brother, in Yeats's terms, embodies the truth even if he does not know it; and both sets of parents—let us say, the members of society—know the truth, and so does the natural world, which is the significance of "Red Willow," the title of the story.

It is not about how the willow became red. It is a story of the declaration of a truth and the human decision to ignore it, for the best of reasons, reasons best revealed by what Dante called the beautiful lies of poetry.

The beautiful Nahuatl songs of native Mexico have been surrounded by deception for five hundred years. In *Cantares Mexicanos: Songs of the Aztecs*, a work that complements Gary Urton's work on the Inka khipu (this volume), John Bierhorst tells us that the Spanish invaders allowed these marvelous songs to survive because the Aztecs told them they were historic preconquest songs, from the previous century, describing ancient battles and rituals.[13] Some, the Aztecs told the Catholic priests, were even written by famous Aztec kings—Nezahualcoyotl was the most famous of these singers. The example of Plato conservatively banning poets from the republic because they were liars serves to remind us of an ancient connection between poetry and lies. Bierhorst tells us that there is no evidence that any of the kings ever wrote any songs at all and that these songs were postconquest, not preconquest; that is, they were contemporary expressions, clothed in deceptions that were so complete the Spanish priest even allowed them to be sung in the courtyards of churches. Furthermore, the priests wrote imitations of these songs, converting them to Christian terms, and the young Aztec novitiates likewise imitated the songs, inserting Christian saints into them—but, as Bernardino de Sahgun, a contemporary Spaniard, adds, "cloaked in many errors and heresies."

These songs, through an intricate elite code that Bierhorst elaborates, are evidence of a revivalist movement in response to the conquerors, songs that were chanted for a day when the slain warriors of the past would return as brightly colored birds and blossoms, and the conquerors would disappear. Of course, the Spanish were not aware of this aspect of the songs, and neither were we until the second half of the 20th century. This cult has analogies with the North American Native Ghost Dance religion, wiped out by the cavalry at Wounded Knee. The colorful, winged *voladores* (flyers), men still seen flying from tall poles in Mexico City, probably descend, whether consciously or not, from that Aztec tradition. Certainly, the Guadalupe cult comes from this movement, whose triumph has culminated in the Christian worship of an Aztec goddess.

It is virtuous to lie to oppressive power. Bierhorst has published a marvel of a book, *Doctor Coyote*, a collection of stories the conquering priests had young Aztec boys translate from the fables of Aesop, tales about wit overcoming superior force.[14] The young Aztecs turned the heroes of these tales into Coyote, their trickster. Similarly, the Uncle Remus stories Joel Chandler Harris collected take as their hero that African and African American trickster, Brer Rabbit, who, when Brer Fox is ready to kill him, begs not to be thrown into the briar patch (in fact, his native turf). Roast me, he begs, hang me, drown me, "'skin me, . . . snatch out my eyeballs, t'ar out my years by de roots, en cut off my legs,' sezee, 'but do please, Brer Fox, don't fling me in dat briar patch.'" Manifesting everything one needs to know about slavery, Brer Fox immediately throws Brer Rabbit into the briar patch, and as the trickster escapes, he hollers: "'Bred an bawn in a briar patch, Brer Fox—bred an bawn in a briar patch,' an wid dat he skip out des ez lively ez a cricket in the embers."[15]

What would it be like to have a god who stood for deception, for lying and stealing and making us laugh? For the Greeks, this was Hermes, a trickster who, when he was a day-old baby, got out of his cradle and carried off several of Apollo's cattle while wearing backwards something like snowshoes to throw the god off his track. He butchered and cooked and ate the cattle, and when Apollo found him, he denied it. Furious, Apollo brought the baby before Zeus, and Hermes lied to Zeus, saying he did not even know what cattle were, he was only born yesterday—surely the first instance of this phrase, from the Homeric Hymn to Hermes. Zeus laughs, and because Hermes has made him laugh, he gives him a special place among the gods.

Odysseus, a prodigious liar, gets his name—Trouble—from his grandfather, Autolycus, the lone wolf whose patron is Hermes, god of cattle thieves and liars. Throughout *The Odyssey* we are reminded of Agamemnon, who, after a long time away from home, rushed to see his wife ("Honey, I'm home!") and was killed by her and her lover. Odysseus is craftier when he returns to Ithaca and lies to nearly everyone he meets, even to Athena, his own goddess, who is delighted that he lies to her. Here is my version of their encounter, from my 1981 book, *The Odysseus Manuscripts*:[16]

> **Athene**
> Lying again, and in disguise? What stories!
> I love you best of all, Odysseus.
> Like Hermes, when he still was in his crib,
> "Born yesterday," a cattle thief and trickster,
> Lying to Apollo and, worse, even to Zeus,
> Making them laugh, and getting off the hook,

Winning a special place among the gods,
You lie to me, and are the best of men,
Suspicious, calculating. The old folks say,
"Man is the animal who hesitates."
In Hades, you heard the story from his shadow,
How foolish Agamemnon, the impulsive leader,
After enduring all the usual troubles—
You know them well, and more—eagerly rushed home
To an exceedingly eager wife, and his last day.
Now you hold off, and lie to me. Old man,
The stubble shows what the gold corn was like.
The bow, the lyre—his power and his spirit—
Long-haired Apollo plays them cautiously,
Brings them to fullness, like the holy sunlight
Quick in your hair right now. And the corn comes back
And ripens in its time. You are the man,
I am the man yourself: the accumulated
Wisdom of your long life. In a short time
You will be ready, no more hesitations;
You need not fear those who would waste away
The granary of your perfected will;
Soon you will show them inspiration born
Of labor and long patience. Weathered and clear,
You will rain sunlight down upon them. Struck
As if by music, they will know, too late,
Straightforwardness, that comes from many turnings,
Justice, a plain song, intricate as fate.

I want to end where I started, with the Shakespeare sonnet I quoted from
in my opening: When my love swears that she is faithful to me, I do believe
her even though I know she sleeps around—a rough paraphrase that brings
another turn to our verb, *to lie*. The sonnets are taken to be the highest expression of love in English, and surely the book is still exchanged by lovers
everywhere. And yet, "Let us not to the marriage of true minds / Admit im-
pediments" notwithstanding, the book tells a story of betrayal, contempt,
self-hatred, recrimination, depression, aging, and jealousy—come to think
of it, it may well be our highest expression of love. Shakespeare identifies the
lies—that his lover is faithful and that he is not old—and concludes with a

melancholy pleasure; is there anything more poignant than "Although she knows my days are not the best?"

> When my love swears that she is made of truth
> I do believe her, though I know she lies,
> That she might think me some untutored youth,
> Unlearnéd in the world's false subtleties.
> Thus, vainly thinking that she thinks me young
> Although she knows my days are not the best,
> Simply I credit her false-speaking tongue:
> On both sides thus is simple truth suppressed.
> But wherefore says she not she is unjust?
> And wherefore say not I that I am old?
> O love's best habit is in seeming trust,
> And age in love loves not to have years told.
> Therefore I lie with her and she with me,
> And in our faults by lies we flattered be.

Although lies by their nature seem to hide the truth, in fact they also reveal it and elicit from us shrewd analyses that are erotic, psychological, social, and cultural. Tom Lutz's essay on crocodile tears exemplifies the shared complexities of domestic deception. And lies are often fun. Where would we be—where would this book be—without them?

Coda: Bric-a-Brac and Curios

> "Swift perception of relations, hallmark of genius," Pound's elision of Aristotle, demonstrating it. I once heard Grace Paley say, "A story's not a story unless it's two stories." Richard Wilbur, poet: "Works of art attract by a resembling unlikeness." In Athens the public transportation vehicles are called metaphorai.
>
> *Kenneth Fields, Bric-a-Brac*

> Tell all the Truth but tell it slant.
>
> *Emily Dickinson*

The French poet Paul Valéry believed that the world was perpetually threatened by two disasters, order and disorder. Moreover, in order "for [the mind] to carry out its characteristic labor of transformation, it has to be supplied with—*disorder!* . . . And the mind finds its disorder where it can. In itself, outside, everywhere. . . . To function, it must have the differential *Order-Disorder*, just as a heat differential is essential to a machine, or to any phenomenon whatever!"[17] I'm reminded of my trumpet teacher, Glenn Bengry, showing me how to find the center of a note, the sweet spot: "Let the note sag until it gets buzzy" (a sound you do not want); "the fat center is very close to the buzz; all you have to do is make a slight adjustment to find it." This is much more helpful than thinking of the right and the wrong notes as polarized, worlds apart.

In first cultures, worlds that seem to us very far apart are often very close together. Backwards people (humans who ride horses backwards and sit next to the fire in summer, complaining of the cold), clowns, and witches (not equivalent beings but perhaps structurally parallel) fall into clear cultural categories of humanity somewhere between the center and the edge of the harmonic structure of the tribe. The Navajo Night Chant is so holy that any mistake in singing or sand drawing invalidates the eight-and-a-half-day healing ritual that culminates in a night of joyous, communal singing. And yet, at the most important moment, the water sprinkler god enters as a clown, mocking the dancers, missing the steps, dancing backwards, and causing great merriment. In the old days, this was also a time for ribald innuendo and even sexual license.[18]

Plato, that most orderly philosopher, disrupts his carefully arranged discussion of beauty, the *Symposium*, with the intrusion of the drunken young Alcibiades, his hair beribboned and garlanded as if a ribald follower of Bacchus, and it is Alcibiades who identifies Socrates as a satyr in his eulogy and calls him a dissembler. The party is further disrupted by the arrival of drunken revelers and most of the guests passing out; with Socrates drinking all night and staying sober, apparently forcing the few listeners (*apparently* because Aristodemus, the source of the story, did not hear the beginning of the conversation and was more than half asleep during it) "to admit that the same man might be capable of writing both comedy and tragedy—that the tragic poet might be a comedian as well."[19]

Ironic figure of comedy and tragedy, Socrates, according to Alexander Nehamas, was not fully understood even by Plato and left an unsettling, crucial legacy:

[I]n Plato, a radically new sense of *eironeira* emerges for the first time. The *eiron*—the person who uses *eironeia*—is now no longer simply a cunning, dissembling hypocrite, an outright deceiver who intends and needs to escape completely undetected. The *eiron* is now transformed into a much more subtle character who lets part of his audience know that his words do not always mean what he says, and who does not mind if some people are aware of his dissembling. The dissembling is no longer secret, at least not from all of one's audience. This new understanding of the term . . . is made concrete and personified in Socrates.[20]

With Socratic irony we are in the realm of Coyote and art, not far from Mark Frank, who in one of his handouts at our conference remarked, "the ability to lie is cut from the same cloth as our greatest creative/intellectual triumphs." Very close, indeed, to Maureen O'Sullivan's palter parsers and truth wizards, whose very names suggest a complex of intellectual and intuitive skills. This is true both for liars and for those who somehow know how to read their creations, both negotiating the web of inference and implication, acutely aware of social convention without being frozen by it. Herman Melville, commenting on his doomed figure of innocence, Billy Budd, says he lacks the "sinister dexterity" necessary to survive in this world. The phrase does not simply mean a skill for dealing with evil, but something more contradictory, like "deft left-handed right-handedness." Surely those of us working at order, a crucial human endeavor, can appreciate Barbara Babcock-Abrahams's characterization of the trickster as an "interstitial figure," one who slips into the cracks between things. I take a certain stylistic comfort in her title, "A Tolerated Margin of Mess."[21]

Made up of thousands of stories, the trickster—whether Coyote, Spider, or Raven—is a bricolage; and because he uses whatever is at hand, he is also a *bricoleur*, working by innuendo and surprise. He is the enigmatic embodiment of multiplicity, of diversity. First cultures tell us that knowing these stories and getting a feeling for their styles is a matter of survival. When wonderful Hany Farid remarked over coffee that as a young man he had not valued literature and a little later that he loved Richard Feynman as scientist, I thought a couple of things: (1) the Tower of Power song, "You're Still a Young Man (Baby)," and (2) *Surely You're Joking, Mr. Feynman?* Who could be a more engaging literary figure than Feynman, whose archive in the broad sense includes accounts of essays he wrote in freshman Composition and the voices of bartenders, hustlers, and bar girls met in the vagaries of his unconventional academic life? Anyone called by Freeman Dyson "50 percent buffoon and 50 percent genius," who then revised it to "100 percent buffoon and 100 percent genius," has a place in the Coyote Hall of Fame.

In addition to the invigorating presence of Brooke Harrington, the *brico-leuse* who brought together this volume's remarkable group of scientists and scholars (and made the little coterie of mere litterateurs feel welcome), one of the unforgettable joys of this collaboration was the genial and sometimes intimidating presence of Murray Gell-Mann, cofounder of the Santa Fe Institute, who discovered the quark and named it from a passage in James Joyce's *Finnegans Wake.* When I was talking about Shakespeare's pun on the word *lie,* Murray looked up from under his eyebrows and, smiling, asked if I did not think Shakespeare had not got it right when he was translating Schlegel's original. I burst out laughing, "Murray, you are Coyote!" It is bracing to be reminded that Coyote is still in these mountains, where he has prowled, watching birds sidewise, for thousands of years.

In fact, to tell the truth at least this one time, I have felt wholly at ease at the Santa Fe Institute, and I know my colleagues share my gratitude. I hope these wandering remarks, at least in spirit, pay tribute to Murray Gell-Mann, who is attentive to the tension between the "universality envisioned by the Enlightenment and our need for the preservation of cultural diversity" and warns against the exploitations of particularity "by unscrupulous leaders."[22] Gell-Mann goes on to say:

> And yet at the same time, cultural diversity is itself a valuable heritage that should be preserved: that Babel of languages, that patchwork of religious and ethical systems, that panorama of myths, that potpourri of political and social traditions. One of the principal challenges to the human race is to reconcile universalizing factors such as science, technology, rationality, and freedom of thought with particularizing factors such as local traditions and beliefs, as well as simple differences in temperament, occupation, and geography.[23]

The competing claims for our attention, which Gell-Mann wants to keep in complex relation to each other, are always threatened by partition. Only special kinds of minds and special institutions can appreciate and pursue this arduous task, as Gell-Mann makes clear early in *The Quark and the Jaguar:*

> The philosopher F.W.J. von Schelling introduced the distinction (made famous by Nietzsche) between "Apollonians," who favor logic, the analytical approach, and a dispassionate weighing of evidence, and "Dionysians," who lean more

toward intuition, synthesis, and passion. These traits are sometimes described as correlating very roughly with emphasis on the use of the left and right brain, respectively. But some of us seem to belong to another category: the "Odysseans," who combine the two predilections in their quest for connections among ideas. Such people often feel lonely in conventional institutions, but they find at SFI a particularly congenial environment.[24]

Notes

Introduction

This volume grew out of a series of workshops at the Santa Fe Institute (SFI), a research institution devoted to cross-disciplinary research on complex adaptive systems in the biological, computational, social, and political sciences. The institute provides a unique setting in which scholars who would not ordinarily cross paths can exchange ideas on broad topics of shared interest. A project like this one would simply not have been possible without SFI and the support of President Geoffrey West, Vice President Chris Wood, and the Science Steering Committee. We are also deeply grateful to Professor Persi Diaconis of Stanford University, whose work inspired this project, and Bill Miller, chairman of SFI's Board of Trustees, who provided the financing. Finally, all the contributors wish to thank the remarkable Wayne Coté, Ginny Greninger, and Laurie Innes for making our time at SFI so pleasant and productive.

1. Leó Szilárd, *His Version of the Facts: Selected Recollections and Correspondence*, ed. Spencer Weart and Gertrud Szilárd (Cambridge, MA: MIT Press, 1979), xii.

2. St. Thomas Aquinas, "Question 110: On Lying," *Summa Theologiae: Vol. 41, Virtues of Justice in the Human Community* (Cambridge: Cambridge University Press, 2006), 147–68.

3. Plato, *The Republic*, trans. Benjamin Jowett (New York: Vintage, 1991), 3.389.

4. Winston Churchill, *The Second World War: Closing the Ring*, vol. 2 (New York: Houghton-Mifflin, 1951 [1943]), 4.

5. Sissela Bok, *Lying: Moral Choice in Public and Private Life* (New York: Pantheon Books, 1999). See also, Sissela Bok, *Secrets: On the Ethics of Concealment and Revelation* (New York: Pantheon Books, 1989).

6. Lawrence Henderson, "Physician and Patient as a Social System," *New England Journal of Medicine* 212 (1935): 49.

7. Carl Bergstrom and P. Godfrey-Smith, "Pure Versus Mixed Strategists: The Evolution of Behavioral Heterogeneity in Individuals and Populations," *Biology and Philosophy* 13 (1998): 205–31. See also M. Lachman, S. Számadó, and C. Bergstrom, "Cost and Conflict in Animal Signals and Human Language," *Proceedings of the National Academy of Sciences, USA* 98 (2001): 13189–94.

8. Bella DePaulo and D. Kashy, "Everyday Lies in Close and Casual Relationships," *Journal of Personality and Social Psychology* 74 (1998): 63–79.

9. R. Feldman, J. Forrest, and B. Happ, "Self-Presentation and Verbal Deception: Do Self-Presenters Lie More?" *Journal of Basic and Applied Social Psychology* 24 (200): 163–70.

10. G. Steiner, *After Babel: Aspects of Language and Translation* (New York: Oxford University Press, 1998).

11. Francois de La Rochefoucauld, *Maxims*, trans. Leonard Tancock (New York: Penguin, 2001 [1665]), 48.

12. Joan Didion, *Slouching Towards Bethlehem: Essays* (New York: Farrar, Strauss & Giroux, 1990 [1968]), 143.

13. James March and Herbert Simon, *Organizations* (New York: Wiley, 1958).

Chapter 1

1. "Oh what a tangled web we weave / When first we practise to deceive!" Sir Walter Scott, *Marmion*, canto vi, stanza 17.

2. J. Maynard Smith and E. Szathmáry, *The Major Transitions in Evolution* (Oxford: Oxford University Press, 1995).

3. E. Szathmáry and J. Maynard Smith, "The Major Evolutionary Transitions," *Nature* 374 (1995): 227–32.

4. J. R. Krebs and R. Dawkins, *Animal Signals: Mind Reading and Manipulation* (Oxford: Blackwell Scientific, 1984), chap. 15, 380–402.

5. M. Lachmann, G. Sella, and E. Jablonka, "On the Advantages of Information Sharing," *Proceedings of the Royal Society of London, B* 267 (2000): 1287–93.

6. Letter: Thomas Jefferson to Isaac McPherson (August 13, 1813) in *The Writings of Thomas Jefferson*, vol. 13 (Washington, DC: Thomas Jefferson Memorial Association of the United States, 1903), 333–34.

7. Anglerfish: T. W. Pietsch and D. B. Grobecker, "The Compleat Angler: Aggressive Mimicry in an Antennariid Anglerfish," *Science* 201 (1978): 369–70; flycatcher: C. A. Munn, "Birds that 'Cry Wolf,'" *Nature* 319 (1986): 143–45; bluegill sunfish: W. J. Dominey, "Maintenance of Female Mimicry as a Reproductive Strategy in Bluegill Sunfish (Lepomis macrochirus)," *Environmental Biology of Fishes* 6 (1981): 59–64; mimic octopus: M. D. Norman, J. Finn, and T. Tregenza, "Dynamic Mimicry in an Indo-Malayan Octopus," *Proceedings of the Royal Society of London, B* 268 (2001): 1755–58; fireflies: James E. Lloyd, "Aggressive Mimicry in Photuris: Firefly Femmes Fatales," *Science* 149 (1965): 653–54; fiddler crab: P. R. Y. Backwell, J. H. Christy, S. R. Telford, M. D. Jennions, and N. I. Passmore, "Dishonest Signalling in a Fiddler Crab,"

Proceedings of the Royal Society of London, B 267 (2000): 719–24; *caterpillars:* T. Akino, J. J. Knapp, J. A. Thomas, and G. W. Elmes, "Chemical Mimicry and Host Specificity in the Butterfly Maculinea Rebeli: A Social Parasite of Myrmica Ant Colonies," *Proceedings of the Royal Society of London, B* 266 (1999): 1419–26; stomatopods: R. Steger and R. L. Caldwell, "Intraspecific Deception by Bluffing: A Defense Strategy of Stomatopods (Arthropoda, Crustracea)," *Science* 221 (1983): 558–60.

8. J. Maynard Smith and D. G. C. Harper, "Animal Signals: Models and Terminology," *Journal of Theoretical Biology* 177 (1995): 305–11.

9. M. Lachmann and C. T. Bergstrom, "The Disadvantage of Combinatorial Communication," *Proceedings of the Royal Society of London, B* 271 (2004): 2337–43.

10. The term "legitimate participants" is a shorthand for describing those individuals whose historical participation in the interaction was causally responsible for the emergence of the signaling system in the first place.

11. P. Resnick and R. Zeckhauser, "Trust among Strangers in Internet Transactions: Empirical Analysis of eBay's Reputation System," in *The Economics of the Internet and E-Commerce,* ed. M. R. Baye (Amsterdam: Elsevier Science, 2002); J. Boyd, "In Community We Trust: Online Security Communication at eBay," *Journal of Computer-Mediated Communication* 7, no. 3 (2002).

12. eBay, "Spoof Email Tutorial," http://pages.ebay.com/education/spooftutorial/index.html (accessed November 2007).

13. A. M. Spence, "Job Market Signalling," *Quarterly Journal of Economics* 87, no. 3 (1973): 355–74; A. M. Spence, "Time and Communication in Economic and Social Interaction," *Quarterly Journal of Economics* 87, no. 4 (1973): 651–60; A. Zahavi, "Mate Selection: A Selection for a Handicap," *Journal of Theoretical Biology* 53 (1975): 205–14; A. Zahavi, "The Cost of Honesty (Further Remarks on the Handicap Principle)," *Journal of Theoretical Biology* 67 (1977): 603–5.

14. *Contra:* G. W. F. Davis and P. O'Donald, "Sexual Selection for a Handicap: A Critical Analysis of Zahavi's Model," *Journal of Theoretical Biology* 57 (1976): 345–54; J. Maynard Smith, "Sexual Selection and the Handicap Principle," *Journal of Theoretical Biology* 57 (1976): 239–42; M. Kirkpatrick, "The Handicap Mechanism of Sexual Selection Does Not Work," *American Naturalist* 127 (1986): 222–40. *Pro:* N. Nur and O. Hasson, "Phenotypic Plasticity and the Handicap Principle," *Journal of Theoretical Biology* 110 (1984): 275–97; A. Grafen, "Biological Signals as Handicaps," *Journal of Theoretical Biology* 144 (1990): 517–46; J. Maynard Smith, "Honest Signalling: The Philip Sidney Game," *Animal Behaviour* 42 (1991): 1034–35.

15. Zahavi's original formulation of the handicap principle differs from its modern interpretation; I will follow the modern view here. The difference is this: in his original papers on the handicap principle, Zahavi viewed handicaps as credible because they cause natural selection to "screen" signalers more intensely. Carrying a handicap—and surviving nonetheless—serves as a statistical signal of strength. When biologists think about costly signals today, they typically assume instead that a signaler makes a strategic choice of how large of a handicap to produce, taking into

account both the cost of doing so and the benefit that will come from the response of the signal receiver. This choice need not be a conscious decision or calculation on the part of the signaler; it can be a decision rule that is encoded by the genes and tuned through the action of natural selection. Relative to weak individuals, strong individuals can bear greater handicaps at lower costs, and so they will choose to produce larger ornaments. As a result, handicap size serves as a reliable signal of strength—and thus the receivers' preference for large handicaps is justified.

16. C. T. Bergstrom, S. Számadó, and M. Lachmann, "Separating Equilibria in Continuous Signalling Games," *Philosophical Transactions of the Royal Society of London* 357 (2002): 1595–606.

17. Nur and Hasson, "Phenotypic Plasticity"; M. Lachmann, S. Számadó, and C. T. Bergstrom, "Cost and Conflict in Animal Signals and Human Language," *Proceedings of the National Academy of Sciences, USA* 98 (2001): 13189–94.

18. C. T. Bergstrom and M. Lachmann, "Signalling among Relatives, Vol. 1: Is Costly Signalling Too Costly?" *Philosophical Transactions of the Royal Society of London Series B* 352 (1997): 609–17.

19. S. Rohwer, "The Social Significance of Avian Winter Plumage Variability," *Evolution* 29 (1975): 593–610; D. P. Whitfield, "Plumage Variability, Status Signalling and Individual Recognition in Avian Flocks," *Trends in Ecology and Evolution* 2 (1987): 13–18; J. Maynard Smith and D. G. C. Harper, "The Evolution of Aggression: Can Selection Generate Variability?" *Philosophical Transactions of the Royal Society of London, Series B* 319 (1988): 557–70.

20. Rohwer, "The Social Significance of Avian Winter Plumage Variability"; S. Rohwer, "Status Signaling in Harris Sparrows: Some Experiments in Deception," *Behavior* 61 (1975): 107–29; A. P. Moller, "Social Control of Deception among Status Signalling House Sparrows Passer domesticus," *Behavioral Ecology and Sociobiology* 20 (1987): 307–11.

21. Lachmann, Számadó, and Bergstrom, "Cost and Conflict in Animal Signals and Human Language."

22. Ibid.

23. Ibid.

24. Lachmann and Bergstrom, "The Disadvantage of Combinatorial Communication."

25. P. Hammerstein, ed., *Genetic and Cultural Evolution of Cooperation* (Cambridge, MA: MIT University Press, 2003); C. T. Bergstrom, J. L. Bronstein, R. Bshary, R. C. Connor, M. Daly, S. A. Frank, H. Gintis, L. Keller, O. Leimar, R. Noë, and D. C. Queller, "Interspecific Mutualism: Puzzles and Predictions Regarding the Emergence and Maintenance of Cooperation between Species," in *Dahlem Conference Report: Genetic and Cultural Evolution of Cooperation*, ed. S. Bowles and P. Hammerstein (Cambridge, MA: MIT University Press, 2003).

26. Resnick and Zeckhauser, "Trust among Strangers in Internet Transactions."

27. C. Anderson, "The Long Tail," *Wired* 12, no. 10 (2004).

28. L. R. Gooding, "Virus Proteins that Counteract Host Immune Defences," *Cell*

71 (1992): 5–7; D. M. Haig, "Subversion and Piracy: DNA Viruses and Immune Invasion," *Research in Veterinary Science* 70 (2001): 205–19.

29. A. Liston and S. McColl, "Subversion of the Chemokine World by Microbial Pathogens," *BioEssays* 25 (2003): 478–88.

30. Not only do viruses practice trickery by spoofing immune signals and fashioning decoy signal receptors, but their very ability to do so has also been acquired by a sort of trickery. In many cases, the genes that the virus uses to tamper with a host's immune system have been stolen from the host species' genome at some earlier point in the virus's evolutionary history. By virtue of replicating within host cells using the host's genetic machinery, viruses have "access" to the full genomes of the host and can incorporate modified versions of host genes into their own viral genomes.

31. The familiar vertebrate adaptive immune system is only one of many immune systems that have evolved in the biological world. For example, bacteria rely on simple immunelike pathways known as restriction-modification systems to detect and destroy viral DNA. Many eukaryotes from yeast to plants to insects use RNA interference (RNAi) as a form of intracellular immune response against viral infection. Plants and animals have evolved diverse and extensive mechanisms of innate immunity. Some immune systems even operate at the colony level: in addition to their individual immune systems, social insects use smell to distinguish between members of the colony and potentially dangerous outsiders.

32. C. T. Bergstrom and R. Antia, "How Do Adaptive Immune Systems Control Pathogens while Avoiding Autoimmunity?" *Trends in Ecology and Evolution* (January 2006).

33. Ibid.

34. R. C. Dorf and R. H. Bishop, *Modern Control Systems,* 10th ed. (Upper Saddle River, NJ: Prentice Hall, 2004).

35. H. Kitano, "Computational Systems Biology," *Nature* 420 (2002): 206–10.

36. S. Kaech and R. Ahmed, "Memory CD8+ T Cell Differentiation: Initial Antigen Encounter Triggers a Developmental Program in Naive Cells," *Nature Immunology* 2 (2001): 415–22; R. Antia, C. T. Bergstrom, S. Pilyugin, S. M. Kaech, and R. Ahmed, "Models of CD8+ Responses. 1. What Is the Antigen-Independent Proliferation Program?" *Journal of Theoretical Biology* 221 (2003): 585–98.

37. C. T. Bergstrom and R. Antia, "How Do Adaptive Immune Systems Control Pathogens while Avoiding Autoimmunity?" *Trends in Ecology and Evolution* (January 2006).

Chapter 2

1. Immanuel Kant, "On a Supposed Right to Tell Lies from Benevolent Motives," in *Kant's Critique of Practical Reason and Other Works on the Theory of Ethics,* ed. Thomas K. Abbott (London: Longmans, Green, 1898); Immanuel Kant, in *The Metaphysics of Morals,* ed. Mary Gregor (Cambridge: Cambridge University Press, 1996); Aristotle, *Nicomachean Ethics* Bk. IV (1127a): 28–30; Augustine, "Against Lying," in

Treatises on Various Subjects, ed. R. J. Deferrari (New York: Fathers of the Church, 1952); Thomas Aquinas, *Summa Theologiae*, vol. 41 (2a2ae 110): 3.

2. Sissela Bok, *Lying: Moral Choice in Public and Private Life* (New York: Pantheon Books, 1978).

3. Jeremy Bentham, *The Theory of Legislation*, ed. C. K. Ogden (New York: Harcourt, Brace, 1931), 170.

4. The effect is typically produced by the victim's belief in the sincerity of the liar's assertion, and so we might include this belief by the victim as a separate component of what constitutes a lie.

5. Or consider the situation, one that most academics have experienced, in which a smiling and grateful student announces that she has been offered the job or place in graduate school for which she thinks you have recommended her, when in fact you have still not gotten around to writing the letter. When you respond by saying that you are happy for her, or even "you're welcome," you have paltered, even though you have not lied.

6. Causation would be less important to a Kantian liar-focused account of the wrong of lying, but we believe it relatively noncontroversial under most other accounts to maintain that a lie derives part of its wrongfulness from the actual way in which it causes a recipient either to come to false belief or to be reinforced in a false belief.

7. Larry Alexander and Emily Sherwin, "Deception in Morality and Law," *Law and Philosophy* 22 (2003): 393–450.

8. When houses are sold in Cambridge, Massachusetts, it is now the norm that the seller is asked to respond to a questionnaire. One question is whether the house has leaked recently. But consider a response of "A few years ago, during that very rainy summer, there was mild seepage into the basement, perhaps a cup of water overall." If the roof has been leaking since then, however, this would be a palter. The potential buyer will not be suspicious, but leaving the question blank would raise suspicions, and stating explicitly that there were no roof leaks would be actionable.

9. We acknowledge, but nevertheless bracket, the agency problem in the example, such that the parent is trying to get the child to make the decision that the parent would prefer, and not necessarily the decision that even a well-informed child would make.

10. And especially so when the role of the person making the statement—car dealers, carpet salesmen, and so on—causes recipients of the messages to have their antennae up.

11. Robert Solo was a well-regarded economist at Michigan State University who undoubtedly had many temptations to use palters of omission when people were impressed upon meeting him because of the similarity of his name to that of the considerably more famous Robert Solow of MIT.

12. Amos Tversky and Daniel Kahneman, "Judgment under Uncertainty: Heuristics and Biases," *Science* 211 (1974): 1124–30; Amos Tversky and Daniel Kahneman, "Availability: A Heuristic for Judging Frequency and Probability," *Cognitive Psychology* 5 (1973): 207–32.

13. See Thomas Lutz, this volume, who also addresses the social impact of mis-

leading or false actions and words. For example, he observes that having his then-girlfriend see through his crocodile tears was important to their relationship.

14. It may be that the very teaching of this tale about George Washington itself involves some paltering. Teachers and parents suspect the story may be apocryphal, but they resolve the uncertainty in the way that assists the lesson they wish to impart, rather than in the way they believe most likely true.

15. The tree might have had a disease, for example, a disease that young George could have accurately described in order to avoid the fact that, disease notwithstanding, he chopped down the tree just for fun.

16. Clinton obviously miscalculated on this occasion, partly because he may have overestimated by orders of magnitude the number of people who would treat oral sex and sexual relations as different categories. Even so, Clinton still had the implausible but not completely impossible defense that he thought of the two as falling in significantly different categories, and therein lies the core of the idea of deniability.

17. Among these harms are various externalities, especially the way in which both paltering and lying tend to hurt people who do not engage in the practice. The more untruths that are told, the harder it is for the truth teller to be believed, as any honest used-car dealer or carpet salesman will tell you. Honest people must then either suffer the consequences of not being believed or spend additional resources—such as hiring intermediaries, offering special warranties, or paying for inspections—in order to be believed. Yet their counterparts in professions where liars and palterers are scarce face no such costs.

18. Section 12(2) of the Securities Act of 1933, for example, prohibits not only making an "untrue statement of a material fact," but also the omission of "a material fact necessary in order to make the statements, in light of the circumstances in which they were made, not misleading."

19. See *Restatement (Second) of Torts* §550 (1977) (literally true statements intentionally creating misimpressions); §527 (partial truths); see, generally, W. Page Keeton, Dan B. Dobbs, Robert E. Keeton, and David G. Owen, *Prosser and Keeton on the Law of Torts*, 5th ed. (St. Paul, MN: West, 1984), 725–38.

20. See *Model Penal Code* §223.3.

21. And so, too, for closely related reasons, for burglary. An increase in burglary in a neighborhood will increase the watchfulness of neighbors, the prevalence of alarm systems, and the frequency of police patrols. Thus the more burglary there is, the harder it is for the individual burglar; and the less burglary that exists, the easier it will be for an individual burglar to burgle undetected.

22. Of course, the trade-off rate is likely to increase with the intensity of rejection, because heterogeneity almost certainly exists among messages. Thus, some palters are relatively easy to detect, implying that eliminating them would entail few Type I errors. As the costs in Type I errors to avoid Type II errors becomes greater, the possibility curve showing the possible values for the two types of errors bulges toward (is convex to) the origin.

23. This huckster-sucker example points to why, popular conception aside,

retail establishments are very interested in finding out the names and identifying information of people who have declared personal bankruptcy. People in this category may be poor credit risks, but interest rates can offset any potential losses; more important to many retailers is that people who have declared personal bankruptcy are especially likely to be vulnerable to sales pitches and to spend beyond their means.

24. See Frederick Schauer, *Profiles, Probabilities, and Stereotypes* (Cambridge: Harvard University Press, 2003), 311–28.

25. See Frederick Schauer and Richard Zeckhauser, "On the Degree of Confidence for Adverse Decisions," *Journal of Legal Studies* 25 (1996): 27–52.

26. The success of eBay in promoting trust is due in large part to its system of rating reputations, in which buyers are asked to rate sellers after each transaction and in which reputations are posted. See Paul Resnick and Richard Zeckhauser, "Trust Among Strangers in Internet Transactions: Empirical Analysis of eBay's Reputation System," in *The Economics of the Internet and E-Commerce*, ed. M. R. Baye (Amsterdam: Elsevier Science, 2002), 127–57.

Chapter 3

1. Charles Darwin, *The Expression of the Emotions in Man and Animals*, 3rd ed., with commentary by Paul Ekman (New York: Oxford, 1998 [1872]).

2. Mark L. Knapp and Judith A. Hall, *Nonverbal Communication in Human Interaction* (London: Thomson Learning, 2002).

3. Bella M. DePaulo, Deborah A. Kashy, Susan E. Kirkendol, Melissa M. Wyer, and Jennifer A. Epstein, "Lying in Everyday Life," *Journal of Personality and Social Psychology* 70, no. 5 (1996): 979–95.

4. Maureen O'Sullivan, "The Fundamental Attribution Error in Detecting Deception: The Boy-Who-Cried-Wolf Effect," *Personality and Social Psychology Bulletin* 29, no. 10 (2003): 1316–27.

5. Hee Sun Park, Timothy R. Levine, Steven A. McCornack, Kelly Morrison, and Merissa Ferrara, "How People Really Detect Lies," *Communication Monographs* 69, no. 2 (2002): 144–57.

6. Robert S. Feldman, James A. Forrest, and Benjamin R. Happ, "Self Presentation and Verbal Deception: Do Self-Presenters Lie More?" *Basic and Applied Social Psychology* 24, no. 2 (2002): 163–70.

7. Suzanne Hala, Michael Chandler, and Anna S. Fritz, "Fledgling Theories of Mind: Deception as a Marker of Three-Year-Olds' Understanding of False Belief," *Child Development* 62, no. 1 (1991): 83–97.

8. Thomas Suddendorf and Andrew Whiten, "Mental Evolution and Development: Evidence for Secondary Representation in Children, Great Apes, and Other Animals," *Psychological Bulletin* 127, no. 5 (2001): 629–50.

9. Todd K. Shackelford, "Perceptions of Betrayal and the Design of the Mind," in *Evolutionary Social Psychology*, ed. Jeffry A. Simpson and Douglas T. Kenrick (Hillsdale, NJ: Erlbaum, 1997), 73–108.

10. Jeffrey J. Haugaard and N. Dickon Repucci, "Children and the Truth," in *Cognitive and Social Factors in Early Deception*, ed. Stephen J. Ceci, Michelle DeSimone-Leichtman, and Maribeth E. Putnick (Hillsdale, NJ: Earlbaum, 1992).

11. Paul Ekman, *Telling Lies: Clues to Deceit in the Marketplace, Politics, and Marriage*, 3rd ed. (New York: Norton, 2001).

12. Ibid.

13. Mark Curriden, "The Lies Have It," *ABA Journal* 81 (1995): 68–72.

14. Suddendorf and Whiten, "Mental Evolution and Development."

15. Ekman, *Telling Lies*.

16. Park et al., "How People Really Detect Lies."

17. Paul Ekman and Mark G. Frank, "Lies That Fail," in *Lying and Deception in Everyday Life*, ed. Carolyn Saarni and Michael Lewis (New York: Guilford, 1993); John E. Hocking and Dale G. Leathers, "Nonverbal Indicators of Deception: A New Theoretical Perspective," *Communication Monographs* 47, no. 2 (1980): 119–31.

18. Bella M. DePaulo, James J. Lindsay, Brian E. Malone, Laura Muhlenbruck, Kelly Charlton, and Harris Cooper, "Cues to Deception," *Psychological Bulletin* 129, no. 1 (2003): 74–118.

19. Bella M. DePaulo, Julie Stone, and Daniel Lassiter, "Deceiving and Detecting Deceit," in *The Self and Social Life*, ed. Barry R. Schlenker (New York: McGraw-Hill, 1985), 323–70; Paul Ekman, W. V. Friesen, and K. Scherer, "Body Movement and Voice Pitch in Deceptive Interaction," *Semiotica* 16, no. 1 (1976): 23–27.

20. Stephen Porter and John C. Yuille, "Credibility Assessment of Criminal Suspects Through Statement Analysis," *Psychology, Crime & Law* 1, no. 4 (1995): 319–31.

21. Udo Undeutsch, "The Development of Statement Reality Analysis," in *Credibility Assessment*, ed. John C. Yuille (New York: Kluwer Academic/Plenum, 1989).

22. John C. Yuille, *Credibility Assessment* (New York: Kluwer Academic/Plenum, 1989).

23. Miron Zuckerman and Robert E. Driver, "Telling Lies: Verbal and Nonverbal Correlates of Deception," in *Multichannel Integrations of Nonverbal Behavior*, ed. A. W. Siegman and S. Feldstein (Hillsdale, NJ: Erlbaum, 1985).

24. Ekman, *Telling Lies*.

25. Paul Ekman, "Strong Evidence for Universals in Facial Expression: A Reply to Russell's Mistaken Critique," *Psychological Bulletin* 115, no. 2 (1994): 268–87; Paul Ekman, *Emotions Revealed* (New York: Henry Holt, 2003); Nico H. Frijda, *The Emotions* (Cambridge: Cambridge University Press, 1986).

26. Paul Ekman, Robert W. Levenson, and Wallace V. Friesen, "Autonomic Nervous System Activity Distinguishes between Emotions," *Science* 221, no. 4616 (1983): 1208–10; Robert W. Levenson, Paul Ekman, and Wallace V. Friesen, "Emotion and Autonomic Nervous System Activity in the Minangkabau of West Sumatra," *Journal of Personality and Social Psychology* 62, no. 6 (1992): 972–88.

27. Carroll E. Izard, "Innate and Universal Facial Expressions: Evidence from Developmental and Cross-Cultural Research," *Psychological Bulletin* 115, no. 2 (1994): 288–99.

28. Paul Ekman, Wallace V. Friesen, and Maureen O'Sullivan, "Smiles When Lying," *Journal of Personality and Social Psychology* 54, no. 3 (1988): 414–20.

29. Paul Ekman, *Emotions Revealed: Recognizing Faces and Feelings to Improve Emotional Life* (New York: Henry Holt, 2003); Alan J. Fridlund, *Human Facial Expression: An Evolutionary View* (San Diego: Academic Press, 1994); Andrew Ortony and Terence J. Turner, "What's Basic About Basic Emotions?" *Psychological Review* 97, no. 3 (1990): 315–31.

30. Darwin, *The Expression*.

31. Ekman, *Emotions Revealed*.

32. Darwin, *The Expression*.

33. Ekman, "Strong Evidence"; Izard, "Innate and Universal Facial Expressions"; Robert Plutchik, *The Emotions: Facts, Theories, and a New Model* (New York: Random House, 1962).

34. Frijda, *The Emotions*.

35. Ekman, *Emotions Revealed*.

36. Ekman, "Strong Evidence"; Ekman, *Telling Lies*; Paul Ekman, Wallace V. Friesen, Maureen O'Sullivan, Anthony Chan, Irene Diacoyanni-Tarlatzis, Karl Heider, Rainer Krause, William Ayhan LeCompte, Tom Pitcairn, Pio E. Ricci-Bitti, Klaus Scherer, Masatoshi Tomita, and Athanase Tzavaras, "Universals and Cultural Differences in the Judgments of Facial Expressions of Emotion," *Journal of Personality and Social Psychology* 53, no. 4 (1987): 712–17; Dacher Keltner, "The Signs of Appeasement: Evidence for the Distinct Displays of Embarrassment, Amusement, and Shame," *Journal of Personality and Social Psychology* 68, no. 3 (1995): 441–54; Carroll E. Izard and O. Maurice Haynes, "On the Form and Universality of the Contempt Expression: A Challenge to Ekman and Friesen's Claim of Discovery," *Motivation and Emotion* 12, no. 1 (1988): 1–16; Kenneth M. Prkachin, "The Consistency of Facial Expressions of Pain: A Comparison Across Modalities," *Pain* 51, no. 3 (1992): 297–306.

37. Paul Ekman and Wallace V. Friesen, "Felt, False, and Miserable Smiles," *Journal of Nonverbal Behavior* 6, no. 4 (1982): 238–52; Mark G. Frank and Paul Ekman, "Not All Smiles Are Created Equal: The Differences Between Enjoyment and Non-enjoyment Smiles," *Humor: The International Journal for Research in Humor* 6, no. 1 (1993): 9–26.

38. Paul Ekman, Wallace V. Friesen, and Sonia Ancoli, "Facial Signs of Emotional Experience," *Journal of Personality and Social Psychology* 39, no. 6 (1980): 1125–34; Ekman et al., "Autonomic Nervous System Activity"; Robert W. Levenson, Paul Ekman, and Wallace V. Friesen, "Voluntary Facial Action Generates Emotion-Specific Autonomic Nervous System Activity," *Psychophysiology* 27, no. 4 (1990): 363–84; Levenson et al., "Emotion and Autonomic Nervous System Activity."

39. Ekman, *Emotions Revealed*.

40. Adolf Miehlke, *Surgery of the Facial Nerve* (Philadelphia: Saunders, 1973); Ronald E. Myers, "Comparative Neurology of Vocalization and Speech: Proof of a Dichotomy," *Annual Review of the New York Academy of Sciences* 280, no. 1 (1976): 745–57; K. Tschiassny, "Eight Syndromes of Facial Paralysis and their Significance in Locating the Lesion," *Annual Review of Otology, Rhinology, and Laryngology* 62 (1953): 677–91.

41. Alf Brodal, *Neurological Anatomy: In Relation to Clinical Medicine* (New York: Oxford University Press, 1981); L. J. Karnosh, "Amimia or Emotional Paralysis of the Face," *Diseases of the Nervous System* 6 (1945): 106–8.

42. William DeMyer, *Technique of the Neurological Examination* (New York: McGraw-Hill, 1980).

43. Ekman and Friesen, "Felt, False, and Miserable Smiles"; William E. Rinn, "The Neuropsychology of Facial Expression: A Review of the Neurological and Psychological Mechanisms for Producing Facial Expressions," *Psychological Bulletin* 95, no. 8B (1984): 52–77.

44. Guillaume B. Duchenne, *The Mechanism of Human Facial Expression or an Electro-Physiological Analysis of the Expression of the Emotions,* trans. A. Cuthbertson (New York: Cambridge University Press, 1990 [1862]).

45. Ekman and Friesen, "Felt, False, and Miserable Smiles."

46. Ibid.

47. Crow's-feet are the reliable indicator for enjoyment only in medium to subtle smiles. When someone is feigning enjoyment by performing a very big smile, the actions of the cheeks can cause the crow's-feet to appear. However, in the interest of clarity, the crow's-feet denotation will be used as a shorthand to describe all enjoyment smiles, although not technically accurate.

48. Mark G. Frank, "Getting to Know Your Patient: How Facial Expression Reveals True Emotion," in *The Clinical Application of Facial Measurement: Methods and Meanings,* ed. Mary Katsikitis (Dordrecht: Kluwer, 2003); Frank and Ekman, "Not All Smiles Are Created Equal."

49. Mark G. Frank, Paul Ekman, and Wallace V. Friesen, "Behavioral Markers and Recognizability of the Smile of Enjoyment," *Journal of Personality and Social Psychology* 64, no. 1 (1993): 83–93.

50. Ekman et al., "Smiles When Lying."

51. Paul Ekman, Richard J. Davidson, and Wallace V. Friesen, "The Duchenne Smile: Emotional Expression and Brain Physiology II," *Journal of Personality and Social Psychology* 58, no. 2 (1990): 342–53.

52. Nathan A. Fox and Richard J. Davidson, "Patterns of Brain Electrical Activity During Facial Signs of Emotion in 10–Month-Old Infants," *Developmental Psychology* 24, no. 2 (1988): 230–36.

53. Daniel S. Messinger, Alan Fogel, and K. Laurie Dickson, "All Smiles Are Positive, But Some Smiles Are More Positive than Others," *Developmental Psychology* 37, no. 5 (2001): 642–53.

54. Klaus R. Scherer and Grazia Ceschi, "Criteria for Emotion Recognition from Verbal and Nonverbal Expression: Studying Baggage Loss in the Airport," *Personality and Social Psychology Bulletin* 26, no. 3 (2000): 327–39.

55. Veikko Surakka and Jari K. Hietanen, "Facial and Emotional Reactions to Duchenne and non-Duchenne Smiles," *International Journal of Psychophysiology* 29, no. 1 (1998): 23–33.

56. Klaus Schneider, "Achievement-Related Emotions in Preschoolers," in *Motivation, Intention, and Volition,* ed. F. Halisch and J. Kuhl (Springer: Berlin, 1987).

57. Willibald Ruch, "Exhilaration and Humor," in *The Handbook of Emotion,* ed. M. Lewis and J. M. Haviland (New York: Guilford Publications, 1993).

58. George A. Bonanno and Dacher Keltner, "Facial Expressions of Emotion and the Course of Conjugal Bereavement," *Journal of Abnormal Psychology* 106, no. 1 (1997): 126–37.

59. Daphne B. Bugental, Jay Blue, and Jeffrey Lewis, "Caregiver Cognitions as Moderators of Affective Reactions to "Difficult" Children," *Developmental Psychology* 26, no. 4 (1990): 631–38.

60. Howard Berenbaum and Thomas F. Oltmanns, "Emotional Experience and Expression in Schizophrenia and Depression," *Journal of Abnormal Psychology* 101, no. 1 (1992): 37–44; Mary Katsikitis and Issy A. Pilowsky, "A Controlled Quantitative Study of Facial Expression in Parkinson's Disease and Depression," *Journal of Nervous and Mental Disease,* 179, no. 11 (1991): 683–88.

61. Rainer Krause, Evelyne Steimer, Cornelia Sanger-Alt, and Gonter Wagner, "Facial Expressions of Schizophrenic Patients and Their Interaction Partners," *Psychiatry* 52, no. 1 (1989): 1–12.

62. F. Steiner, "Differentiating Smiles," in *FACS in Psychotherapy Research,* ed. E. Branniger-Huber and F. Steiner (Zurich: Department of Clinical Psychology, Universitat Zurich, 1986).

63. Paul Ekman, David Matsumoto, and Wallace V. Friesen, "Facial Expression and Affective Disorders," in *What the Face Reveals: Basic and Applied Studies of Spontaneous Expression using the Facial Action Coding System (FACS),* ed. Paul Ekman and Erika L. Rosenberg (New York: Oxford University Press, 1997).

64. Harold A. Sackheim, Ruben C. Gur, and M. C. Saucy, "Emotions Are Expressed More Intensely on the Left Side of the Face," *Science* 202, no. 4366 (1978): 434–36; Martin Skinner and Brian Mullen, "Facial Asymmetry in Emotional Expression: A Meta-Analysis of Research," *British Journal of Social Psychology* 30, no. 2 (1991): 113–24; but see also Paul Ekman, Gowen Roper, and Joseph C. Hager, "Deliberate Facial Movement," *Child Development* 51, no. 3 (1980): 886–91.

65. Paul Ekman, Joseph C. Hager, and Wallace V. Friesen, "The Symmetry of Emotional and Deliberate Facial Actions," *Psychophysiology* 18, no. 2 (1981): 101–6.

66. Alf Brodal, *Neurological Anatomy: In Relation to Clinical Medicine* (New York: Oxford University Press, 1981).

67. Frank, "Getting to Know Your Patient."

68. Friedbert Weiss, Gerald S. Blum, and Lisa Gleberman, "Anatomically Based Measurements of Facial Expressions in Simulated Versus Hypnotically Induced Affect," *Motivation and Emotion* 11, no. 1 (1987): 67–81.

69. Daphne B. Bugental, "Unmasking the 'Polite Smile': Situational and Personal Determinants of Managed Affect in Adult-Child Interaction," *Personality and Social Psychology Bulletin* 12, no. 1 (1986): 7–16.

70. Mark G. Frank, Paul Ekman, and Wallace V. Friesen, "Behavioral Markers and Recognizability of the Smile of Enjoyment," *Journal of Personality and Social Psychology* 64, no. 1 (1993): 83–93.

71. Kathryn L. Schmidt, Jeffrey F. Cohn, and Yingli Tian, "Signal Characteristics of Spontaneous Facial Expressions: Automatic Movement in Solitary and Social Smiles," *Biological Psychology* 65, no. 1 (2003): 49–66.

72. Ursula Hess and Robert E. Kleck, "Differentiating Emotion Elicited and Deliberate Emotional Facial Expressions," *European Journal of Social Psychology* 20, no. 5 (1990): 369–85; Ursula Hess, Arvid Kappas, Gregory J. McHugo, Robert E. Kleck, and John T. Lanzetta, "An Analysis of the Encoding and Decoding of Spontaneous and Posed Smiles: The Use of Facial Electromyography," *Journal of Nonverbal Behavior* 13, no. 2 (1989): 121–37.

73. Hess and Kleck, "Differentiating Emotion."

74. Frank et al., "Behavioral Markers."

75. Ekman, *Telling Lies*.

76. Paul Ekman, Gowen Roper, and Joseph Hager, "Deliberate Facial Movement," *Child Development* 51, no. 3 (1980): 886–91.

77. Ekman and Friesen, "Felt, False, and Miserable Smiles"; Frank et al., "Behavioral Markers"; Frank and Ekman, "Not All Smiles Are Created Equal," 9–26; Frank, "Getting to Know Your Patient"; Schmidt et al., "Signal Characteristics."

78. Ekman, *Telling Lies*; Ekman et al., *Face, Voice, and Body*; Mark G. Frank and Paul Ekman, "The Ability to Detect Deceit Generalizes across Different Types of High Stake Lies," *Journal of Personality and Social Psychology* 72, no. 6 (1997): 1429–39.

79. Ekman, *Telling Lies*.

80. Frank and Ekman, "Ability to Detect Deceit."

81. Ekman, *Telling Lies*; Ekman et al., "Smiles When Lying."

82. Frank and Ekman, *The Ability to Detect Deceit*; Mark G. Frank and Paul Ekman, "Appearing Truthful Generalizes Across Different Deception Situations," *Journal of Personality and Social Psychology* 86, no. 3 (2004): 486–95.

83. Klaus R. Scherer and Harald G. Wallbott, "Evidence for Universality and Cultural Variation of Differential Emotion Response Patterning," *Journal of Personality and Social Psychology* 66, no. 2 (1994): 310–28.

84. Lynn A. Streeter, Robert M. Krauss, Valerie Geller, Christopher Olson, and William Apple, "Pitch Changes During Attempted Deception," *Journal of Personality and Social Psychology* 35, no. 5 (1977): 345–50.

85. Klaus Scherer, "On the Nature and Function of Emotions: A Component Process Approach," in *Approaches to Emotion*, ed. Klaus Scherer and Paul Ekman (Hillsdale, NJ: Erlbaum, 1984).

86. See a review by Knapp and Hall, *Nonverbal Communication*.

87. Paul Ekman and Wallace V. Friesen, "Nonverbal Leakage and Clues to Deception," *Psychiatry* 32, no. 1 (1969): 88–105.

88. Paul Ekman and Wallace V. Friesen, "Detecting Deception from the Body or Face," *Journal of Personality and Social Psychology* 29, no. 3 (1974): 288–98.

89. Ekman, *Telling Lies*.

90. Fred E. Inbau, John E. Reid, and Joseph P. Buckley, *Criminal Interrogation and Confessions* (Baltimore, MD: Williams and Wilkins, 1986).

91. DePaulo et al., "Cues to Deception."

92. Ekman, *Telling Lies.*

93. Ekman and Friesen, "Detecting Deception"; Aldert Vrij, Lucy Akehurst, and Paul M. Morris, "Individual Differences in Hand Movements During Deception," *Journal of Nonverbal Behavior* 21, no. 6 (1997): 87–102.

94. Robert M. Krauss, "Why Do We Gesture When We Speak?" *Current Directions in Psychological Science* 7, no. 2 (1998): 54–60.

95. Ekman, *Telling Lies.*

96. Stan B. Walters, *Principles of the Kinesic Interview* (Boca Raton, FL: CRC Press, 1998).

97. DePaulo et al., "Cues to Deception."

98. DePaulo et al., "Deceiving and Detecting Deceit."

99. Reviewed in Frank, "Getting to Know Your Patient."

100. Aldert Vrij, Katherine Edward, and Ray Bull, "Police Officers' Ability to Detect Deceit: The Benefit of Indirect Deception Detection Measures," *Legal and Criminological Psychology* 6, no. 2 (2001): 185–96.

101. Ekman, *Telling Lies.*

102. Ibid.

103. DePaulo et al., *Deceiving and Detecting Deceit*; M. Zuckerman, Bella M. DePaulo, and Robert Rosenthal, "Verbal and Nonverbal Communication of Deception," in *Advances in Experimental Social Psychology*, vol. 14, ed. Miron Zuckerman, Bella M. DePaulo, and Robert Rosenthal (San Diego, CA: Academic Press, 1981).

104. Mark G. Frank, John D. Yarbrough, and Paul Ekman, "Improving Interpersonal Evaluations: Combining Science and Practical Experience," in *Investigative Interviewing: Rights, Research, Regulation* (Portland, OR: Willan, 2006).

105. Bella M. DePaulo and Roger L. Pfeifer, "On-the-Job Experience and Skill at Detecting Deception," *Journal of Applied Social Psychology* 16 (1986): 249–67; Paul Ekman and Maureen O'Sullivan, "Who Can Catch a Liar?" *American Psychologist* 46, no. 9 (1991): 913–20; Paul Ekman, Maureen O'Sullivan, and Mark G. Frank, "A Few Can Catch a Liar," *Psychological Science* 10, no. 3 (1999): 263–66; Robert E. Kraut and Donald Poe, "Behavioral Roots of Person Perception: The Deception Judgments of Customs Inspectors and Laymen," *Journal of Personality and Social Psychology* 39, no. 5 (1980): 784–98.

106. Frank et al., "Improving Interpersonal Evaluations."

107. Christian A. Meissner and Saul M. Kassin, "'He's Guilty!': Investigator Bias in Judgments of Truth and Deception," *Law and Human Behavior* 26, no. 5 (2002): 469–80.

Chapter 4

1. Gideons International, *The Holy Bible* (Nashville, TN: Gideons International, 1985).

2. Charles F. Bond, Jr., and Bella M. DePaulo, "Accuracy of Deception Judgments," *Personality and Social Psychology Review* 10, no. 3 (2006): 214–34.

3. Although the Bible story may suggest that women are more gullible than men, there is no research evidence suggesting that men are better lie catchers than women.

4. John Strausbaugh, "When Barnum Took Manhattan," *New York Times* (November 9, 2007), E-31.

5. Edward Munnich (personal communication, September 17, 2007).

6. William I. Miller, *Faking It* (Cambridge: Cambridge University Press, 2003).

7. Adam Phillips, *On Flirtation* (Cambridge, MA: Harvard University Press, 1994). Other observations about the role of flirtation, deception, and self-deception can be found in Maureen O'Sullivan, "Deception and Self-Deception as Strategies in Short and Long-Term Mating," in *Mating Intelligence: Sex, Relationships, and the Mind's Reproductive System*, ed. Glenn Geher and Geoffrey Miller (New York: Erlbaum, 2008).

8. A theoretical analysis of the cognitive construction of romantic love may be found in Robert C. Solomon, *About Love: Reinventing Romance for Our Time* (New York: Simon & Schuster, 1988). Empirical studies examining differing ideas about romantic love over time and across cultures include Susan Sprecher, Arthur Aron, Elaine Hatfield, Anthony Cortese, Elena Potapova, and Anna Levitskaya, "Love: American Style, Russian Style, and Japanese Style," *Personal Relationships* 1 (1994): 349–69; Susan Sprecher and Sandra Metts, "Romantic Beliefs: Their Influence on Relationships and Patterns of Change over Time," *Journal of Social and Personal Relationships* 6 (1999): 387–411.

9. F. Scott Fitzgerald, "The Crack-Up," *Esquire* 5 (February 1936).

10. David Dunning, Chip Heath, and Jerry M. Suls, "Flawed Self-Assessment: Implications for Health, Education, and the Workplace," *Psychological Science in the Public Interest* 5 (2004): 69–106; Brent W. Pelham, Mauricio M. Carvallo, and Andrew J. T. Jones, "Implicit Egotism," *Current Directions in Psychological Science* 14 (2005): 106–9.

11. Geoffrey Miller (personal communication, January 30, 2006).

12. Paul Ekman, Wallace V. Friesen, Maureen O'Sullivan, and Klaus R. Scherer, "Relative Importance of Face, Body and Speech in Judgments of Personality and Affect," *Journal of Personality and Social Psychology* 38, no. 2 (1980): 270–77; Maureen O'Sullivan, Paul Ekman, Wallace V. Friesen, and Klaus R. Scherer, "What You Say and How You Say It: The Contribution of Speech Content and Voice Quality to Judgments of Others," *Journal of Personality and Social Psychology* 48, no. 1 (1985): 54–62.

13. Bella M. DePaulo and B. M. May, "Deceiving and Detecting Deceit: Insights and Oversights from the First Several Hundred Studies" (address to the American Psychological Society, Washington, DC, 1998); Samantha Mann and Albert Vrij, "Police Officers' Judgments of Veracity, Tenseness, Cognitive Load and Attempted Behavioral Control in Real-Life Police Interviews," *Psychology, Crime and Law* 12, no. 3 (2006): 307–19.

14. Richard Byrne and Andrew Whiten, eds., *Machiavellian Intelligence: Social Expertise and the Evolution of Intellect in Monkeys, Apes, and Humans* (Oxford, UK: Oxford University Press, 1988). See also Carl Bergstrom's chapter in this volume.

15. Ziva Kunda, "The Case for Motivated Reasoning," *Psychological Bulletin* 108, no. 3 (1990): 480–98; Douglas S. Krull and Darin J. Erickson, "Judging Situations: On

the Effortful Process of Taking Dispositional Information into Account," *Social Cognition* 13, no. 4 (1995): 417–38.

16. Daniel Kahneman won the Nobel Prize in 2002 for the application of his work on judgment uncertainty to economic decisions. A representative publication is Amos Tversky and Daniel Kahneman, "Judgment under Uncertainty: Heuristics and Biases," *Science* 185 (1974): 1124–31.

17. Jennifer Steinhauer, Cheryl Camp, and Alain Delaqueriere, "Posing as Family, Sex Offenders Stun Schools and the Neighbors," *New York Times* (February 1, 2007), 1.

18. Hee Sun Park and Timothy R. Levine, "A Probability Model of Accuracy in Deception Detection Experiments," *Communication Monographs* 68 (2001): 201–10. The study testing this model is described in Timothy R. Levine, Rachel K. Kim, Hee Sun Park, and Mikayla Hughes, "Deception Detection Accuracy Is a Predictable Linear Function of Message Veracity Base-Rate: A Formal Test of Park and Levine's Probability Model," *Communication Monographs* 73 (2006): 243–60.

19. The Innocence Project is a legal activity focused on exonerating wrongly convicted criminals, usually through DNA evidence. Information about Paul Ekman's program of research on lie detection, including a description of deceptiveness bias, can be found in Paul Ekman, *Telling Lies: Clues to Deceit in the Marketplace, Politics, and Marriage*, 3rd ed. (New York: Norton, 2001). Although training and education may have diminished deception bias in many U.S. police departments, researchers are still examining what they now label the "investigator response bias"—namely, the tendency for police interrogators to presume deceptiveness on the part of those they are interviewing. This new label, however, is merely deceptiveness bias applied to police interrogators. See Christian A. Meissner and Saul M. Kassin, "'He's Guilty!': Investigator Bias in Judgments of Truth and Deception," *Law and Human Behavior* 26, no. 5 (2002): 469–80.

20. An example of the response to information of expert and nonexpert therapists can be found in Thomas Anstadt, Joerg Merten, Burkhard Ullrich, and Rainier Krause, "Affective Dyadic Behavior, Core Conflict Relationship Themes, and Success of Treatment," *Psychotherapy Research* 7, no. 4 (1997): 397–417. Information about the differential lie detection accuracy of different police groups can be found in Maureen O'Sullivan, "Home Runs and Humbugs: A Comment on Bond and DePaulo (2008)," *Psychological Bulletin* 134, no. 4 (2008), 493–97.

21. Lee Ross and Richard Nisbett, *The Person and the Situation: Perspectives of Social Psychology* (New York: McGraw-Hill, 1991); Emily Pronin, Daniel Y. Lin, and Lee Ross, "The Bias Blind Spot: Perceptions of Bias in Self versus Others," *Personality and Social Psychology Bulletin* 28, no. 3 (2002): 369–81; Vincent Y. Yzerbyt, Olivier Corneille, Muriel Dumont, and Kirsten Hahn, "The Dispositional Inference Strikes Back: Situational Focus and Dispositional Suppression in Causal Attribution," *Journal of Personality and Social Psychology* 81, no. 3 (2001): 365–76.

22. Maureen O'Sullivan, "The Fundamental Attribution Error in Detecting Deceit: The Boy-Who-Cried-Wolf Effect," *Personality and Social Psychology Bulletin* 29, no. 10 (2003): 1316–27.

23. Miron Zuckerman, Richard Koestner, Michelle J. Colella, and Audrey O.

Alton, "Anchoring in the Detection of Deception and Leakage," *Journal of Personality and Social Psychology* 47, no. 2 (1984): 301–11; Maureen O'Sullivan, Paul Ekman, and Wallace V. Friesen, "The Effect of Comparisons on Detecting Deceit," *Journal of Nonverbal Behavior* 12, no. 3 (1988): 203–15.

24. Susan T. Fiske, "Thinking Is for Doing: Portraits of Social Cognition from Daguerreotype to Laser Photo," *Journal of Personality and Social Psychology* 63, no. 6 (1992): 877–89.

25. Paul Ekman, Wallace V. Friesen, and Maureen O'Sullivan, "Smiles When Lying," *Journal of Personality and Social Psychology* 54, no. 3 (1988): 414–20; Mark G. Frank, Paul Ekman, and William V. Friesen, "Behavioral Markers and Recognizability of the Smile of Enjoyment," *Journal of Personality and Social Psychology* 64 (1993): 83–93; David Matsumoto and Bob Willingham, "The Thrill of Victory and the Agony of Defeat: Spontaneous Expressions of Medal Winners at the 2004 Athens Olympic Games," *Journal of Personality and Social Psychology* 91 (2006): 568–81.

26. Paul Ekman, *Emotions Revealed: Recognizing Faces and Feelings to Improve Emotional Life* (New York: Henry Holt, 2003).

27. Robert J. Sternberg, ed., *Handbook of Intelligence* (Cambridge: Cambridge University Press, 2000); Maureen O'Sullivan, "Emotional Intelligence and Detecting Deception: Why Most People Can't 'Read' Others, but a Few Can," in *Applications of Nonverbal Communication*, ed. Ronald E. Riggio and Robert S. Feldman (Mahwah, NJ: Erlbaum, 2005).

28. Maureen O'Sullivan and Paul Ekman, "The Wizards of Deception Detection," in *The Detection of Deception in Forensic Contexts*, ed. Pär Anders Granhag and Leif A. Strömwall (Cambridge: Cambridge University Press, 2004).

29. Paul Ekman and Maureen O'Sullivan, "Who Can Catch a Liar?" *American Psychologist* 46, no. 9 (1991): 913–20; Paul Ekman, Maureen O'Sullivan, and Mark G. Frank, "A Few Can Catch a Liar," *Psychological Science* 10, no. 3 (1999): 263–66.

30. Herbert A. Simon and William G. Chase, "Skill in Chess," *American Scientist* 61, no. 4 (1973): 394–403.

31. K. Anders Ericsson, "The Acquisition of Expert Performance: An Introduction to Some of the Issues," *The Road to Excellence: The Acquisition of Expert Performance in the Arts and Sciences, Sports, and Games* (Mahwah, NJ: Erlbaum, 1996).

32. Maureen O'Sullivan, "Unicorns or Tiger Woods? Are Expert Lie Detectors Myths or Rarities? A Response to: 'On Lie Detection Wizards' by Bond and Uysal," *Law and Human Behavior* 30, no. 1 (2007): 117–23.

Chapter 5

This work was supported by a Guggenheim Fellowship, a gift from Adobe Systems, Inc., a gift from Microsoft, Inc., and a grant from the United States Air Force (FA8750-06-C-0011), as well as by the Institute for Security Technology Studies at Dartmouth College under grant 2005-DD-BX-1091 from the Bureau of Justice Assistance and award number 2006-CS-001-000001 from the U.S. Department of Homeland Security. Points of view or opinions in this chapter are those of the author and do not represent the official position or policies of the U.S. Department of Justice, the U.S. Department of Homeland Security, or any other sponsor.

1. Micah K. Johnson and Hany Farid, "Exposing Digital Forgeries by Detecting Inconsistencies in Lighting," in *Proceedings of the 7th Workshop on Multimedia and Security*, ed. Ahmet M. Eskicioglu, Jessica J. Fridrich, and Jana Dittmann (New York: ACM Press, 2005).

2. Micah K. Johnson and Hany Farid, "Exposing Digital Forgeries through Specular Highlights on the Eye," in *Proceedings* (9th International Workshop on Information Hiding, Saint Malo, France, June 11–13, 2007).

3. Ko Nishino and Shree K. Nayar, "The World in an Eye," in *Proceedings* (2004 IEEE Computer Society Conference on Computer Vision and Pattern Recognition, Washington, DC, June 27–July 2, 2004).

4. Alin Popescu and Hany Farid, "Exposing Digital Forgeries by Detecting Duplicated Image Regions" (technical report, Department of Computer Science, Dartmouth College, TR2004–515, 2004).

5. Jessica Fridrich, David Soukal, and Jan Lukas, "Detection of Copy-Move Forgery in Digital Images," in *Proceedings* (Digital Forensic Research Workshop, Cleveland, Ohio, 2003).

6. Woo Suk Hwang et al., "Evidence of a Pluripotent Human Embryonic Stem Cell Line Derived from a Cloned Blastocyst," *Science* 303, no. 5664 (2004): 1669–74.

7. Donald Kennedy, Editorial Retraction, *Science* 211, no. 5759 (2006): 335.

8. Helen Pearson, "Image Manipulation: CSI: Cell Biology" *Nature* 434 (2005): 952–53.

9. Alin Popescu and Hany Farid, "Exposing Digital Forgeries in Color Filter Array Interpolated Images," *IEEE Transactions on Signal Processing* 53, no. 10 (2005): 3948–59.

10. Hany Farid, "Digital Image Ballistics from JPEG Quantization" (technical report, Department of Computer Science, Dartmouth College, TR2006–583, 2006).

11. Jan Lukas, Jessica Fridrich, and Miroslav Goljan, "Digital Camera Identification from Sensor Noise," *IEEE Transactions on Information Security and Forensics* 1, no. 2 (2006): 205–14; Jan Lukas, Jessica Fridrich, and Miroslav Goljan, "Detecting Digital Image Forgeries Using Sensor Pattern Noise," in *Proceedings* (SPIE Electronic Imaging, Photonics West, San Jose, California, January 2006).

12. Hany Farid and Mary J. Bravo, "Photorealistic Rendering: How Realistic Is It?" (presented at Vision Sciences, Sarasota, Florida, 2007).

13. Siwei Lyu and Hany Farid, "How Realistic Is Photorealistic?" *IEEE Transactions on Signal Processing* 53, no. 2 (2005): 845–50.

14. Maryanne Garry and Kimberly Wade, "Actually, a Picture Is Worth Less than 45 Words: Narratives Produce More False Memories than Photographs," *Psychonomic Bulletin and Review* 12 (2005): 359–66; Dario Sacchi, Franca Agnoli, and Elizabeth Loftus, "Doctored Photos and Memory for Public Events," *Applied Cognitive Psychology* 21 (2007): 1005–22; Kimberly Wade, Maryanne Garry, J. Don Read, and D. Stephen

Lindsay, "A Picture Is Worth a Thousand Lies," *Psychonomic Bulletin and Review* 9 (2002): 597–603.

15. Wade et al., "A Picture Is Worth a Thousand Lies."

16. Garry and Wade, "Actually, a Picture Is Worth Less than 45 Words."

17. Sacchi, Agnoli, and Loftus, "Doctored Photos and Memory for Public Events."

Chapter 6

1. Patricia Wallace, *The Psychology of the Internet* (Cambridge: Cambridge University Press, 1999).

2. John W. Thibaut and Harold H. Kelly, *The Social Psychology of Groups* (New York: Wiley, 1959).

3. Fred B. Schneider, *Trust in Cyberspace* (Washington, DC: National Academy Press, 1999).

4. Herbert H. Clark and Susan E. Brennan, "Grounding in Communication," in *Perspectives on Socially Shared Cognition*, ed. Lauren B. Resnick, John M. Levine, and Stephanie D. Teasley (Washington, DC: American Psychological Association, 1991).

5. Federal Trade Commission, "Prepared Statement of the Federal Trade Commission on 'Unsolicited Commercial Email'" (presented to the U.S. Senate Committee on Commerce, Science and Transportation, 2003).

6. Markus Jakobsson, "The Human Factor in Phishing," *Privacy and Security of Consumer Information* (2007), http://www.informatics.indiana.edu/markus/papers/aci.pdf (accessed January 23, 2008).

7. Daniel E. Slotnik, "Too Few Friends? A Web Site Lets You Buy Some (and They're Hot)," *New York Times* (February 26, 2007), http://www.nytimes.com/2007/02/26/technology/26fake.html.

8. Jeffrey T. Hancock, "Digital Deception: When, Where, and How People Lie Online," in *Oxford Handbook of Internet Psychology* (Oxford: Oxford University Press, 2007).

9. John A. Bargh, Katelyn Y. A. McKenna, and Grainne M. Fitzsimons, "Can You See the Real Me? The Activation and Expression of the 'True Self' on the Internet," *Journal of Social Issues* 58 (2002): 33–48; Joshua Berman and Amy Bruckman, "The Turing Game: Exploring Identity in an Online Environment," *Convergence* 7 (2001): 83–102; Joseph B. Walther and Malcolm R. Parks, "Cues Filtered Out, Cues Filtered In: Computer-Mediated Communication and Relationships," in *Handbook of Interpersonal Communication*, 3rd ed. (Thousand Oaks, CA: Sage, 2002).

10. Sherry Turkle, *Life on the Screen: Identity in the Age of the Internet* (New York: Simon & Schuster, 1995).

11. Judith S. Donath, "Identity and Deception in the Virtual Community," in *Communities in Cyberspace* (New York: Routledge, 1998).

12. Amotz Zahavi, "The Fallacy of Conventional Signaling," *The Royal Society Philosophical Transaction* 340 (1993): 227–30.

13. Walther and Parks, "Cues Filtered Out, Cues Filtered In."

14. Donath, "Identity and Deception in the Virtual Community."

15. Berman and Bruckman, "The Turing Game"; Susan C. Herring and Anna Martinson, "Assessing Gender Authenticity in Computer-Mediated Language Use: Evidence from an Identity Game," *Journal of Language and Social Psychology* 23 (2004): 424–46; Turkle, *Life on the Screen*.

16. Jeffrey T. Hancock, Catalina Toma, and Nicole Ellison, "The Truth about Lying in Online Dating Profiles," in *Proceedings of the ACM CHI 2007 Conference on Human Factors in Computing Systems* (New York: ACM Press, 2007), 449–52.

17. Ralph Keyes, *The Post-Truth Era: Dishonesty and Deception in Contemporary Life* (New York: St. Martin's, 2004), 198.

18. Bella M. DePaulo, James J. Lindsay, Brian E. Malone, Laura Muhlenbruck, Kelly Charlton, and Harris Cooper, "Cues to Deception," *Psychological Bulletin* 129 (2003): 74–118.

19. Jeffrey T. Hancock, Michael Woodworth, and Saurabh Goorha, "See No Evil: The Effect of Communication Medium and Motivation on Deception Detection," *Group Decision and Negotiation* (in press).

20. For a more complete treatment on what factors are important in deception detection in mediated communication, see John R. Carlson, Joey F. George, Judee K. Burgoon, Mark Adkins, and Cindy H. White, "Deception in Computer-Mediated Communication," *Group Decision and Negotiation* 13 (2004): 5–28.

21. Adam N. Joinson and Carina B. Paine, "Self-Disclosure, Privacy, and the Internet," in *Oxford Handbook of Internet Psychology*, ed. Adam Joinson, Katelyn McKenna, Tom Postmes, and Ulf-Dietrich Reips (Oxford: Oxford University Press, 2007).

22. Nora C. Schaeffer, "Asking Questions about Threatening Topics: A Selective Overview," in *The Science of Self-Report: Implications for Research and Practice* (Mahwah, NJ: Erlbaum, 2000).

23. Wallace, *The Psychology of the Internet*.

24. Thibaut and Kelly, *The Social Psychology of Groups*.

25. Bargh et al., "Can You See the Real Me?"

26. Adam N. Joinson, "Self-Disclosure in Computer-Mediated Communication: The Role of Self-Awareness and Visual Anonymity," *European Journal of Social Psychology* 23 (2001): 177–92.

27. Herbert H. Clark, *Using Language* (Cambridge: Cambridge University Press, 1996).

28. Jeffrey T. Hancock, Jennifer Thom-Santelli, and Thompson Ritchie, "Deception and Design: The Impact of Communication Technologies on Lying Behavior," *Proceedings of Conference on Computer-Human Interaction* 6 (New York: ACM Press, 2004), 130–36; Jeffrey T. Hancock, Jennifer Thom-Santelli, and Thompson Ritchie, "What Lies Beneath: The Effect of the Communication Medium on the Production of Deception" (presented at the annual meeting of the Society for Text and Discourse, Chicago, 2004).

29. Bella M. DePaulo, Susan E. Kirkendol, Deborah A. Kashy, Melissa M. Wyer, and Jennifer A. Epstein, "Lying in Everyday Life," *Journal of Personality and Social Psychology* 70, no. 5 (1996): 979–95.

30. Tom Postmes, Russell Spears, and Martin Lea, "The Formation of Group Norms in Computer-Mediated Communication," *Human Communication Research* 26 (2000): 341–71.

31. Clark, *Using Language*.

32. Adam N. Joinson and Beth Dietz-Uhler, "Explanations for the Perpetration of and Reactions to Deception in a Virtual Community," *Isocial Science Computer Review* 20, no. 3 (2002): 275–89.

33. Avner Caspi and Paul Gorsky, "Online Deception: Prevalence, Motivation, and Emotion," *Cyberpsychology and Behavior* 9 (2006): article 1.

34. Nicole Ellison, Rebecca Heino, and Jennifer Gibbs, "Managing Impressions Online: Self-Presentation Processes in the Online Dating Environment," *Journal of Computer-Mediated Communication* 11 (2006): article 2, http://jcmc.indiana.edu/vol11/issue2/ellison.html (accessed September 2, 2006).

35. Hancock, Thom-Santelli, and Ritchie, "Deception and Design" and "What Lies Beneath."

36. Hancock, Toma, and Ellison, "The Truth about Lying."

37. Kimberly J. Mitchell, David Finkelhor, and Janis Wolak, "Risk Factors and Impact of Online Solicitation of Youth," *Journal of the American Medical Association* 285 (2001): 3011–14.

38. Jonathan Knight, "The Truth about Lying," *Nature* 428 (2004): 692–94.

Chapter 7

1. George Cybenko, Annarita Giani, and Paul Thompson, "Cognitive Hacking: A Battle for the Mind," *IEEE Computer* 35, no. 8 (2002): 50–56.

2. Peter Sayer, "Clever Fake of WTO Web Site Harvests E-mail Addresses," *NetworkWorldFusion* (October 31, 2001), http://www.networkworld.com/news/2001/1031wto.html (accessed January 31, 2008).

3. Markus Jakobsson and Steven Myers, eds., *Phishing and Countermeasures: Understanding the Increasing Problem of Electronic Identity Theft* (Hoboken, NJ: Wiley, 2007), 1.

4. Bill Mann, "Emulex Fraud Hurts All," *The Motley Fool* (August 28, 2000), http://www.fool.com/news/foolplate/2000/foolplate000828.htm (accessed January 31, 2008).

5. Cybenko et al., "Cognitive Hacking."

6. Brian Krebs, "E-Mail Scam Sought to Defraud PayPal Customers," *Newsbytes* (December 19, 2001), http://www.mail-archive.com/cybercrime-alerts@topica.com/msg00613.html (accessed January 31, 2008); James E. Combs and Dan Nimmo, *The New Propaganda: The Dictatorship of Palaver in Contemporary Politics* (New York: Longman, 1993).

7. Dorothy Denning, *Information Warfare and Security* (Reading, MA: Addison-Wesley, 1999).

8. Lina Zhou, Douglas P. Twitchell, Tiantian Qin, Judee K. Burgoon, and Jay F. Nunamaker, "An Exploratory Study into Deception in Text-Based Computer-

Mediated Communications," *Proceedings* (36th Hawaii International Conference on Systems Sciences, Big Island, Hawaii, January 6–9, 2003).

9. The Coalition for Networked Information is "an organization dedicated to supporting the transformative promise of networked information technology for the advancement of scholarly communication and the enrichment of intellectual productivity"; see http://www.cni.org/ (accessed February 1, 2008).

10. Clifford Lynch, "When Documents Deceive: Trust and Provenance as New Factors for Information Retrieval in a Tangled Web," *Journal of the American Society for Information Science and Technology* 52, no. 1 (2001): 12–17.

11. Frederick Mosteller and David L. Wallace, *Inference and Disputed Authorship: The Federalist* (Reading, MA: Addison-Wesley, 1964).

12. Douglas Biber, *Dimensions of Register Variation: A Cross-Linguistic Comparison* (Cambridge: Cambridge University Press, 1995); Douglas Biber, "Spoken and Written Textual Dimensions in English: Resolving the Contradictory Findings," *Language* 62, no. 2 (1986): 384–413; Jussi Karlgren and Douglass Cutting, "Recognizing Text Genres with Simple Metrics Using Discriminant Analysis," in *Proceedings* (15th Conference on Computational Linguistics, 2, Kyoto, Japan, August 5–9, 1994).

13. Brett Kessler, Geoffrey Nunberg, and Hinrich Schütze, "Automatic Detection of Genre," *Proceedings of the 35th Annual Meeting of the Association for Computational Linguistics and 8th Conference of the European Chapter of the Association for Computational Linguistics* (San Francisco: Morgan Kaufmann, 1997), 32–38.

14. Zhou et al., "An Exploratory Study."

15. James Thornton, *Collaborative Filtering Research Papers*, http://jamesthornton.com/cf/ (accessed January 31, 2008); R. Yahalom, B. Klein, and Th. Beth, "Trust Relationships in Secure Systems—A Distributed Authentication Perspective," in *Proceedings* (IEEE Symposium on Research in Security and Privacy, Oakland, California, May 24–26, 1993); Chrysanthos Dellarocas, "Building Trust On-line: The Design of Reliable Reputation Reporting Mechanisms for Online Trading Communities," Center for eBusiness@MIT, paper 101 (2001).

16. Josyula R. Rao and Pankaj Rohatgi, "Can Pseudonymity Really Guarantee Privacy?" *Proceedings* (9th USENIX Security Symposium, Denver, Colorado, August 14–17, 2000).

17. International Association of Forensic Linguists, http://www.iafl.org/ (accessed January 31, 2008); *Forensic Linguistics: The International Journal of Speech, Language and the Law* (Birmingham, UK: University of Birmingham, 1994–), *http://www.equinoxjournals.com/ojs/index.php/IJSLL* (accessed November 16, 2008). This journal was founded in 1994 as *Forensic Linguistics* and changed to its present title in 2003.

18. Donald W. Foster, "Policing Anonymity," *Ideas in American Policing* 5 (December 2001), http://www.policefoundation.org/pdf/foster_anonymity.pdf (accessed January 31, 2008).

19. James W. Pennebaker, Martha E. Francis, and Roger J. Booth, *Linguistic Inquiry and Word Count (LIWC): LIWC2001* (Mahwah, NJ: Erlbaum, 2001).

20. Harold Love, *Attributing Authorship: An Introduction* (Cambridge: Cambridge University Press, 2002).

21. Gabriel Mateescu, Masha Sosonkina, and Paul Thompson, "A New Model for Probabilistic Information Retrieval on the Web" (paper presented at the 2nd SIAM International Conference on Data Mining [SDM 2002] Workshop on Web Analytics, Arlington, Virginia, April 11–13, 2002).

22. David B. Buller and Judee K. Burgoon, "Interpersonal Deception Theory," *Communication Theory* 6, no. 3 (1996): 203–42; Karen M. Cornetto, "Identity and Illusion on the Internet: Interpersonal Deception and Detection in Interactive Internet Environments" (PhD thesis, University of Texas at Austin, 2001); Judee K. Burgoon, J. P. Blair, Tiantian Qin, and Jay F. Nunamaker, "Detecting Deception through Linguistic Analysis," *NSF/NIJ Symposium on Intelligence and Security Informatics, Lecture Notes in Computer Science* (Berlin: Springer-Verlag, 2003), 91–101.

23. Zhou et al., "An Exploratory Study."

24. Jinwei Cao, Janna M. Crews, Ming Lin, Judee K. Burgoon, and Jay F. Nunamaker, "Designing Agent99 Trainer: A Learner-Centered, Web-Based Training System for Deception Detection," *NSF/NIJ Symposium*, 358–65; Joey F. George, David P. Biros, Judee K. Burgoon, and Jay F. Nunamaker, "Training Professionals to Detect Deception," *NSF/NIJ Symposium*, 366–70.

25. Lina Zhou, Judee K. Burgoon, and Douglas P. Twitchell, "A Longitudinal Analysis of Language Behavior of Deception in E-mail," *NSF/NIJ Symposium*, 102–10; Zhou et al., "An Exploratory Study."

26. Hsinchun Chen, Daniel D. Zeng, Jenny Schroeder, Richard Miranda, Chris Demchak, and Therani Madhusudan, eds., *NSF/NIJ Symposium*.

27. Paul Thompson, "Semantic Hacking and Intelligence and Security Informatics," *NSF/NIJ Symposium*, 390.

28. J. B. Bell and B. Whaley, *Cheating and Deception* (New Brunswick, NJ: Transaction, 1991).

29. Martin Libicki, "The Mesh and the Net: Speculations on Armed Conflict in an Age of Free Silicon" (National Defense University McNair Paper 28, 1994).

30. *Proceedings* (2nd International Workshop on Adversarial Information Retrieval on the Web—AIRWeb 2006, Seattle, August 10, 2006).

31. Robert H. Anderson, Thomas Bozek, Tom Longstaff, Wayne Meitzler, Michael Skroch, and Ken Van Wyk, *Research on Mitigating the Insider Threat to Information Systems #2: Proceedings of a Workshop Held August 2000*, RAND Technical Report CF163 (Arlington, Virginia, August 30–September 1, 2000).

32. J. C. Munson, and S. Wimer, "Watcher: The Missing Piece of the Security Puzzle" (paper presented at the 17th Annual Computer Security Applications Conference [ACSAC '01], New Orleans, Louisiana, December 10–14, 2001).

33. Office of Science and Technology Policy and National Science Foundation, "Behavioral, Psychological and Physiological Aspects of Security Evaluations: Report on a Series of Workshops," 2007.

34. Paul Thompson, George Cybenko, and Annarita Giani, "Cognitive Hacking

and the Economics of Misinformation," in *The Economics of Information Security*, ed. L. Jean Camp and Stephen Lewis (London: Springer, 2004): 255–87.

35. Jakobsson and Myers, *Phishing and Countermeasures*.

Chapter 8

I am grateful to Patrik Aspers, John Booth, Brooke Harrington, Sascha Münnich, Richard Priem, Sabine Stumpf, Antoinette Weibel, Nicholas Wheeler, and the participants of the Santa Fe Institute Workshop on Deception in March 2007 for their great help and feedback.

1. Sheldon Rampton and John Stauber, *Weapons of Mass Deception: The Uses of Propaganda in Bush's War on Iraq* (New York: Tarcher / Penguin, 2003); see also Nicholas J. O'Shaughnessy, *Politics and Propaganda: Weapons of Mass Seduction* (Ann Arbor: University of Michigan Press, 2004).

2. Onora O'Neill, *A Question of Trust* (Cambridge: Cambridge University Press, 2002), 4–19.

3. Georg Simmel, *The Sociology of Georg Simmel* (New York: Free Press, 1950 [1908]), 313.

4. Erving Goffman, *The Presentation of Self in Everyday Life* (London: Penguin, 1959), 65; Paul Ekman, "Why Don't We Catch Liars?" *Social Research* 63, no. 3 (1996): 801–17, 806.

5. Denise M. Rousseau, Sim B. Sitkin, Ronald S. Burt, and Colin Camerer, "Not So Different after All: A Cross-Discipline View of Trust," *Academy of Management Review* 23, no. 3 (1998): 393–404, 395.

6. See Guido Möllering, *Trust: Reason, Routine, Reflexivity* (Amsterdam: Elsevier, 2006), 111, for a detailed elaboration of this understanding of trust.

7. My perspective is limited to social relationships, and I would not speak of trust and deception in relation to entities that do not have intentions, expectations, and a degree of autonomy in their capacity to act. Whether it makes sense to speak of trust and deception in very young children, animals, or unanimated objects depends on whether we attribute agency to them.

8. The insight that the deceiver's true knowledge and intentions are unknown to the deceived has been noted, for example, by Simmel, *Sociology of Georg Simmel*, 312; and Paul Ekman, *Telling Lies: Clues to Deceit in the Marketplace, Politics, and Marriage* (New York: Norton, 2001 [1985]), 41.

9. Goffman, *The Presentation of Self*. Goffman's view is still very topical, as can be seen, for example, in research on the role of deception in the workplace by David Shulman, *From Hire to Liar: The Role of Deception in the Workplace* (Ithaca, NY: Cornell University Press, 2007).

10. For core contributions to the rational choice perspective on trust, see Partha Dasgupta, "Trust as a Commodity," in *Trust: Making and Breaking Co-Operative Relations*, ed. Diego Gambetta (Oxford: Basil Blackwell, 1988), 49–72; James S. Coleman, *Foundations of Social Theory* (Cambridge, MA: Harvard University Press, 1990); Russell Hardin, *Trust and Trustworthiness* (New York: Russell Sage Foundation, 2002).

11. See the ethnographic studies by James M. Henslin, "Trust and the Cab Driver," in *Sociology and Everyday Life*, ed. Marcello Truzzi (Upper Saddle River, NJ: Prentice Hall, 1968), 138–58; and Diego Gambetta and Heather Hamill, *Streetwise: How Taxi Drivers Establish Their Customers' Trustworthiness* (New York: Russell Sage Foundation, 2005).

12. Roger C. Mayer, James H. Davis, and F. David Schoorman, "An Integrative Model of Organizational Trust," *Academy of Management Review* 20, no. 3 (1995): 709–34.

13. Michael Bacharach and Diego Gambetta, "Trust in Signs," in *Trust in Society*, ed. Karen S. Cook (New York: Russell Sage Foundation, 2001), 148–84, 159. Their argument takes up issues raised by Dasgupta, *Trust as a Commodity*. The specific theoretical background is signaling theory, A. Michael Spence, *Market Signaling: Informational Transfer in Hiring and Related Screening Processes* (Cambridge, MA: Harvard University Press, 1974). In his chapter on deception in biology in this volume, Carl Bergstrom also uses signaling theory and the idea that honesty occurs when deception is too costly.

14. See Georg Simmel, *The Philosophy of Money* (London: Routledge, 1990 [1907]), 179; Guido Möllering, "The Nature of Trust: From Georg Simmel to a Theory of Expectation, Interpretation and Suspension," *Sociology* 35, no. 2 (2001): 403–20.

15. Möllering, *The Nature of Trust*, 414.

16. *Aufheben* captures the dialectical principle of synthesis, transcending thesis and antithesis and thereby simultaneously preserving and rescinding them; see Georg W. F. Hegel, *Phänomenologie des Geistes* (Frankfurt: Suhrkamp, 1973 [1807]), 94.

17. Kevin D. Mitnick and Willam L. Simon, *The Art of Deception: Controlling the Human Element of Security* (Indianapolis, IN: Wiley, 2002), 41.

18. Goffman, *The Presentation of Self*, 65.

19. See, for example, Peter Fleming and Stelios C. Zyglidopoulos, "The Escalation of Deception in Organizations," Working Paper 12/2006 (Cambridge: Judge Business School, 2006).

20. Simmel, *Sociology of Georg Simmel*, 348.

21. See, for example, Eric M. Uslaner, *The Moral Foundations of Trust* (Cambridge: Cambridge University Press, 2002).

22. J. David Lewis and Andrew J. Weigert, "Trust as a Social Reality," *Social Forces* 63, no. 4 (1985): 967–85, 969, 971 (emphasis in original).

23. Robert W. Mitchell, "The Psychology of Human Deception," *Social Research* 63, no. 3 (1996): 819–61, 840.

24. Niklas Luhmann, *Trust and Power: Two Works by Niklas Luhmann* (Chichester: Wiley, 1979), 32.

25. Ibid., 62; see also Anthony Giddens, "Risk, Trust, Reflexivity," in *Reflexive Modernization*, ed. Ulrich Beck, Anthony Giddens, and Scott Lash (Cambridge: Polity Press, 1994), 184–97.

26. Mitchell, *Psychology of Human Deception*, 841.

27. Alfred Schütz, *The Phenomenology of the Social World* (Evanston, IL: Northwestern University Press, 1967 [1932]), 98.

28. These examples are taken from Thomas C. Schelling, "The Mind as a Consuming Organ," in *The Multiple Self*, ed. Jon Elster (Cambridge: Cambridge University Press, 1986), 177–95.

29. David Shapiro, "On the Psychology of Self-Deception," *Social Research* 63, no. 3 (1996): 785–800, 799.

30. Luhmann, *Trust and Power*, 32.

31. William James, *Essays in Pragmatism* (New York: Hafner Press, 1948 [1896]), 107.

32. On the relationship between trust and control, see Guido Möllering, "The Trust/Control Duality: An Integrative Perspective on Positive Expectations of Others," *International Sociology* 20, no. 3 (2005): 283–305.

33. See, for example, the Special Topic Forum on "Repairing Relationships Within and Between Organizations," *Academy of Management Review* 34, no. 1 (2009).

34. See, for example, Unni Kjærnes, Mark Harvey, and Alan Warde, *Trust in Food: A Comparative Institutional Analysis* (Basingstoke, UK: Palgrave Macmillan, 2007).

35. Baron Münchhausen is an 18th-century historical figure from Germany who liked to tell tall tales to his friends, but who only became a popular literary character later on as others wrote books about the incredible stories he allegedly related about his adventures, always insisting that they were true, as is expected in this genre of entertainment. Many of the tall tales were not invented by the historical Baron himself, such as the incident of Münchausen pulling himself and the horse on which he was sitting out of a swamp by his own hair; see especially Gottfried A. Bürger, *Münchausen* (Ditzingen: Reclam, 2004 [1786]). Bürger added the swamp stunt, which is not mentioned in the most popular English account of Münchhausen stories by Rudolf E. Raspe.

Chapter 9

This paper was originally prepared for the conference, "Deception: Methods, Motives, Contexts, and Consequences," which was organized by Brooke Harrington at the Santa Fe Institute in Santa Fe, New Mexico, on April 1–3, 2005. The paper was rewritten following its initial presentation and was subsequently presented in a more complete form in the follow-up meeting at the Santa Fe Institute on March 2–4, 2007. I express my sincere thanks to Brooke for the invitation to the two wonderful meetings at the SFI and to my fellow conferees for their questions and comments on the two presentations made at those conferences. Thanks to my wife, Julia Meyerson, for reading and commenting on an earlier version of this paper. I express my great appreciation to Carrie Brezine, who served as administrator of the Khipu Database Project at Harvard University from 2002 to 2005 and who helped in collecting and analyzing data used in this study. Finally, I express my appreciation to the National Science Foundation for research grants that made possible the creation and development of the Khipu Database Project (2002–3: BCS-0228038; 2003–4: BCS-0408324; and 2006–7: BCS-0609719). Finally, I express sincere thanks to the MacArthur Foundation for a fellowship that supported my research on the Inka khipus from 2001 to 2005.

1. Kathryn Burns, "Notaries, Truth, and Consequences," *The American Historical Review* 110, no. 2 (2005): 350–79.

2. Frank Salomon, *The Cord Keepers: Khipus and Cultural Life in a Peruvian Village* (Durham and London: Duke University Press, 2004).

3. Pedro de Cieza de Leon, *El Señorio de los Incas* (Lima: Instituto de Estudios Peruanos, 1967 [1551]), 36 (my translation).

4. For a discussion of how such cumulative, synthetic accounts may have been structured, see Gary Urton and Carrie J. Brezine, "Khipu Accounting in Ancient Peru," *Science* 309 (2005): 1065–67; and G. Urton and C. J. Brezine, "Information Control in the Palace of Puruchuco: An Accounting Hierarchy in a Khipu Archive from Coastal Peru," in *Variations in the Expression of Inka Power*, ed. Richard L. Burger, Craig Morris, and Ramiro Matos Mendieta (Washington, DC: Trustees of Dumbarton Oaks, 2007).

5. See M. Ascher and R. Ascher, *Mathematics of the Incas: Code of the Quipus* (New York: Dover, 1997 [1981]); and Gary Urton, *Signs of the Inka Khipu: Binary Coding in the Andean Knotted-String Records* (Austin: University of Texas Press, 2003).

6. Friar Martín de Múrua, *Historia General del Perú* (Madrid: Dastin Historia, 2001 [1613]), 361.

7. Gary Urton, "Khipu Archives: Duplicate Accounts and Identity Labels in the Inka Knotted String Records," *Latin American Antiquity* 16, no. 2 (2005): 147–67.

8. Tristan Platt, "'Without Deceit or Lies': Variable Chinu Readings during a Sixteenth-Century Tribute-Restitution Trial," in *Narrative Threads: Accounting and Recounting in Andean Khipu*, ed. Jeffrey Quilter and Gary Urton (Austin: University of Texas Press, 2002); and Gary Urton, "From Knots to Narratives: Reconstructing the Art of Historical Record-Keeping in the Andes from Spanish Transcriptions of Inka Khipus," *Ethnohistory* 45, no. 3 (1998): 409–38.

9. Guido Möllering, "The Trust / Control Duality: An Integrative Perspective on Positive Expectations of Others," *International Sociology* 20, no. 3 (2005): 284.

10. Ibid., 287–88.

11. Ibid., 288–89.

12. Photos and observations on khipu samples may be viewed at http://khipuka mayuq.fas.harvard.edu/; http://instruct1.cit.cornell.edu/research/quipuascher/.

13. For general works on khipu structures, see Ascher and Ascher, *Mathematics of the Incas*; William J. Conklin, "A Khipu Information String Theory," in Quilter and Urton, *Narrative Threads*; Carlos Radicati di Primeglio, *Estudios sobre los Quipus*, intro. and ed. Gary Urton (Lima: Fondo Editorial Universidad Nacional Mayor de San Marcos, 2006); Gary Urton, "A New Twist in an Old Yarn: Variation in Knot Directionality in the Inka Khipus," *Baessler-Archiv Neue Folge* 42 (1994): 271–305; and Urton, *Signs of the Inka Khipu*.

14. L. L. Locke, *The Ancient Quipu, or Peruvian Knot Record* (New York: American Museum of Natural History, 1923); and Hugo Pereyra, "Notas sobre el Descubrimiento de la Clave Numeral de los Quipus Incaicos," *Boletín del Museo de Arqueología y Antropología* 4, no. 5 (2002): 115–23.

15. Locke, *The Ancient Quipu*.

16. Ascher and Ascher, *Mathematics of the Incas*; and Urton, *Signs of the Inka Khipu*.

17. Ascher and Ascher, *Mathematics of the Incas*, 151–52.

18. Gary Urton, "A Calendrical and Demographic Tomb Text from Northern Peru," *Latin American Antiquity* 12, no. 2 (2001): 127–47; and Gary Urton, "Recording Signs in Narrative-Accounting Khipu," in Quilter and Urton, *Narrative Threads*.

19. Salomon, *The Cord Keepers*; and Gary Urton, *The Social Life of Numbers: A Quechua Ontology of Numbers and Philosophy of Arithmetic* (Austin: University of Texas Press, 1997).

20. Cieza de Leon, *El señorío de los Incas*, 67 (my translation and emphasis).

21. José de Acosta, *Natural and Moral History of the Indies* (Durham and London: Duke University Press, 2002 [1590]), 343 (my emphasis).

22. Garci Diez de San Miguel, *Visita hecha a la Provincia de Chucuito* (Lima: Ediciones de la Casa de la Cultura del Perú, 1964 [1567]), 89.

23. Juan Pérez Bocanegra, *Ritual Formulario e Institucion de Curas para Administrar a los Naturals de Esta Reyno los Santos Sacramentos . . .* (Lima: Geronymo de Contreras, 1631); see Regina Harrison, "Pérez Bocanegra's Ritual Formulario: Khipu Knots and Confession," in Quilter and Urton, *Narrative Threads*; Bruce Mannheim, *The Language of the Inka since the European Invasion* (Austin: University of Texas Press, 1991), 146.

24. Cited in Harrison, "Pérez Bocanegra's Ritual Formulario," 280.

25. Cited in Carlos Sempat Assadourian, "String Registries: Native Accounting and Memory According to the Colonial Sources," in Quilter and Urton, *Narrative Threads*, 138.

26. Archivo General de Indias (Seville, 1579), 409v (my translation and emphasis).

27. Jose de Acosta, *Natural and Moral History*, 343 (my emphasis).

28. John Hemming, *The Conquest of the Incas* (New York: Harcourt Brace Jovanovich, 1970).

29. El Inca Garcilaso de la Vega, *Royal Commentaries of the Incas*, trans. H. V. Livermore, 2 vols. (Austin: University of Texas Press, 1966 [1609]), 331 (my emphasis).

30. Diez de San Miguel, *Visita hecha a la Provincia . . .* , 64, 74.

31. Garcilaso de la Vega, *Royal Commentaries*, 275.

32. Hernando Pizarro, "A los Señores Oydores de la Audiencia Real de Su Magestad," in *Informaciones sobre el Antiguo Perú*, Colección de Libros y Documentos Referentes a la Historia del Perú, vol. 3, 2nd series (Lima: Sanmartí y Ca., 1920 [1533]), 175, 178.

33. Urton, "Khipu Archives."

34. Ibid., 150–51.

35. Urton and Brezine, "Information Control in the Palace of Puruchuco."

36. Möllering, "The Trust/Control Duality," 286.

37. Anthony Giddens, *Central Problems in Social Theory: Action, Structure and Contradiction in Social Analysis* (London: Macmillan, 1979); R. Garud and P. Karnøe, "Path Creation as a Process of Mindful Deviation," in *Path Dependence and Creation* (Mahwah, NJ: Erlbaum, 2001).

38. Möllering, "The Trust/Control Duality," 287.

39. Ibid., 295–96.

40. Ibid., 296.

41. Garcilaso de la Vega, *Royal Commentaries*, 276–85, 552–55, 556–58.

42. One could point to two accounts that might be thought to contradict the claims just made. First, Garcilaso de la Vega states that he knew how to read khipus as a young man in Cuzco and that he commonly read the tribute records of Indians who worked on his father's estate at their request, since, as he says, the Indians did not trust the Spaniards' own written tribute accounts (*Royal Commentaries*, 333; see my commentary on this and related passages in Urton, "Recording Signs"). This is indeed the gist of testimony provided by this noted mestizo chronicler. However, Garcilaso nowhere details for us how to read a khipu and certainly he does not do so in a way that has proved productive for our efforts at deciphering extant samples. And second, a fairly detailed reading of information encoded in an exemplary khipu appears in Antonio de la Calancha, *Crónica Moralizada del Orden de San Agustín en el Perú con Sucesos Ejemplares en Esta Monarquía*, 6 vols. (Lima: Universidad Nacional Mayor de San Marcos, 1974 [1638]), 206. Still, Calancha does not claim to have been reading an actual sample but rather to be reporting methods of recording information that were described to him by a native informant. As with the account of Garcilaso, while Calancha's data have helped generate models or paradigms for reading khipus, such as Martti Pärssinen, *Tawantinsuyu: The Inca State and Its Political Organization*, Studia Historica 43 (Helsinki: Societas Historica Finlandiae, 1992), we have not successfully employed his methods to read an extant sample.

43. Garcilaso de la Vega, *Royal Commentaries*, 331.

44. Platt, "Without Deceit or Lies"; and Urton, "From Knots to Narratives."

45. Juan de Solórzano y Pereyra, *Política Indiana*, Biblioteca de Autores Españoles 2 (Madrid: Lope de Vega 1972 [1736]), 308–9 (my translation and emphasis).

46. Cited in Platt, "Without Deceit or Lies," 239.

47. Cited in Harrison, "Pérez Bocanegra's Ritual Formulario," 275.

48. Ibid., 277.

49. Cited in ibid., 282–83.

50. See Platt, "Without Deceit or Lies."

51. Steven Stern, *Peru's Indian Peoples and the Challenge of Spanish Conquest* (Madison: University of Wisconsin Press, 1993).

52. Felipe Guaman Poma de Ayala, *El Primer Nueva Corónica y Buen Gobierno*, critical edition by John V. Murra and Rolena Adorno; trans. and textual analysis Jorge L. Urioste, 3 vols. (Mexico City: Siglo Veintiuno, 1980 [1615]).

53. Ibid., 655, 694.

54. Burns, "Notaries, Truth, and Consequences," 350–79.

55. Ibid., 352.

56. Ibid., 353.

57. Cited in ibid., 361.

58. Ibid., 365.

59. Jeffrey Quilter and Gary Urton, *Narrative Threads*.

60. Cited in Sempat Assadourian, "String Registries," 134.

61. Möllering, "The Trust/Control Duality," 300.

Chapter 10

1. Patricia Turner, *I Heard It through the Grapevine: Rumor in African-American Culture* (Berkeley: University of California Press, 1993), 165.

2. Ralph L. Rosnow and Gary Alan Fine, *Rumor and Gossip: The Social Psychology of Hearsay* (New York: Elsevier, 1976), 11.

3. Erving Goffman, *Frame Analysis: An Essay on the Organization of Experience* (Cambridge, MA: Harvard University Press, 1974).

4. Linda Dégh, *Legend and Belief: Dialectics of a Folklore Genre* (Bloomington: Indiana University Press, 2001).

5. J. L. Austin, *How to Do Things with Words* (Cambridge: Harvard University Press, 1975).

6. C. Wright Mills, "Situated Actions and Vocabularies of Motive," *American Sociological Review* 5 (1940): 904–13; Marvin Scott and Stanford Lyman, "Accounts," *American Sociological Review* 33 (1968): 46–62.

7. Tamotsu Shibutani, *Improvised News: A Sociological Study of Rumor* (Indianapolis: Bobbs-Merrill, 1966), 31.

8. Linda Dégh and Andrew Vázsonyi, "Legend and Belief," in *Folklore Genres*, ed. Dan Ben-Amos (Austin: University of Texas Press, 1976), 93–123.

9. A. Chorus, "The Basic Law of Rumor," *Journal of Abnormal and Social Psychology* 48 (1953): 313–14.

10. Gary Alan Fine, *Manufacturing Tales: Sex and Money in Contemporary Legends* (Knoxville: University of Tennessee Press, 1992); Frederick W. Koenig, *Rumor in the Marketplace: The Social Psychology of Commercial Hearsay* (Dover, MA: Auburn House, 1985).

11. Deirdre Boden, "The World as It Happens: Ethnomethodology and Conversation Analysis," in *Frontiers of Social Theory: The New Synthesis*, ed. George Ritzer (New York: Columbia University Press, 1990), 185–213.

12. Dégh and Vázsonyi, "Legend and Belief"; Robert Georges, "Toward an Understanding of Storytelling Events," *Journal of American Folklore* 82 (1969): 313–28.

13. Eviatar Zerubavel, *Social Mindscapes: An Invitation to Cognitive Sociology* (Cambridge, MA: Harvard University Press, 1997).

14. Jean-Noël Kapferer, *Rumor: Uses, Interpretations, and Images* (New Brunswick, NJ: Transaction Publishers, 1990); Nicholas DiFonzo and Prashant Bordia, *Rumor Psychology: Social and Organizational Approaches* (Washington, DC: American Psychological Association, 2007).

15. Raymond A. Bauer and D. B. Gleicher, "Word-of-Mouth Communication in the Soviet Union," *Public Opinion Quarterly* 17 (1953): 297–310.

16. Herbert C. Kelman, "Violence without Moral Restraint: Reflections on the Dehumanization of Victims and Victimizers," *Journal of Social Issues* 29 (1973): 25–61.

17. Pamela Donovan, *No Way of Knowing: Crime, Urban Legends and the Internet* (New York: Routledge, 2004); Gary Alan Fine and Patricia Turner, *Whispers on the Color Line: Rumor and Race in America* (Berkeley: University of California Press, 2001).

18. David Maines, "Information Pools and Racialized Narrative Structures," *Sociological Quarterly* 40 (1999): 317–26; Fine and Turner, *Whispers on the Color Line.*

19. Turner, *I Heard It through the Grapevine,* chap. 4.

20. Robert H. Knapp, "A Psychology of Rumor," *Public Opinion Quarterly* 8 (1944): 22–27.

21. Véronique Campion-Vincent, "From Evil Others to Evil Elites: A Dominant Pattern in Conspiracy Theories Today," in *Rumor Mills: The Social Impact of Rumor and Legend,* ed. Gary Alan Fine, Véronique Campion-Vincent, and Chip Heath (New Brunswick, NJ: Aldine/Transaction, 2005), 103–22.

22. Barry O'Neill, "The History of a Hoax," *New York Times Magazine* (March 6, 1994): 46–49.

23. Gordon Allport and Leo G. Postman, *The Psychology of Rumor* (New York: Holt, 1947); Frederick Bartlett, *Remembering* (Cambridge, MA: Cambridge University Press, 1932).

24. Warren Peterson and Noel Gist, "Rumor and Public Opinion," *American Journal of Sociology* 57 (1951): 159–67.

25. Goffman, *Frame Analysis.*

Chapter 11

1. Thomas Jefferson, *Papers,* vol. 10 (Princeton, NJ: Princeton University Press, 1950), 450.

2. Jean-Paul Sartre, *The Emotions: Outline of a Theory* (New York: Philosophical Library, 1948).

Chapter 12

1. R. J. Blendon, J. M. Benson, C. M. DesRoches, W. E. Pollard, C. Parvanta, M. J. Herrmann, "The Impact of Anthrax Attacks on the American Public," *Medscape General Medicine* 4, no. 2, http://www.medscape.com/viewarticle/430197 (accessed March 20, 2002).

2. Stephen Prior, Robert Armstrong, Ford Rowan, and Mary Beth Hill-Harmon, *Weathering the Storm: Leading Your Organization Through a Pandemic* (Washington, DC: Center for Technology and National Security Policy, National Defense University, 2006). My chapter builds on material I wrote for this volume.

3. Dorothy Nelkin and Sander Gilman, "Placing Blame for Devastating Disease," *Social Research* 55, no. 3 (1988).

4. Baruch Fischhoff, "Evaluating the Success of Terror Risk Communications," *Biosecurity and Bioterrorism* 1, no. 4 (2003), 255.

5. Prior et al., *Weathering the Storm,* 24–27.

6. D. B. Reissman, E. A. Whitney, and T. H. Taylor, Jr., "One-Year Health

Assessment of Adult Survivors of Bacillus Anthracis Infection," *Journal of the American Medical Association* 291 (2004): 1994–98.

7. Prior et al., *Weathering the Storm*, 25.

8. Vincent T. Covello and Peter M. Sandman, "Risk Communication: Evolution and Revolution," in *Solutions to an Environment in Peril*, ed. A. Wolbarst (Baltimore, MD: Johns Hopkins University Press, 2001), 164–78; Peter M. Sandman, "Hazard Versus Outrage in the Public Perception of Risk," in *Effective Risk Communication: The Role and Responsibility of Government and Nongovernment Organizations*, ed. V. T. Covello, D. B. McCallum, and M. T. Pavlova (New York: Plenum Press, 1989), 45–49.

9. National Research Council, *Improving Risk Communication* (Washington, DC: National Academy Press, 1989), 21.

10. Prior et al., *Weathering the Storm*.

11. Ibid.

12. D. Powell and W. Leiss, *Mad Cows and Mother's Milk: The Perils of Poor Risk Communication* (Montreal: McGill-Queen's University Press, 1997).

13. R. E. Kasperson, O. Renn, P. Slovic, H. S. Brown, J. Emel, R. Goble, J. X. Kasperson, and S. Ratick, "The Social Amplification of Risk: A Conceptual Framework," *Risk Analysis* 8, no. 2 (1988): 177–87.

14. Peter M. Sandman, "Definitions of Risk: Managing the Outrage Not Just the Hazard," in *Regulating Risk: The Science and Politics of Risk*, ed. T. A . Burke, N. L. Tran, J. S. Roemer, and C. J. Henry (Washington, DC: International Life Sciences Institute, 1993).

15. Prior et al., *Weathering the Storm*.

16. Paul Slovic, "Perceived Risk, Trust and Democracy," *Risk Analysis* 13 (1993): 675–82.

17. M. Siegrist, G. Cvetkovich, and C. Roth, "Salient Value Similarity, Social Trust and Risk / Benefit Perception," *Risk Analysis* 20, no. 3 (2000): 353–62.

18. L. Sjoberg, "Factors in Risk Perception," *Risk Analysis* 20, no. 1 (2000): 1–11.

19. M. Siegrist and G. Cvetkovich, "Better Negative than Positive? Evidence for a Bias for Negative Information about Possible Health Dangers," *Risk Analysis* 21, no. 1 (2001): 199–206.

20. L. Sjoberg, "Limits of Knowledge and the Limited Importance of Trust," *Risk Analysis* 21, no. 1 (2001): 189–98.

21. Vincent T. Covello, "Risk Perception, Risk Communication and EMF Exposure: Tools and Techniques for Communicating Risk Information," in *Risk Perception, Risk Communication, and Its Application to EMF Exposure: Proceedings of the World Health Organization / ICNRP International Conference*, ed. R. Matthes, J. H. Bernhardt, and M. H. Repacholi (Vienna, Austria: International Commission on Non-Ionizing Radiation Protection, 1998), 179–214; R. G. Peters, V. T. Covello, and D. B. McCallum, "The Determinants of Trust and Credibility in Environmental Risk Communication: An Empirical Study," *Risk Analysis* 17, no. 1 (1997): 43–54; R. E. Kasperson, O. Renn, P. Slovic, H. S. Brown, J. Emel, R. Goble, J. X. Kasperson, and S. Ratick, "The Social Amplification of Risk: A Conceptual Framework," *Risk Analysis* 8, no. 2 (1988): 177–87.

22. Paul Ekman, *Telling Lies: Clues to Deceit in the Marketplace, Politics, and Marriage*, 3rd ed. (New York: Norton, 2001).

23. Ibid., 343–44.

24. M. P. Lynch, *True to Life: Why Truth Matters* (Cambridge, MA: MIT Press, 2005), 152.

25. Quoted by P. Thomas, "The Anthrax Attacks," Century Foundation's Homeland Security Project (2003), http://www.tcf.org/list.asp?type=PB&pubid=221 (accessed October 29, 2008).

26. P. Caplan, *Risk Revisited* (London: Pluto Press, 2000), 21.

27. *New York Times* (October 16, 2001).

28. *Newsday* (October 8, 2002).

29. E. Gursky, T. V. Inglesby, T. O'Toole, "Anthrax 2001: Observations on the Medical and Public Health Preparedness," *Biosecurity and Bioterrorism: Biodefense Strategy, Practice and Science* 1, no. 2 (2003): 97–110.

30. Ibid., 104.

31. Bill Frist, *When Every Moment Counts* (New York: Rowman and Littlefield, 2002).

32. Ibid., 164.

33. M. W. Thompson, *The Killer Strain: Anthrax and a Government Exposed* (New York: HarperCollins, 2003), 184.

34. *New York Times* (October 18, 2001).

35. *Time* magazine (October 29, 2001).

36. Blendon et al., "The Impact of Anthrax Attacks."

37. Ibid.

38. J. Barbera, A. Macintyre, L. Gostin, T. Inglesby, T. O'Toole, C. DeAtley, K. Tonat, and M. Layton, "Large-Scale Quarantine Following Biological Terrorism in the United States: Scientific Examination, Logistic and Legal Limits, and Possible Consequences," *Journal of the American Medical Association* 286 (2001): 2711–17.

39. Quoted in N. Ethiel, ed., *Terrorism: Informing the Public* (Chicago: McCormick Tribune Foundation, 2002), 99.

40. P. A. Singer, S. R. Benatar, M. Bernstein, A. S. Daar, B. Dickens, S. MacRae, R. Upshur, L. Wright, and R. Z. Shaul, *Ethics and SARS: Learning Lessons from the Toronto Experience,* working paper of the University of Toronto Joint Center for Bioethics (2003), www.utoronto.ca/jcb/SARS_workingpaper.asp (accessed March 4, 2004).

41. T. Beauchamp and L. Walters, *Contemporary Issues in Bioethics*, 6th ed. (Belmont, CA: Wadsworth, 1999).

42. T. Beauchamp and J. Childress, *Principles of Biomedical Ethics,* 5th ed. (Oxford: Oxford University Press, 2001).

43. D. E. Beauchamp, "Community: The Neglected Tradition of Public Health," *Hasting Center Report* 15 (1985), 28–36

44. L. C. Leviton, "Health Risk Notification in a Small Town," in *Confronting Public Health Risks: A Decision Maker's Guide,* ed. L. C. Leviton, C. E. Needleman, and M. A. Shaprio (Thousand Oaks, CA: Sage, 1998), 119.

45. B. Pearson, F. Sy, K. Holton, B. Govert, and A. Liang, "Fear and Stigma: The Epidemic within the SARS Outbreak," *Emerging Infectious Diseases* 10, no. 2 (2004).

46. J. F Childress, R. Faden, R. Gaare, L. Gostin, J. Kahn, R. J. Bonnie, N. Kass, A. C. Mastroinanni, J. D. Moreno, and P. Nieburg, "Public Health Ethics: Mapping the Terrain," *Journal of Law, Medicine and Ethics* 30 (2002); J. D. Moreno, *In the Wake of Terror: Medicine and Morality in a Time of Crisis* (Cambridge, MA: MIT Press, 2003).

47. Singer et al., *Ethics and SARS.* The quotations are from the working paper (see note 40). The Toronto group published its final paper at: http://www.bmj.com/cgi/content/full/327/7427/1342?maxtoshow=&HITS=10&hits=10&RESULTFORMAT=1&title=SARS+ethics&andorexacttitle=and&andorexacttitleabs=and&andorexactfulltext=and&searchid=1&FIRSTINDEX=0&sortspec=relevance&resourcetype=HWCIT (accessed October 28, 2008).

48. Ibid. The solidarity recommendation did not survive in the final version.

49. Vamik Volkan, *Blind Trust: Large Groups and Their Leaders in Times of Crisis and Terror* (Charlottesville, VA: Pitchstone, 2004), 13.

50. Ibid., 166.

51. Aristotle, *On Rhetoric: A Theory of Civic Discourse,* trans. G. A. Kennedy (New York: Oxford University Press, 1991).

Chapter 13

1. Ralph Waldo Emerson, "Journal entry," in *Selected Writings of Ralph Waldo Emerson,* ed. William H. Gilman (New York: Signet, 1857), 160.

2. *Business Week* (January 28, 2002).

3. Erving Goffman, "On Cooling the Mark Out: Some Aspects of Adaptation to Failure," *Psychiatry* 15 (1952): 451–63.

4. Hersh Shefrin and Meir Statman, "The Disposition to Sell Winners Too Early and Ride Losers Too Long: Theory and Evidence," in *Advances in Behavioral Finance,* ed. Richard Thaler (New York: Russell Sage Foundation, 1993). See also Hersh Shefrin and Meir Statman, "Behavioral Portfolio Theory," *Journal of Financial and Quantitative Analysis* 35 (2002): 127–51.

5. Goffman, "On Cooling the Mark Out," 452.

6. Friedrich Von Hayek, "The Pretence of Knowledge" (Nobel Prize address, Stockholm, 1974).

7. Albert Hirschman, *The Strategy of Economic Development* (New Haven, CT: Yale University Press, 1967).

8. June 10, 1999; the full text of the commencement address is available at http://www.federalreserve.gov/boarddocs/speeches/1999/ 199906102.htm.

9. Paul Povel, Rajdeep Singh, and Andrew Winton, "Booms, Busts and Fraud," *Review of Financial Studies* 20 (2007): 1220.

10. T. S. Eliot, *Four Quartets* (Orlando, FL: Harcourt, 1971 [1943]), 2.

11. John Kenneth Galbraith, *A Short History of Financial Euphoria* (New York: Penguin, 1994), 52.

12. Charles Geist, *One Hundred Years of Wall Street* (New York: McGraw-Hill, 1999).

13. National Association of Securities Dealers (NASD), *National Investor Survey* (Washington, DC: Peter D. Hart Research Associates, 1997).

14. Richard Thaler, *The Winner's Curse* (Princeton, NJ: Princeton University Press, 1994).

15. NASD, *National Investor Survey.*

16. Povel, Singh, and Wilton, "Booms, Busts and Fraud," 1249.

17. Ibid., 1250.

18. Brooke Harrington and Gary Fine, "Opening the 'Black Box': Small Groups and Twenty-First-Century Sociology," *Social Psychology Quarterly* 63 (2000): 312–23.

19. Erving Goffman, "The Nature of Deference and Demeanor," *American Anthropologist* 58 (1956): 47–85.

20. Brooke Harrington, *Pop Finance: Investment Clubs and the New Investor Populism* (Princeton, NJ: Princeton University Press, 2008).

21. National Association of Investors Corporation (NAIC), *NAIC Factbook* (2002), http://www.better-investing.org/about/fact.html; figures as of December 31, 2002.

22. Goffman, "On Cooling the Mark Out," 460.

23. Elisabeth Kubler-Ross, *On Death and Dying* (New York: Scribner, 1969).

24. Goffman, "On Cooling the Mark Out," 454.

25. John Meyer and Brian Rowan, "Institutionalized Organizations: Formal Structures as Myth and Ceremony," *American Journal of Sociology* 83 (1977): 340–63.

26. Mark Peyrot, "Institutional and Organizational Dynamics in Community-Based Drug Abuse Treatment," *Social Problems,* 38 (1991): 20–33.

27. Barry Staw, "Knee-Deep in the Big Muddy: A Study of Escalating Commitment to a Chosen Course of Action," *Organizational Behavior and Human Performance* 16 (1976): 27–44.

28. Gregory Curtis, "Corporate Crooks and Investor Trust," *Greycourt White Paper Series* 22 (Pittsburgh, PA: Greycourt, 2002), 1.

29. Alex Berenson, "Tweaking Numbers to Meet Goals Comes Back to Haunt Executives," *New York Times* (June 29, 2002), A1.

30. Keith Hart, "The Idea of Economy: Six Modern Dissenters," in *Beyond the Marketplace,* ed. R. Friedland and A. F. Robertson (New York: Aldine de Gruyter, 1990), 120.

Chapter 14

The contents of this chapter were presented at the Santa Fe Institute Workshop on Deception: Methods, Motives, Contexts, and Consequences in Santa Fe, New Mexico, on March 2–4, 2007. Its contents reflect the author's personal views and are not necessarily endorsed by the Chief of Naval Operations, Strategic Studies Group, the Naval War College, or the Department of the Navy.

1. Niccolo Machiavelli, *The Discourses Upon the First Ten (Books) of Titus Livy,* bk. 3, chap. 40, http://www.constitution.org/mac/disclivy (accessed on February 1, 2007).

2. General Waldemar Erfurth, *Surprise,* trans. Stefan T. Possony and Daniel Vilfroy (Harrisburg, PA: Military Service, 1943), 51. Although a German, Erfurth was

used by the U.S. Army before, during, and after World War II as a primary source for the education of the American officer corps on matters of strategy.

3. It is important to recognize that in the world of the 21st century, the differentiation between peace and war may be neither accurate nor useful. Military operations, including strategic and operational deception, occur in war, in peace, and in that widely variant area in between. Furthermore, a nation may be at war with one nation while in a crisis with others. For simplicity and clarity, the term *war* will be used throughout this chapter to mean military operations in which the primary activity involves the use of violence. In this context of war, military deception is acceptable. During military operations that are primarily peaceful in nature and in which the primary activity does not involve the use of violence, military deception is generally not acceptable.

4. John Gooch and Amos Perlmutter, eds., *Military Deception and Strategic Surprise* (Totowa, NJ: Frank Cass, 1982), 1.

5. See, for example, Milan Vego, *Operational Warfare* (Newport, RI: Naval War College, 2000); Milan Vego, *Operational Warfare Addendum* (Newport, RI: Naval War College, 2002); and Milan Vego, "Operational Deception in the Information Age," *Joint Force Quarterly* (Spring 2002): 60–66, among others.

6. Brian R. Reinwald, "Forsaken Bond: Operational Art and the Moral Element of War" (unpublished monograph, School of Advanced Military Studies, U.S. Army Command and General Staff College, Fort Leavenworth, Kansas, 1998), 8.

7. The use of the term *military deception* is for simplicity and clarity. This narrow definition should not be construed to mean that in the conduct of military operations there is no place for surprise, propaganda, camouflage, or strategic communications. It should also not be implied that there is no need to coordinate military deception, information operations, psychological operations, and strategic communications. In an environment heavily influenced by information, all activities intended to compete in this environment must be coordinated.

8. Department of the Army, *Field Manual 90-2, Battlefield Deception* (Washington, DC: Department of the Army, 1988), 2-9 (hereafter *FM 90-2*).

9. Michael Dewar, *The Art of Deception in Warfare* (New York: Sterling, 1989), 69.

10. Ibid., 69–77. For a more complete discussion about military deception in World War II and as part of Operation Overlord, see Anthony Cave Brown, *Bodyguard of Lies* (New York: Harper and Row, 1975).

11. Gooch and Perlmutter, *Military Deception and Strategic Surprise*, 36–37.

12. Ibid., 90.

13. Bradley K. Nelson, *Battlefield Deception: Abandoned Imperative of the 21st Century* (unpublished monograph, School of Advanced Military Studies, U.S. Army Command and General Staff College, Fort Leavenworth, Kansas, 1997), 20.

14. Gooch and Perlmutter, *Military Deception and Strategic Surprise*, 124.

15. Department of Defense, *Joint Publication 3-13.4, Military Deception* (Washington, DC: Joint Chiefs of Staff, 2006), I-2, I-4, I-8, II-1, II-3 (hereafter *JP 3-13.4*).

16. Dewar, *Art of Deception in Warfare*, 68–69.

17. Carl von Clausewitz, *On War*, ed. and trans. Michael Howard and Peter Paret (Princeton, NJ: Princeton University Press, 1976), 202.

18. Ibid., 202–203.

19. Sun Tzu, *The Art of War*, trans. Samuel B. Griffith (New York: Oxford University Press, 1971), 66–70.

20. This obvious dilemma between military deception and honesty, unlike in other social interactions, was pointed out to me by Dr. Brooke Harrington after her review of an earlier version of this chapter.

21. *FM 90-2*, 1-1.

22. Nelson, *Battlefield Deception*, 22.

23. See, for example, Richard H. Shultz and Ruth Margolies Beitler, "Tactical Deception and Strategic Surprise in Al-Qai'da's Operations," *Middle East Review of International Affairs* 8, no. 2 (June 2004), http://meria.idc.ac.il/journal/2004/issue2 (accessed December 21, 2006); and Devin D. Jessee, "Tactical Means, Strategic Ends: Al Qaeda's Use of Denial and Deception," *Terrorism and Political Violence* 18 (2006): 367–88, http://www.international.ucla.edu (accessed December 21, 2006).

24. See, for example, Caitlin Hall, "The Office of Strategic Deception," *Arizona Daily Wildcat* (February 27, 2002), http://wc.arizona.edu/papers/95/109/03_2 (accessed December 21, 2006); Vernon Loeb and Dana Milbank, "New Defense Office Won't Mislead, Officials Say," *Washington Post* (February 21, 2002), http://www.washingtonpost.com/ac2/wp-dyn/A42427-2002Feb20 (accessed on March 31, 2007); and James Dao and Eric Schmitt, "A 'Damaged' Information Office Is Declared Closed by Rumsfeld," *New York Times* (February 27, 2002), http://query.nytimes.com/gst/fullpage.html?res=9906E6DB1431F934A15751C0A9649C8B63 (accessed on March 31, 2007).

25. The debate between truth and deception by the U.S. military has reemerged based on the experiences in Iraq. See, for example, Julian E. Barnes, "Pentagon Weighing News and Spin," *Los Angeles Times* (April 18, 2007), http://www.latimes.com/news/printedition/asection/la-na-pentagon (accessed May 17, 2007).

26. Military deception may have unintended results, and those results may be outside of the military realm, such as occurred in the Falklands War of the early 1980s. As a strategic signal to the Argentine government, the United Kingdom attempted a military deception by announcing that Royal Navy submarines had deployed to the South Atlantic Ocean well before the submarines were actually in the area. The objective of this strategic deception was to cause the Argentine leaders to acquiesce in the face of a strong U.K. military position and thus avoid a conflict. Instead, believing the deception, the Argentine public rioted against the British, forcing the Argentine government to declare war. See Max Hastings and Simon Jenkins, *The Battle for the Falklands* (New York: Norton, 1983), 60–67.

27. *FM 90-2*, 4-6, 4-9.

28. Graham T. Allison and Philip D. Zelikow, *Essence of Decision: Explaining the Cuban Missile Crisis*, 2nd ed. (New York: Longman, 1999), x–xi. Allison and Zelikow offer three frameworks through which to view the Cuban Missile Crisis: the Rational

Actor, Organizational Behavior, and Governmental Politics. Similar mechanisms are at play in deception at the strategic and operational levels of war.

29. Movement of information and modern technology have allowed the manner in which military capabilities are developed to dramatically change over the past 10 to 15 years. Commonly referred to as network-centric warfare, the geographic, functional, and temporal nature of the warfighting environment has changed requiring the principles underlying and methods of executing military deception to change. In his book, *Distributed Networked Operations: The Foundation of Network Centric Warfare* (Lincoln, NE: iUniverse, 2005), Jeffrey Cares presents a cogent discussion of the theory and practice of network-centric warfare.

30. Applying principles of virology and bacteriology, such as how infections propagate through a population, provides useful insights into how ideas propagate through a population. When coupled with principles of the behavior of herds or flocks, one can start to gain a better understanding of the behavior of a group, social network, or organization. The notions of information movement and group behavior are central to military deception, although neither is part of current U.S. military deception doctrine.

31. Alfred Thayer Mahan as quoted in Milan Vego, *Operational Warfare* (Newport, RI: Naval War College, 2000), 619.

32. Dewar, *Art of Deception in Warfare*, 20.

Chapter 15

1. Alfred North Whitehead, *The Function of Reason* (Boston: Beacon Press, 1970 [1929]), 10, 40.

2. Edgar Bowers, *Collected Poems* (New York: Knopf, 1999), 154. "The Prince" is one of the poems growing out of Bowers's service in Army intelligence in Germany, as part of the post-WWII de-Nazification project.

3. Gary Alan Fine, *Manufacturing Tales: Sex and Money in Contemporary Legends* (Knoxville: University of Tennessee Press, 1992), 141–59.

4. Thom Gunn, *Collected Poems* (New York: Farrar, Straus & Giroux 1993), 290–91. Used with permission.

5. Barre Toelken and Tacheeni Scott, "Poetric Retranslation and the 'Pretty Languages' of Yellowman," in *Traditional Literatures of the American Indian: Texts and Interpretations*, 2nd ed., ed. Karl Kroeber (Lincoln and London: University of Nebraska Press, 1997), 128.

6. Jarold Ramsey, *Coyote Was Going There* (Seattle and London: University of Washington Press, 1977), 36.

7. Toelken and Scott, "Poetric Retranslation," 102, 109.

8. Alan Stephens, "Moments in a Glade," *Between Matter and Principle* (Denver, CO: Swallow Press, 1963). This poem can be found in Yvor Winters and Kenneth Fields, *Quest for Reality: An Anthology of Short Poems in English* (Chicago: Swallow Press, 1969), 181–82.

9. Frank Russell, *The Pima Indians* (Tucson: The University of Arizona Press, 1975,

1980), 312. Originally published as part of the *Twenty-sixth Annual Report of the Bureau of American Ethnology, 1904–05.*

10. Ramsey, *Coyote Was Going There,* 100–101, 272; Dell Hymes, *In Vain I Tried to Tell You* (Lincoln and London: University of Nebraska Press, 2004).

11. Kroeber, *Traditional Literatures,* 11–18.

12. Karl Kroeber, "The Wolf Comes: Indian Poetry and Linguistic Criticism," in Brian Swann, *Smoothing the Ground: Essays in Native American Oral Literature* (Berkeley, Los Angeles, London: University of California Press, 1983), 106.

13. John Bierhorst, "Part One: General Introduction," *Cantares Mexicanos: Songs of the Aztecs* (Stanford: Stanford University Press, 1985), 3–122. This work is of utmost importance for the study of Aztec poetics. It is a superb account, too, of a wholesale religious deception that worked for nearly 500 years.

14. John Bierhorst, *Doctor Coyote: A Native American Aesop's Fable* (New York: Macmillan, 1987).

15. Joel Chandler Harris, *Uncle Remus: His Songs and His Sayings,* intro. Robert Hemenway (New York: Viking Penguin, 1982). Hemenway's introduction throws a good deal of light on our subject.

16. Kenneth Fields, *The Odysseus Manuscripts* (Chicago: Elpenor Books, 1981), 34–35.

17. Paul Valéry, *Idée Fixe,* trans. David Paul (New York: Pantheon Books, 1965).

18. "The Night Chant: A Navajo Ceremonial," in *Four Masterworks of American Indian Literature,* ed. John Bierhorst, trans. Washington Matthews (Tucson: University of Arizona Press, 1974), 281–347.

19. Plato, "Symposium," in *The Collected Dialogues of Plato,* ed. Edith Hamilton and Huntington Cairns; trans. Michael Joyce (New York: Pantheon, 1961), 574.

20. Alexander Nehamas, *The Art of Living: Socratic Reflections from Plato to Foucault* (Berkeley, Los Angeles, London: University of California Press, 1998), 50.

21. Barbara Babcock-Abrahams, "A Tolerated Margin of Mess: The Trickster and His Tales Reconsidered," *Journal of the Folklore Institute* 11, no. 3 (1975): 147–86.

22. Murray Gell-Mann, *The Quark and the Jaguar: Adventures in the Simple and the Complex* (New York: Henry Holt, 1994), 341.

23. Ibid.

24. Ibid., xiii.

Index

Italic page numbers refer to figure captions.

accountability: dialectic of trust and, 151, 160–62; human demand for, 234
accuracy: anthrax attacks of 2001 and need for, 223–28; in credibility of officials, 216, 235
accusatory reluctance, 7, 79, 148, 208
Acosta, José de, 164, 167
Adam's Rib (film), 207–8
adaptation to failure, 237, 238–40, 251
adultery (infidelity), 138, 147, 204
advertising, paltering used in, 44
Aesop, 83, 281
African Americans: "Lights Out" rumor about, 197; racialized claims to knowledge by, 196; rumors among, 196, 197–98; Tropical Fantasy rumor among, 183–84
Akerloff, George, 24
Alcibiades, 285
alibi agencies, 112–13
alibi and excuse clubs, 113
Allied invasion of Normandy, 260–61, 274
Allison, Graham, 269, 325n28
Allport, Gordon, 198
al-Qaeda, 216, 266, 274

altered photographs, 95–108; angry reactions to, 138; of celebrities, 96–98; cloning in, 102–3; collusion in acceptance of, 91; and computer-generated images, 105–7; as digital deception, 110; exposing digital forgeries, 100–106; growing frequency and sophistication of, 95, 98; historically significant photographs, 8, 95–96; lighting in, 100–102; of Lincoln, 8, 95–96, *96*; market pressures resulting in, 126; memory affected, 107; photographic ballistics for detecting, 104–5; retouching in, 103–4; seen as frauds, 5; trust eroded by, 8, 107–8; in wartime, 98, 99, 108, 271–72
Altman, Lawrence, 225
Amazon.com, 132
American Idol (television program), 100–102, *101*
anchoring effect, 84
anglerfish, 21
animals: absence of intent in deception in, 3; chimpanzees, viii, x, 58; deception by society members in, 22;

insects: caterpillars, 22; fireflies, viii, 6,
21; monarch and viceroy butterflies,
viii, x
insider misuse of information, 131–132
instant messaging, 114, 117, 118, 133
institutions, 213–88; deception in, 12–15;
divisive rumors undercut authority
of, 197–98. *See also* financial markets;
government; military deception
intelligence, general, 85
intentionality: deception distinguished
from other forms of conveying
misleading information by, vii, 11;
deception without, 3, 11, 15, 141; in
lying, vii, 3, 38, 39, 41–42, 57, 110; in
paltering, 42, 43
Internal Revenue Service, 44
International Association of Forensic
Linguists, 127
Internet: chat rooms, 110, 115, 117–18, 123,
133; deception in digital age, 109–20;
dot-com bubble, 237, 238, 240, 242,
243, 244, 246; newsgroups, 115, 118, 123,
126; "no one knows you're a dog" on,
113; PayPal, 123; perceived anonymity
on, 116; in rumor diffusion, 194–95.
See also e-mail; World Wide Web
interpretation, mechanisms in, 7
investment clubs, 241; annual rate
of return in 1990s, 245; denial as
adaptation in, 248–49; findings on
response to financial fraud, 245–51;
in growth of investment population,
241; loose coupling between payoffs
and perseverance in, 245; maintain
their lines of action via their identity-related interactions, 245, 251–52;
sample in this study, 243–45; see no
alternative to remaining invested,
246–47; self-blame response to corporate corruption in, 249–51, 252;
stay invested in stock market despite
frauds, 238–39, 242, 245, 251, 253; stock
holdings after burst of dot-com
bubble, 242
investor class, growth of, 241
IQ, 85

Iraq war, 216, 325n25
Ironside, 261
irony, 141, 285–86
isolation of ill individuals, 229, 230

James, William, 151
Jefferson, Thomas, 21, 204, 205
Joinson, Adam N., 116
Joint Center for Bioethics (University of
Toronto), 229
Jolie, Angelina, 97, 98, 100, 101
Journal of Cell Biology, 103
JPEG quantization tables, 104–5
judgment, cultures of, 192

Kahneman, Daniel, 81, 304n16
Kant, Immanuel, 38
Katrina, Hurricane, 189, 196, 215, 217, 221,
231–33, 235
Kennedy, John F., assassination of, 189
Kerrigan, Nancy, 97
Kerry, John, 97, 98, 107
Kessler, Brett, 125
Keyes, Ralph, 115
khipus, 154–82; accounting for truthfulness of, 168–74; checks and balances
in system of, 159–60, 168–71; close
matches, 170, 171; colors in, 162; commoners and keepers of, 161, 172–74,
180; for communicating over distance, 111; confessions recorded on,
165, 166, 176–77; destruction of, 181–82;
keeper reporting to an overseer, 169;
keepers as constitutionally trustworthy, 10, 84, 160, 164–68, 181–82;
keepers as simultaneously truthful
and accountable, 151; knot types
in, 162–63; limitations on modern
interpretation of, 159; matching,
170; numerical representation of
information in, 163; pendant cords,
162, 163; photograph of, 157; provincial administrator with pair of, 158;
rectitude-seeking calculation as
principle of, 163–64; Spaniards fail
to learn to read, 174, 317n42; Spanish
administrative officials and keepers

from, 45; pleasures of, 275–88; in propaganda and disinformation campaigns, 12; rumor compared with, 184–85; seen as absolutely wrong, 38–39; as standard operating procedure in financial markets, 14; succeeds because we want the lie to be true, 75–76, 80; thoughts and feelings and, 55–73; voice in, 68; what happens when a person lies, 59–69; what is a lie, 56–59. *See also* lie detection; white lies

Lynch, Michael, 223

Machiavelli, Niccolo, 254
magic tricks, 5, 11, 76
Mahan, Alfred Thayer, 273
Major Transitions in Evolution, The (Maynard Smith and Szathmáry), 20–21
manipulators, 68–69
Mann, Samantha, 79
manufacturing tales, 191
Mao Zedong, 265
markets, financial, *see* financial markets
mating: deception's value in, 4. *See also* love
Matrix (film), x
Mayer, Roger, 143
Maynard Smith, John, 20–21, 22
McCain, John, 13
medicine: biomedical ethics, 229–30; deception as necessary in, 4. *See also* health care crises
Melville, Herman, 286
memory: altered photographs affect, 107; clues for distinguishing real from fabricated, 60–61; dynamics of, 198; false, 57; individual versus collective, 192, 197
mental effort in lying, 60–61
metadata, 131
microexpressions, 67, 85, 211
military deception, 254–74; altered photographs in, 98, 99, 108, 271–72; Churchill on necessity of, 3; Clausewitz and Sun Tzu on, 263–65; current

U.S. military approach to, 254–55, 265–67, 268, 269, 272, 273; defined, 255–57; as different from other forms of deception, 254, 257; elements of interaction in, 267; environment for today, 267–72; historical examples of, 259–262; human considerations in, 268–69; human factors in, 256–57; inferring adversary's intent, 129–30; information availability and movement considerations for, 270–71, 326n30; and levels of war, 257–59; limitations on use of, 256; operational deception, 262–63; perfidy distinguished from legitimate, 256; principles of, 263; as proactive, 257; psychological operations distinguished from, 263; role in strategy reconsidered, 14; shifting from single leader to collective organizations, 273–74; strategic deception, 259, 262, 324n7; surprise compared with, 257; technology in, 256, 265, 271–72, 274; as "Third World technique," 266; time considerations in, 269–70; as time-sensitive competition, 255; unintended results of, 325n26; in U.S. military doctrine, 262–63

Miller, Geoffrey, 78
Miller, George, ix
Miller, William I., 77
mimic octopus, 21, 201, 202
mimicry, Batesian, viii
Miss Marple effect, 88–89
mistaken recall, 57
Mitchell, Robert, 147–48, 149
Mitnick, Kevin, 145
Möllering, Guido, 10, 11, 70, 71, 124, 160–61, 172–73, 182, 186, 209, 210, 216, 233, 240
monarch butterflies, viii, x
Montgomery, Bernard, 258
moon landing, 8
Mosteller, Frederick, 125, 127
Münchausen, Baron, 153, 314n35
Munn, Charlie, ix
Munson, J. C., 132